Future Issues for
Social Work Practice

Future Issues for Social Work Practice

Edited by

Paul R. Raffoul
University of Houston

C. Aaron McNeece
Florida State University

Allyn and Bacon
Boston • London • Toronto • Sydney • Tokyo • Singapore

Vice President, Social Science: Susan Badger
Executive Editor: Karen Hanson
Managing Editor, Social Work: Judy Fifer
Series Editorial Assistant: Jennifer Jacobson
Executive Marketing Manager: Joyce Nilsen
Editorial-Production Service: Electronic Publishing Services Inc.
Manufacturing Buyer: Aloka Rathnam
Cover Administrator: Suzanne Harbison

Copyright © 1996 by Allyn & Bacon
A Simon & Schuster Company
Needham Heights, Massachusetts 02194

Library of Congress Cataloging-in-Publication Data

Future issues for social work practice / edited by Paul R. Raffoul &
    C. Aaron McNeece.
        p.   cm.
    Includes bibliographical references.
    ISBN 0-205-17429-9
    1. Social service—United States—Forecasting.   2. Social
prediction—United States.   I. Raffoul, Paul R.   II. McNeece, Carl
Aaron.
    HV91.F87   1996
    361.3'2—dc20   95-25264
                                                                                        CIP

Printed in the United States of America
10   9   8   7   6   5   4   3   2   99   98   97

To
Social Workers of the Future

Contents

Part IV   *Gerontology*   *115*

Part V   *Women, Children, and Families*   *139*

Part VI   *Administration*   *189*

Preface

Editing a book on the future of social work is a formidable challenge, so we took the coward's way out by seeking safety in numbers. We called on those persons with reputations for being the most knowledgeable in the field to assist us with this task. Sometimes there was agreement on the major issues confronting us, sometimes not. Only rarely did we reach a consensus about what is likely to happen in a given field of practice. Nevertheless, what the reader will find in the following pages represents the collective wisdom of hundreds of years of practice, research, teaching, and policy experience. The task we set out to accomplish was to prepare a book that might assist in preparing students and practitioners for the rapidly changing future that will inevitably confront all social workers. We expect that we will be wrong about some of our predicted issues and outcomes, at best because we have stimulated enough thought and discussion to push us toward more attractive "alternative" futures, at worst because we just are not very skilled at this type of prognostication.

Part I begins with a discussion of the implications of demographic changes on social welfare services in the next century. These changes almost certainly mean that social welfare as we currently know it will cease to exist in the near future. This is followed by a discussion of how social work is going digital, and whether we will be able to adapt to rapid technological change, especially changes in information technology. The final chapter is about accountable practice in the next century and predicting how social work effectiveness will be measured, and it discusses the benefits and problems related to future technological innovations and suggests ways of preparing ourselves for future accountable practice.

Parts II through VII deal with future issues in several different fields of social work practice. Part II, deals with potentially explosive issues such as health care rationing, new paradigms for health care, and the dramatic increase in HIV and AIDS, especially among adolescents. It also examines the impact of all of these changes on health care social work. Part III looks at the changes in mental health, clinical, and private practice. One author examines the refinement of empirical social work practice. Another discusses the impact of managed care on mental health services. Still another speculates about some alternative modes of private practice in the next century. The role and function of the DSM-IV and its impact on clinical practice is also reviewed. The authors of Part IV examine the major issues of aging: services needed by a rapidly growing older population, alternative models for providing services to the elderly, the role of universities in training social work aging specialists, and the impact of caregiver stress. Part V deals with issues relevant to women, children, and families. The first two chapters paint a stark picture of current services for children and adolescents and the crisis in foster care. The next presents a detailed analysis of the problem of violence against women. Another looks at the ever-changing structure of American families, and the final chapter focuses on the problem of teenage pregnancy. Part VI is concerned with social services administration. These three chapters present different perspectives on new organizational forms, privatization, the decline of professionalism, the impact of technology on management and control, multiculturalism, and empowerment. Part VII looks at policy, politics, and activism in social work. One author examines the future prospects for radical social work, and another examines the relationship between activism and professionalism. Still another chapter describes a widening gap between the ideal social welfare policy and what can realistically be expected beyond the year 2000, and the final chapter in this section predicts that political social work will become a legitimized activity within social work practice and social work education by the year 2000.

In Part VIII, the concluding section, the first chapter examines the current status and future prospects for social work research, and the other deals with how social workers might prepare for the changes that technology, computers, and the Information Revolution will bring, and what kind of value conflicts those technological changes will create.

We don't offer a single vision of the future but rather several alternative visions. It is our hope that the profession of social work will be able to weave its way between the bleakest and more dire of these alternatives and arrive at a future that holds out the promise of a better life for those we serve.

Paul R. Raffoul, Ph.D.
C. Aaron McNeece, Ph.D.
St. George's Island, FL

Part I

Overview

The first two chapters set the tone of the discussion for the rest of the book. Chapter 1 is the only chapter written entirely by scholars outside the profession of social work. Demographers Murdock and Michael take a close look at the ever-changing population of the United States and the implications of those changes on the demands for social welfare services in the next 50 years. Readers should keep in mind questions such as the following:

1. How can we address the increased demand for services in a system that is increasingly constrained by limited resources?
2. Are there ways to alter the historical relationships between certain demographic characteristics and the levels of socioeconomic resources?
3. Can we make social, political, cultural, or programmatic changes to compensate for the seemingly inevitable demographic changes?

In Chapter 2 Wally Gingerich and Ronald Green describe the "explosion of information technology" that faces our profession and trends that will completely change the way we will work in the twenty-first century. Some of the questions the reader may want to ponder at the end of Chapter 2 include the following:

1. What are the implications for social workers' having a potentially infinite number of information sources to which they will have immediate access?
2. How will the automation of routine tasks (determination of eligibility for services, screening, diagnosis, and the like) affect the profession?
3. In what ways will social work education need to change in order to provide students with the appropriate technical skills needed in the next century?

In Chapter 3 Berit Ingersoll-Dayton and Srinika Jayaratne address the issues of effectiveness and accountability in social work practice. They predict the development of uniform outcome measures and centralized, mandatory data-gathering banks. Both social workers and clients will be computer literate and clients will enter self-observation data into their home computers. These authors also see computer technology having an equally important impact on agency management, especially in matters of cost containment. Finally, potential benefits and problems of the technology revolution are discussed. Important questions raised include the following:

1. Will the drive for accountability lead to "cutting corners" on services?
2. To what extent will professional social work functions be performed by computers?
3. What are the implications of technological change for accountable social work practice and education?

Chapter *1*

Future Demographic Change

The Demand for Social Welfare Services in the Twenty-First Century

STEVE H. MURDOCK, PhD and MARTHA MICHAEL, MS

Texas A & M

Welfare reform is a major social and political issue in the United States, and it promises to occupy a central position in policy debates in the remainder of the 1990s and beyond (Bane & Ellwood, 1994; Karger & Stoesz, 1994). The underlying patterns of dependency and poverty that necessitate such social programs are also receiving renewed attention as attempts are made to identify the determinants of welfare dependency and alternatives to the present welfare system (Danziger et al., 1994).

The debate has become increasingly intense because of the rapid growth in the dependent population and because of the difficulty of projecting future demands for social programs. Extensive attention has been given to the impact of changing eligibility requirements and changes in the social, economic, and cultural characteristics of eligible populations (U.S. House of Representatives, Committee on Ways and Means, 1993; U.S. House of Representatives, Congressional Research Service, 1993). Demographic factors have also received extensive analysis historically (O'Hare, 1987; Soldo, 1988; Berger, 1993), and attention has recently focused on the impacts of immigrants on social service expenditures (Huddle, 1993; Passel, 1994; Clark, 1994). However, the implications of the most recent national projections, which assume extensive level of immigration, have been much less thoroughly analyzed, particularly in regard to the role

3

that future demographic change may play in determining the number of persons requiring assistance.

One of the reasons demographic factors often receive less attention than other dimensions is that they are not direct determinants of socioeconomic need. Rather, the effects of demographic factors on the demand for social programs depend on the nature of relationships between demographic characteristics and socioeconomic need. If need were equally distributed among members of the population of the United States, then the growth in demand for social welfare services would simply be a function of the overall increase in the population. As is clear in Tables 1–1 and 1–2, however, such is not the case.

Table 1–1 provides data on the distribution of poverty in the United States by key social and demographic characteristics, which show a disproportionate concentration of poverty among specific population segments. Similarly, those utilizing social welfare services have specific characteristics. Table 1–2 shows key demographic characteristics for recipients of means-based assistance (such as AFDC, Medicaid, and Food Stamps) in the

TABLE 1–1   Selected Characteristics of Persons and Families in Poverty in the United States in 1990

Total number of persons in poverty	33.6 million
Percentage of all persons in poverty	13.5
Percentage of persons in poverty by age	
< 15 years of age	21.4
15–24	16.1
25–44	10.4
45–54	7.8
55–59	9.0
60–64	10.3
65+	12.2
Percentage of persons in poverty by race and Hispanic origin	
White	10.7
Black	31.9
Hispanic	28.1
Percentage of families in poverty by type (N = 66.3 million)	
Married couples	5.7
Male household, no spouse	12.0
Female household, no spouse	33.4

Source: "Poverty in the United States: 1990" *Current Population Reports*, P-60, No. 175, Washington, DC: U.S. Government Printing Office, 1991.

TABLE 1–2   Selected Characteristics of Persons Receiving Means-Based Assistance, 1990 (Numbers in Thousands)

Characteristics	Number	Percentage
Total receiving assistance	53,249	21.4
Age		
<18	21,428	32.9
18–24	5,390	21.6
25–34	8,586	20.0
35–44	6,093	15.8
45–54	3,522	13.7
55–59	1,506	14.1
60–64	1,557	14.6
65+	5,167	17.2
Sex		
Males	24,210	20.0
Females	29,039	22.8
Race/ethnicity		
White	35,526	17.0
Black	15,046	48.8
Hispanic	9,161	42.8
Household type		
All families	46,359	22.0
Married couple families	25,802	15.3
Female householder families	18,186	53.8

Source: "Poverty in the United States: 1990" *Current Population Reports*, P-60, No. 175, Washington, DC: U.S. Government Printing Office, 1991.

United States. Owing to a variety of discriminatory, historical, and access-related factors, poverty and accompanying need are disproportionately experienced by minority populations and by the youngest and oldest and those in certain household types in American society (Danziger et al., 1994; Rural Sociological Society, 1993).

Although it is hoped that the relationships between socioeconomic need and demographic characteristics will change over time, it is nevertheless useful to examine what projected demographic trends in the United States are likely to mean for the demand for welfare services in the United States in the coming years. This chapter presents such an analysis, examining projections of future demographic change in the United States and evaluating what such change may mean for levels of socioeconomic need and related program use in the United States.

Future Demographic Trends in the United States

Table 1–3 presents four alternative projections of the population of the United States completed by personnel from the U.S. Bureau of the Census (Day, 1992) and analyzed recently in a work by Murdock (1995). These projections combine different assumptions about the demographic processes of fertility, mortality, and immigration. Under the low-growth scenario, fertility is assumed to be at a total level of 1.8 births per woman, life expectancy at birth would be at the 1990 level of 75 years, and immigration is assumed to be at a very low level of 350,000 per year. Under the middle- and zero-immigration scenarios, fertility would be at the 1990 level of 2.1 births per woman and life expectancy is projected to increase to 82 years; under the zero-immigration scenario no immigration is projected to occur (or immigration and emigration are assumed to be equal), whereas under the middle scenario immigration is expected to be maintained at a level of 880,000 per year. Under the high scenario, the birth rate is assumed to climb to 2.5 births, life expectancy to reach 87 years, and immigration to be 1,370,000 per year. The middle scenario is that which the U.S. Census Bureau suggests has the highest likelihood of prevailing over time.

As is evident in the data in Table 1–3, there is substantial uncertainty about the size of the future population of the nation. The total population projected for 2050 varies from only 275 million, or about 27 million more people than were counted in the 1990 census, to 507 million, 259 million more than in 1990. The differences are much less in the short term, with the differences among scenarios being 16 million by 2000, 40 million by 2010, and 75 million by 2020. Despite such uncertainty about the total size likely to be attained by the U.S. population, several common patterns in these alternative projections merit attention by those involved in the examination of welfare in the United States.

First, as is evident in Table 1–4, the patterns of growth shown under these projections are generally lower than historical patterns for the total and for majority or Anglo populations but are very rapid for minority populations. Whereas the population of the United States increased by 9.8 percent from 1980 to 1990 and by 11.4 percent from 1970 to 1980, there is only one decade (1990 to 2000) under the low-, middle-, and zero-immigration scenarios in which the projected rate of future growth for the total population is not lower than that experienced by the United States in the 1980s. Only under the highest-growth scenario are rates of growth as high as those experienced during the 1970s.

Slow growth is especially evident for the Anglo population. It would decrease for the total 60-year projection period under both the low- and zero-immigration scenarios, increase by only 7 percent under the middle scenario, and increase by 38 percent under the high-growth scenario. Although the Anglo population increased by only 4 percent from 1980 to 1990, it would grow even more slowly under most scenarios and would decline in absolute terms in all but the 1990-to-2000 decade, under the low-growth scenario, and during the two last decades of the projection period under the middle scenario.

By contrast, growth among minority population groups is pervasive (it occurs in all but one decade for all except one group). The growth in the Anglo population for the total 60-year projection period is projected to be only 7.3 percent under the middle scenario, but the Black population is projected to increase by 96.2 percent, the Hispanic population by 260.9 percent, and the Other population is projected to increase by 375.4 percent from

TABLE 1–3   U.S. Bureau of the Census' Projections of the Population in the United States by Race/Ethnicity* from 1990 to 2050 under Alternative Scenarios

Year	Race/Ethnicity				Total Population
	Anglo	Black	Hispanic	Other	

Low Scenario

Year	Anglo	Black	Hispanic	Other	Total Population
1990	188,128,296	29,216,293	22,354,059	9,011,225	248,709,873
2000	193,877,343	33,094,398	28,692,581	12,443,453	268,107,775
2010	193,018,640	35,596,370	33,827,982	15,638,510	278,078,502
2020	189,931,046	37,560,108	38,866,493	18,842,024	285,199,671
2030	182,603,708	38,666,601	43,464,839	21,975,182	286,710,320
2040	170,986,916	39,047,263	47,390,943	24,860,638	282,285,760
2050	158,340,427	38,980,851	50,790,117	27,535,149	275,646,544

Middle Scenario

Year	Anglo	Black	Hispanic	Other	Total Population
1990	188,128,296	29,216,293	22,354,059	9,011,225	248,709,873
2000	196,700,935	33,834,463	30,602,142	13,677,925	174,815,465
2010	201,668,449	38,200,689	39,311,562	18,928,373	298,109,073
2020	206,161,770	42,910,788	48,951,768	24,577,377	322,601,703
2030	207,674,257	47,551,578	59,197,188	30,528,356	344,951,379
2040	205,586,784	52,284,693	69,827,229	36,650,334	364,349,040
2050	201,840,533	57,315,588	80,675,012	42,842,948	382,674,080

High Scenario

Year	Anglo	Black	Hispanic	Other	Total Population
1990	188,128,296	29,216,293	22,354,059	9,011,225	248,709,873
2000	199,638,719	34,485,466	32,342,744	14,839,110	281,306,039
2010	211,185,161	40,346,047	44,328,371	22,035,208	317,894,787
2020	224,370,664	47,187,279	58,445,123	30,119,472	360,122,538
2030	236,654,055	54,682,389	74,717,255	39,076,094	405,129,793
2040	248,211,126	63,013,832	93,465,608	48,996,204	453,686,770
2050	259,720,826	72,277,469	114,903,956	59,837,914	506,740,165

Zero-Immigration Scenario

Year	Anglo	Black	Hispanic	Other	Total Population
1990	188,128,296	29,216,293	22,354,059	9,011,225	248,709,873
2000	194,965,334	33,231,157	27,309,887	10,477,149	265,983,527
2010	197,663,449	36,770,881	31,524,275	11,538,507	277,497,113
2020	199,648,747	40,533,600	35,966,836	12,602,334	288,751,517
2030	198,445,572	44,094,173	40,199,015	13,574,332	296,313,092
2040	193,514,146	47,629,160	44,096,785	14,365,552	299,605,643
2050	186,906,199	51,690,897	47,644,286	15,098,474	301,009,856

Source: Data derived from "Population of the United States by Age, Sex, Race, and Spanish Origin, 1992–2050" by Jennifer Cheeseman Day, *Current Population Reports*, P-25, No. 1092, Washington, DC: U.S. Bureau of the Census, 1992.
* The racial/ethnic groupings used in this and all subsequent tables are four mutually exclusive categories. Anglo consists of White non-Hispanics, Black of Black non-Hispanics, Other of persons in all other (except White and Black) racial groups who are not Hispanic, and Hispanic refers to Hispanics of all races.

TABLE 1–4   Percentage Change in the U.S. Bureau of the Census'
Projections of the Population in the United States by Race/Ethnicity from
1990 to 2050 under Alternative Scenarios

Time	Anglo	Black	Hispanic	Other	Total
		Low Scenario			
1990–2000	3.1	13.3	28.4	38.1	7.8
2000–2010	-0.4	7.6	17.9	25.7	3.7
2010–2020	-1.6	5.5	14.9	20.5	2.6
2020–2030	-3.9	2.9	11.8	16.6	0.5
2030–2040	-6.4	1.0	9.0	13.1	-1.5
2040–2050	-7.4	-0.2	7.2	10.8	-2.4
1990–2050	-15.8	33.4	127.2	205.6	10.8
		Middle Scenario			
1990–2000	4.6	15.8	36.9	51.8	10.5
2000–2010	2.5	12.9	28.5	38.4	8.5
2010–2020	2.2	12.3	24.5	29.8	8.2
2020–2030	0.7	10.8	20.9	24.2	6.9
2030–2040	-1.0	10.0	18.0	20.1	5.6
2040–2050	-1.6	9.6	15.5	16.9	5.0
1990–2050	7.3	96.2	260.9	375.4	53.9
		High Scenario			
1990–2000	6.1	18.0	44.7	64.7	13.1
2000–2010	5.8	17.0	37.1	48.5	13.0
2010–2020	6.2	17.0	31.8	36.7	13.3
2020–2030	5.5	15.9	27.8	29.7	12.5
2030–2040	4.9	15.2	25.1	25.4	12.0
2040–2050	4.6	14.7	22.9	22.1	11.7
1990–2050	38.1	147.4	414.0	564.0	103.7
		Zero-Immigration Scenario			
1990–2000	3.6	13.7	22.2	16.3	6.9
2000–2010	1.4	10.7	15.4	10.1	4.3
2010–2020	1.0	10.2	14.1	9.2	4.1
2020–2030	-0.6	8.8	11.8	7.7	2.6
2030–2040	-2.5	8.0	9.7	5.8	1.1
2040–2050	-3.4	7.8	8.0	5.1	0.5
1990–2050	-0.6	75.8	113.1	67.6	21.0

Source: See source note for Table 1–3.

1990 to 2050. In fact, under the middle scenario 90 percent of the projected net increase in
the population from 1990 to 2050 of nearly 134 million persons would be due to minority
populations. As a result, as shown in Table 1–5, the proportion of the population that is
minority increases dramatically over time such that by 2050 more than 47 percent of the

TABLE 1–5   U.S. Bureau of the Census' Projections of the Percentage of the Population in the United States by Race/Ethnicity from 1990 to 2050 under Alternative Scenarios

Year	Anglo	Black	Hispanic	Other
Low Scenario				
1990	75.7	11.7	9.0	3.6
2000	72.4	12.3	10.7	4.6
2010	69.4	12.8	12.2	5.6
2020	66.6	13.2	13.6	6.6
2030	63.6	13.5	15.2	7.7
2040	60.6	13.8	16.8	8.8
2050	57.5	14.1	18.4	10.0
Middle Scenario				
1990	75.7	11.7	9.0	3.6
2000	71.6	12.3	11.1	5.0
2010	67.7	12.8	13.2	6.3
2020	63.9	13.3	15.2	7.6
2030	60.1	13.8	17.2	8.9
2040	56.3	14.4	19.2	10.1
2050	52.7	15.0	21.1	11.2
High Scenario				
1990	75.7	11.7	9.0	3.6
2000	70.9	12.3	11.5	5.3
2010	66.5	12.7	13.9	6.9
2020	62.3	13.1	16.2	8.4
2030	58.5	13.5	18.4	9.6
2040	54.7	13.9	20.6	10.8
2050	51.2	14.3	22.7	11.8
Zero-Immigration Scenario				
1990	75.7	11.7	9.0	3.6
2000	73.3	12.5	10.3	3.9
2010	71.1	13.3	11.4	4.2
2020	69.1	14.0	12.5	4.4
2030	66.9	14.9	13.6	4.6
2040	64.6	15.9	14.7	4.8
2050	62.1	17.1	15.8	5.0

Source: See source note for Table 1–3.

population would be composed of members of minority groups. Population growth in the United States will be largely attributable to growth in minority populations.

A second important aspect of the projected patterns is the effect of immigration on future population growth. This can be determined by comparing the values for the middle scenario to those for the zero-immigration scenario, because the zero-immigration scenario is identical in its assumptions to the middle scenario except that it assumes no net immigration. Such a comparison shows that immigration would account for 81.7 million additional persons by 2050 compared with what would have been in the population if only natural increase had occurred between 1990 and 2050. Because the total population growth projected under the middle scenario is roughly 134 million, this means that 61 percent of the total net increase in the U.S. population from 1990 through 2050 is projected to be due to immigrants and their descendants. It is maintained (Huddle, 1993) that recent immigrants have socioeconomically disadvantaged characteristics, so the needs of immigrants may well play a role in the growth in demand for social services in the coming decades.

A third trend of significance is that of the aging of the population. The data in Table 1–6 provide information on the aging of the population of the United States. In 1990, 12.6 percent of the population of the United States was 65 years of age or older, but by 2030, when all of the baby boomers (those born between 1946 and 1964) will be 65 years of age or older, 20.2 percent of the population will be 65 years of age or older. Although the percentage of persons under 18 will decline by 2 percent by 2050, the combination of young minority populations and older Anglo populations will result in an increase of 5.6 percent in the population in dependent ages. Given the projected population increase, this indicates a projected increase from 95 million persons in dependent ages of less than 18 and 65 years of age or older in 1990 to 167.6 million persons in these ages by 2050. Of particular significance for Medicare and related costs is the fact that it is the number of the very old who are the most likely to be in long-term care who will show the largest increase. Whereas those 75 years of age or older accounted for 5.3 percent of the population, or 13.2 million persons, in 1990, by 2050 persons 75 years of age or older would account for 11.4 percent of the population, or 43.6 million persons. The aging of the population will likely affect the need for services, particularly for the elderly.

Overall, then, to the extent that socioeconomic need remains concentrated in minority populations and in older and younger populations, future demographic patterns suggest increased levels of need for social services. The effects of such demand are examined in greater detail in the following section.

Implications of Future Population Change for Socioeconomic Need and Social Service Usage in the United States

What are the implications of the projected demographic changes noted above for social welfare needs in the United States in the coming years? To address this, the following paragraphs examine the likely implications of such changes for levels of socioeconomic resources and for selected health and long-term care services.

As noted in Tables 1–1 and 1–2, increased levels of poverty and related forms of need are associated with specific patterns of household composition. Table 1–7 shows projected patterns of household change for all households and projected changes in households by type in the United States assuming that 1990 patterns of household composition by age and race/ethnicity prevail in 2050. These data suggest several patterns of importance. First, unlike recent patterns of faster growth among nonfamily relative to family households, the higher proportion of minority populations in family households will lead to faster future

Table 1–6 U.S. Bureau of the Census' Projections of the Percentage of the Population in the United States by Age and Median Age by Race/Ethnicity from 1990 to 2050 under the Middle Scenario

Age Group	Percentage of Population by Age and Race/Ethnicity				
	Anglo	Black	Hispanic	Other	Total
		1990 Census			
1990					
<18	23.3	31.9	34.7	30.2	25.6
18–24	10.0	12.3	14.2	12.2	10.7
25–34	16.9	18.0	19.7	19.0	17.4
35–44	15.5	14.0	13.2	16.4	15.1
45–54	10.7	8.7	7.7	9.7	10.1
55–64	9.2	6.6	5.3	6.3	8.5
65–74	8.3	5.1	3.2	4.1	7.3
75–84	4.7	2.6	1.6	1.7	4.1
85+	1.4	0.8	0.4	0.4	1.2
Median age	34.8	28.0	25.3	29.1	32.9
2000					
<18	23.1	32.0	33.9	29.6	25.7
18–24	8.8	11.1	11.6	10.7	9.5
25–34	12.8	14.3	17.0	16.6	13.6
35–44	16.4	15.7	15.7	16.5	16.3
45–54	14.5	11.6	9.9	12.0	13.5
55–64	9.6	6.9	5.7	7.1	8.7
65–74	7.6	4.8	3.7	4.6	6.6
75–84	5.3	2.6	1.9	2.2	4.5
85+	1.9	1.0	0.6	0.7	1.6
Median age	38.4	30.1	28.1	30.9	35.6
2030					
<18	19.8	29.6	29.7	26.4	23.4
18–24	8.0	10.6	10.9	10.3	9.1
25–34	11.3	13.0	14.3	14.8	12.3
35–44	12.7	12.6	13.0	14.1	12.9
45–54	11.8	10.3	10.5	11.7	11.4
55–64	11.6	9.3	9.1	9.5	10.7
65–74	13.1	8.7	7.4	7.2	10.9
75–84	8.7	4.4	3.8	4.2	6.9
85+	3.0	1.5	1.3	1.8	2.4
Median age	43.4	32.8	31.8	33.9	39.0
20/50					
<18	19.2	29.4	27.9	24.8	23.2
18–24	7.8	10.4	10.4	9.9	9.0
25–34	11.5	12.9	14.0	14.3	12.5
35–44	11.8	11.9	12.6	13.7	12.2
45–54	11.7	10.4	10.8	11.9	11.4
55–64	12.5	9.7	9.4	9.8	11.1
65–74	11.0	7.5	7.1	7.4	9.2
75–84	8.5	4.6	5.0	5.0	6.8
85+	6.0	3.2	2.8	3.2	4.6
Median age	44.6	33.2	33.5	35.6	39.3

Source: See source note for Table 1–3.

TABLE 1–7   Number of Households by Type in the United States and Percentage Change in the Number of Households by Type, from 1990 to 2050 under the Middle Scenario

Household Type	Number		Percentage Change
	1990	2050	
Family households	65,329,955	109,660,675	67.9
Married Couple			
With own children	24,512,124	42,690,107	74.2
Without own children	27,155,876	40,521,533	49.2
Male householder with no spouse present			
With own children	1,331,025	2,674,385	100.9
Without own children	1,729,275	3,385,195	95.8
Female householder with no spouse present			
With own children	6,031,320	12,089,964	100.5
Without own children	4,570,335	8,299,491	81.6
Nonfamily households	26,617,456	40,917,753	53.7
Total households	91,947,411	150,578,428	63.8

Source: Derived from Steve H. Murdock, *An America Challenged: Population Change and the Future of the United States*, Boulder, CO: Westview Press, 1995.

growth in family than nonfamily households. Thus the number of family households would increase by nearly 68 percent from 1990 to 2050, compared to 54 percent for nonfamily households. The data also suggest, however, that growth will be most substantial among single-parent households with children. Since these are the household types most likely to need social services, this finding suggests that future demographic patterns will likely lead to a larger number of households that have higher levels of need.

By applying 1990 income levels for households with heads with different racial/ethnic statuses to the projected patterns of population change shown in Table 1–7, some indication can be obtained of how future levels of socioeconomic resources are likely to be altered as a result of demographic change (and in the absence of changes in the historical relationships between demographic and socioeconomic factors). Tables 1–8 and 1–9 present information on both aggregate income and poverty levels (in 1990 dollars) resulting from the projected patterns of demographic change.

The data in Table 1–8 shows aggregate income by racial/ethnic group assuming 1990 patterns of income by race/ethnicity of the householder. These data show a shift in the overall proportion of aggregate income accounted for by Anglo and minority households as a result of large increases in the number and proportion of minority households. However, the net effects on income growth is of even more importance. The growth in the total number of households (as shown in Table 1–7) is 63.8 percent versus an overall growth in

TABLE 1–8   Aggregate and Average Per-Household Income by Race/Ethnicity of the Householder in 1990 and Projected for 2050 Assuming 1990 Race/Ethnicity Composition (Aggregate Income in Thousands of 1990 Dollars)

	1990		2050		
	Aggregate Income	Percentage	Aggregate Income	Percentage	Percentage Change, 1990–2050
Anglo	$2,967,995,019	85.0	$3,566,695,797	65.8	20.2
Black	252,684,462	7.2	552,827,760	10.2	118.8
Hispanic	181,860,688	5.2	813,452,899	15.0	347.3
Other	89,202,918	2.6	486,397,473	9.0	445.3
Total	3,491,743,087	100.0	5,419,373,929	100.0	55.2
Average per-household income	$37,975	—	$35,990	—	-5.2

Source: See source note for Table 1–7.

income of 55.2 percent. As a result, there is a decline in average per household income of 5 percent. Because of changes in the composition of households, the average household may be poorer in 2050 than in 1990.

The data in Table 1–9 also suggest that demographic trends will likely increase the number of families in poverty. Again, the data in this table assume that poverty levels by race/ethnicity and household type in 1990 would prevail in 2050. What these data suggest is that poverty levels would increase for all households by more than 3 percent and would increase most rapidly for those households with children, both married couples and single parents. Clearly, then, the changes projected are likely to further impoverish the population of the United States, unless the historical relationships between specific household forms, socioeconomic resources, and race/ethnicity status are changed.

The data in Tables 1–10 and 1–11 show the incidence of diseases and disorders by race/ethnicity and the change in proportion of incidences by type likely to be attributable to persons from different racial/ethnic groups. These data show a marked shift of health care needs toward minority populations. This is especially true for such health occurrences as those related to pregnancy and infants. In these health care areas, minority populations would account for 56 percent of all cases involving pregnancy and for 66 percent of cases involving disorders among newborns and neonates by 2050. Health care needs may also shift toward populations with fewer resources to address such needs.

Table 1–12 provides an example of what the aging of the population may mean for long-term care needs in America. In this table nursing home care populations and monthly costs are shown assuming that the age, sex, and race/ethnicity patterns of long-term needs in 1990 prevailed in 2050 and population increased according to the patterns projected under the middle scenario. The data in this table show a substantial growth in need. The number of persons in nursing homes would increase from 1.5 million in 1990 to 5.8

TABLE 1–9   Number and Percentage of Families in Poverty by Family Type in 1990 and Projected for 2050 under the Middle Scenario

Family Type	1990 Number	1990 Percentage	2050 Number	2050 Percentage	Percentage Change 1990–2050
Married couple	3,025,963	5.9	6,536,639	7.9	116.0
With children < 18 yrs of age	688,416	12.5	1,736,869	16.6	152.3
No children < 18 yrs of age	1,096,179	4.0	1,995,366	4.9	82.0
Male householder with no spouse present	409,086	13.4	953,631	15.7	133.1
With children < 18 yrs of age	64,607	31.7	171,810	35.3	165.9
No children < 18 yrs of age	143,777	8.3	331,342	9.8	130.5
Female householder with no spouse present	3,093,965	29.2	6,823,513	33.5	120.5
With children < 18 yrs of age	784,174	63.9	1,846,954	66.5	135.5
No children < 18 yrs of age	508,243	11.0	1,113,326	13.4	119.1
Total households	6,529,014	10.0	14,313,773	13.1	119.2

Source: See source note for Table 1–7.

million in 2050, an increase of 292.5 percent. This rate of increase is more than five times the rate of population growth from 1990 to 2050. Growth in need is particularly accentuated among the oldest of the elderly. Whereas the number of residents in the age group of 65 to 74 years of age would increase by 94.5 percent from 1990 to 2050, the number of residents 75 to 84 years of age would increase by 158.7 percent and the number of residents 85 years of age or older would increase by 473.1 percent.

In sum, whether examined in terms of changes in levels of socioeconomic resources or in terms of direct demands on services such as health care and long-term care services, the demographic changes projected for the United States in the coming years are likely to substantially affect the size of the populations in need of social, health, and related services. Such increases have clear implications for those involved in the delivery of social and health-related services and the development of policies to address the need for such services.

Implications of Future Demographic Trends for Welfare Programs

The trends projected for the U.S. population will have substantial impacts on the demand for social services in the United States. The increasing size of minority populations, the growth in immigrant populations, and the increasing number of single-parent households and of elderly persons will increase the number of persons likely to require such services. What are the implications of such findings, and how can these increased needs be addressed?

First, the data reported here suggest that those who see the difficulties surrounding the provision of social assistance as a short-term phenomenon are likely to be discom-

TABLE 1–10   Projections of the Incidences and Percentage Change in the Incidences of Diseases/Disorders in the United States by Race/Ethnicity from 1990 to 2050 under the Middle Scenario

Year	Anglo	Black	Hispanic	Other	Total
			Incidences by Race/Ethnicity		
1990	651,760,177	83,918,053	59,163,781	27,500,015	822,342,026
2000	694,052,322	98,824,620	83,583,207	43,988,342	920,448,491
2010	727,979,527	114,836,156	111,465,938	62,264,604	1,016,546,225
2020	765,731,227	132,472,484	143,499,310	82,630,767	1,124,333,788
2030	797,398,740	150,468,408	179,192,943	104,706,048	1,231,766,139
2040	802,062,803	167,550,328	217,013,366	127,678,839	1,314,305,336
2050	787,170,309	184,243,762	254,087,541	151,029,549	1,376,531,161
		Percentage Change in Incidences by Race/Ethnicity			
1990–2000	6.5	17.8	41.3	60.0	11.9
2000–2010	4.9	16.2	33.4	41.5	10.4
2010–2020	5.2	15.4	28.7	32.7	10.6
2020–2030	4.1	13.6	24.9	26.7	9.6
2030–2040	0.6	11.4	21.1	21.9	6.7
2040–2050	-1.9	10.0	17.1	18.3	4.7
1990–2050	20.8	119.6	329.5	449.2	67.4

Source: See source note for Table 1–7.

forted by these findings. In fact, these data strongly suggest that determining more effective means to provide social welfare services and to move populations from dependence to independence will become even more important in the coming years. The welfare problem will not go away but will likely be accentuated by projected population patterns.

It is also important to note that one means of addressing the likely implications of future demographic change on social service needs is to institute programs that alter the historical relationships between certain demographic characteristics and levels of socioeconomic resources. Programs to improve the socioeconomic opportunities of minority residents and immigrants thus become both a means of improving the lives of individual members of such groups and of reducing the likely demand on public resources. It is critical that policy makers come to recognize in their formulation of programs, and policy researchers in their analyses of the impacts of programs on clients, the ways in which different types of needs interact to accentuate public welfare needs or to decrease such needs. Analyzing the impacts of policy change on discrete programs without examining the impacts of such changes on other programs has limited value. The costs of not providing care in one area (such as workforce training) may markedly affect needs in other areas (such as AFDC and Medicaid). Altering the levels of socioeconomic resources associated with given demographic groups is one means of altering the long-term need for social welfare programs.

TABLE 1–11   Projections of the Incidences of Diseases/Disorders in the United States Accounted for by Anglos by Type of Disease/Disorder, 1990 and 2050 under the Middle Scenario

Disease/Disorder	1990	2050
Nervous system	79.1	58.0
Eye	81.0	60.6
Ear, nose, and throat	77.6	54.6
Respiratory system	78.5	56.1
Circulatory system	81.8	59.8
Digestive system	80.1	59.0
Hepatobiliary system	80.7	59.2
Musculoskeletal system	81.4	59.4
Subcutaneous tissue and breast	79.3	57.7
Endocrine, nutritional, and metabolic	75.9	51.9
Kidney and urinary	78.9	57.0
Male reproductive system	80.0	59.1
Female reproductive system	75.1	50.7
Pregnancy and childbirth	71.5	44.4
Newborns and other neonates	58.2	34.3
Blood and immunological	73.8	52.1
Myeloproliferative	75.4	52.4
Infectious and parasitic	80.7	58.0
Mental	75.1	51.1
Substance abuse	68.8	40.9
Drug poisoning	80.7	58.8
Burns	59.0	35.9
Other	75.1	52.3

Source: See source note for Table 1–7.

If one assumes that mitigating the demographic-need linkages described above will, at best, only partially alleviate the growth in demand for services, the sheer size of the likely increases suggests the need for additional experimentation and innovation in the development of programs for the delivery of social services. We must develop more effective means for moving persons from poverty as children to full participation in the economy as adults and must similarly more effectively integrate newly arrived immigrants into the U.S. economy. We must develop more effective means of managing long-term care, or the costs of such care are likely to be prohibitive. These and other needs must be addressed with whatever type of program will most effectively provide the services needed by dependent population groups while providing a path to future independence and a reduction in the level of the public's burden of support. The use of new and innovative approaches of a variety of types is likely to be essential for the United States to address its future social service needs adequately.

The demographic changes impacting the future of welfare service needs in the United States represent only some of the many dimensions that will likely affect the future of such services in the United States. Economic, social, political, cultural, programmatic, and other

TABLE 1–12   Projected Number of Nursing Home Residents and Total Monthly Costs (in 1990 Dollars) in the United States by Age of Resident and Year for the Middle Scenario

Year/Age of Resident	Residents	Total Monthly Costs
1990		
65–74	226,332	$ 310,527,477
75–84	580,180	851,703,844
85+	678,560	1,015,804,843
Total	1,485,072	2,178,036,164
2000		
65–74	228,219	$ 313,116,893
75–84	712,013	1,045,234,878
85+	944,760	1,414,305,166
Total	1,884,992	2,772,656,937
2030		
65–74	473,318	$ 649,392,584
75–84	1,361,303	1,998,393,405
85+	1,846,273	2,763,870,112
Total	3,680,894	5,411,656,101
2050		
65–74	440,206	$ 603,962,234
75–84	1,500,657	2,202,964,784
85+	3,888,664	5,821,330,008
Total	5,829,527	8,628,257,026

Source: See source note for Table 1–7.

factors may be as important as or more important than demographic factors. We believe, however, that knowledge of the likely demographic changes underlying such service needs is a basic prerequisite to the development of effective policies for serving the social welfare needs of Americans in the remainder of this decade and the next century.

References

Bane, M. J., & Ellwood, D. T. (1994). *Welfare realities: From rhetoric to reform.* Cambridge, MA: Harvard University Press.

Berger, M. C. (1993, April 1–3). *The aging of the population, Medicaid expenditures, and the duration of Medicaid spell.* Paper presented at the Annual Meeting of the Population Association of America, Cincinnati, OH.

Clark, R. L. (1994). The cost of providing public assistance and education to immigrants. *Program for Research on Immigration Policy,* Washington, DC.

Danziger, S. H., Sandefur, G. D., & Weinberg, D. H. (1994). *Confronting poverty: Prescriptions for change.* New York: Harvard University Press.

Day, J. F. (1992). Population projections of the United States by age, sex, race, and Spanish origin,

1992–2050. *Current Population Reports,* Series P-25, No. 1092. U.S. Bureau of the Census. Washington, DC: U.S. Government Printing Office.

Huddle, D. (1993). *The costs of immigration.* Washington, DC: Carrying Capacity Network.

Karger, H. J., & Stoesz, D. (1994). *American social welfare policy: A pluralist approach* (2nd ed.). White Plains, NY: Longman.

Murdock, S. H. (1995). *An America challenged: Population change and the future of the United States.* Boulder, CO: Westview Press.

O'Hare, W. P. (1987). America's welfare population: Who gets what?. *Population Trends and Public Policy No. 13,* Washington, DC: Population Reference Bureau.

Passel, J. S. (1994). Immigrants and taxes: A reappraisal of Huddle's "The cost of immigrants." *Program for Research on Immigration Policy,* Washington, DC: The Urban Institute.

Rural Sociological Society Task Force on Persistent Rural Poverty. (1993). *Persistent poverty in rural America.* Boulder, CO: Westview Press.

Soldo, B. J. (1988). America's elderly. *Population Bulletin, 43,* 1–53. Washington, DC: Poplulation Reference Bureau.

U.S. Bureau of the Census. (1991). Poverty in the United States: 1990. *Current Population Reports,* Series P-60, No. 175, Washington, DC: U.S. Government Printing Office.

U.S. House of Representatives, Congressional Research Service. (1993). *Medicaid source book: Background data and analysis (a 1993 update).* Washington, DC: U.S. Government Printing Office.

U.S. House of Representatives, Committee on Ways and Means. (1993). *Overview of entitlement programs.* Washington, DC: U.S. Government Printing Office.

Information Technology

How Social Work Is Going Digital

WALLACE J. GINGERICH, PhD, and RONALD K. GREEN, JD, ACSW
Case Western Reserve University

The Information Technology Explosion

Social workers are currently faced with an explosion of information technology. A critical issue facing our profession is whether we will be able to adapt to this explosion and harness it for the good of our consumers, or whether by the year 2000 and beyond we will simply be "blown away" by it.

The rapidly increasing capability of information technology combined with dramatically decreasing costs is now almost commonplace. Today's battery-operated notebook computers have more computing power inside their small cases than the room-filling mainframe computers of the mid-1970s, and they can be purchased for several thousand dollars instead of millions. This is a startling development when one considers that the first personal (desktop) computer was invented only 20 years ago. And as for large computers, today's machines can perform tasks that were hardly imaginable only 20 years ago—creating virtual realities for research and entertainment, simulating highly complex problems such as weather patterns, and carrying out mathematical calculations that were impossible to do manually.

If the trends of the last 50 years continue into the twenty-first century, as they are expected to do, it is difficult to imagine all of the ways in which social work practice will be affected. We shall try, nonetheless, to identify some impacts information technology will probably have on social work clients, social workers, and the services we deliver.

What Is Information Technology?

Perhaps we should begin by saying what we mean by *information technology*. We use the term to encompass (1) computing technology in its many forms, (2) the electronic networks that tie computers together over long distances, and (3) the capacity of these networks to transmit not only simple text data but voice and images as well. Developments in these technologies are combining to create the information technology explosion. The information technology explosion is already having an impact on social work practice, but the current impact is small compared to what it will become in the early decades of the twenty-first century.

In the short 50-year history of electronic computing, computers have moved out of the research laboratories and universities and onto our office desks, kitchen counters, and even our wrists. Computers now serve us when we go to the bank for cash; they draw three-dimensional pictures of vital human organs; and they help to land airplanes. Computers advise auto mechanics on what repairs to perform, and they help physicians decide which patients can benefit most from scarce medical procedures. Computers are so ubiquitous that they go largely unnoticed.

Information Technology of the Future

As computing technology continues to develop computers will become more humanlike in how they interact with people and, indeed, in the tasks they are able to perform. Computers can already speak and respond to spoken commands, and they can recognize people by seeing them through video imaging. These capabilities are limited now but will become more powerful and commonplace by the year 2000. As computers develop, they will increasingly be able to perform tasks now considered to require human intelligence, tasks such as deciding which clients are eligible for benefits, providing face-to-face (or, should we say, video-to-face) educational and therapeutic services, and advising on critical issues such as whether a child is at risk for abuse or neglect. In fact, computers are already doing all of these things. Currently these applications are largely experimental. By the year 2000 they will be fairly routine.

Following the developments in computing technology, communications are going digital, the language of computers. By the year 2000 the majority of voice, data, graphic, and video transmissions traveling to our homes or offices will be in digital form and carried by a single transmission system. No longer will we have a simple two-wire phone system, a coaxial cable TV system, and a dedicated high-speed digital data line serving a single site. What we now know as television will be carried on the same line (perhaps fiber optic) as voice and data communications, and it will have the capacity for interactive communication. Most individuals will have access to the Internet or its successor through this new communications channel, which will provide for interactive connection with a potentially *infinite number of information sources.* Not only will you be able to select the movie of your choice, see the rerun of the football game you missed, or order the consumer goods you want to purchase, but you will also be able to determine what benefits you are eligible for and take advantage of a wide variety of interactive self-help programs.

With the coming technology people will have the same ease with video (visual) communication from point to point that they have now with the telephone. In the year 2000 the old party-line telephone conversation will have evolved into a video conference between family members, a community committee, or a work group located in dispersed areas of the state or the nation, or around the world. Because of the interconnectivity of the networks, a wide range of fully developed interactive multimedia programs will be accessible from the home or office. Access to virtual reality software will be as close as the local library or your local retailer.

The Information Revolution

The information revolution affects not just social workers and their clients but society at large. Scholars and futurists have referred to the current period of history as the information revolution, following the industrial revolution of the last several centuries and the agrarian society before it. In the information revolution, information is becoming the new capital, replacing money and factories, and the dominant worker function is managing information rather than producing agricultural goods or manufacturing products. With the information revolution, people will no longer be required to live near the factory or office because they will be able to transact much of their business using information networks. Just as the industrial revolution changed the nature of work (from field work in the country to factory work in the city) and the structure of society (from largely self-sufficient rural households to a highly specialized and interdependent urban society), so will the information revolution have far-reaching impacts over the next decades.

Modern computers have greatly enhanced ability to store and process large amounts of information, and with this ability has come the capacity to synthesize and create new information. Increasingly, computers will be able to perform activities that were once considered intelligent, that is, activities that could only be performed by humans. However, as the capabilities of computers continue to increase, they will challenge our accepted definitions of human intelligence and human behavior and will prompt a redefinition and new appreciation of what comes to be understood as essential human qualities. Just as machines greatly enhanced the physical capacities of humans during the industrial period, so information technology will enhance the information-processing capacity of humans in the information revolution. Whether or not these new capabilities are considered truly intelligent, it is clear that computers will increasingly relieve humans of many cognitive activities they now do for themselves—much as the bank's computers do today when they add up account balances at the end of the workday.

Developments in communications and networking over long distances likewise are having an impact on society in general. Electronic networking effectively removes the constraints of distance and scheduling in enabling people to interact with each other at any time of day, and at almost any point around the globe. With the invention of the telephone, social workers could interact with people at a distance, saving the cost and inconvenience of physical travel, and gradually a new type of service developed—the anonymous telephone helpline. Sophisticated communications will bring new capabilities for service and, in all likelihood, new services that haven't even been thought of to date.

It is impossible to predict all of the ways the information revolution will affect social work consumers and social work practice. However, we can predict with some confidence the kinds of changes we will see in the near term, the year 2000 for example, because most of the innovations we will see in day-to-day social work practice are being developed and tested in research labs and demonstration projects. In the pages that follow we will describe some of these innovative developments and the ways they are likely to affect social work practice.

Information Technology and Social Work Practice

Client Records Will Be Automated

By the year 2000 many agencies will have automated their client records. In the short term, information will continue to be entered from the keyboard, but developments in handwriting and speech recognition will soon allow the social worker to write or speak into the computer, and the computer will record the information in text form for later use and analysis. Likewise, instead of reading case records, the busy social worker may have the computer talk to him or her while en route to an appointment. All of the diagnostic and assessment tools will be contained on the computer for immediate use and analysis as needed. In addition, agency policies and procedures will be included for immediate reference, as well as expert system modules that will advise on assessment, goal-setting, treatment selection, and case management strategies.

Because computers will be smaller and more powerful, social workers will carry them along just as we carry appointment books today. And because computers will be able to connect to networks through phone lines and cellular phones, they will interact with the agency's central information bases to upload information, coordinate appointments, and obtain information from resource directories. In addition, because the agency's computer will be connected to the information highway, the social worker will be able to access information and interact with other professionals on the network located anywhere around the world. So, for example, the social worker will be able to search a bibliographic database to find the latest information on a new intervention, consult an authoritative state-of-the-art expert system for advice on a specialized problem, or access a nationally coordinated resource directory for needed services.

With automated client records will come the capacity to conduct analyses of one's practice to identify which interventions and programs are effective and which are not. Such automated programs will also have the capacity to advise the worker on which clients need service and what type of service is needed. These tools will function much like an assistant to the social worker, looking after many of the routine information management tasks of practice and freeing the social worker to engage in the more innovative and highly skilled aspects of practice.

Will computerized recording take care of the chief complaint of social workers today, paperwork? Perhaps, but probably not. One of the laws of the information explosion seems to be that the volume of information gathered expands to take up the increased capacity to manage it. So whether or not social workers spend less time documenting and analyzing services, it is almost certain that they will be maintaining more and better information about their cases.

Routine Tasks Will Be Automated

As any practicing social worker knows, many of the tasks in day-to-day practice do not require specialized judgment expertise. Determining eligibility for benefits or services is one example. Teaching well-defined social skills may be another such task, and delivering a structured self-help intervention may be another. Increasingly, computers will begin to assist with such routine tasks or even do them themselves. Rule-based expert systems are ideally suited for many of these tasks.

Self-Help Technologies

Through the use of interactive TV, compact disc–interactive (CD-I), and other interactive multimedia technologies, a whole new set of psychosocial interactive intervention supports will be available. These interactive technologies will allow the participant to actively engage with the program they are "watching." For example, a person selecting a movie on interactive TV will control the level of violence, type of ending, gender of the lead, and otherwise directly shape the nature of the program he or she will watch. Likewise, self-help programs using CD-I technology will allow a parent to view a video scenario of a parent-child interaction, select a parenting response, and immediately view the effect of the choice on the child. Such tools will be accessible from home or from psychosocial support interactive technology centers. If the person is unclear about exactly what is needed, an automated self-help kiosk will carry on an interactive assessment dialog to identify the type of skill or advice that is desired, and then will show a listing of relevant interactive tools.

As multimedia self-help technology becomes more prevalent, a new social work role will emerge in which the social worker is the content specialist on the multimedia development team. The use of multimedia technology for self-help interventions will not be without problems, however. There will probably be a need for some type of screening system to make the more emotionally powerful interactive programs available only through licensed mental health practitioners. Further, legal issues of professional liability for interventions mediated through information technology have yet to be worked out.

Community Will Be Defined Electronically

Electronic networks will allow communities of people to form and interact without requiring participants to gather in a single physical place. Community practitioners will be able to develop "digital groups." Community meetings of neighborhood groups or public housing residents could be held without individuals' having to leave their apartments. As a result, those previously excluded, such as people with disabilities, frail elderly, or those afraid to go out at night, can now participate through technology such as video conferencing or interactive TV.

The role of the community practitioner will be to help residents learn how to use the technology as well as to promote the involvement and empowerment process. In order to ensure equal access to the new electronic community, programs providing supports to low-income persons will need to include information technology supports. Social workers will need to be outspoken advocates for policies supporting equal access. Public housing will need to be wired to support the digital link to the information networks. Federal, state, and local governments will need to provide tax incentives or other supports for current home-owners to complete local links to the networks. Perhaps an approach similar to the public policies providing incentives to make homes and commercial buildings more energy efficient will need to be adopted.

Access to Services Will Be Immediate

Caseworkers will be able to help link clients with other needed resources in real time. Utilizing portables and video conferencing techniques, a client and a referral source can be introduced, relevant client records faxed, transportation identified (through geocoded resource identification techniques), transportation arranged (such as electronic scheduling of community responsive transit), and an electronic reminder created to ensure follow up.

All service and self-help information will be accessible from single entry points, either from home or a nearby community resource such as a neighborhood center, community elementary school, or library. From these entry points to the information highway, community residents will be able to access needed information that they previously obtained from service providers. Those eligible for public benefits of various kinds will be able to check their eligibility on-line and determine exactly what they are entitled to. If a face-to-face interview is required, it will be done on the spot through video conferencing technology. Labor force–related information will be immediately available. Assessment tools of various kinds will be available on-line, and there will be much greater emphasis on self-help. In such an environment, the role of the social worker will be to help the resident to be comfortable with the technology and then help in navigating the system if needed.

Agencies in the business of case management will be reconfigured to use video conferencing techniques extensively to maintain contact with clients. In this way clients will not have to deal with issues of child care and transportation to maintain contact. In those cases in which a family does not have the video conferencing technology at home, there will be neighborhood access points available as mentioned above.

A major new community service will be developed to provide community access points to the new information technologies. An issue will develop as to whether these access points should be from community social service agencies, through information service organizations such as libraries, or through neighborhood schools. The current wave of experimentation of joining the elementary and secondary school with human service organizations to produce family-centered local schools could well provide the most productive base for the development of these access centers, at least for families with school-age children.

Information Technology and Education

The impact of information technology on social work education and training will be profound. It will have a major impact on both the educational techniques that will be utilized to assist with the mastery of social work knowledge and skills and the content of the knowledge and skills that will be required for effective practice in the information age. This impact will be felt in the educational methods used to train social workers and the retooling needed to equip current practitioners for twenty-first-century practice.

Educational Methods

By the year 2000 we will probably see significant variances between those social work educational programs that fully incorporate information technologies as a regular part of their educational approach and those that do not. The difference between the early achievers and late adopters will be startling.

Digital courseware will be available to students for access from home, office, or classroom. With the advent of the information highway, courses developed by the most knowledgeable social work educators can be available to students anywhere around the world. There will be an increase in the use of individual interactive educational technologies for self-paced learning. There will also be an increase in the use of interactive technologies to assess student learning. The use of such technologies as simulations and virtual reality will provide for standardized assessment of students and the shaping of individualized educational plans.

With the use of video conferencing, a course emanating from one point in the nation will be accessible to students anywhere. The concept of a university without walls will become much more advanced. In 1995, for example, the University of Akron and Cleveland State University initiated an MSW program where half of the classes originate from Akron and the other half from Cleveland, with the students at the other campus participating in real time by remote audio and video. By the year 2000 this will become common practice.

Those schools of social work who can afford it will bring on faculty experts who may reside anywhere in the world but be available to students through the use of information technology. Students will be able to take course work from their work settings, field placements, or even homes. These developments will place new requirements on social work educators. Educators will need to be competent in distance teaching methods and video conferencing technology as well as in their social work subject matter. With increased use of broad-based dissemination capacity comes the issue of how to protect the intellectual property rights of the author of the material presented. It is anticipated that by the year 2000 metering technologies will have advanced sufficiently to permit wide access to information while still protecting the commercial interest of the developer.

Educational Content

As discussed earlier in this chapter, by the year 2000 and beyond, the practice of social work will be heavily affected by the availability of information technologies. This shift in the practice paradigm will require significant curricular shifts in social work educational programs and a major retooling of current social workers. Social workers will need to be fully competent in the use of information technologies. They will need to know what, how, and when to use interactive assessment tools; what, how, and when to use multimedia interactive interventions; and how to use technology to provide sound practice evaluation information.

To effectively utilize these tools social workers will still need a solid grounding in the social science of person in environment, interpersonal helping skills, and the policy framework within which they practice. In order to provide the old content with the new within two years, social work educational programs will have to rely to a much greater extent on the power of individualized interactive multimedia programs to facilitate the learning process.

The Retooling of Current Social Workers

Probably a more prodigious task than overhauling social work higher education will be bringing those social workers who were educated and trained prior to the information technology explosion into the information age. By the year 2000 those who chose social work because it was not viewed as a technical field of practice will be faced with making critical career decisions, either to embrace information technology or to choose another profession. By the turn of the century it is highly likely that there will be a major shakeout in the profession that will effect both individual workers and educational and practice organizations.

This scenario of social work practice in the twenty-first century suggests that there will be a major role for continuing education programs in helping current workers move into the information age. By the year 2000 there will be a range of continuing education and training programs utilizing the latest in interactive training technologies to assist those late adapters who want to retool for the information age. Perhaps we will also see the development of certification programs in social work information technology. Certainly, licensing and accreditation examinations will need to be updated.

Some Reflections on Going Digital

Historically, social work has not embraced information technology. There are good reasons for this. Social work and social workers are "high touch" by nature, not "high tech." Further, until recently computers were not adept at many of the tasks social workers do, tasks involving human communication and human interaction. The early adopters of information technology were found in industries such as banking, commercial airlines, and retailing, whose tasks consisted largely of number crunching and data processing and were easily adapted to the new technology. Although social work has not adopted information technology in any significant way up to now (except for administrative functions), it will be impossible to avoid using information technology in the future. Information technology will permeate our homes and schools and, indeed, our workplaces.

Our main purpose in this chapter has been to speculate how information technology will affect social work practice in the year 2000 and beyond. We have described changes we are already seeing and developments that we expect to see during the next decade. But our speculations are conservative—they are really only extrapolations of what we are currently seeing. Although our speculations are probably realistic, they understate the impact that information technology will have on social work practice in the following decades. This is where our crystal ball becomes more hazy, but it might be useful to consider for a moment where the information revolution could lead a bit further down the road.

In the coming decades the new capabilities opened up by information technology will begin to challenge some cherished ideas about what is good social work practice. As hinted above, the ability to span time and distance in real time will begin to challenge accepted views of community. Community may come to be defined electronically by who one interacts with over the information network rather than geographically by where one lives or functionally by what one does. Electronic community may open up new possibilities, but it may have its downside as well. Will there continue to be the social supports available to people in today's geographically defined communities? What will happen to the social fabric of community life—the norms and values that depend on a shared sense of community?

The information revolution will make its affect felt on a more personal level as well. As we are able to interact electronically, will we have less face-to-face contact? If so, will we experience a loss of essential aspects of human experience? Business and professional transactions can be carried out via electronic networks, but how about family and social interactions? Will electronic networking simply add to our social world, or will it begin to replace face-to-face interactions? How will such change affect the social well-being of our clients? How will it affect the kinds of services that social workers can and will provide?

As computers become more powerful and interact with us more naturally (that is, have more humanlike interfaces), they will begin to challenge some of our long-held ideas about the nature of intelligence. New computing architectures designed more like the human brain may enable computers to perform activities previously thought to be the sole province of humans—activities such as *understanding* human speech, *recognizing* the identity of a person in a never-before-seen photograph, or *learning* new classification rules after processing many cases. Does such cognitive processing ability represent intelligence? What is intelligence, really, and if machines can be made to do intelligent things that would assist social workers in their work, should they be used? Our profession has long held that human interaction is essential in helping individuals and families. But what is it about the human relationship that is essential? As machines take on more humanlike capacities, social workers may need to rethink their answers to this question and begin to consider new possibilities as well.

The information revolution is forcing us to reexamine other issues. As information systems become more prevalent, and there is more and more information circulating about each of us, the issue of personal privacy arises: the extent to which we as individuals own the "rights" to information about ourselves. Or put another way, what does confidentiality mean in the information age, and who is in charge of confidentiality issues?

As we noted earlier, the increasing use of self-help interventions disseminated via information technology will raise new issues of legal and professional liability. Who is responsible for the outcome when an intervention (such as a parent training program on CD-ROM) is designed and delivered to someone whom the practitioner has never met? Or what about support group interventions delivered via the Internet or an electronic bulletin board? Just what is the practitioner's liability? Clearly, our legal system and professional ethics will need to address these issues in the near future.

Information technology is providing new opportunities for social work, but it also brings new challenges. We hope that our predictions have been informative and thought provoking. We hope, too, that you have begun to see some new possibilities for creative use of information technology, as well as becoming aware of some of the challenges that the technology creates for the clients and the profession. Our hope is that as the profession goes digital, as it inevitably will, social workers will not just go along but will be prepared to lead the way for creative and constructive new solutions.

Chapter 3

Measuring Effectiveness of Social Work Practice

Beyond the Year 2000

BERIT INGERSOLL-DAYTON, PhD and SRINIKA JAYARATNE, PhD
University of Michigan

As the beginning of the twenty-first century approaches, social workers are in a unique position to reflect on their experiences and ponder the future. They have seen the emergence of many serious social issues (such as drug and alcohol abuse, family violence, and teen pregnancy) and an explosion of new practice innovations and technologies. With the advent of managed care, dramatic changes in the service delivery structure, and significant cost containment efforts, the role of social workers will inevitably change. Learning from the past and looking to the future would enable social workers to consider ways to reorient the practice of social work. This chapter will forecast trends in accountable practice, describe our predictions concerning how social work effectiveness will be measured, discuss benefits and problems related to future technological innovations, and suggest ways of preparing for future accountable practice.

Future Trends in Accountable Practice

Several recent societal trends are likely to change the face of future social work practice. Federal and state funding for social services can no longer be taken for granted. Instead, social workers will need to advocate for and demonstrate the effectiveness of their programs. Insurance companies that provide third-party payment for social work treatment will increase their emphasis on cost containment and are likely to link reimbursement to demonstrated improvement. Further, as social work services increasingly fall under the umbrella of managed care, there will be efforts to establish uniform criteria for the definition of effectiveness and treatment success.

Each of these trends will influence social work practice and its accountability in several ways. First, in an effort to contain costs, there will be increased pressure to provide short-term intervention. Second, to ensure high-quality results, public and private funding sources will insist on results-oriented outcomes. As social work agencies contract with or join managed care organizations, there will be more emphasis on uniformity of outcome criteria across social work settings. Third, this emphasis on cost containment and uniform outcome indicators will inevitably lead to the use of more automated procedures in social work settings.

At the direct practice level, there are many new private-sector opportunities for the provision of social work services. Employee assistance programs, for example, are increasingly likely to contract out services to private social work practitioners. Concomitant with these new roles, however, will be a growing pressure to demonstrate practice effectiveness using uniform assessment and evaluation tools. To minimize intervention and evaluation time, funding sources will insist that practitioners use specific rapid-assessment instruments in relation to certain clinical problems. For example, if a client presents with anxiety and depression, the social worker will be required to administer two short standardized questionnaires that concern each of these problem areas. These same questionnaires will then be administered periodically throughout treatment to determine the client's progress over time.

As our society becomes increasingly multicultural, there will be pressure to ensure that such instruments are reliable and valid for a variety of client groups. Many existing rapid-assessment tools have not been tested extensively within various racial and ethnic groups. It is crucial that, as practitioners adopt a uniform set of measurement instruments, such instruments are thoroughly evaluated for their psychometric characteristics as well as their sensitivity to change among a wide variety of client groups. It will also be important to have established norms on these instruments with respect to gender, ethnicity, and race.

The use of uniform outcome indicators will allow for the development of centralized data-gathering banks at the community, state, and national levels. We predict that agencies will be required to report to such banks concerning their clients' demographic characteristics, their target problems, the interventions used, and the intervention outcomes. States may use these data to distribute future funds to agencies and communities. States, in turn, may have to use these data to justify the receipt of federal funds.

With the increasing emphasis on results-oriented outcomes, professional groups such as the NASW are likely to become more involved in establishing and maintaining standards of accountable practice. With increasing privatization in service delivery, there will likely be increased competition for resources. Undoubtedly, this kind of scenario could lead to "cutting corners" and the potential to provide the cheapest services possible. To counteract the negative consequences of such a system, social work practitioners, administrators, and researchers will need to collaborate and play a more proactive role in this process of defining service adequacy and evaluative criteria. The results of such an effort should be the development of evaluation tools and national standards for effective social work practice.

Measuring Practice Effectiveness in the Next Century

Within the next few decades the United States will have spawned a generation of children who are computer literate. These children are the social workers and clients of the future who will be comfortable interacting with computers at home and in an agency setting. Virtual reality and cyberspace will be integrated into the daily life and work of future generations. Computers and related technologies will become essential to social work practice at both the client and agency level. The use of such technology will enable social work administrators and practitioners to gather systematic data about their client populations, evaluate their interventions, and determine their effectiveness.

Future Technological Innovations in Direct Social Work Practice

A social work intake interview during the next century will look quite different from current procedures. Rather than being asked to fill out multiple forms before meeting with a social worker, the client may be asked to enter basic demographic data directly into a computer in the agency waiting room. Similarly, after the social worker has met the client and established some rapport, she may enter additional data on her own laptop during the interview. This direct entry of information by the client and worker will provide crucial data for the agency's demographic profile of clients, allow for the collection of baseline data on the client's presenting problems, and alleviate the time-consuming step of entering data from a series of intake forms completed by hand.

Computers will also be used in the development of treatment programs and continued monitoring of treatment progress. Expert systems, perhaps tied to centralized databases reflecting relative success with specific populations and problems, may be an on-line requirement. Thus not only will workers be guided by empirical data referencing appropriate treatment protocols, but the determination of effectiveness will be based on standardized measures (such as self-esteem or depression) related to their treatment goals.

In the future, clients may routinely respond on the computer to a standardized set of questions about their problem areas before their weekly appointment with a social worker. Case managers housed in managed care operations may use this information to direct clients to appropriate resources. Scores from these responses will be converted to graphic form and used as baseline data to be compared with future scores. These data in turn will be available to both client and social worker as they discuss treatment progress. A few practice settings have already begun to experiment with this kind of monitoring, and continued progress in this direction is likely.

When the monitoring function requires the use of daily measures of client's feelings, thoughts, or behaviors, computers will help clients track their own observations and communicate these observations to the social worker. Clients will be able to enter their self-observations directly onto their home computers. Perhaps a few decades from now, for example, a social worker will be treating a father who is physically punishing his son. The social worker may establish a contract with the father who agrees to refrain from physical punishment and instead make use of time-outs as a way of establishing limits. The social worker could ask the father to enter onto the computer at the end of the day the number of times he disciplines physically and the number of times he uses time-outs. To obtain alternative sources of data measurement, the mother and the child might also be asked to report on their observations concerning the use of physical punishment and time-outs in the same manner. If it were important that the social worker see such data between treatment sessions, it would be possible to have the data transmitted directly to the social worker's computer. In so doing, the social worker would be able to monitor the client's progress on a daily basis. If problems were maintaining or increasing (for example, the father was using more physical discipline), the social worker could contact the father immediately either via the telephone or electronic mail to determine the appropriate course of action. Other technologies will also be useful in helping clients track their self-observations. For clients who do not have computers or who find the tracking of their daily observations difficult, the use of telephone voice mail may provide an alternative monitoring device. In such cases, the telephone would be programmed to call the client at a prespecified time each day with a series of questions regarding the client's observations. These responses could then be transmitted to a computer scoring program that would take the verbal answers and transform them into a graph that would be available for both the client and the social worker.

This kind of telephone technology would also be applicable to the gathering of follow-up data on clients' progress following social work intervention. At present, social workers rarely have the opportunity to contact clients with whom they have terminated treatment to determine their continued level of functioning. A reprogrammed telephone voice mail system could, however, inquire about the ongoing status of clients relative to their presenting problems. The information resulting from such follow-up questions could be transmitted to the social worker to help ascertain the long-term effects of the intervention and would also identify those clients who need additional social work intervention.

Future Technological Innovations in Administrative Practice

Computers and related technologies will also become crucial to administrators of social work agencies. With increased pressure to contain costs and demonstrate high-quality service, administrators will need to implement numerous data recording and reporting systems.

As they advocate for public funding, administrators will have to demonstrate a need for services among specific populations of potential clients. Agency administrators may be required to compile such data by surveying community needs. Rather than mailing surveys or using staff for in-person interviews, administrators will make use of computers and telephone voice mail systems. Through random-digit dialing, the computer will establish an adequate sample of potential clients. The preprogrammed voice mail system will then inquire about whether the telephone respondent is in need of specific services.

In addition to using telephone technology to complete a survey of needs assessments, administrators will also use such technology to establish service needs for all potential clients who contact an agency. Prior to receiving services, these clients will be asked to complete a brief voice mail interview about the kinds of services they need. In this interview, they will be asked to choose from a list of possible service needs. As in the telephone survey, their responses will be transmitted to a computer that will compile the data into categories of needed services for use by the administrator who is advocating for additional funding for social work programs.

Computer technology will also play a vital role in cost containment and the evaluation of service delivery effectiveness. As mentioned earlier, each direct service social worker will be collecting information on individual client's progress. These data can then be aggregated at the agency level to examine service delivery among all social workers on a number of dimensions. First, it will be possible to determine how many sessions clients have with social workers. Such basic treatment data are crucial to the cost containment constraints of managed care organizations. Second, these data will indicate the extent to which clients are experiencing both short-term and long-term improvement. As funding becomes contingent on the ability to demonstrate progress, such data will be necessary to maintain the viability of social work services. Third, it will be possible to determine what kinds of client problems experience the most dramatic improvement and which social workers have the most clients who are improving. Such data are important to administrators as they plan for staff development. If it is possible to identify which kinds of client problems are less responsive to current social work practice, then administrators can plan together with the direct service staff to develop alternative social work interventions. Likewise, if certain social workers are less successful at helping clients to change, administrators can help them find additional training opportunities to further develop their skills.

Potential Benefits and Problems Related to Future Technological Innovations

The scenarios portrayed here concerning the future of accountable social work practice may seem either exciting or frightening. The use of computers and other technologies to examine social work effectiveness is likely to be accompanied by a host of benefits as well as problems.

Potential Benefits

As increasing numbers of people in the society are computer literate, clients and social workers will be more comfortable directly interacting with a computer. As clients they may feel even more comfortable interacting with a computer than with a social worker. When clients are asked during an intake interview to describe their presenting problem or to monitor their self-observations over time, their responses may be more accurate if they do so with a computer than with a social worker whom they want to please or impress.

Using technological innovations to monitor client progress may be particularly beneficial for frail social work clients who are seen infrequently. Future social workers are likely to assist increasing numbers of older clients and clients with mental illnesses. These are individuals whose service needs may change dramatically at any time. If social workers could be alerted to their relapses either from data that the client has entered into the computer or from data generated by the daily voice mail monitoring, they would be able to provide assistance in a more timely fashion.

Likewise, making use of technology to assist in follow-up assessments would be a marked improvement on current practice. Today, most social workers are far too burdened by their present caseload to be able to engage in any systematic follow-up of previous clients. Indeed, in this era of cost containment, any agency that currently engages in follow-up phone calls, letters, or visits is likely to drop this practice because of the effort and expense associated with relying on agency staff to fulfill these time-consuming tasks. By using telephone and computer technology, social workers and their agencies will need to expend minimal effort on these tasks. Instead, the technology would provide them with more information about the long-term results of their interventions and would alert them to clients who have suffered a setback and need additional support.

Associated with the demands of managed care and the use of technology will be a move toward increasing specificity of treatment goals and the use of standardized measures of client problems. One benefit of this trend will be that social workers will be encouraged to be more precise about the desired outcomes of their interventions and clearer about their treatment plans. Another benefit will be that, as treatment goals and measures become less idiosyncratic, there will be more opportunity to aggregate client outcome data and compare the effects of different treatment with specified kinds of problems. The knowledge derived from such comparative approaches will aid in determining which kinds of social work interventions are most effective. Such information can then be organized and used to further refine and develop expert systems.

Finally, these future scenarios seek to empower clients further by having them integrally involved in assessing their progress. Their participation is a key element in our vision of the future. They will be involved in helping to specify clear intervention goals, collecting information on their own progress, and examining graphic representations of their progress. In conjunction with the social worker, they will review changes over time and participate in decisions about the need for further kinds of social work intervention. As clients are involved in each of these stages, we would expect that they would be further motivated to seek change and to accept ownership for their improvement.

Potential Problems

This vision of future social work accountability is heavily reliant on the use of technological innovations. Although future generations may be increasingly comfortable with computer technology, some clients may find that talking to a voice mail recording about their thoughts or entering numbers into a computer about their behaviors only exacerbates their feelings of isolation and alienation. Social workers may also feel that the picture painted here seems devoid of human contact and seriously impinges on their clinical judgment. What happens, for example, when after the presenting problem has been identified and appropriate measurements selected, a more fundamental problem emerges? To the extent that future intervention is likely to be short-term and measured by standardized rapid-assessment tools, the flexibility of social workers with regard to changes in treatment direction may be hampered.

Another concern is that the use of automated procedures, such as transmission of data between the client's computer and the social worker's, makes it increasingly difficult for social workers and social service agencies to have control over who has access to such information. Ensuring confidentiality when, in fact, multiple people may have access to computer records becomes problematic. Also, the use of preprogrammed telephone interviews for follow-up will create further problems with respect to confidentiality. For example, how can we be sure that, when the telephone recording begins discussing the client's previous treatment issues, that the telephone is communicating with the same client?

This vision of practice effectiveness measurement presumes that some social workers will be identified as being less effective than others. The ability to evaluate social workers in this way may seriously affect the climate of social service agencies, fostering mistrust and competition. Some social workers may be induced to fake their clients' data rather than appear to be ineffective. Agency administrators might use effectiveness data as a basis for firing social workers rather than as a way of identifying those who need additional training.

Perhaps the most serious concern about this possible future is that it relies so heavily on technological innovation that it may ignore those for whom such innovations are not available. Although it is likely that computer and telephone technologies will become increasingly commonplace, there may still be a substantial proportion of social work clients who do not have access to them. Social workers traditionally work with the poor and disenfranchised. It is very difficult to conceive of how social workers could monitor the progress of a homeless client using computer or telephone technology. Indeed, if social workers orient their assessment, monitoring, and evaluation procedures toward technologies that are not available to all clients, the clients' voices will be lost in the social workers' assessments of their needs and in the evaluation of practice. Further, to the extent that funding becomes heavily reliant on computerized data gathering, social work practice with populations that have no access to such technology may be less easily funded. Specialized agencies and differentiated practice may emerge in relation to sources of funding. Results-oriented funding would be available to social workers providing computerized data-gathering services, whereas only flat-rate funding would be available to those providing non-computerized services.

Preparing Ourselves for Future Accountable Practice

The trends toward cost containment, uniformity of outcome criteria, and use of technological innovations seems quite clear. This discussion has highlighted some of the possibilities and problems associated with a few potential scenarios concerning accountable practice. What then are the implications for how social workers should position themselves to meet such challenges?

First, it is vital that social workers educate themselves about ways of determining practice effectiveness. Traditional pre- and post-treatment designs comparing clients in an intervention group with those in a control group are generally not practical for social workers who need rapid feedback about progress on client-specific interventions and do not find it ethically acceptable to withhold treatment from a control group. Instead, single-system design, an alternative form of measuring practice effectiveness, allows social workers to collect ongoing information about a single client's progress. Within this evaluation approach, clients become their own controls as data collected prior to social work intervention is compared with data collected during and after intervention. Further, single-system design requires that practitioners identify target problems, clearly specify treatment goals, and then select measures relevant to target problems on which data will be collected multiple times to determine client progress. Each of these components of single-system design is consistent with the ever-increasing demands among insurance agencies and managed care organizations for greater accountability. Thus, despite the current criticism of single-system methodology, its future importance either in its current form or some other form will be central.

Second, it is crucial that social workers take a proactive position in developing usable and flexible measures of client progress. By taking such a position, social workers can begin to develop model evaluation procedures that can be adopted by others rather than having such procedures imposed on them by funding sources. A few social workers have already assumed a leadership position in this area by developing standardized measures that are used by social workers as well as other mental health professionals.

Third, it is important that social workers appreciate the ways in which technology can enhance as well as limit their practice effectiveness. At present, many social workers remain "computer phobic." Social workers need to overcome their aversion to computers by taking workshops and learning from more experienced peers. Social service agencies will inevitably hire and retain professionals with significant knowledge of computer systems. The profession may need to explore the value of training social workers in such technologies through joint degree programs with computer science because workers with a background in social work could better respond to the needs of clients and practitioners than workers trained in computers alone.

However, increased knowledge concerning computer technology should also be tempered with an awareness of possible liabilities associated with such technology. Social workers need to ensure, for example, that data entered into the computer directly or via telephone voice mail will be accessible only to those involved in services to their clients. Social workers must carefully think through how data will be used when such data demonstrate that some social workers are less effective than others. Finally, social workers must be vigilant that innovations in measurement do not overlook the poor and disenfranchised who have no access to computer technology. As the close of the twentieth century approaches, social workers should be open to new innovations while still retaining those aspects of traditional social work practice that best meet the needs of their clients.

Part *II*

Health Care

The health care field is one of the most volatile areas for social work practice at the present time. Rationing of health care is already a reality, and both the federal and state governments are considering new criteria for rationing. The AIDS epidemic is still a major source of anguish and expense among a growing number of people. Health care policy and reform are currently in the news and are being debated on both the national and local levels. Traditionally, medical social work has been highly visible in the health care system. However, this visible role is changing and, in many instances, being subsumed under other departments, such as nursing. Part II contains five chapters on the future of health care for social work.

In Chapter 4, George Magner presents a future scenario on health care and rationing that has already begun to take place implicitly in the United States today. Looking ahead to the year 2015, this chapter raises several questions for social work to consider:

1. What is the role of private market competition in the delivery of future health care services (and to whom) in our society?

2. What will be the impact of the changing role of private health care insurance providers in the delivery of future health care services?

3. What is the impact on social workers of the proletarianization of the profession (that is, the acceptance of wages within large corporations that establish conditions of work)?

Chapter 5 examines the future incidence and prevalence of HIV and AIDS, a major topic in health care now and probably in the future, especially among adolescents. Sly and Montgomery raise the following questions for the reader:

1. What are the possible conditions that might lead to new viral diseases which are currently unknown?

2. What is the future course of HIV transmission among adolescents beyond the year 2000?

3. What are the factors that will directly determine the number of adolescent HIV infections and transmission of HIV among the adolescent population in the future and their implication for social work practice with this target population?

Stephen Gorin and Cynthia Moniz speculate about the health care system in the year 2004 and beyond to 2010 from the present context of health care reform and consider prospects for social work in that time frame. They present the reader with a number of questions to consider:

1. What are the origins of single-payer systems of managed health care in America? In Canada? What are the differences between the two systems?

2. What are some of the limitations of medical care in promoting health?

3. What is unique about social work's biopsychosocial perspective in the planning of future health policy for the next century?

In Chapter 7 Cathy Clancy presents a personal picture of hospital-based social work practice in the year 2000. In her speculative description a number of questions are addressed:

1. What technological advances in medicine, computers, and information technology are presumed in this description of hospital social work in the year 2000?

2. What social changes are assumed in this scenario that might be challenged by recent events in our society?

3. What are the changes in social work education for health care students mandated by the dramatic changes in health care practice outlined in this chapter?

4. What will be the role of the social worker on the primary health care team within the multiservice health care center of the future?

C h a p t e r *4*

Health Care and Rationing

GEORGE MAGNER, PhD
University of Houston

In a traditional sense, rationing simply is the allocation of scarce resources: the triage of military hospitals under combat conditions or overstretched urban emergency rooms, or the allocation of consumer goods such as gasoline, sugar, or meat during periods of wartime shortages. In the latter instance, not experienced in the United States since World War II, it was caused by intervention of a federal government as a means of sustaining a wartime military effort by the diversion of essential goods from a civilian population to military forces.

For the most part, health care, except under unusual circumstances just noted, has not been subjected to such explicit, policy-decreed rationing. Indeed, the national response has been to counter shortage by the production of additional resources. As early as 1946 the Hill–Burton Act provided federal funds to assist in overcoming the scarcity of hospitals and hospital beds—a legacy of the Great Depression of the 1930s and minimal construction during World War II. Later, by way of capitation grants and other support for expanded training programs, federal policy targeted the shortfall of critical health care personnel.

It is interesting to note that although these strategies tended to follow a traditional economic model—increasing supply to meet demand—it was not by investment of the private sector, although this was involved, but heavily *via* federal policy and financing. The effort to produce additional goods and services has been successful. Sadly, of course, there has been no concomitant guarantee of equal or equitable distribution of these increased resources; nor did their presence create the promised competition that would lower costs. More has not become less, in terms of costs, and more has not filtered down to guarantee access to all segments of our population.

What has been learned is that the equation of increased supply equals increased competition equals greater choice and lower prices does not work in health care. As Weiner (1992) notes, "The rate of increase in health care spending has not substantially declined. Rightly or wrongly, it is widely perceived that our bag of tricks for cost containment is fairly empty" (p. 14).

Rationing Today

Although we may have no explicit national policy that mandates rationing of health care resources, there are many policies, practices, and regulations that do, in fact, serve as means of rationing. Indeed, retaining much of health care within the private sector suggests an implicit recognition that some will get more and some will get less. At this point in the discussion it should suffice to simply list the current mechanisms that, together, constitute very real rationing of health care. Consider the following:

a. The millions of uninsured persons who do receive fewer health care resources than those with insurance (or money).
b. The almost universal use of cost sharing, deductibles, and exclusions, although often touted as a means of encouraging *prudent consumerism,* which are remarkably effective rationing mechanisms.
c. The widely adopted model of the Medicare prospective payment system (PPS) with its diagnostically related groups (DRG). In concert with peer review and sanctions, there is a stress on constraining use of health care resources: fewer hospital days, fewer admissions, reliance on alternative care, and limitations on diagnostic and therapeutic procedures.
d. The enormous expansion of managed care, which has brought to most Americans a firsthand exposure to the many sophisticated means by which to restrict utilization. Prior authorization, stringent gatekeeping, second opinions, utilization review, policy exclusions, concrete limitations on length and types of service, heavy use of nonphysician personnel, and guarded access to specialty care: These all are an intimate part of the corporate, large scale, often for-profit health care bureaucracy.
e. Explicit rationing by way of public policy, which has finally emerged in the state of Oregon. Designed as a trade-off for the expansion of Medicaid to all persons below the poverty threshold, it has critics who question the targeting of *only* the state's poorest population. Nonetheless, some of those close to the policy debate view it as a positive move.

Philosopher Robert Baker wrote the following:

From a moral and philosophical perspective, the Oregon initiative is a watershed in the history of non-market provision of health care. For the first time, a funds-providing body has publicly admitted the impossibility of providing unlimited access to health care, eschewed abstruse reality disguising budgetary devices, and opted for an allocation process that makes the realities of rationing explicit and visible to all. For this reason, if for no other, the Oregon experiment deserves to be tried. It may well prove to be the most significant event in the provision of health care since the "appointed day." (Baker, 1992, p. 225)

No one doubts that rationing of health care exists. From a perspective of justice and fairness, question certainly can be raised as to the manner in which rationing takes place. As long as health care is maintained largely within the private sector, in which insurance or money is a requisite to access, the rationing will be carried out in an unsystematic and inequitable fashion. This may work for automobiles; it will not work as a just means of meeting a basic human need.

But this chapter is not about the situation in 1995. I move to the future to determine what the policy process has provided and whether the subject of rationing remains one of concern.

Twenty Years Later

In 2015 it is tempting to look back at the multiple lost opportunities for the attainment of a true national health insurance program: the elimination of a health insurance title in the Social Security Act of 1935, the efforts led by then-senator Ted Kennedy in the 1960s, and the tragic health care debate of 1993–94.

It is tempting, but also futile. The great political shift alluded to by Kevin Philips (1990) that "a new U.S. political cycle might begin in the 1990s" (p. 221) did not occur. In health care, the effort has moved from dramatic change to incremental change in those few areas where bipartisan political support can be found. We did see, in 1999, insurance reform that mandated the use of community rather than experience rating. This has lessened the earlier phenomenon of "job-lock" in which the potential loss of insurance coverage precluded job mobility. It was a costly policy initially. The paucity of effective risk analysis methodology forced health care premiums even higher.

We also saw, in the year 2000, tort reform aimed at establishing additional order in the medical malpractice maze. Depending on one's perspective, it has either provided needed protection to insurers and providers, or it has been a barrier to consumer recourse from negligence or mistreatment. It has proven to be of little consequence to the cost of health care.

Rather than a cycle of political and social reform as suggested by Philips, we saw a conservative move to slow change and to maintain the status quo. We have now, in 2015, a health care scene that more closely resembles that prophesied by Paul Starr (1982) in his magnificent social history of American medicine written over 30 years ago:

The failure to rationalize medical services under public control meant that sooner or later they would be rationalized under private control. Instead of public regulation, there will be private regulation, and instead of public planning, there will be private planning. Instead of public financing for pre-paid plans that might be managed by the subscribers' chosen representatives, there will be corporate financing for private plans controlled by conglomerates whose interest will be determined by the rates of return on investments. This is the future toward which American medicine now seems to be headed. (p. 449)

Starr was correct. Certainly for the majority of Americans who obtain health insurance through employment, the management of available health care resources by large conglomerates has become a reality of their lives.

For those who expected health care policy to keep pace with health care technology, there has been disillusionment. Policy change has come slowly and in small increments. The total financial burden has not loosened, although the rate of annual increase has slowed. This year, the estimated aggregate cost will be 2.5 trillion dollars, some 16.5 percent of our gross domestic product. To understand the nature of health care rationing in 2015, one must first understand the context within which such rationing takes place.

There are today three tiers of health care financing and delivery.

- *Tier One:* Occupied by some 10 percent to 15 percent of the population, it provides health indemnity insurance that allows members full access to all available health care resources, a choice of providers, and a range of amenities. Among the providers are the few remaining fee-for-service practitioners.
- *Tier Two:* Here are to be found the bulk (some 70 percent to 75 percent) of the population. It includes most persons who attain health coverage through employment and the recipients of the two largest federal programs, Medicare and Medicaid. In one form or another, all receive health care on a per capita basis from one of the large health provider corporations (HPCs).
- *Tier Three:* This is the residual tier that serves those persons with no coverage via employment or who are not eligible for one of the public programs. Here remain the public charity hospitals and medical centers.

Within this context, cost containment has been a driving force, although the results have been modest. Public programs have taken the lead. In Medicare, for example, the earlier national payment schedules represented a serious attempt to restrain prices. Unfortunately, this also led to a negative reaction in the medical community, as fewer and fewer physicians chose to participate in the program. The severity of this problem led to the 2004 legislation that channeled all Medicare recipients into membership in one of the health provider corporations (HPCs).

Of course, Medicaid recipients have long been relieved of any choice of provider. One provision of the Omnibus Reconciliation Act of 2002 mandated that all states utilize competitive bidding with HPCs. With state and federal approval, the HPCs have moved to restrict the number and type of procedures to which Medicaid recipients are entitled. This has nicely supplemented (or implemented) the actions of 23 states to replicate the great social experiment of Oregon in the 1990s. Simply put, although it has been anything but simple, these states have introduced explicit rationing for Medicaid recipients. The legal and ethical challenges have been powerful, but the goal of providing a "limited but adequate" package of benefits for the poor, and within the budget constraints of the states, has prevailed.

So in the year 2015 the first level of rationing can be identified. It is explicit, it is public, and it results from policy decisions at the state level. It is targeted to a specific population. It quite likely is not, however, the result envisioned by a liberal Congress in 1965 when the Medicaid legislation was enacted.

It is with less clarity that one provides an analysis of health care and rationing outside the public programs. What you must know is that there has been a repeated repudiation of any increased public role. For most, the delivery of health care remains a private-sector issue.

The private market competition has become fierce. Of the 1,300 to 1,500 private health insurance companies that were in business 20 years ago, less than 100 remain. Three of those, Aetna, Prudential, and Sanya, a Japanese-held firm, control almost 50 percent of the private health insurance market. This has resulted in major savings. The massive companies have been successful in simplifying the claims and adjustment process, and their health status cards allow providers to ascertain immediately and electronically the insurance status and benefits eligibility of each patient. In the private market, the consolidation of so many insurance carriers has been a natural and perhaps essential progression. As the similar consolidation of providers into the giant HPCs occurred, effective negotiations on price and benefits could be carried on only by insurers representing billions of consumer premium dollars.

It is also to be noted, of course, that the role of insurance has been diminished. Many large corporations negotiate directly with an HPC, thereby providing their employees with a uniform benefit package. A very real loss, although it no longer seems as significant as it did 20 years ago, is that of choice. The typical consumer today has *no* choice of individual provider, *no* choice of specialist, and *no* choice of institutional setting if such becomes necessary. Given a modified set of expectations, we have a most feasible system for those 70 percent to 75 percent of the population covered. People today do not expect to have a "family physician." In fact, there are very few left. Most physicians in 2015 have been absorbed by the HPCs. Physicians completing their residences now interview with HPCs rather than looking to start a private practice.

Concomitantly, for most Americans, fee-for-service (FFS) medicine is a memory. There are some FFS practitioners left, and people with supplemental and specifically indemnity insurance have a choice among these private practitioners. The choice, of course, is limited; most providers hold a contract or a salary with an HPC. Nonetheless, this relatively small subsystem (the estimate is that 10 percent to 15 percent of the population may be covered in this fashion) provides full access to all available health care resources and usually with all available amenities.

What has happened to the majority of the population—those funneled into the massive HPCs—is never referred to as rationing. It is the provision of cost-effective, highly regimented health care with an emphasis on the maximization of primary care personnel and a minimization of high-cost specialists and procedures. The traditional "gatekeeping" of the HMOs of the 1980s and 1990s, usually assigned to a primary care physician, today occurs at two levels. The first contact is most likely to be with nonphysician personnel (NPP)—a nurse practitioner, a physician's assistant, or a medical assistant. In mental health divisions of HPCs, it will be a psychiatric nurse or a social worker. For nonpsychiatric patients such screening is a prerequisite for access to a primary care physician. These physicians, who now constitute 50 percent of all practitioners completing residences, are extensively trained and are expected to provide care for many conditions that formerly would have sparked automatic referral to a specialist.

There is no question but that the medical care available in the United States in 2015 is the most advanced in the world. The apex of the triangle, where much of this advanced technology rests, is not easily accessed, and the perception of barriers to full care is widespread. Increasingly, the home or community is viewed as the site of care. The typical HPC is a model of vertical integration. The acute care or specialty hospital has become smaller, ambulatory and outpatient units have multiplied and grown, and each HPC has an extensive home health care network.

Thus what we experience in 2015 is a de facto rationing. With corporations and insurers on one side seeking to minimize the cost of providing employee health care and, on the other side, HPCs seeking to maximize profits, a mutual goal has emerged—that of providing a minimally adequate package of benefits at the lowest possible cost.

One should not misconstrue the above. This large middle population, some 75 percent of all U.S. citizens, does receive good health care benefits. This population does not receive all possible benefits. We learned long ago that such a goal was unrealistic and fiscally not sustainable. This population also pays a heavy price. Even with tough negotiations from the powerful insurance groups and corporations, the HPCs have been able to justify a series of upwardly creeping deductibles, cost sharing percentages, and exclusions in coverage. Costs have been slowed. Perhaps more important, the more sophisticated polls suggest a subtle attitudinal change. People seem to be accepting health care delivered in a more structured and impersonal manner and with very real constraints on what will be available. This level of "consumer prudence" represents a major shift and has been one of the outstanding accomplishments within our market economy.

The transformation has not been without incident. An array of antitrust suits have been brought. In some cases, where collusion and/or monopolistic tendencies have been blatant, there has been court-ordered dissolution of HPCs. Perhaps more serious, although difficult to prove, are the allegations that some HPCs have abused their stewardship of large-scale health care resources. There are charges that some advanced technologies simply are not made available, that elderly consumers are denied access to certain procedures, and that excessive use of foreign medical graduates and nonphysician personnel has placed quality of care in jeopardy. Much of what one hears is anecdotal. However, the concern is sufficiently high that the House Subcommittee on Health Affairs began hearings last fall.

To sum up to this point, there are now two tiers of health care serving some 85 percent of all U.S. citizens. The top tier commands all that once was considered the natural expectation: a choice of providers and access to the full array of facilities and procedures. The second tier remains assured of access within a tightly controlled corporate bureaucratic structure. This tier serves the low- and middle-income classes as well as specific publicly entitled population such as the elderly and eligible poor. There is a residual population, not much changed from 20 years ago. Included are illegal immigrants (barred from all entitlement programs in 1999), some of the working poor to whom the nation still has not guaranteed insurance coverage, and a segment of the poverty population not eligible for public programs. For this group, there remain the public charity institutions that have no ties to the private sector.

The changes in the public charity institutions have been subtle but serious. The tightening of public financing has left many county and municipal health units in crisis. Fewer are affiliated with teaching institutions, and the fiscal constraints have rendered staffing problematic. Facilities are not replaced in a timely fashion, and the new technology is available on a limited basis. Staffing required for many intensive care units cannot be maintained. Within this context, rationing is simple. The demand far outstrips the supply, and some go without. The queues are more lengthy, beds are unavailable, clinics must turn away people, and essential but nonurgent, procedures are deferred or denied. By policy (sometimes stated, at times tacit), elderly patients, the terminally ill, high-risk infants, and others often are provided comfort care, with therapeutic procedures forsaken. Here, then, the rationing is *real*. In a classical sense, it is the allocation of scarce resources where the greatest good is likely to occur.

The ethicists have much to say about the public institutions and the slow erosion of access to care under their aegis. There is less said about the increasingly regimented care within the private sector. There is, instead, an apparent acceptance of the natural evolutionary processes of the market. If dramatic reform is in the future of this nation, it remains below the policy agenda horizon.

In the overall health care scheme, high drama has not been the hallmark of policy change. Rather, the process has been gradual, but with an unmistakable display of distaste for further federal intervention, along with a continuing confidence in the ability of the market to provide health care for most Americans. There is little pressure to revive the global goals of the Clinton presidency. As one of the nation's foremost health economist's of that period said in 1994:

> The United States never has had a one-tier health care system, and, as the recent debate on health reform in Congress has demonstrated, the United States never will have a one-tier health care system. A working majority of politicians representing Americans in the policy arena evidently view health care as essentially a private consumption good of which low income families might be accorded a basic ration but whose availability and quality should be allowed to vary with family income. (Reinhardt, 1994, pp. 23–24)

Although many remain disillusioned with the state of affairs in health care, social workers have done very well. For much of its history, social work has been practiced within the structure and value system of an agency. In health care, this was primarily the hospital. However, the shift to a broader community-based health care practice has provided social workers with the opportunity for a more autonomous and less restricted practice than did the authoritarian and hierarchical acute care or specialty hospital setting.

The HPCs, by which most health care social workers are employed, also have discovered that social work is a most cost-effective means by which to extend their programs into the community. The older "bridge" function seems to have given fresh life and vigor to social work practice in health care.

The rationing, both explicit and tacit, that this paper has addressed does pose moral and philosophical problems for social work. Universal coverage, preferably under a single-payer system, remains a goal for the major professional organization (NASW). This has been advocated with less and less vigor as the organizational effort has shifted to negotiating efforts with the HPCs that employ social workers. Although unionization is not in full bloom, the NASW has had significant success in establishing salary scales and related benefits for BSW and MSW social workers. As the professional organization focused in the 1980s and 1990s on third-party payment for its private practice members, today it represents a far greater proportion of the membership in labor negotiations. The result has been striking. Recognizing the concrete benefits to NASW membership, new members, especially at the BSW level, have boosted the NASW total membership to 218,000. This in turn has greatly added to its bargaining strength.

The career diversity of social work under this health care system is more limited. Most private practitioners, like their counterparts in medicine, could not survive in the limited and competitive fee-for-service market and have moved into the HPCs. Similarly, most MSW social workers have abandoned the public health care arena (the charity hospitals and clinics) for the HPCs. The profession, in its health care role, has become a integral part of the private health care corporate structure.

Conclusion

Despite years of political debate and a continuation of painful fiscal consequences, the United States, in 2015, has reaffirmed a core belief that the delivery of health care services is a proper function of the private market. There is recognition of the need for limited public participation, both of a social insurance and public assistance nature. Much, although not all, of such public participation is financial, with beneficiaries obtaining actual services in the private sector. Only a small residual group (perhaps 10 percent of the population) is served directly by public institutions.

Health care today is dominated by the large corporate bureaucracies. On the one side, those include the surviving private insurance carriers, the large businesses that prefer to negotiate their own contracts for employee coverage, and the representatives of public agencies that finance health coverage. On the other side, there are the remarkably well-integrated (both horizontally and vertically) health provider corporations. Years of competition have resulted, on both sides of the equation, in mergers, consolidations, and buyouts. The old term *cottage industry* no longer applies to medicine in particular or health care in general.

In the negotiations related to the cost of today's health care, representatives of the large insurer groups, with their billions of consumer premium dollars in hand, sit across from the equally powerful HPCs, which bring to the table the array of providers, facilities, and technology. The individual consumer and, in most cases, the individual provider have little say in the process or results of the negotiations. To the side, and uninvolved in such arrangements, are the remaining public charity institutions that provide direct service to the uninsured residual population.

Within this vast health care arena in 2015, rationing is alive and well. It can be identified under three specific circumstances:

a. Explicit rationing has been adopted by a number of states, specifically targeting those covered under the federal-state categorical program of Medicaid. Despite concerns of a social justice nature—that is, the failure to treat all citizens equally—this type of rationing has been widely accepted. It allows, say its advocates, an expansion of Medicaid to cover more of the poor while allowing states to allocate resources within their realistic fiscal constraints.

b. Tacit rationing takes place within the enormous HPCs. Such rationing is not publicly acknowledged, nor is it sanctioned by specific public statute. It is, instead, initiated by introducing cost factors as an integral part of the diagnostic and therapeutic processes of health care practice. It demands a modification in the behavior of clinical personnel. It demands an acceptance of limits on the resources to be expended in any given clinical situation. Simply put, through a variety of intrusive mechanisms, it demands a limit to utilization in order to maximize return on corporate investment. Interestingly, the evidence available suggests that this type of highly structured, tightly managed corporate health delivery has become acceptable to most of the population.

c. For the residual group, rationing is of a more traditional nature, that is, sufficient restraint of supply (personnel, facilities, and other goods) that results in an inability to serve all those in need. This entire public subsystem, serving perhaps the most disadvantaged among us, has come to resemble a huge triage operation. Always, with the imbalance of need and supply, some will be left waiting, and some will be left out.

Social workers have adapted well to the evolving system. The expansion of professional boundaries beyond the central hospital has provided a host of more independent (and lucrative) roles. Like most physicians and dentists, social workers have not found great disharmony with the "proletarianization" of the profession—the acceptance of wages within large corporations that establish conditions of work. Unionlike organization and bargaining have been effective in the enhancement of the social work reward system.

Sadly, even while social workers enjoy their new roles and benefits, there has been a concomitant diminishment in the thrust to universal coverage and increased equity for all. Having established a satisfying and essential niche within the private, corporate health care market, the social work health care community seems less interested in the moral imperative to serve the least advantaged and more interested in its enhanced economic and professional status.

References

Baker, R. (1992). The inevitability of health care rationing: A case study of rationing in the British national health service. In M. A. Strosberg, J. M. Weiner, R. Baker with I.A. Fein (Eds.), *Rationing America's medical care: The Oregon plan and* *beyond* (p. 225). Washington, DC: The Brookings Institution.

Philips, K. (1990). *The politics of rich and poor: Wealth and the American electorate in the Reagan aftermath.* New York: Random House.

Starr, P. (1982). *The social transformation of American medicine.* New York: Basic Books.

Reinhardt, U. (1994).Germany's health care system: It's not the American way. *Health Affairs, 13*(4), 23–24.

Weiner, J. M. (1992). Rationing in America: Overt and covert. In M. A. Strosberg, J. M. Weiner, R. Baker, with I. A. Fein (Eds.), *Rationing America's medical care: The Oregon plan and beyond* (p. 14). Washington, DC: The Brookings Institution.

$$Chapter \quad 5$$

HIV/AIDS and Adolescents
Future Trends and Changing Sexual Mores

DAVID F. SLY, PhD and DIANNE F. HARRISON, PhD
Florida State University

Under current definitions of disease, the future incidence and prevalence of STDs, including HIV-infected persons and persons with AIDS, is going to be strongly influenced by teenage sexuality. Although this chapter will focus primarily on current definitions of sexually transmitted disease, and on HIV/AIDS in particular, it is important at the outset to alert the reader that these definitions may, in fact, change markedly over the next 10 to 25 years. At the present time STDs are defined in terms of transmission routes for bacteria and viruses; those agents of disease that are transmitted via some mode of sexual intercourse are considered sexually transmitted diseases. Definitional changes are likely to emerge for two primary reasons. First, what is considered disease-causing sexual behavior is likely to change; and second, the evolution of existing viruses, bacteria, and parasites already known to cause disease, to say nothing of ones not yet known or in existence, may be transmittable via sexual as well as nonsexual behaviors.

To some these concerns may seem remote, but both are already happening in subtle yet potentially profound ways. For example, today touching another person, looking at another person, or saying something to another person is considered a sexual behavior by many administrative and professional codes if it is interpreted as sexual by either party to the interaction. Although this definition is generally used only for legal and ethical harassment and discrimination purposes currently, it could easily be extended (as it already has in at least one prominent U.S. university) to define sexual behavior generally or for medical purposes. On the microbial side it has already been learned that this is an extremely adaptable world; parasites, bacteria, and viruses have all demonstrated an amazingly rapid ability to become drug resistant. In addition, it is also possible that human attempts to manipulate, regulate, and control the world at this level directly will bring about changes that may make some of the microbes that are transmittable only through sexual intercourse at one point in time transmittable via either sexual intercourse or some other way or both at another point in time. This transmission ambiguity is currently reflected in the case of HIV, which may be transmitted through sexual intercourse (using current definitions) or through blood exchange mechanisms. Similarly, alternative routes of transmission, including sexual, appear to transmit some forms of the hepatitis virus.

The discussion that follows will focus on describing the incidence and prevalence of HIV/AIDS in the future, as well as some other sexually transmitted diseases, using current definitions. However, before we do this it is important that we first discuss the possibility of, and some of the factors that are likely to influence, the emergence and spread of new disease-causing agents more generally. This consideration is important both because of the general threat with which these will challenge us, and because many of the factors that will influence the emergence and spread of new diseases more generally will also influence the spread of HIV and other sexually transmitted diseases. To keep this discussion focused on the present topic, we will center it on the emergence and spread of HIV and what can be learned from this disease thus far.

The Potential for New Disease Emergence

Humankind has faced epidemics in the past, but there has never been a global epidemic that emerged under the social, political, and economic conditions, or at a time of technological transitions, such as existed in the pre- and present HIV era. Any effort to discuss the transmission and prevention of HIV transmission in the future must be done in the context of these conditions, and with the understanding that HIV/AIDS represents only a single viral emergence in what is likely to be an era of microbial epidemics emanating not only from viruses but also from bacteria and parasites. Indeed, one can make a case that it is fortunate to have had HIV as a "first alert" of what may come. Imagine, for example, what might have occurred (or could be occurring) if HIV were more easily transmitted via alternative routes, or if the immunodeficiency of AIDS took much longer to manifest itself, or if it had produced far more common opportunistic infections than the early and obvious ones that it did. One can even say that in some sense it was fortunate that the virus spread into the developed world where surveillance systems and detection technology existed, and that once there its early concentration was in a cooperative and politically astute gay population that provided many key clues and took organized action to assist health officials and researchers.

The 30 to 35 years or so that preceded the emergence of HIV (in its life-threatening form) was a period of nearly incomprehensible change. On the technological front change and innovation directly related to control of the microbial world moved at an astounding pace and gave the public an unprecedented faith in science and the medical profession. These accomplishments cannot all be reviewed here, but consider how antibiotics and immunizations influenced the public's and many physicians' views of disease. The introduction of antibiotics and immunizations convinced nearly everyone that bacterial and viral diseases could be eliminated at will. Tuberculosis, scarlet fever, diphtheria, many types of pneumonia, polio, rubella, and influenza went from being major causes of death to diseases of little or no significance. By 1965 the pharmaceutical industry had developed more than 25,000 antibiotics, and most laymen and many physicians believed that what an increased dosage of one could not cure another could. The faith placed in antibiotics and immunizations in the developed world nearly completely shifted the fear of disease from microbe-causing agents to chronic and degenerative causes.

The medical-technological revolution of this period was not confined to attacks on the microbial world of disease-causing agents. Another major accomplishment came through the production of synthetic hormones (estrogen and progesterone), which when put in a pill in correct dosages inhibited maturation of egg follicles and ovulation. This, in turn, offered the unique opportunity for people to engage in sex free of inhibiting physical barriers for the first time in history, nearly completely independent of concern of a pregnancy. Sex became something to enjoy, something that could be pursued for purely (or partly) hedonistic reasons, something that could be separated from the reproductive function of sex and the long-term emotional, social, economic, and legal relationships of a pregnancy. Sex became something that no one needed to deny themselves (or others) out of the fear of producing a child, and something that became increasingly difficult to deny more rational younger adults. Such young adults, accustomed to having their needs and wants satisfied immediately, were increasingly exposed to sexuality and, specifically, sexual intercourse portrayed as the ultimate pleasure and defining rite of passage of adulthood. The pill and other chemical-hormonal methods of contraception protected individuals from pregnancy and encouraged sex for pleasure but offered no protection from the threats of disease that could result from sex.

Advances in nonmedical technology during this period have also had important implications for the microbial world of infectious and parasitic disease and its transmission. Again, we cannot list all of these here or consider the implications of any one in depth, but their potential can be illustrated with a few examples. Many people believe that globalization is something that began only in the last few years, a phenomenon that many people in the United States became aware of during the 1992 presidential elections. In fact, globalization began decades before this and was perhaps nearly completed by this time. For example, global attempts to eradicate some diseases using medical technology had succeeded by this time (smallpox), whereas others had failed miserably (malaria). Two world wars were largely global conflicts, and many of the subsequent political and economic aid efforts brought important global structures into existence. Nonmedical technology played a particularly important role in the globalization process, and perhaps the most important innovations marking the ending of this era came from the space and aeronautics programs.

The space program launched a new transportation revolution, but far more important than the transport of a few people into space was the technological cargo that rockets could move. Space transportation made orbiting satellites possible, and the latter made it possible for all kinds of information to be transported instantly to all corners of the globe. When this technology was combined with television, Western lifestyles could be viewed and aspired to firsthand anyplace in the world where there was electricity and reception/transmission capabilities. What could not be viewed live was frequently available on videotape for replay. By the mid-1970s many (if not most) young people on a global scale, even in remote rural areas, were forming their expectations and having their behavior influenced by Western television's portrayal of "how everybody in the United States and Europe lives" based on popular shows such as *Dallas* and, lately, *Beverly Hills 90210.*

The intercontinental mass transportation of people, other animals, vegetables, fruits, and flowers, all potential transporters of the disease-causing agents of the microbial world, also began in this era. The introduction of the 747 and wide-bodied airplanes during this period coupled with increased business activity and tourism took hundreds of thousands of people routinely and daily to the most remote parts of the world, where they could be exposed to microbes totally nonexistent in their native environments. Frequently overlooked is the fact that these airplanes also facilitated the mass transportation of fresh flowers, fruits, and unprocessed foods, to say nothing of the transport capabilities of massive sea ships. Scientists in search of miracle cures went into jungles, rain forests, and savannahs in increasing numbers. Even the many animals needed for experimentation, although known to carry diseases potentially lethal to humans, were now shipped with great speed and ever-increasing numbers from one part of the world to another.

What we want to emphasize is that these are only a few of the examples of some of the factors that were in place at the time that HIV emerged, and that these same factors could, and probably will, lead to the emergence and rapid spread of other new viruses, bacteria, and parasites that will cause diseases not yet known. Moreover, these factors highlight the fact that communicable disease emergence must be seen in a global context; there will probably never again be a new disease transmittable from one human to another, particularly a sexually transmitted disease (using current definitions), that will not spread intercontinentally with the same or greater speed than did HIV.

The Future Course of HIV/AIDS among Adolescents

In discussing the future course of HIV/AIDS it is important to bear in mind that at the present time no one knows how many HIV-infected persons there are in the world, let alone in developed countries such as the United States. Moreover, because of the long and substantially varying incubation period between infection and the onset of the disease AIDS, it is frequently difficult to establish when a person became infected. The known age distribution of infections and AIDS cases, however, have led most researchers to believe that an increasing number of infections are occurring among adolescents, and that for each known infection there are as many as 10 undetected infected persons. Given the lethal nature of the disease and its social and economic costs, including the loss of human resources at a time when society has invested in education and training and reaped few of the returns from the individual, what might be most important to bear in mind is that the general trend and order of magnitude are more important than precise figures.

The World Health Organization (WHO) estimates that there were 17 million persons worldwide infected with the AIDS virus in 1994, and that by the year 2000 this number will increase to at least 30 million persons. Moreover, many experts believe that these are only conservative to moderate estimates, and not estimates purposively made high to increase awareness and action. Particularly important for our purposes are two additional observations that can be made from the WHO data. First, some 24 million of the projected 30 million HIV infections in the year 2000 are expected to be among persons from less-developed countries, with the countries of Asia alone accounting for about 19,200,000 of the world's infections. Second, WHO estimated that by 1994 one-half of the world's infected population was in the 15–24 age group, strongly suggesting that HIV was already spreading most rapidly among adolescents.

Clearly, then, between now and the turn of the century HIV infection is going to spread rapidly throughout the world. Its prevalence is going to escalate dramatically in the less-developed countries, and its transmission is going to become increasingly concentrated in the adolescent population. Although some minor advances have been made in the treatment of the syndrome of diseases associated with AIDS, there has not been significant progress in the development of either an immunization against the HIV virus or a cure for the disease. In fact, it would not be an exaggeration to state that as more has been learned about the HIV virus (and its different forms), the one thing that is clear is that finding an effective cure and an immunization may be more difficult than originally thought. Moreover, the implications of this difficulty for the future are that there is not likely to be a medical solution to the problem (with one exception, to be discussed later), and that far greater emphasis needs to be placed in finding behavioral and social solutions.

HIV Transmission beyond the Turn of the Century among Adolescents

There are two proximate factors that will directly determine the number of adolescent HIV infections and the transmission of HIV in the adolescent population in the future. The first of these is the number of adolescents and the second is the number of adolescents who will be engaging in behaviors that will put them at risk of being infected. In 1990 there were 1.039 billion adolescents in the world, and adolescents represented nearly one in every five persons at a global scale. Over the next two decades, according to the United Nations' mid-range projections, the number of adolescents is expected to increase by some 127 and 139 million, respectively, before increasing by a more moderate 46 million between 2010 and 2020. Thus, over the whole period, the number of adolescents will increase by about 312 million, and by the year 2020 adolescents will comprise over 1.351 billion persons; however, their percentage of the total population will have declined from the present 20 percent to about 16.5 percent. Throughout the whole period the largest absolute number of adolescents will be concentrated in Asia, where the number will peak in 2010 at nearly 775 million before it begins to decline to about three-quarters of a billion by 2020. The most rapidly growing adolescent population will be in Africa, where the number of adolescents is projected to increase dramatically from 145 million in 1990 to over 316 million by 2020, an increase of 117 percent.

Among the remaining regions of the world, changes in the number of adolescents will be considerably less dramatic from a demographic perspective in both absolute number and the rate of change, but from an epidemiological perspective they are nevertheless significant. In Oceania, where the population is small, the number of adolescents will increase by nearly one-third, but this means an absolute increase of about 1.5 million. In each of the remaining regions, except Europe, where the number of adolescents is actually expected to decline by nearly 6 million, the increase in adolescents will vary between a modest 15 and 17 percent; in absolute terms, these percentages translate into increases of between 8 and 15 million more adolescents.

Thus over the interval examined there is going to be a particularly large concentration of adolescents in Asia and a dramatic increase in the number of adolescents in Africa. Together, these two regions are expected to account for some 92 percent of the world's total increase of nearly 312 million adolescents. Only Europe is expected to see a decrease in its adolescent population, but even here the number of adolescents by 2020 will still exceed 66 million. Among the regions of the world where more modest increases in the adolescent population are expected, the numerical increases will be significant, ranging from about 6 million to 15 million. These numbers are significant because they suggest that even if current levels of infection were maintained, that is, if there was no increase or decrease in the rates of infection, the simple demographic impact alone would produce an additional 5.1 million HIV-infected adolescents in the population by the year 2020, and that the total number of HIV-infected adolescents would be in the range of 20.125 million.

Whether the number of HIV infections reaches this figure, exceeds it, or falls short of it will largely depend on the second proximate factor, the level of risk behaviors, and the phenomena that influence these behaviors. Not a great deal is known about the levels of sexual risk behavior among adolescents or the factors that influence these. There is an overwhelming tendency in the literature to argue that levels of adolescent sexual behavior have risen dramatically in recent years, but there is surprisingly little direct evidence to demonstrate this clearly. What has risen is the number of out-of-wedlock births to teenage mothers, but it is important to realize that this may be more influenced by dramatic increases in the age at first marriage, changed mores and values, and the decreased likelihood of a pregnancy to result in a marriage than in the level of sexual activity among adolescents. Moreover, no one knows the extent to which direct reports (from surveys) of sexual activity among adolescents are overstated (or understated) across time, or the extent to which these reports at different points in time have been influenced by real or imagined perceptions of the acceptability of the behavior and expectations of the time.

However, two things are known. First, largely economic considerations are not likely to lead to a declining age at marriage in the developed countries in the future, and in less-developed countries (particularly many in Asia and some in Africa) there is a clearly emerging trend of sharp rises in the age at marriage as young adults are in school longer and education is more generally available to females. Second, as adolescents delay marriage the probability that sexual activity will begin prior to marriage increases. Within the context of this latter point, however, it is important to note that the onset of sexual activity prior to marriage does not necessarily mean that this will be risky sexual behavior.

Young people who have aged into adolescence during the early to mid-1990s were largely socialized to sex and sexual behavior during the 1980s. These people were exposed to a more positive image of sex and sexual behavior through the mass media than young people who were born in the late 1980s and 1990s, who are aging into adolescence with a far more negative and confusing image of sex and sexual behavior. The children born during this later period have been exposed to media campaigns that tell them that you can get

AIDS through sex (even though they may not completely understand it, or even know what it is) and that "AIDS Kills." Exposing young children to this kind of message while exposing current adolescents and adults to the message does not mean that it will have the same effect on each group. It may, in fact, have its greatest effect in the future on the youngest. Among young children, the logical link between sex and AIDS and AIDS and death may appear clear, but to expose children from the youngest ages, when their cognitive abilities do not allow them to understand many of the complexities of sex or disease, may lead them to avoid the behavior as sexual maturity is reached. Similarly, children born after 1990 in Western countries will enter adolescence as the first cohorts who have been socialized through the media to accept and have a positive image of condoms as part of their sexual behavior. We do know that in some Western European countries where young children have been exposed to condoms from a young age, condom use is far more readily accepted by the young. In short, many of our current efforts to alter the behavior of today's adolescents (and adults) may have a greater impact on tomorrow's adolescents even though they were not directly designed to do this.

The emerging political conservatism in many parts of the world may well bring about a halt to the mass media's presentation of many of these current messages. If this happens, the potential to alter the behavior of future generations of adolescents may be short-lived. This would mean that either there would be no programs to alter behavior or that different programs would emerge. Any new programs that do emerge within this political context are likely to move toward an increased emphasis on the family as the agent responsible for controlling and altering sexual behavior. The role of the state within this philosophical approach will be to protect individuals (economically and socially) who are responsible and who make the right choices from those individuals who make the wrong choices with negative sanctions or disincentives for making the wrong choices. The appeal of this philosophy is likely to heighten as the number of people with AIDS and the cost of treating HIV-infected persons and maintaining persons with AIDS increases. This seems even more likely in the United States, where there is increasing emphasis being placed, even within the scientific community, on the idea that AIDS is emerging as a disease of the underclass. The precursors to this type of reasoning are clearly evident in the current welfare and crime reform debates and was one of the cornerstones in the defeat of President Clinton's health care reforms.

A central question in this sense might well be what sanctions could be imposed to eliminate sexual risk behaviors among adolescents. Within the context of the family responsibility–choice model there are many, but they would probably begin with well-defined laws making sex between unmarried (even consenting) persons under some specified age illegal, or they might alternatively specify certain conditions under which the behavior would be legal. For example, sex might be specified as legal for persons who carried HIV (or STD) insurance. In most states in the United States, such sanctions might simply result from stricter enforcement of existing state laws that prohibit sexual acts between nonmarried individuals and children who have not reached the age of majority. Further, it is likely that any state or federal benefits in the form of economic, health, or educational assistance might be denied those who do not eliminate sexual risk behaviors. Any STD diagnosis could be used as evidence that risk behaviors had occurred.

Implications for Social Work

Given the future continued spread of HIV infection, the possible future threats of new disease emergence, the increase in the absolute numbers of adolescents worldwide, and the delay in age before marriage and subsequent increase in sexual activity among teenagers, it is incumbent, as stated earlier, that greater emphasis be placed on seeking behavioral and social solutions to these future health problems. As these trends can provide ammunition to conservatives who may seek to limit sexual activity to heterosexual, monogamous, married individuals and to place severe negative sanctions on those who violate these standards, social workers need to be prepared with solutions that are realistic, humane, and compatible with our professional values and ethics. We recommend strategies that encompass efforts in the areas of social policy, direct practice, and community development, strategies that focus primarily on prevention and that have application worldwide.

On the policy level, social workers need to advocate for programs and services that are cost-effective, community based, and gender neutral. The last characteristic refers to placing as much emphasis on male responsibility and involvement in disease prevention as is currently placed on female responsibility. It also is apparent that future policies will need to take a clear, rational position on the morality of teenage sexuality and premarital sex. Rather than denying its existence, as is the case in many abstinence-only programs for adolescents, we believe that the range of adolescent sexual activity and mores should be acknowledged and that some type of universal agreement be reached regarding the timing, content, philosophy, and objectives of sex education and STD prevention programs. With increased collaboration among advocates and researchers cross-nationally, it is conceivable that such an agreement might affect both developed and less-developed nations. AIDS is a problem that will continue to affect adolescents worldwide. Social workers will need to take a global perspective in the future design and analysis of policies and programs.

Related to community development, we anticipate trends in service delivery that go beyond school- and clinic-based prevention programs to programs that are community-wide in involvement and orientation. A variety of community systems, beyond the health and educational ones, should be integrated into the prevention of HIV and other STDs, including religious organizations, libraries, media, parent and other adult groups, law enforcement, business interests, and adolescent clubs and organizations. The use of a variety of settings and systems for communicating consistent messages and options to teenagers may create a strong sense of sexual responsibility and reduce risk taking.

One of the major challenges on the direct practice level is how to convey the message of safety and responsibility without making sexuality and sexual activity totally aversive. As we discussed earlier, future generations of adolescents will have been reared in a society where issues of sex, disease, and even death have been commingled. It is probable that some teens will respond to these messages by developing, at the least, anxiety about sexual activity and, at worst, sexual aversions and phobias. Realistic discussions need to take place with adolescents about sex and disease, precautions and risk, and various sexual practices. In the absence of such discussions, social workers in the future can anticipate increased numbers of clients with sexual dysfunctions resulting from fear-based sex education.

The content of preventive sex education programs must include skill-based instruction on sexual decision making, problem solving, and self-esteem enhancement, preferably using peer educators. Although adolescents frequently have an almost insurmountable feeling of invulnerability toward risks and hazards, and current adolescents have had few peers directly experience HIV infection or AIDS, future trends would indicate that an unfortunate increase in the number of peer examples will likely result. The use of such peers and other peer models as educators may help to alleviate the tendency by most teenagers to discount the dangers to themselves.

We believe that educational efforts, even skill-based programs, are not sufficient in themselves to create and maintain long-term behavior changes among adolescents. Both behavioral and dramatic cultural changes in the form of values and mores around sexuality and disease prevention will be necessary to produce positive future outcomes. In general, typical adolescents are not futuristically oriented. Social workers have the opportunity and responsibility to plan and implement strategies that will reduce the spread of HIV infection and AIDS among young people now and in the future.

Chapter 6

From Health Care to Health

A Look Ahead to 2010

STEPHEN GORIN, PhD and CYNTHIA MONIZ, PhD
Plymouth State College

Our health care system today, in 2004, is very different from the system of a decade ago. This chapter will present an overview of how these changes came about and consider prospects for social work in the decade ahead.

The Emergence of the Current System

Since 2000 the United States has had a health care system based on a single payer with managed competition. The roots of this system go back to the 1920s, when regulation of the medical profession ended pure competition, (i.e., competition based largely on price) in health care. Price competition was further diluted with the emergence of third-party payers and, particularly, Medicare and Medicaid in the 1960s.

During the 1970s, two schools of procompetitive reform emerged. The first approach emphasized the lack of competition over prices and the role of government and other third party-payers in distorting the health care market and encouraging consumers to engage in wasteful spending (Marmor & Boyum, 1993).

A second approach, called managed competition, emerged under the leadership of Alain Enthoven, an economist at Stanford. As envisioned by Enthoven, managed competition would encourage competition among groups of providers to restrain growth and health care costs. At the same time, it relied on public, or government, sponsors to structure the health care market and enforce rules for competition. In effect, managed competition

58

acknowledged the failure of "patient-driven" competition and shifted focus to "provider-driven" competition (Dranove, 1993).

During the 1992 presidential campaign Bill Clinton expanded Enthoven's version of managed competition. He called for "competition within a budget" as a means of achieving universal health care coverage and controlling costs (Starr & Zelman, 1993). After the election Clinton's health care task force further developed this notion, resulting in the Health Security Act of 1993.

Despite the failure of the Health Security Act, pressure for change continued to build. The health care system increasingly fell under the control of what observers, as early as the 1970s, had called a medical-industrial complex (Kotelchuck, 1976). Through mergers and acquisitions, nonprofit institutions gave way to profit-making organizations and managed care replaced fee for service (Eckholm, 1994). Concern over access, cost, and quality grew.

In 2000 the nation adopted a single-payer system with managed competition. This approach, which built on the work of several analysts (Starr, 1994; Relman, 1992; Rachlis & Kushner, 1994), combined regulation and competition with universal coverage.

Under a single-payer system, the government serves as sole insurer and covers everyone. The single-payer also negotiates fees, or global budgets, with providers who remain independent practitioners. It is financed through the tax system. A single-payer enabled Canada to provide universal coverage and control costs (U.S. Government Accounting Office, 1991).

Despite this success, the Canadian system faced problems of its own during the 1990s. In the face of escalating costs and inefficiencies, Rachlis and Kushner (1994) and others proposed sweeping changes in the delivery of Canadian health care. These included a shift from fee for service to capitation, particularly in primary care; emphasis on prevention and the treatment and care of population groups; reliance on outpatient and community-based facilities; consumer participation; a team approach to health care; and expansion of non-physician and nontraditional services (Rachlis & Kushner, 1994).

In the United States, a similar model was proposed by Arnold Relman, the longtime editor of the *New England Journal of Medicine* (Relman, 1992). He advocated state or regional single-payers, which would insure all individuals and set payments to providers. The latter would be organized in nonprofit, group-model HMOs that would compete on the basis of quality. Providers would negotiate salaries with HMO boards. The federal government would license and assist in the organization of the HMOs. The HMOs would also receive a global budget that they could spend as they choose.

While some argued that managed care did not save money, Relman disagreed. Although managed care originally referred to prepaid, or capitated, group care or staff model HMOs, it came to include almost any approach that limited or regulated consumer choice, such as utilization review, preferred provider networks, and independent practice associations (Starr, 1992). Relman suggested that for-profit HMOs were unsuccessful because they undermined physicians' morale by "permitting business managers to determine the conditions under which the doctors work" (Relman, 1992).

The Rand Health Insurance Experiment found that nonprofit, staff-model HMOs, such as the Group Health Cooperative of Puget Sound, did have lower average patient costs, without reduced quality, than fee-for-service physicians. In Canada nonprofit HMOs also saved money without reducing quality (Rachlis & Kushman, 1994). As a result, Relman correctly concluded that a single-payer with a system of nonprofit HMOs would yield significant savings in both the administrative and delivery systems (Relman, 1992).

The Limits of Medical Care

The single-payer has focused renewed attention on the limits of medical care in promoting health. Although life expectancy in the West has dramatically increased during the last few centuries, due primarily to a decline in mortality from infectious diseases such as cholera, typhoid, and tuberculosis, advances in health care have played a minimal role in this development.

Thomas McKeown (1994) found that changes in mortality actually preceded the development of medical treatments for infectious diseases. For example, in England and Canada death rates from tuberculosis, long a major killer, had fallen for years before the development of streptomycin in 1947. In the United States, deaths from pneumonia began to fall before the discovery of sulfa drugs and other therapeutic agents. A similar pattern exists for many other diseases. In short, the emergence of medical treatments accelerated but did not create declines in mortality.

The limits of medicine are also evident in the health status of populations with universal health care coverage. In England and Canada, national health care failed to prevent disparities in health status or longevity among social classes (Rachlis & Kushner, 1994; Naylor, 1991). This has also been true in the United States.

If medical care cannot explain the improvement in life expectancy, what can? McKeown (1994) argued that the primary factors were rising incomes, improved nutrition, and public health efforts. Reves (1985) suggested that family planning and smaller families also played key roles in extending life expectancy by improving conditions for women and children. Fogel (1994) emphasized the link between improved nutrition and reductions in mortality.

Scholars in Western Europe and Canada also found evidence of a health gradient. Economic development does play a crucial role in reducing mortality, but beyond a certain point increasing national wealth does not necessarily contribute to better health (Wilkinson, 1994). Studies of the European countries showed that those with the least income inequality had the greatest life expectancy (Wilkinson, 1994). Most importantly, within nations even small differences in income levels resulted in marked differences in health status and mortality. People from middle-income groups were in better health than those from lower-income groups, and they were in worse health than those with higher incomes.

This focus on inequality dovetailed with a recognition that poverty and income inequality lay at the root of many health problems in the United States. As a result of the nation's failure to address the widening gap between rich and poor, many problems linked with inequality were mistakenly identified as medical problems. Among these, Schwartz (1994) identified alcohol and drug abuse, gambling, violence, motor vehicle accidents, and infant mortality. Recognition of the social determinants of health, and the link between equality and health, led to the creation of a National Institute of Social Health (NISH) in 2000 (Hurowitz, 1993).

A New Paradigm for Health

In 2004 the NISH proposed a new model for the U.S. health care system based on the seminal work of Canadian economists Robert Evans and Greg Stoddart (1994). The Canadian provinces of British Columbia and Ontario experimented with such an approach in the 1990s. According to Evans and Stoddart, traditional approaches to health policy were based on a narrow "thermostat" model, which viewed illness as a deviation from an otherwise normal state of health. Just as one would respond to a cold wind by turning up the thermostat, one responds to illness by turning up the level of health care treatment and services. Based on this assumption, universal coverage was conceived as the ultimate goal of the nation's health care system.

From the perspective of Evans and Stoddart (1994), the key elements in determining health status are the physical and social environments, biological endowment, individual responses, and national wealth (Ontario Premier's Council on Health Strategy, 1991a). Medical and hospital treatment can do little to alter the effects of these factors. To improve the overall health of a population, overall conditions must be improved. Investments must be made not only in the health care system but in other arenas as well, including employment, education, family support, and the physical environment.

A New Role for Social Work

Emphasis on the social environment, individual responses, and national wealth were particularly congruent with the social work biopsychosocial perspective. For example, research found that job-related stress and unemployment played key roles in limiting health and longevity; conversely, those with social supports tended to live longer and enjoy better health (Ontario Premier's Council on Health Strategy, 1991a). Other studies suggested that social factors play a key role in the development of the brain and other aspects of human physiology (Cynader, 1994; Ontario Premier's Council on Health Strategy, 1991a). Finally, Wilkinson (1994), Marmot (1994), and others demonstrated the impact of income and relative deprivation on health status.

With the NISH's shift from a medical model to a biopsychosocial model of health, a parallel shift occurred in the hierarchy of professions in health and mental health care. Social work, given its focus on the interactions between human behavior and the social environment, was called on by NISH to play a leading role in the formulation of health policy.

Between 2000 and 2003 a number of social welfare policy experts and social work practitioners served as leading members of NISH's Task Force on Health Care in the Twenty-First Century. Social workers participated as key planners in the development of goals and objectives for the new health care system.

In 2003 the final report of the task force, *A Vision of Health for the United States,* was released. The task force stressed the need for new attitudes and ideas about health. To achieve new directions in health policy, new priorities would be needed. These priorities were as follows (Ontario Premier's Council on Health Strategy, 1990):

> *Goal 1:* To emphasize health promotion and disease prevention
>
> *Goal 2:* To create strong families and communities
>
> *Goal 3:* To create a safe, clean physical environment
>
> *Goal 4:* To advance the longevity of U.S. citizens and reduce the incidence of illness, disability, and premature death
>
> *Goal 5:* To provide universal accessible, affordable, comprehensive services

This framework has created new opportunities for social work. The profession has long recognized the link between private troubles and public issues, and as far back as the 1970s NASW Delegate Assemblies were on record in support of strong social supports for individuals, families, and communities. The new framework eliminates artificial barriers between social problems and health problems and makes the social work perspective public policy.

Implications for Practice and Education

Although each of the five goals established by NISH has enormous implications for social work practice, Goal 2 is particularly significant and gives new meaning to social work intervention with families and communities. The provision of social supports to families contributes not only to the emotional and social well-being of families but also to their physical well-being.

To realize Goal 2 the NISH task force identified a number of priorities for social work practice for the next decade. Working with the National Association of Social Workers and the Council on Social Work Education, the NISH Subcommittee to Create Strong Families and Communities developed the following objectives (Ontario Premier's Council on Health Strategy, 1991a):

- To expand economic opportunities, particularly for low-income individuals and families
- To empower people to influence public policy and the distribution of resources
- To expand access to adequate housing and recreational facilities
- To expand access to educational resources
- To expand social supports and networks

The first four objectives provide opportunities for social welfare planners, educators, researchers, and practitioners to work together with other health care providers to redesign income maintenance, employment, housing, and education policies. Because income affects access to adequate housing, food, and other basic needs, the federal government will need to redefine poverty. Unemployment affects not only income but self-esteem and emotional health, so strategies to create jobs, provide retraining for displaced workers, and develop programs for employable disabled and older persons must be developed.

Because good health is associated with self-determination, individuals and communities need greater opportunities to participate in decisions that control their lives. The notion of maximum feasible participation that emerged in the 1960s needs further study for implementation. Inadequate housing threatens good health, thus new efforts to create affordable housing, as well as transitional and emergency housing, must be pursued. Education is linked to health in a variety of ways, including job opportunities, job security, and knowledge of health care, so barriers to education must be removed; in addition, health education must be emphasized in school curricula.

Not since the Great Society in the 1960s have social workers had such an enormous opportunity to affect social policy. Whether the nation will be able to embrace the kind of major social welfare reform necessary to a new paradigm of health is yet to be seen. However, the fifth objective provides the most immediate promise for social work practice with families and communities.

To implement this objective, the subcommittee developed five targets. First, beginning in 2005 the number of licensed child care opportunities should be expanded at a rate of 12 percent per year. As understood here, child care goes beyond traditional day care and encompasses a range of services—toy-lending services, parenting workshops, community centers, and information services, as well as day and evening care (Ontario Premier's Council on Health Strategy, 1991b).

Second, beginning in 2005 policies should be implemented to assist parents in balancing work and family obligations. This would include expanded family and medical leave and flexible work arrangements.

Third, by 2010 the resources allocated for community services and facilities should be doubled. These include public health agencies, community mental health clinics, group homes, halfway houses, and home and hospice care.

Fourth, by 2010 violence against women and children should be reduced by 50 percent. This would require a variety of interventions, including public education campaigns, parenting workshops, and counseling programs. At the same time, although domestic violence can occur in any family, it tends to be concentrated among extremely poor families. Therefore, reducing domestic violence would also necessitate the expansion of opportunities for low-income people, particularly women.

Fifth, by 2010 the number of school-based social service programs should be increased by 25 percent. Schools are an essential link between families and the community and play a critical role in the development of healthy communities. School-based programs should address a variety of areas including alcohol- and drug-related problems, family counseling, before- and after-school programs, and parent education. Schools should build on the success of Head Start by developing programs that intervene with more children at younger ages. In addition, because intervention can be successful at later stages of development, the schools should also develop programs that address the needs of middle and high school students.

These targets expand opportunities for social work practice. They will give rise to demand for social workers in the such areas as public health, community mental health, school social work, child welfare, and adult day care.

Finally, the new paradigm for health has broad implications for social work education and training. Moore and Webb (1986) and Weil (1988) pointed out that for many years medicine was dominated by mechanistic and reductionistic thinking, resulting in overspecialization and reliance on technology and drugs. The new approach focuses on systems, interconnections, and complexity (Moore and Webb, 1986).

This framework has given impetus to greater integration of the professional foundation areas and the advanced generalist approach in social work education. With the community as the focus, the curriculum now places greater emphasis on policy and the social determinants of health. The goals and objectives created by NISH have led to new outcome measures for health and new approaches to evaluating service delivery in health care. Recognition of the social determinants of health has also led to a reconceptualization of macropractice, which is now viewed as an essential component of the health care system.

References

Cynader, M. S. (1994). Mechanisms of brain development and their role in health and well-being. *Daedalus, 4,* 155–166.

Dranove, D. (1993). The case for competitive reform in health care. In R. J. Arnould, R. Rich, & W. D. White (Eds.), *Competitive approaches to health care reform* (pp. 67–82).Washington, DC: Urban Institute Press.

Eckholm, E. (1994, December 18). While congress remains silent, health care transforms itself. *The New York Times,* p. 1.

Evans, R., & Stoddart, G. (1994). Producing health consuming health care. In P. R. Lee & C. L. Estes (Eds.), *The nation's health* (4th ed., pp. 14–33). Boston: Jones & Bartlett Publishers.

Fogel, R. W. (1994, April). *Economic growth, population theory, and physiology: The bearing of long-term processes in the making of economic policy.* Working Paper No. 4638. Cambridge: National Bureau of Economic Research.

Hurowitz, J. C. (1993). Sounding board—Toward a social policy for health. *New England Journal of Medicine, 2,* 130–133.

Kotelchuck, D. (1976). The health-care delivery system. In D. Kotelchuck (Ed.), *Prognosis negative: Crisis in the health care system* (pp. 5–30). New York: Vintage Books.

Marmor, T. R., & Boyum, D. A. (1993). The political considerations of procompetitive reform. In R. J. Arnould, R. F. Rich, & W. D. White (Eds.), *Competitive approaches to health care reform* (pp. 245–256). Washington, DC: Urban Institute Press.

Marmot, M. G., et al. (1994). Health inequalities and social class. In P. R. Lee & C. L. Estes (Eds.), *The nation's health* (4th ed., pp. 34–40). Boston: Jones & Bartlett Publishers.

McKeown, T. (1994). Determinants of health. In P. R. Lee & C. L. Estes (Eds.), *The nation's health* (4th ed., pp. 6–13). Boston: Jones & Bartlett Publishers.

Moore, R., and Webb, G. (1986). *The K factor.* New York: Pocket Books.

Naylor, C. D. (1991). A different view of queues in Ontario. *Health Affairs, 4,* 110–128.

Ontario Premier's Council on Health Strategy. (1990). *A vision of health—Health goals for Ontario.* Toronto.

Ontario Premier's Council on Health Strategy. (1991a). *Nurturing health—A framework on the determinants of health.* Toronto.

Ontario Premier's Council on Health Strategy. (1991b). *Toward health outcomes—Goals 2 & 4: Objectives & targets.* Toronto.

Rachlis, M., and Kushner, C. (1994). *Strong medicine: How to save Canada's health care system.* Toronto: HarperCollins Publishers.

Relman, A. S. (1992, August). *The choices for health care reform.* Camp Hill, PA: Pennsylvania Blue Shield Institute.

Reves, R. (1985). Declining fertility in England and Wales as a major cause of the 20th century decline in mortality. *American Journal of Epidemiology, 122,* 112–126.

Schwartz, L. L. (1994, April). *The medicalization of social problems: America's special health care dilemma—Special report.* Washington, DC: American Health Systems Institute.

Starr, P. (1994). *The logic of health care reform: Why and how the President's plan will work.* New York: Penguin Books.

Starr, P., and Zelman, W. A. (1993). Bridge to compromise: Competition under a budget. *Health Affairs,* supplement, 7–23.

U.S. Government Accounting Office. (1991). *Canadian health insurance: Lessons for the United States.* Washington, DC: U.S. Government Printing Office.

Weil, A. (1988). *Health and healing.* Boston: Houghton Mifflin.

Wilkinson, R. G. (1994). The epidemiological transition: From material scarcity to social disadvantage? *Daedalus, 4,* 61–77.

Chapter 7

═══════════════════════════════

Beyond 2000

The Future of Hospital-Based Social Work Practice

CATHERINE A. CLANCY, PhD, LMSW-ACP

The health care system of today looks very different from what it was just 20 years ago in 1990. Our focus is no longer on the treatment of disease but on the prediction of and prevention of disease. The Human Genome Project revealed the location of the DNA molecules of each gene and determined precisely which genes do what (Fisher, 1992). This enabled scientists to make great advances in genetic engineering. With these advances and advances in molecular biology, biotechnology, and pharmacology, many dread diseases of the 1990s such as cancer, AIDS, cardiovascular disease, and diabetes have been eradicated; new and effective treatments have been developed. New developments in transplantation have made it possible to buy needed organs off the shelf; organ rejection is a thing of the past. All forms of addiction and mental illness can now be successfully treated. Much research is being done in the area of total health enhancement so that healthy individuals can improve both physical and emotional components of their lives. Great strides have been made in dealing with the aging process, and a life expectancy of 100 years is now the norm.

Dramatic advances in technology have given individuals much more responsibility for and involvement in their total health care. Routine laboratory tests can now be performed at home without drawing blood. Shower heads contain optical computer scanners and periodic body assessments are routine (Fisher, 1992). Biosensors resembling wrist watches are worn to continually monitor general health status. All these data are fed into the centralized information center at the individual's assigned multisystem health care center, and people are automatically alerted to any health deviation. Treatment for deviations are relayed via home computer links from the assigned multisystem health care center, and often people are simply told which genetically engineered medication to pick up from the pharmacy. More complicated deviations may require a video office visit with the primary care physician, and the most serious complications may bring one into the multisystem health care center for more complicated diagnostic testing or emergency or extended care.

Everyone carries a credit-card-sized health information card that contains all vital health history and current information. This information for the entire population is stored in a national data bank for instant access by any treating professional. Confidentiality is a concept of the past, but people are willing to give up confidentiality to receive enhanced treatment.

We have moved from a medical disease/treatment paradigm to a more comprehensive health care delivery system. Health care now encompasses the responsibility for health policy formulation, as well as improvements in the social environment and human behavior of the population, instead of just illness care. We have clearly moved from the notion that health care's only responsibility is treating the sick to the notion that it is the responsibility of the health care system to improve overall health status.

Universal health care coverage based on a single-payer system is now a reality, and health care is delivered by large health care systems that are responsible for the total health care needs of the community they serve. The whole range of health care customers and the entire community are involved in designing the health care system that best fits its needs (Hancock & Bezold, 1994).

The term *hospital* has been replaced by the notion of a group of related health care facilities. This is not a single building, as was the hospital of old, but a total system of services. One part of this system is community health clinics that provide wellness services, health-enhancement services, and outpatient treatment. Another facility, the multiservice health care center, provides emergency, intensive care, and complex diagnostic services. This facility most resembles the hospital of the 1990s because it provides inpatient care. However, its role is much expanded in that it acts as the data hub for the entire system and is the operation center of the system. Another facet of the system is the multiple healthy living communities for aging citizens who no longer wish or are no longer able to live in an independent environment. These are not facilities where people go to grow old but where they learn to live more productive, healthy lives.

Health Care Social Workers

With such dramatic changes in health care technology and redesign of the way health care is delivered, what has happened to the traditional role of the hospital social worker of the 1990s? The job title of hospital social worker no longer exists; it has been replaced by a new position known as the *health care social worker*. Health care social workers are employed by all the health care systems and fulfill three major functions within these systems.

Community Practice

Because of their knowledge of human behavior and the social environment and their expertise in community practice, some health care social workers function as strategic planners in the development and implementation of systemwide programs to improve the social environment of the community served by their health care system. They are also instrumental in designing programs to enhance the mental health of their community. They work with other key players within their system to develop humane policies and procedures for all facets of the health care system, and to develop systemwide outcomes measures.

These workers are skilled in epidemiology and broad areas of research design and are trained to function across professional boundaries. Their major area of expertise is in program design, implementation, and evaluation, but they are also involved in providing input into the national, state, and local political process as it relates to health care issues important to their individual systems. These community practice health care workers sit as representatives of their systems on regional and national planning councils whose responsibility it is to develop plans to improve national health status.

Community practice health care social workers are seen as making vital contributions to all health care systems and often hold high administrative positions within the system. They are in constant data communication with all other health care social workers employed by the health care system and use their input extensively for program design and implementation, policy formulation, and political advocacy activities.

Community Treatment

Other health care social workers work in the multiple community health clinics and the healthy-living communities operated by the health care system. These workers have expertise in clinical treatment, but they also have strong educational skills; the main focus of community health clinics and healthy-living communities is to encourage wellness and optimal functioning. Many of the services provided by this type of health care social worker are group focused. The groups may meet within the facilities, at places of employment, or in client homes. They may be traditional face-to-face groups or they may serve clients from multiple locations through interactive video networks. This social worker must be especially skilled in group techniques and appreciate the value of support groups and networks in enhancing wellness.

Aside from group skills, these health care social workers must possess much greater knowledge of educational techniques than was required in the social work curriculum of the 1990s. Adult education theory and practice principles are now required in the training of all health care social workers. Major educational areas of practice for these health care workers may include teaching optimal parenting, maximal physical fitness, and healthy aging.

Another area of growing importance for health care social workers based in community clinics or healthy-living communities is the new area of health enhancement. Because there are now fewer sick people, health care is dealing with enhancing the lives of the well. People will come to community clinics and will live in healthy-living communities with the purpose of getting better. The community-based health care social worker will be a major player in determining the ethics of health enhancement, in making the selection of who will receive this service and to what degree.

Community-based health care social workers will be in ongoing data contact with the community practice health care social workers and the soon-to-be-discussed multiservice health care center social worker. This loop will also contain all multidisciplinary members of the primary care teams at the multiservice health care center. The community-based workers will provide vital information for the community practice health care workers, and these workers in turn will use data to design new programs for the community health care workers.

Multiservice Center Practitioner

Although the inpatient facility that was referred to in the 1990s as the hospital still exists, inpatient care has been reduced by 50 to 90 percent of what it was in the 1980s and 1990s (Hancock & Bezold, 1994). The buildings formerly occupied by inpatient facilities have now become multiservice health care centers, or the hub of a system that provides seamless care to clients through the life cycle. These multiservice health care centers are the nerve centers that coordinate the services provided in the multiple community outpatient centers and the healthy-living communities. They also act as the staging center for health treatment administered at home through interactive television by physicians and all members of the allied health team ("2013: The Hospital Is Not a Place," 1993).

The health care social worker employed in the multiservice health care center functions as both a client (no longer a patient, because the emphasis is on wellness) case manager and a clinical social worker. Whereas the community-based health care social worker focuses on treatment of groups and group related problems, the social worker at the multiservice health care center emphasizes work with individuals. It is the function of this worker to manage all aspects of a client's psychosocial care from entry into the health care system throughout the life cycle. Referrals to community health clinics and to healthy-living communities all come through the multiservice health care center social worker, and information from social workers in both these areas is fed back to the multiservice worker.

Multiservice health care center social workers function most like the former hospital social worker in that they are the only ones of the three types of health care social workers who actually do some work in the inpatient setting. However, the scope of coverage of clients is much greater than their counterparts of the 1990s because of such extensive coverage and case management responsibilities that extend beyond the inpatient setting. In fact, the majority of these workers' time is focused on work done in clients' homes or other areas of the outpatient environment.

Service Delivery

The structure of social work service delivery provided by the worker in the multiservice health care center is very different from what it was in the traditional hospital of the 1990s. Large, centralized allied health departments are a thing of the past. Health care social workers employed at multiservice health care centers are basically independent practitioners who function as members of primary health care teams led by a primary care physician. These teams are composed of a mix of allied health professionals who provide direct service to clients. Clients are assigned to the primary care teams by the health system designated to provide their coverage through the life cycle. These teams have information on clients' genetic makeup, family health and behavioral history, and current health, as well as computer-generated predictions about future health and the likelihood of a future chronic illness. They are able to monitor the client's health status constantly through the use of biosensor self-care devices that relay health data to a centralized information system (Bergman, 1993).

Social workers who work on these teams must be generalists, as specialized practice does not fit the needs of the primary care model. In this sense they are multiskilled workers with extensive knowledge of health needs throughout the life cycle. Their clinical skills have been expanded beyond past clinical functions to include more knowledge of various treatment modalities, alternative therapies, and educational interventions. The distinctions between psychiatric and medical social work are no more, and workers are charged with managing and treating the psychosocial implications of physical and emotional problems.

It is the responsibility of the health care social worker employed at the multiservice health care center to manage the psychosocial health care status of clients assigned to the team. Quarterly contact is maintained with all clients to monitor their adherence to healthy lifestyle prescriptions given to them by the primary care team. These contacts also are used to monitor client lifestyle adjustment, provide any needed treatment, and coordinate treatment for psychosocial and environmental problems identified between the multisystem worker and the community health center workers.

All client contact outside the multiservice health care center is done through interactive video sessions with the client. All treatment is done according to computer-generated optimal protocols of care developed by recognized social work experts. A fully automated health care record has made paper obsolete in health care.

In addition to quarterly contact with clients, multiservice health care system social workers maintain on-line contact with their peers in the multiple community health centers. This contact makes possible an ongoing communication loop regarding needed referrals and follow-up care provided. This information is added to all other health information about clients that is collected by other members of the primary health care team and their community counterparts. This information is processed by an extremely complex, but user-friendly, central information system that can provide an instant report on the health status of any client covered by the health care system.

Client problems that are identified by a number of social workers both in the multiservice health care center and by the community workers are then fed back to the system's community practice social workers, whose job it is to design systemwide programs to improve the social environment and behavioral health of all clients served by the system. These workers make extensive use of advanced simulations and video teleconferencing with social work experts contracted by the health care system in their efforts to design programs. In this way they can simulate the real world or an artificial world, or combine the best of both worlds in their program design (Burrus, 1993). For example, if a number of multisystem health care workers identified a statistically significant group of clients as experiencing marital discord, a geographically appropriate community-based marital treatment program would be developed by the community practice health care social worker through consultation with recognized experts in marital therapy. Advanced simulations using this new treatment program would be done until all aspects of the program were perfected. This new marital treatment program would then be released to the health care social workers in the appropriate community health centers for implementation. Through the use of many forms of interactive technology, this program would quickly be available to all clients desiring intervention, and results of the intervention would then be fed back to the primary health care teams responsible for that client.

These three functional roles of the health care social worker-planner, educator/therapist, and client health care manager/therapist have expanded the scope and influence of social work in the health field. The transition from 100 years of traditional hospital social work practice to these new and expanded roles has not always been smooth. Changes in three areas are immediately apparent.

Graduate Training

The graduate social work curriculum of today is very different from what it was in the 1990s. Students still choose areas of specialization such as health care, but teaching methods are very different. University faculty act much more as coaches and facilitators of the educational process. In the best tradition of adult education, faculty members work with students to design a curriculum plan based on the students' past experience and technology-projected future needs. Actual instruction is most often done by renowned experts both in health care social work practice and health care fields outside the university setting. These master teachers provide the content using all forms of interactive information technology, and it is the job of university faculty to work with the student to tie all the information into a meaningful whole.

As mentioned earlier, training must prepare generalist practitioners who have a broad knowledge base in health care needs throughout the life cycle. The days of specialized disease-specific practice are over, as most chronic diseases have now been eradicated or are easily controlled by genetic engineering and biotechnology. In addition to this, the ability to predict disease occurrence and to treat most conditions is so advanced as to have caused radical change in the psychosocial and emotional consequences of illness. Today the students must be taught much more about the ethical considerations of total health care than about disease-specific treatment.

Technology in the health care field has exploded, and students must leave the university setting with the ability to utilize advanced technology in their practice. The use of advanced technology has also affected the old notion of field training of students. Students must leave the university much better prepared to act as independent practitioners. For this reason, field instruction is based much more broadly than in the past and relies on actual client contact much less. Advanced simulation using advanced expert systems (Burrus, 1993) is the most common tool for field instruction in health care today. It is imperative that all knowledge gained by today's student be on the cutting edge of technology, or the knowledge is useless for practice.

Supervision

With the advent of independent, interdisciplinary team-centered practice and the move away from centralized departmental-focused practice, health care social workers no longer use on-site peer consultation or have a designated social work supervisor. If it were not for technological advancements, this would be a serious problem. Now expert consultation and supervision are as close as the interactive video monitor. Master supervisors on contract to the health care system are available to all three types of heath care social workers on a moment's notice. Through the use of electronic data interchange, interactive video, and simulations, supervision and consultation have reached a new level of excellence.

Continuing Education

As technology has raised supervision to the next level, it has done the same for the notion of continuing education for health care social workers. Health care systems no longer strive for a well-trained workforce but a workforce that is capable of being retrained again and again (Burrus, 1993). With the rapid expansion of health care technology to prevent or treat health conditions, knowledge may become obsolete soon after it is gained, and health care social workers have accepted that change is a constant. Health care systems have now moved to the notion of "just-in-time training" (Burrus, 1993, p. 63) and multimedia interactive technology is the trainer of choice. As with students and field instruction, advanced expert systems and advanced simulations have made traditional continuing education a concept of the past.

These improvements in the processes of graduate education, supervision, and continuing education have challenged health care social workers to demonstrate continuing competence to practice. Again, advanced technology has made this possible. Competencies have been developed by experts for all areas of health care social work practice on an ongoing basis. Workers are tested to identify areas of practice where new skills should be learned or old skills should be improved. The results of these tests are analyzed, and a customized instructional program is developed to enhance knowledge and practice skills.

Conclusion

Health care social work is different in many ways from the hospital social work of the 1990s. The prevention of health problems has become the most important component of health care practice (Fisher, 1992). The social and emotional components of health have been given a much more important place in all areas of health care practice, as advanced technology works toward conquering or controlling most of the dread diseases of the 1990s. The ability of social workers to take a leading role in working toward the elimination of such health-related societal problems as crime, poverty, illiteracy, environmental pollution, and poor nutrition has given the profession a greatly expanded role in the health care delivery system. The clinical and educational expertise of health care social workers is well recognized, and social work functions in these areas continue to expand. Health care social workers have finally claimed their rightful place as the true health care case managers for all clients.

Just as the role of health care social work has been elevated, so have the demands of practice. As advances in health care continue at an ever-accelerated pace, it is the obligation of health care social workers to strive for optimal levels of continuing professional competence in all areas of health care social work practice.

References

Bergman, R. L. (1993). Quantum leaps. *Hospitals & Health Networks, 67*(28-31), 34–35.

Burrus, D. (1993). *Technotrends.* New York: Harper Business.

Fisher, J. A. (1992). *Our medical future.* New York: Pocket Books.

Hancock, T., & Bezold, C. (1994). Possible futures, preferable futures. *Healthcare Forum Journal, 37,* 23–29.

2013: The hospital is not a place. (1993). *Hospitals & Health Networks, 67,* 29.

Part *III*

Mental Health

We begin this part by looking at Bruce Thyer's vision of social work in Chapter 8 as a developing empirical clinical science in the year 2006. His description presents social work as a highly refined science in which myths and practice wisdom are relegated to a lesser role, and only the most reliable, *proven,* techniques are practiced when known. The reader may want to ask:

1. Is the daily routine of a social worker he describes appealing? Is this the kind of career to which you aspire?

2. Is social work likely to ever become this scientific? If so, what professional and political obstacles would we have to overcome?

In Chapter 9 Robert Paulson presents two visions of managed care in mental health. He addresses three major policy issues: the fate of Medicaid, long-term care, and ancillary social services. Under one scenario *profit* is the driving force in managed care, and it leads to "the worst fears of social work clinicians." The other scenario assumes that *wellness* is the driving force and that high-quality services can be realized under managed care. Obvious questions are:

1. Which of the two scenarios is the most likely to occur, and what impact will the previously described changes in the population have on mental health practice, the spread of HIV/AIDS, and in continuing improvements in technology on mental health practice?

2. Would social work continue to have a significant role in a profit-driven system?

Kimberly Strom presents a thoughtful appraisal of the future of private practice in Chapter 10. After examining its history and the current trends, she describes the structure, funding sources, services, clientele, and clinician characteristics of two alternative models. Remembering previous chapters, the reader will probably want to ask:

1. Given the constraints of managed care, how likely is private practice to survive at all?

2. Will there really be any difference between private practice and doing social work in the context of a large, for-profit agency?

3. Will there still be opportunities for solo practice?

4. Won't there be enormous differences in the training requirements for successful private practice and other types of social work practice?

Gayle Klabor looks at the future of the DSM-IV in Chapter 11. She concludes that in order for social work to maintain its professional standing, it is essential for us to become both knowledgeable and skilled in its use. This is not an assertion that will be supported by those (including most of the authors in Part 7) who believe that the DSM-IV represents a foreign intrusion into the profession which has detracted us from our principal mission in assisting the poor and disadvantaged. One is compelled to ask:

1. Why should social workers be held hostage by an instrument created by and for another profession?

2. What impact will the changes in managed care and private practice have on our use of the DSM-IV?

3. Will social work ever develop a diagnostic tool of its own that will be accepted, especially for third-party reimbursements?

Chapter **8**

Social Work Practice in the Year 2006

A Developing Empirical Clinical Science

BRUCE A. THYER, PhD
University of Georgia

Pat Wilkes leaned the chair back and reviewed the daily schedule displayed on the work pad. Not too bad; three clients in the morning, some time for reviewing journals, hospital rounds in the afternoon, an hour for reviewing notes, and a grand round presentation. The first client, a Mrs. Myers, was due in 30 minutes, time for a cup of tea and a review of the assessment materials that Mrs. Myers had completed after making the initial appointment.

Sipping the soothing brew, Pat looked over the intake forms and rapid-assessment instruments that Mrs. Myers had filled out after completing the computer-based interview covering the criteria found in the DSM-VI. After the DSM workup, the computer automatically displayed several rapid-assessment instruments that seemed relevant to Mrs. Myers's presenting problem, in this case the Beck Depression Inventory–revised, and the Hudson Generalized Contentment Scale, version 3.5. Mrs. Myers had indicated her responses, and the computer automatically scored and graphed the results for Pat to examine prior to meeting the client for the first time. This new system, the Clinical Assessment System for the Social Services (CASSS) was working out well. It saved Pat a lot of time by covering some fairly routine stuff before the initial interview, leaving time to converse with the client about more substantive issues. CASSS even covered the latest criteria found in the DSM-VI, the *Diagnostic Manual of Behavior, Emotional, and Cognitive Disorders* (formerly the *Diagnostic and Statistical Manual of Mental Disorders*). It was still called the DSM, even though it had moved away from the antiquated notion of "mental disorders." Pat's provisional diagnosis was major depression, because Mrs. Myers appeared to meet the DSM criteria for this disorder, and this impression was collaborated by her scores on the Beck and Hudson rapid-assessment instruments.

Mrs. Myers arrived on time, and Pat conducted a typical initial session: some introductions, general remarks, and questions, followed by more specific inquiries, plenty of time for Mrs. Myers to tell her story. The provisional diagnosis seemed to be corroborated by the personal interview, and Pat outlined several treatment options for Mrs. Myers. Among the first-choice treatment options approved by the Federal Health Maintenance Organization (FHMO) were individual or group cognitive-behavioral therapy, third-generation tricyclic antidepressants, and individualized applied behavior analysis. Each of these was well supported by extensive clinical research as efficacious in the treatment of major depression and were services reimbursable by the FHMO.

Ever since the National Association of Social Workers revised its *Code of Ethics* four years ago (NASW, 2002), requiring clinical social workers to provide clients with empirically supported interventions as a first-choice treatment, the profession had undergone a revolution in service provision. Of course, this was buttressed by the Council on Social Work Education's including in its own accreditation standards (CSWE, 2002, 2003) the coordinated mandate that schools of social work provide training in practice methods with a sound empirical foundation. Bogus or ineffective therapies had faded from the social work picture relatively quickly. It was hard to find an accredited school offering training in neurolinguistic programming, object relations theory, or sand tray therapy any more. Even long-venerated giants such as systems theory and the so-called ecological perspective could hardly be found, and in another generation the remaining faculty and practitioners advocating such approaches would be gone from the scene. All this had been made possible by the collaboration between the NASW and CSWE back at the turn of the century, when these organizations took decisive moves toward adopting an empiricist agenda for social work education and practice, as had been advocated by so many social workers in the previous two decades (such as Thyer, 1995).

Of course, the social work professional organizations had been coerced into adopting this empiricist orientation, following the historic lawsuit (*Bordnick v. NASW*) of 1998. Mr. Bordnick, suffering from erectile failure, sought treatment from a social worker who provided him with months of verbal psychotherapy. Predictably, treatment failed to produce any firm results, and Mr. Bordnick discontinued social work treatment and received care from a psychologist providing a Masters and Johnson–type program (Masters & Johnson, 1970), which rapidly effected a cure. Bordnick sued the social worker, contending that she failed to provide him with a first-choice treatment for his condition when such treatments did exist. A codefendant was the National Association of Social Workers, because they had credentialed the clinical social worker in question. As a part of his successful argument, Bordnick noted that the NASW had previously established as a standard of treatment that it is *unethical* to provide a therapy that lacks credible empirical evidence of effectiveness and that is supported only by anecdotal reports.

It was a dramatic moment in the courtroom when Bordnick's lawyer read the following statement, which was an official NASW position:

Proponents of reparative therapies claim—without documentation—many successes. They assert that their processes are supported by conclusive scientific data which are in fact *little more than anecdotal.* NCOGLI protests these efforts to "convert" people through irresponsible therapies . . . empirical research does not demonstrate that . . . sexual orientation (heterosexual or homosexual) can be changed through these so-called reparative therapists. (NASW, 1992, p. 1, italics added)

This statement turned out to be a precedent-setting position, perhaps unintentionally established by the NASW's National Committee on Lesbian and Gay Issues who were concerned with efforts to change homosexual individuals into heterosexual ones in the name of mental health treatment. This precedent, of course, was seen as extending to *all* social work clinical services, not just to reparative therapies.

Arguing that because the NASW had previously contended that is a violation of its *Code of Ethics* to offer clinical services that lack empirical research (having only supportive anecdotal reports) and Bordnick's social worker was credentialed by the NASW, the social worker was obviously in violation of the *Code of Ethics* by providing verbal psychotherapy and not well-supported behavioral intervention, and the NASW was culpable for her actions because that organization certified her as a diplomate in clinical social work. Following the multimillion dollar payout to Mr. Bordnick, the NASW quickly moved to forestall similar lawsuits by including in its *Code of Ethics* the following new standard, which revolutionized social work practice:

Clients should be offered as a first-choice treatment interventions with some significant degree of empirical support, where such knowledge exists, and should be provided other treatments only after such first-choice treatments have been given a legitimate trial and been shown not to be efficacious. (NASW, 2002, p. 3)

Mrs. Myers opted for cognitive-behavioral group work and Pat checked the electronic schedule. A new group was beginning Tuesday, and Mrs. Myers's name was added to the roster. Pat knew the group worker, Ashley Stewart, to be a competent and caring therapist, trained at the Beck Memorial Center for Cognitive Therapy in Philadelphia two years ago. Ashley specialized in helping clients with affective disorders such as major depression and regularly offered group and individual sessions at the agency. More and more it seemed that new social workers such as Ashley were electing to focus their clinical training into relatively narrow fields. This was becoming increasingly necessary with each new development in effective psychosocial treatments for specific conditions. The days of the generalist clinical social worker with a diverse caseload were almost gone, Pat ruefully reflected. Although this meant that some of the diversity of daily work was missing, it also meant that genuine expertise in a focused area became possible.

Using the office computer Mrs. Myers completed another user-friendly version (psychometrically comparable to the ones she filled out two weeks ago) of the Beck and

Hudson rapid-assessment instruments while Pat processed her paperwork. Mrs. Myers's FHMO card was run through the reader and Pat typed in the required information about diagnosis, provider number, and recommended treatment. Payment was immediately approved, and Pat reflected on how nice it was to have a national payroll tax in place providing for Mrs. Myers's FMHO membership. It was certainly a surprise to have President Dole support that legislation eight years ago, but the provisions that mandated providing only empirically supported treatments and the ongoing evaluation of practice outcomes using single-case research designs overcame the objections of most conservatives to the FMHO concept. Limiting reimbursement to empirically supported treatments resulted in more people receiving effective services and ended up costing the system *less* money. It was hard to imagine that barely a decade ago social workers could provide literally *anything* to clients in the name of therapy, no matter what the research evidence had to say about its efficacy, and still receive insurance reimbursement. Those days were gone.

A few private practitioners lingered on, seeing wealthy clients seeking the panache of talking about "my therapist," but most had climbed aboard the FMHO bandwagon, particularly because social workers, psychologists, and psychiatrists were reimbursed at the same rate. It was ironic how Senate Majority Leader Mikulski (one of 16 senators who were social workers) exacted that concession from President Dole in return for her support of the president's health care bill. The result of such parity was that schools of social work were bulging with applicants clamoring for admission to the standard three-year MSW program in lieu of the five-year psychology Ph.D. degree. Psychiatric residency programs were barely staying alive, and those that were doing well did so by focusing on pharmacotherapy. Hardly any psychiatrists are providing psychosocial treatments nowadays. Even so, with extensive practice guidelines for primary care, general medical practitioners, clinical psychologists, and nurse practitioners were providing almost all of the psychotropic medication prescriptions, making the lot of the average psychiatrist that much more difficult.

As Mrs. Myers left, Pat thought about the tremendous strides that had been made in treating so-called mental disorders. Virtually all clients had access to genuinely effective interventions delivered by skilled social workers well trained in these services. Persons with what used to be called chronic mental illness or schizophrenia were provided with state-of-the-art inpatient treatment when necessary, based on the landmark program developed and evaluated by Paul and Lentz (1977; Paul & Menditto, 1992). Once in the community, assertive case management teams using a family-based psychoeducational model (Hogarty et al., 1991) helped these discharged patients live as independently as possible, obtain rewarding employment, and have an enjoyable social life. Children with autism and their families received intensive behavioral intervention modeled after the treatment developed by Ivar Lovaas (1987; McEachin, Smith, & Lovaas, 1993), who had received the 1998 National Science Medal from Vice-President Colin Powell, in recognition of his service as a clinical researcher. Persons who drank too much and wanted to quit were enrolled in the latest version of Azrin's Community Reinforcement Approach to alcoholism treatment (Azrin, Sisson, Meyers, & Godley, 1982), an approach that had proven effective back in the 1970s and 1980s but received widespread application only during the late 1990s. Clients experiencing panic attacks were offered as a first-choice treatment Barlow and

Cerny's (1988) comprehensive treatment program involving exposure therapy, breathing training, cognitive therapy, relaxation training, and other elements, another empirically supported intervention that unfortunately required a decade or two before being widely disseminated and adopted.

Pat's revery was interrupted by low music from the desk pad, a reminder of the approaching appointment at 1000 hours. This was with Mr. Donald Scott, a recovering abuser of alcohol who had been participating in a combined community reinforcement approach for substance abuse and job-finding club (Azrin, Flores, & Kaplan, 1975) for the past two months. In reviewing the CASSS file, Pat recalled that Mr. Scott had landed a job six weeks ago, and that the disulfiram implantation procedure last month had gone well. The nurse practitioner found that Mr. Scott had not experienced any side effects from the medication, and his blood enzyme analysis corroborated complete abstinence from alcohol for over eight weeks. Disulfiram, also known as Antabuse, inhibited the breakdown of alcohol by the liver, producing severe nausea in people who drank alcohol while taking Antabuse. For decades social workers wrung their hands over the problem of ensuring that patients regularly took their Antabuse, before the FMHO mandated the well-established implantation procedure as a condition of receiving long-term services for persons who drank too much.

Pat had been working with Mr. Scott ever since the client's discharge from Mary Richmond Hospital two months ago, after a six-day stay on the D & A detoxification unit. An unemployed veteran of Operation Alamo, as the nine-day North Mexican war was popularly known, Mr. Scott had a tough time adjusting to civilian life. As his case manager, Pat coordinated the numerous services Mr. Scott was receiving. Today was a mandated quality-assurance meeting to assess Mr. Scott's satisfaction with the services he was receiving. Following a 15-minute getting-reacquainted conversation, Pat completed a semistructured client satisfaction interview with Mr. Scott and set him up to answer a couple of additional rapid-assessment measures being used as individualized outcome measures. The new job appeared to be working out well, and Mr. Scott had just received his four-week continuous-employment bonus check from the plant. He had used it to upgrade his wardrobe and was already planning on how to spend his eight-week bonus paycheck. These continuous-employment bonuses were proving their weight in gold. Subsidized by the state, they resulted in formerly unemployed persons keeping jobs far longer than would otherwise be the case, and ended up saving the state money.

It's time for a break and another cup of tea. Pat checked in with CASSS and watched a recorded digital message from a colleague, a reminder about Pat's case presentation scheduled for 1600 hours today at Mary Richmond Hospital, where Pat held a clinical faculty appointment and retained admitting privileges. Social workers with such admitting and staff privileges were commonplace now, even outside of the network of NASW-owned hospitals (acquired at bargain-basement prices during the great proprietary hospital sell-off of 1999, when the FMHO legislation was passed). Pat acknowledged the message and paged through a recent issue of *Research on Social Work Practice.* Originally the first of the social work journals to be made available electronically, it remained the best of over 10 top-quality practice research social work publications, 8 of which could be read using e-mail. Pat downloaded and printed one article on the psychosocial treatment of bipolar disorder, to be read at leisure later. It was time for the next appointment.

This one promised to be particularly interesting. Mrs. Soufer was a middle-aged woman who met the DSM criteria for Tourette's disorder (TD). TD appearing in a woman was unusual enough (almost all cases were among men). Pat heard Mrs. Soufer arrive in the waiting room before the secretary announced her presence. Her vocal tic was particularly loud and obscene today, which Pat attributed to Mrs. Soufer's nervousness over meeting Dr. Krebbs. Pat fetched Mrs. Soufer and closed the office door behind her as she sat down. Pat explained once more that the office video camera would allow Dr. Krebbs, staff neurologist at Mary Richmond Hospital, to see Mrs. Soufer, while the monitor displayed Dr. Krebbs to Pat and Mrs. Soufer in the office. Real-time conversation was both possible and natural. As scheduled, Dr. Krebbs appeared on the screen and introduced herself to Mrs. Soufer. Krebbs reviewed the client's history with her; this was more to put the patient at ease, because all of this was well known and accessible to the neurologist via CASSS. Obligingly but unconsciously Mrs. Soufer displayed her typical array of facial and vocal tics and spasmodic neck movements. Dr. Krebbs took Mrs. Soufer's blasphemous and obscene characterizations of Krebbs's personal character and ancestry in stride. Pat admired Krebbs's aplomb during this first meeting with Mrs. Soufer. It had taken Pat several sessions to accept and ignore the characteristic coprolalia emitted by the client.

Mrs. Soufer had conscientiously worn the microphone provided by Pat 16 hours a day for the past two weeks, and after the data were downloaded and graphically displayed, Pat, Dr. Krebbs, and Mrs. Soufer could see a fairly stable but high rate of vocal tics. They didn't seem to fluctuate much by day of the week, and the data seemed to show a very good pattern for baseline purposes. As had been tentatively arranged, Krebbs was to call in a prescription for a newly developed dopamine receptor-blocker recently approved for the treatment of Tourette's. Mrs. Soufer would begin the medication tomorrow morning and would continue to wear the vocal tic monitor as before. In a week she would come in for another visit with Pat, who would download and graph the past seven days' worth of data, review possible side effects with Mrs. Soufer, obtain the client's own impressions of how she was responding to the medication, and transmit the graphed data via CASSS to Dr. Krebbs. In effect, Pat, Krebbs, and Mrs. Soufer planned an A-B single case study (see Bloom, Fischer, & Corcoran, 2001). If results were not satisfactory some additional treatment options would be discussed with Mrs. Soufer, but Dr. Krebbs was fairly confident that the new medication would prove immensely helpful.

It was now time for lunch. Pat reviewed the notes and transparencies for the case conference presentation at the hospital later in the day while munching down a lunch delivered by the local Chinese eatery. Everything was in order, and after a quick car trip Pat was at Mary Richmond Hospital by 1300. The first patient was Mrs. Niver, hospitalized a week ago for an intensive behavior therapy regimen designed to alleviate her incapacitating panic attacks and related agoraphobia. After reviewing the chart, Pat dropped by Mrs. Niver's room where she was resting after lunch. She perked up when she saw Pat, and proceeded to describe her day's activities. She was enjoying the relaxation training sessions in the morning and the cognitive-behavioral group work, but she was finding the exposure therapy exercises as difficult as she had expected. She was enjoying working with Mrs. Lynn, the social work student completing her internship on the Anxiety Disorders Unit, who accompanied Mrs. Niver and helped support and facilitate Mrs. Niver's exposure exercises. Yesterday they had been to the mall, a place Mrs. Niver avoided for years because she had had a terrible panic attack there. Ms. Lynn had helped Mrs. Niver to become comfortable riding the mall's escalators, a process that took over two hours of work. Mrs. Niver had some troubling dreams last night about the mall, but she was quite proud of her newfound ability to enter such phobic situations. Today Mrs. Niver's husband would accompany Ms. Lynn and his wife back to the mall, where Mrs. Lynn would guide him in helping his wife with the exposure program. This would greatly help with maintaining and generalizing the patient's treatment gains once she was discharged.

The graphs on Mrs. Niver's charts displayed a dramatic reduction in spontaneous panics (assessed using a portable monitor worn by the patient 24 hours a day, coupled with her self-reports), situational anxiety, and anticipatory fears. Tomorrow would begin a brief group therapy program designed to help her learn to regulate her breathing, because subtle hyperventilation had been shown to be etiologically related to most so-called panic attacks. Mrs. Niver and her husband had been conscientiously reading the books and articles that Pat had provided them on the nature and treatment of panic and agoraphobia, and Pat answered some of her questions. If she continued to make progress, she could expect to be discharged in another five days, to be then enrolled in a follow-up aftercare program. Both Pat and Mrs. Lynn would continue to work with her, providing for continuity of care. Normally hospital-based treatment of panic attacks was not necessary, because the disorder could be cared for as an outpatient service, but Mrs. Niver's case was of such severity and duration that the more intensive program seemed to be indicated.

Pat congratulated the patient on her hard work and effort in dealing with the panic attacks, dictated a few notes for the chart, and called on the other two patients scheduled for that day's visits. Both were clients with severe obsessive-compulsive disorder (OCD) receiving a rigorous regimen of exposure therapy and response prevention, following the treatment protocol developed by social worker Gail Steketee over 15 years ago, which had now become the treatment of choice for OCD (Steketee, 1987; Steketee & White, 1990). The social work intern, Mrs. Lynn, was also conducting these two patients' exposure programs, and she brought Pat up to date on the conduct of the sessions. Both were complying with the program, but one of them didn't seem to habituate as quickly as normal during the exposure exercises. Pat made a mental note to discuss this case more fully with Ms. Lynn during their clinical supervision scheduled for tomorrow. It was possible that the patient was engaging in some form of covert avoidance behavior that was impairing the effectiveness of the exposure work.

It was time for a break in the doctor's lounge, where Pat brushed up once more on the presentation notes. The actual lecture shouldn't be a problem, as Pat had presented this case, a single-system research evaluation of six chronically disabled patients, at last month's annual conference of the Society for Social Work and Research held in New York. Over 300 people attended Pat's presentation, almost 10 percent of the entire group of registrants, so today's collection of 40 or so hospital staff and interns should be a piece of cake. And so it proved to be. One of the psychiatrists had posed some really challenging questions during the discussion period, and Pat was hard-pressed to explain why a multiple-baseline design was not suitable for evaluating this group of clients. Even conceding this point, Pat had no regrets, when serving as chair of the hospital's recruitment committee, about hiring this particular psychiatrist two years ago. She had proved to be a valuable asset to the medical staff of the hospital and had adapted well to the interdisciplinary and egalitarian organization of the professional services.

By 1830 Pat was home, eating a light dinner with the kids. After some family time, 2100 found Pat asleep, with an unread article on bipolar disorder on the floor beside the recliner and a lukewarm cup of tea cooling on the end table.

With a sudden start, Pat awoke. Blinking, the outlines of the psychoanalyst's office came into focus. "Oh my God! Dr. Streen, I must have dozed off during my session. I had the most horrible nightmare about social work practice 10 years from now."

"Please tell me about it," came Dr. Streen's soothing voice from behind Pat.

"Well, it all began. . . ."

References

Azrin, N. H., Flores, T., & Kaplan, S. J. (1975). Job-finding club: A group-assisted program for obtaining employment. *Behaviour Research and Therapy, 13,* 17–27.

Azrin, N. H., Sisson, R. W., Meyers, R., & Godley, M. (1982). Alcoholism treatment by disulfiram and community reinforcement therapy. *Journal of Behavior Therapy and Experimental Psychiatry, 13,* 105–112.

Barlow, D. H., & Cerny, J. A. (1988). *Psychological treatment of panic.* New York: Guilford.

Bloom, M., Fischer, J., & Corcoran, K. (2001). *Evaluating practice: Guidelines for the accountable professional* (3rd ed.). Itasca, IL: F. E. Peacock.*

Council on Social Work Education. (2002). *Handbook of accreditation standards and procedures.* Alexandria, VA: Author.*

Council on Social Work Education. (2003). *Curriculum policy for the Master's degree and Baccalaureate degree programs in social work education.* Alexandria, VA: Author.*

Hogarty, G., Anderson, C., Reiss, D., Kornblith, S., Greenwald, D., Ulrich, R., & Carter, M. (1991). Family psychoeducation, social skills training, and maintenance chemotherapy in the aftercare treatment of schizophrenia: II. Two-year effects of a controlled study on relapse and adjustment. *Archives of General Psychiatry, 48,* 340–347.

Lovaas, I. (1987). Behavioral treatment and normal education and intellectual functioning in young autistic children. *Journal of Consulting and Clinical Psychology, 55,* 3–9.

Masters, W. H., & Johnson, V. E. (1970). *Human sexual inadequacy.* Boston, MA: Little Brown.

McEachin, J. J., Smith, T., & Lovaas, O. I. (1993). Long-term outcome for children with autism who received early intensive behavioral treatment. *American Journal of Mental Retardation, 97,* 359–372.

National Association of Social Workers—National Committee on Lesbian and Gay Issues. (1992). *Position statement—"Reparative" or "conversion" therapies for lesbians and gay men.* Washington, DC: Author.

National Association of Social Workers. (2002). *Code of Ethics.* Washington, DC: Author.*

Paul, G. L., & Lentz, R. J. (1977). *Psychosocial treatment of chronic mental patients: Milieu versus social learning programs.* Cambridge, MA: Harvard University Press.

Paul, G. L., & Menditto, A. A. (1992). Effectiveness of inpatient treatment programs for mentally ill adults in public psychiatric facilities. *Applied and Preventive Psychology, 1,* 41–63.

Steketee, G. (1987). Behavioral social work with obsessive-compulsive disorder. *Journal of Social Service Research, 10*(2/3/4), 53–72.

Steketee, G., & White, K. (1990). *When once is not enough: Help for obsessive compulsives.* Oakland, CA: New Harbinger.

Thyer, B. A. (1995). Promoting an empiricist agenda in the human services: An ethical and humanistic imperative. *Journal of Behavior Therapy and Experimental Psychiatry, 26,* 93–98.

*Fictitious reference.

Swimming with the Sharks or Walking in the Garden of Eden

Two Visions of Managed Care and Mental Health Practice

ROBERT I. PAULSON, PhD
Portland State University

One of the few things experts and prognosticators agree on is that managed care and health care reform are inevitable. What they will look like, however, and how mental health practice will be affected is subject to much speculation and disagreement. Depending on the outcome, two completely different scenarios could emerge, one (wellness) that would provide a myriad of opportunities for social work, the other (profit) a plethora of threats. Before describing these alternative scenarios, a brief discussion of the current trends and policy issues that will shape these future scenarios is in order.

Current Trends

1. The Merging of Public and Private Sector Care

One of the most important trends is a rapid collapsing of the boundaries between public, not-for-profit, and for-profit care. For years social work, more than any other profession, has worked in either the public or private not-for-profit sectors with publicly funded clients. These vulnerable populations are frequently stigmatized and seen as less deserving and less desirable to work with. Now, however, many private businesses are finding that under the right circumstances, there is profit to be made with these populations. Hence, social work agencies that previously had a monopoly in a publicly funded service area are now facing increasing competition from all sectors. The future portends that privatization will occur on a widespread basis and that few distinctions will remain between the public and private sectors.

2. The Dominance of Managed Care in the Public and Private Sectors

The initial rapid growth in managed care was restricted to private insurers. This is no longer the case. Public payers are swiftly adopting managed care strategies as a method of holding down costs and are increasingly willing to contract with for-profit managed care companies to manage public Medicaid programs.

3. Merger, Acquisition, and Alliance Fever and the Blending of Insurers, Managed Care Entities, and Providers

The capital and information demands of managed care and the growing need for large provider networks have led to an explosion of mergers, acquisitions, and alliances as organizations seek vertical and horizontal integration to better position themselves in a highly competitive market. The result is that traditional organizational configurations no longer apply. For example, insurance companies are developing or acquiring managed care companies, and HMOs and for-profit hospitals are buying not-for-profit hospitals. The result is a blending of these traditionally separate roles and functions.

4. Continued Development of Integrated Provider Networks and Mixed Large-Volume Purchasers

Solo private practice is expected to be extinct within a very short time. The wave of the future is large integrated networks that provide a full array of services and continuum of care. Similarly, on the purchasing side, there is an increasing recognition of the need for mechanisms that join individuals and small employers in the purchase of insurance, and it is likely that large purchasing cooperatives will be either formed voluntarily or mandated by legislation. This will result in purchasers obtaining increasing leverage over insurers and providers.

5. Increased Nongovernmental Regulation of Practice

One of the new utilization management technologies of managed care is the regulation of practice patterns through privileging, staff profiling, and treatment protocols. Privileging is the process by which a practitioner's training and experience is evaluated to determine which treatment interventions will be allowed with which specific target populations. In the past, for example, a clinician could be shifted from serving an older adult population to a children's population for the purpose of meeting staffing needs based solely on the credential of an MSW degree rather than specialized training. At this juncture, however, treatment protocols are being developed for each discrete mental health diagnosis that detail the recommended treatment and expected length of treatment. Managed care organizations regularly develop staff profiles that illustrate an individual clinician's productivity, use of treatment modalities, average length of treatment time, and adherence to treatment protocols in comparison with colleagues within the organization or region as a whole. Practice regulations such as these will be standard throughout the industry whether or not they are willingly accepted by social work practitioners.

6. Greater Risk Sharing among All Parties

Another clear pattern that is developing is the growth of risk sharing. Many managed care contracts are capitated, and the financial risk is passed on through the use of subcapitation to individual providers and to individuals by utilizing copayment schemes.

7. Pressure to Integrate Behavioral and Physical Health Care and Increased Access to Primary Care

The integration of physical and mental health care is the ultimate goal of most policy makers. Short-run concerns that mental health will receive short shrift in the larger health care system have led to mental health carve-outs. This separation, however, is likely to be only an interim step. At the same time, the shared goal of universal health care means that demands for increased access to primary health care will grow.

8. Price, Outcomes, Service, and Quality as Key Buying Factors for Purchasers of Health Care

As mental health providers move into a competitive marketplace they will need to compete and perform in areas that are new to public and private not-for-profit providers. One of the greatest challenges will be for organizations and their staffs to be held accountable for outcomes rather than process measures, such as the number of hours of service. Competing in the arena of price, outcomes, service, and quality will demand that practice patterns and information systems be radically altered in the future.

9. Continued Advances in Neuroscience, Psychopharmacology, Genetics, and Biotechnology

Current progress in the understanding of the brain, the etiology of serious and persistent mental illness, the biological components of these illnesses including genetic markers and genetic predispositions, can only accelerate. Ongoing breakthroughs in discovering new classes of drugs such as Respiradol can be expected with increased knowledge of brain chemistry. Although it is highly unlikely that a magical treatment will be discovered that will cure or completely control all symptoms of mental illness, advances in drug therapies should make an increasing number of persons amenable to psychosocial rehabilitative interventions. This is particularly true of certain subgroups (such as young adults) with frequent comorbidity between primary diagnoses and substance abuse and/or personality disorders, unless medical advances take place that better control these problems.

It is also likely that in a number of situations genetic markers will be discovered that will identify persons who are predisposed to these illnesses so that careful monitoring and preventive measures can be established. Further, it is possible that genetic defects that affect brain chemistry may be identified and therapeutic techniques developed that will lead to less intrusive and more effective management of these illnesses.

10. Necessity for the Development of Community-Based Innovations

The shift to capitated forms of financing and outcome measurement will produce a constant impetus for ongoing innovations in community-based services. There will be a shift in emphasis from facility-based "medically necessary" services to wrap-around, flexible support services that can be adjusted to the immediate needs of the consumer at a particular time.

11. Increasing Roles for Consumers and Family Members (Secondary Consumers)

The growth of the family movement (National Alliance for the Mentally Ill and the Federation of Families for Children with Serious Emotional Disorders) and the consumer movement is profoundly affecting the mental health system. As a matter of federal law (and in many instances state law as well) the participation of consumers in policy making has been mandated, and their participation in treatment planning encouraged and protected. The involvement of consumers as providers in their own right, as participants in their own treatment, and as watchdogs and advocates, will continue and expand into the next century.

12. Expansion of Need and Demand Populations

Current demographic and epidemiological trends all point to the rapid growth in high-demand populations that will stress current and future resources beyond their limits (see Chapter 1). The needs of the populations to be cared for will be more difficult to meet and will require innovations in services that are responsive to special needs. This resource demand will further focus concerns on efficiency and cost containment.

Given these trends, it is certain that social workers in the mental health field will be working exclusively in integrated consumer-sensitive networks of health care as providers in some form of a managed care.

13. Technological Advances in Computers, Communications, and Management Information Systems

Managed care, especially in capitated systems, requires extremely sophisticated on-line computer information systems. The emphasis on outcomes, service, consumer responsiveness, and quality, which are critical in a competitive environment, requires a rapid response to consumer needs, especially in crisis situations, which necessitates quick transfers of information. New concerns will arise regarding the balance between the needs for quick information sharing and the protection of confidentiality.

Video conferencing will be utilized to reach rural areas or to connect satellite offices of an urban agency to reduce travel costs and better utilize scarce, highly trained, expensive personnel. Where transportation is an issue, or when persons cannot or will not leave their own homes, wider conferencing innovations are likely to play an active role.

Undecided Policy Issues

In the absence of health care reform, the three major policy issues that pertain to the fate of Medicaid, long-term care, and ancillary social services remain undecided. The outcome of these policy debates will have a profound impact on the future of managed mental health care and will influence which of two scenarios is most likely to occur. If Medicaid remains as a separate program, the current distinctions between public and private-pay clients will continue, and a two-tier system of health care will remain and become further accentuated. Most importantly, there is little agreement regarding what is to be done with long-term care. The explosion in high-need populations described above, all of which involve long-term care, is likely to create a major health care crisis both fiscally and in service capacity, without a solution to the problem of long-term care. With respect to mental health, treating persons with major mental illness, chemical dependency, or dementia related to aging or HIV involves long-term, expensive care.

The results of these policy decisions combined with the evolution of current trends could lead to two starkly contrasting possibilities for mental health managed care in the year 2000 and beyond. These are purposely extreme scenarios. As is often the case, what actually happens will most likely be a mix of the two.

Swimming with the Sharks and Barracudas

The first scenario, which we have named *profit,* presumes that the momentum for privatization, less government, and deregulation will continue as large, influential corporate health care interest groups identify substantial money-making potential in managing both the public and private sectors of the health care industry. Under the profit scenario, the worst fears of social work clinicians would be realized.

Large national for-profit managed care organizations (MCOs) would succeed in convincing states that MCOs could operate Medicaid programs more economically and would capture a large share of the employer market. However, in the belief that market competition will hold down costs and improve quality, multiple MCOs would be allowed to compete for Medicaid members, creating a bewildering array of options for persons who are unaccustomed to making such choices. This competitive scramble would lead to a large number of questionable enrollment tactics that would rarely protect consumer interests (such enrollment practices have actually occurred in several states).

If the profit scenario were real, states would not exercise their option to protect their long-term, historic investment in community mental health and substance abuse agencies by requiring managed care entities to contract with these historic providers. Instead, the MCOs would form their own extensive networks by utilizing individual practitioners and group practices. Fearing that they would be left off panels, and being relatively unsophisticated about the nature of such contracts, many social workers would be expected to sign contracts that place them at a disadvantage vis-a-vis the MCOs. Few if any solo practitioners would survive, and the survivors would be restricted to clientele whose treatment was not dependent on insurance reimbursement. Community mental health agencies would survive either by convincing MCOs that it was more economical and efficient to use the existing agencies' infrastructure and to contract with them or by merging with larger health care organizations such as hospitals.

The profit scenario finds national or regional MCOs successfully convincing states that MCOs could save the states money by deliberately pricing initial contracts below cost, and obtaining a "foot in the door" by underbidding local agencies and other local MCO competitors. Only large for-profit ventures with extensive capital reserves could afford to take such risks. As a consequence, public payers would essentially eliminate governmental and private not-for-profit alternatives and leave public payers at the mercy of the corporate health care sector. Prices would soon be raised, which is a strategy that has been used in prior privatization efforts (Paulson, 1988). In such a continuation of the era of privatization and deregulation, states would exercise minimal oversight over service delivery.

One consequence of the profit scenario is that true MCO competition occurs only in desirable, and usually urban, markets. In smaller towns and rural areas consumers may be left with only a single MCO that has a monopoly over services, but no counterbalancing public interest or vehicle for community input and influence, which nonprofit agencies (with community boards of directors) provide. Similarly, once states have turned over their responsibility for care to MCOs, primary and secondary consumer advocacy groups will have considerably less leverage and involvement than they had with state and local governments.

If allowed, MCOs will seek to select healthier, lower-cost clients and intentionally avoid serving persons with chronic conditions. For cases in which fiscal responsibility for hospitalization is not part of the managed care contract, there will be an incentive for shifting difficult clients to state hospitals, depending, of course, on bed availability and local commitment laws. If there is no mental health carve-out or a minimum mental health benefit package included in the contract, this would be an incentive to restrict access to mental health services, which currently occurs in many HMOs. In numerous instances, certainly in HMOs, primary health care providers control referrals to mental health services.

If the primary health care providers' financial gain is determined partly by their success in utilizing specialists only within certain limits, then financial interests, rather than mental health needs, are likely to drive the referral process. If public sector and not-for-profit agencies survive in the profit scenario, they will be the sole providers for persons whose illnesses are difficult to treat and who are not desired by the MCOs.

Under these conditions the incentives are to reduce cost to meet the competition and to maximize profits, and the current insurance/utilization review model of managed care, rather than a community-based capitated model, is likely to remain. The pressure to maximize profits will have considerable implications for the conditions under which social work clinicians practice and could extend and intensify the worst of the current insurance model managed care practices. For instance, as a cost-saving measure, the MCO could hire case managers–utilization reviewers with minimal training and clinical experience whose numbers and availability would greatly restrict their accessibility to authorize services. Reviewers in this system, of course, would be rewarded for containing costs and restricting access. The profit scenario would find social workers restricted to providing services that are "medically necessary," regulated by reviewers who are insensitive to the need for community supports.

This medicalization of mental health would tend to emphasize medication as the major intervention with little or no emphasis on rehabilitation and supplementary community support services. Providers would be compelled to spend considerable time accessing services for clients, undergoing concurrent reviews, justifying service extensions, advocating for clients, and providing guidance in the appeal of service denials. Providers might also find their clinical judgment questioned and their professional autonomy threatened by MCO reviewers. The reliance on medications as the most cost-effective way to treat serious and persistent mental illness would occur in this medicalization profit scenario.

If the mental health industry follows these reasonable conjectures, much tighter standards on the amount of training and prior experience will be necessary to practice a particular modality or with a particular population. For example, a mere day-long workshop that provides training on a particular intervention, disability, or illness will no longer suffice to qualify a clinician to practice in a new specialty area, which is currently possible. Greater restrictions would significantly reduce clinicians' flexibility to shape their own careers because more formalized training would be required to expand practice opportunities and movement into a different practice area. Clinicians will be compared with their peers primarily with respect to utilization patterns and productivity. Outcomes will likely be geared toward the needs of the MCO and major customers, with an emphasis on ease of administration and cost-effective outcome measures.

It is also possible that MCOs will resort to the use of part-time contract workers so that benefit costs can be minimized and staffing easily flexed to meet immediate and changing demands. In addition, there might be a tendency to hire less-experienced, less-expensive workers. In such a situation, it is in the MCO's interest to minimize utilization so that social work's commitment to outreach, particularly with vulnerable populations, will be strongly discouraged. The major concern will not be to meet the psychosocial needs of consumers but to meet the minimum standards outlined in protocols that protect the liability concerns of management. In market areas in which there is heavy competition, greater pressure on workers for increased productivity and reduced cost can be anticipated. If these conditions are realized, social workers may face professional and values conflicts as they strive to practice within such a restrictive environment.

In short, the profit scenario in the year 2000 and beyond would find major social work roles under managed mental health care restricted to the provision of brief therapy, discharge planning, and utilization review. In addition, social workers would utilize advanced information technologies that would focus on accountability to organizational standards, rapid transfer of information, and monitoring of service utilization and cost. Additional technology uses such as computerized assessment and therapy could be expected to dominate if lower costs were promised as a result.

Undoubtedly, the mental health service system as a whole would suffer under these conditions. With this profit model there is no incentive or mechanism for developing more specialized services for which there is limited demand and that are feasible only on a communitywide basis. No identified part of the system is responsible, nor is there a mechanism for the coordination, planning, and development of the community support system to protect the community interest. Furthermore, the real threat exists that, unlike public or private not-for-profit systems where surpluses fund program development or enhancement, profits will probably be removed from the community to flow into the coffers of shareholders.

Walking in the Garden of Eden

The second scenario, which we have named *wellness,* is based on a very different set of premises. It assumes that government does not relinquish its responsibility for mental health services, either because the profit scenario demonstrated that the hypothesized savings were not forthcoming or as a matter of public policy. This wellness scenario delegates the responsibility for providing managed mental health care to county governments, which either provide those services directly or subcontract with community providers. Consequently, the historical investment in community mental health and chemical dependency agencies is preserved by requiring the utilization of existing community providers that have met state certification or licensing standards.

This future possibility retains state government responsibility to establish and monitor standards for the provision of mental health services, focusing on such outcomes as functional levels, symptomatology, community tenure, quality of life, and consumer satisfaction. Here mental health care, including long-term care for persons with chronic conditions, is capitated and integrated with general health care. In the wellness scenario, mental health care has earned parity with health care as part of a minimum benefits package including a continuum of community care, not just inpatient care, which is currently the case with most insurance coverage. Finally, risk is shared by all providers through subcapitation. There are multiple capitation rates for persons with serious and persistent mental illness based on severity of condition and historical use of intensive and expensive services.

Funding agencies that share responsibility for portions of adult and children's care (such as schools and child welfare) would pool their funds that were designated for mental health services or support of long-term clients and transfer the responsibility for providing community support services that would be included in the capitation rate. The system would probably be established by a model of one-time funding of additional community-based services allowing utilization of less-restrictive and less-costly care environments as a trade-off for assuming the risk of inpatient and institutional care. With respect to risk assumption, protection against a series of extremely high-cost incidents would be provided through stop-loss insurance, which includes shared risk as well. The wellness scenario in no way precludes the use of for-profit providers or MCOs; however, in the latter case the MCOs are responsible for an entire population, which prohibits the selection of low users of care; mandates care to high users, with performance regulated and monitored by the state and county.

Under these conditions, prepaid health plans would be responsible for the wellness of a community in a geographic area so that a broad view of supportive and prevention services could become cost-effective. Ironically for mental health, this comes full circle to the original rationale and mandate of the community mental health center movement. Capitation allows for much greater flexibility in service delivery than was true under Medicaid or other categorical funding. In addition, penalties now exist for underserving client needs because inadequate care leads to mental health deterioration over time and requires more intensive and expensive interventions.

Although cost-effectiveness remains an important goal in this more desirable scenario, the overriding motive would be stewardship and careful management of limited resources, not profitability for its own sake. Surpluses would further enhance service development and further reduce costs by utilizing appropriate, less-intensive care settings, or enhance quality through consumer feedback; consumer satisfaction would be an important performance measure for the organization. Consequently, continuous quality-improvement programs would be a regular part of an organization's operations in a real way, not simply as window dressing or as a quick fix. Utilization review would continue to be important; however, it would not be used simply to restrict access and limit costs. This improved process would ensure the appropriate care, provided in the most cost-effective manner—no more and no less. To be successful, this form of utilization review requires well-trained clinicians who understand multiple treatment modalities and are comfortable in the client advocate role. By training, social workers are well equipped with skills to fulfill this role.

Treatment protocols would also be utilized, but much more flexibly, and as a starting point to truly individualize treatment planning. Staff profiling would also likely occur, but again in a more flexible fashion with a focus on client outcomes. Although these changes would require some adjustment for social workers who are currently accustomed to process measures and evaluations, this approach is much more congruent with social work values and the purpose of social work. Furthermore, given the fact that much will remain to be learned about treating and preventing mental illness by the year 2000, these methods should be utilized to inform practice improvements in the spirit of continuous learning, not to punish imperfect performance. In this case, the shift to outcome measurements could be exciting, freeing social workers from relatively meaningless process measures and rigid productivity standards, which appear unrelated to the quality of one's work.

The flexible funding model allows for the development of individualized wraparound service packages designed to maintain persons with chronic conditions in the least restrictive, most normalized community settings. There is also an important role for self-help and community education under the wellness scenario. For example, educating and supporting clients and families in how to cope with serious mental illness, symptom control, and medication management are logical functions of these groups. Similarly, educating and working with community resources on reasonable accommodations for persons with mental illness is another important role social workers could play that would be extremely cost-effective. Because funding is not based on fee for service, there is no longer an incentive to provide more services than necessary or to opt for facility-based services because they capture high reimbursement rates. On the contrary, providing community-based services on a flexible basis is the most appropriate treatment and is also most cost-effective. Similarly, this model bases service planning and service delivery on actual need rather than those services that are reimbursable, and reduces the pressures on social workers to primarily provide billable hours, which typically excludes outreach (with travel time not being reimbursable), collateral contacts, or attendance at multiagency treatment planning meetings.

Social workers would enjoy opportunities for varied and expanded roles. For example, they would design and coordinate wraparound services for individuals, provide community and psychoeducational programs and prevention programs, and develop a variety of self-help groups. These have all been social work roles in the past, which have tended to disappear in the funding cuts of the 1980s, and have not been included under managed care. Although it is certainly true that in the wellness scenario long-term therapy for persons without severe mental health problems is excluded, and an emphasis on brief therapy continues; nonetheless, the needs of consumers will determine the type and length of treatment.

In contrast to the profit scenario, in this improved environment social workers would be encouraged to provide outreach and advocacy services and to generally facilitate access to care to minimize relapse, hospitalization, or other intensive services. Furthermore, a holistic, preventative, rehabilitation model is much more effective in these circumstances than a medical model in the absence of psychosocial interventions, and such a model increases the opportunity for social workers to experience a wide variety of roles in various programs. Innovations in treatment, including psychosocial treatments, would be encouraged in the wellness scenario, as it would be recognized that there is considerable room for improvement in treating serious and persistent mental illness. Therefore, there is a tremendous capacity for creativity and much less likelihood that social workers will find themselves forced into situations that run counter to their values, ethics, and basic job satisfaction.

Implications and Conclusions

Although somewhat extreme, these two scenarios do represent possible alternative futures. In the profit scenario, cutthroat competition and the profit motive would be the prevailing forces shaping the future of managed mental health care. These conditions would create the worst possible situation for independent practitioners and the social work profession as a whole, because of the inevitable ethical and value conflicts that would unfold. The provision of good-quality care to vulnerable populations whose needs have been traditionally championed by social work would certainly fare poorly under such circumstances.

In contrast, it could certainly be argued that the second scenario promises perfection. Taken to its logical extreme, regional capitated managed care systems could move this country toward the model of universalistic social services that is prevalent in most of the industrialized world. If, for example, a single health plan is responsible for the health of an entire community, it must address all issues that affect that community's health. Included would be health-related issues that derive from social problems and would be best served by early intervention, as in the cases of drive-by shootings and substandard housing. Otherwise, the bottom line costs would ultimately be greater. Such circumstances would invite social workers to assume a wide variety of roles that traditionally have been mainstays of the profession. In addition, social workers would have numerous opportunities to assume newer, more innovative roles.

Considering the fact that a very high percentage of social workers practice in the health and mental health settings, the choice of these alternative futures is of extreme importance to the profession. Sustained and powerful advocacy is necessary to advance a sound future for the profession and acceptable care for populations most at risk. Otherwise, the profession will find itself reacting to a future shaped by competing, powerful interest groups. It will be crucial for the profession to develop a strategy of focused political activism in coalition with other invested parties to bring about as many elements of the second scenario as possible and not fall victim to the plight of the first scenario.

Irrespective of which of these two scenarios prevail, social workers will be operating under a managed care model; therefore, formal social work training must prepare practitioners for this new environment. Managed care systems, particularly at-risk capitation models, will require practitioners to conceptualize their practice in an entirely different way. Traditionally, agency-based clinicians have provided essentially unlimited services under fee-for-service arrangements rather than planning services based on a real level of need. Clinical assessments, therapeutic interventions, and practice protocols will be very different under these new circumstances. Not only will new generations of students need to be trained differently, but the traditionally trained clinician will require retraining in order to be effective in the new environment. In addition, social workers who provide care to persons with chronic mental illness must also be trained in the more flexible, wrap-around service approaches and become competent to practice in a wide variety of venues. Therefore, schools of social work must achieve fundamental curriculum changes necessary to reflect these new demands and realities.

We can expect that the policy decisions affecting Medicaid and the place of social services in health care reform will be determined by the more traditional liberal-versus-conservative and democrat-versus-republican coalitions that have historically argued these issues. The extent to which the 1994 elections represent a real shift in the political landscape or are another manifestation of frustration and a "throw the rascals out" mentality remains to be seen. If the new conservatism prevails the likelihood is that entitlements, including Medicaid, will be capped, creating an impetus for delivering the control of Medicaid to the states in exchange for less federal participation. If the movement for national health care reform is halted for any substantial time, or if Medicaid is turned over to the states, the action will shift to the state level and predictions must then be made on a state-by-state basis. It is also clear that under the Contract for America politics, social services will be cut, and any consideration of social services integration with mental health care becomes very unlikely. Furthermore, mental health care is likely to have a minimum, "bare-bones" coverage in mandated minimum benefits packages. Again, all of these forces would tend to favor the profit scenario.

What, then, are the forces that might facilitate the wellness scenario? One vigorous force is the growth in the aging population and HIV-infected persons, making it impossible to ignore the issue of long-term care as the year 2000 approaches. Any comprehensive solution must include integration of care for these populations into the health care system and prohibit health plans from refusing to cover these groups. As previously discussed, the most cost-effective way of serving chronic populations is through capitated community-based care that emphasizes maintenance and prevention. Secondly, as states move ahead with their own reforms, the results of public managed care compared with private for-profit managed care will become available. If, as many believe, the profit scenario fails to produce substantial savings beyond reducing hospitalization rates and underserves and abandons difficult-to-serve populations, whereas public managed care provides comparable savings when serving these populations, the policy makers will likely take notice of the wellness scenario.

These two alternatives present scenarios that illustrate a wide disparity in possible outcomes. Clearly these are possibilities and not certain predictions. Nonetheless, the possibilities are realistic and are derived from the real-world conditions of today. Therefore, they should provide existing and future practitioners with realistic expectations regarding the problems and solutions that will dominate the implementation of managed mental health care in the years to come.

Reference

Paulson, R. (1988). People and garbage are not the same: Issues in contracting for public mental health services. *Community Mental Health Journal, 48* (2), 91–102.

$$C \quad h \quad a \quad p \quad t \quad e \quad r \quad \mathit{10}$$

The Future of Private Practice

KIMBERLY STROM, PhD
University of Minnesota

What does the beginning of the new century hold for the private practice of social work? Some would question whether or not private practice will exist at all in the year 2000, so rapid have been the changes of the late 1980s and early 1990s. Some trends, such as an increased sensitivity to mental health needs and the acceptance of social workers as directly reimbursable service providers, have been a boon to private practice. Other trends, such as increasing concerns about the spiraling expense of mental health care and the lack of predictable, quantifiable outcomes, have threatened the enterprise. How will these and other phenomena influence private practice in the future? How will they shape who enters private practice and how those individuals are trained and supervised? How will the clientele of private practitioners be affected? How will the practices themselves be configured? What services will be provided? What theoretical orientations will prevail?

These are exciting and dynamic times for the profession of social work and for this form of service delivery in particular. Yet in order to understand where private practice is going, it is first important to understand what it is, where it has been, and the conditions that have shaped it to date. This chapter examines the background of private practice, identifies the factors most likely to affect its future development, and sets forth two private practice models for the twenty-first century.

Defining Private Practice

The private practice of social work has traditionally been defined as the provision of social work services outside the auspices of an agency setting. Under this arrangement the social worker is directly responsible for his or her practice and sets the terms and conditions for the provision of services. Sometimes referred to as autonomous or independent practice, it occurs in many forms.

Some social workers operate solo practices, in which they are the only service provider. Others operate in groups, with other social workers or with providers from other disciplines. Some social workers engage in private practice as their full-time job or as their primary work setting, whereas others work elsewhere and do private practice part-time as a secondary job, some for as few as 1 or 2 hours per week. Practitioners may offer services from offices attached to their homes; share an office on alternate days with other providers; use their agency offices for seeing private clients after hours; or sublet, rent, or own their own facilities.

Private practice is often viewed as synonymous with psychotherapy or the provision of clinical social work through one-on-one, conjoint, or family therapy. Yet private practitioners, particularly those who undertake it as their primary work setting, offer a diverse array of services, such as educational programs, consultation to business and industry, supportive and therapeutic groups, and contractual evaluations or consultations. Likewise, their funding may come from a variety of sources: government contracts or fee-for-service arrangements; third-party reimbursement through traditional insurance companies; HMOs, PPOs, or government programs such as Medicare; and direct client payments.

Many different entities, then, constitute private practice, and each entity possesses different attributes and vulnerabilities that will cause it to be differentially affected by the trends of the future. Today's private practices are the result of a long and sometimes conflictual history, shaped by forces from within the social work profession and by larger social trends.

The Background of Private Practice

Since its inception, private practice has been seen as representing a repudiation of the social justice origins of the profession. Some argue that adherents of private practice form a deviant subculture, driven by profit rather than altruistic motives. They maintain that private practice diverts experienced and talented social workers from agency practice and makes their services available to those least in need, the "worried well." Specht and Courtney articulate these concerns well in their recent text, *Unfaithful Angels* (1994). Although they acknowledge that private practice may be an attractive alternative when pay and public recognition for other forms of social work are low, they nevertheless insist that this "defection" be fought at every turn. Whatever the factual basis for these historical assertions, it is clear that they continue to flourish. One result of social work's long-standing ambivalence toward private practice may be delayed and uneven responses to some of the trends that now threaten privately delivered clinical social work services.

The social work profession's struggle with the private delivery of services began as early as 1926, when the American Association of Social Workers, a national organization, ruled that "the private practice of social work was a contradiction, and that without auspices, what was being offered was something other than social work" (Barker, 1992, p. 4). Rather than extinguishing private practice, such edicts evidently succeeded only in driving aspiring private practitioners underground. Published accounts over the ensuing decades document both the profession's aversion to private practice and its simultaneous pursuit by practitioners who carved their identity from sources other than social work (for example by affiliating with psychoanalytic practices and other psychotherapists). For an extended discussion of the history of private practice, see Levenstein (1964).

Larger trends occurring in the 1970s and 1980s enhanced the attraction and viability of private social work practice and foreshadowed some of the forces shaping its future. I have identified four major trends during these two decades that shaped the current picture for private practice:

- The passage of laws licensing or otherwise credentialling social workers protected the title of *social worker* and delineated the educational preparation and competency social workers possess. As such, regulation promoted social work in the public eye and made the labor market increasingly competitive by elevating the qualifications necessary for many positions.
- Social changes and the influence of the media and self-help movements increased public awareness about the range of mental health problems—from stress to depression to family conflict. This increased sensitivity to mental health made it more acceptable to seek professional help for personal problems of all sorts and increased the pool of potential clients needing services.
- Insurance regulations and customer demands resulted in the inclusion of mental health and substance abuse coverage in most health care plans.
- Vendorship legislation, passed in over 30 states, recognized social workers as directly reimbursable providers of mental health services and generally required that their services be paid for in plans offering mental health or substance abuse coverage.

Together these circumstances made private practice an attractive and profitable pursuit for social workers who saw it as an opportunity for professional autonomy, a chance to exercise their well-honed clinical expertise, and a flexible and challenging work setting. Yet the heyday of private practice was short-lived. On the heels of liberalized mental health coverage came spiraling health care costs and subsequent and enduring efforts to limit them.

The dominant strategy in mental health care cost containment is managed care. Managed care refers to a variety of mechanisms in which the payer of services plays an active role in determining how much and what kind of services will be offered, and who will be allowed to provide them. Managed care strategies are evident in programs from traditional indemnity insurance to Medicaid. As it has developed, numerous permutations (hybrids) of the managed care model have emerged, although the essential mechanisms remain the same. Typical cost-containment features include increasing and enforcing client copayments for services, capping the amount of coverage available over the year or over a lifetime, limiting the number of treatment sessions, and covering illnesses only in certain diagnostic categories. Accompanying these strategies is an emphasis on treatment outcomes and in practitioners using the most cost-efficient means of addressing client problems. Thus payers increasingly exert control on treatment planning through utilization reviewers and case managers, and require that clinicians obtain approval before using certain treatment strategies or techniques.

A more recent managed care development involves shifting the risk of coverage to service providers through prepaid capitated contracts. Under such arrangements the mental health service provider contracts to provide a predefined set of services or benefits at a fixed rate prepaid per subscriber per year, regardless of the amount of services actually used. Capitated contracts require that the provider accurately anticipate the utilization rate for the services that he or she intends to offer. Because the provider is fully responsible for providing clinical services to all of those covered, underestimation could ruin the practice. Conversely, such programs have a built-in financial incentive for minimizing services, which could present practitioners with unanticipated ethical and clinical dilemmas.

In some ways, clinicians are caught in a highly competitive and rapidly evolving system in which insurers attempt to offer employers and other "buyers" of insurance coverage a range of quality services at the lowest possible (profitable) cost. The net result is that mental health services today, and for the years to come, will be offered under a system that is increasingly outcome oriented and payer driven. All other trends will likely pale when compared with this one in shaping the future of private practice.

Private Practices of the Future

Given these and other societal developments over the coming decades, what will private practice look like? Probably two models will emerge. The most prevalent will be the adaptive model, which has been shaped to accommodate the evolutions in health care financing. Less prevalent but also viable is the orthodox model, in which practitioners are able to carve a practice niche without acceding to the demands of the payer system. The following sections will describe the models and will discuss the various forces that will shape their structures, funding, clientele, and staff.

The Adaptive Practice

The private practice of the next century that adapts to meet market forces will look much like the human service agencies of old. That is, clinicians will offer their services in medium-to-large group practices that offer a range of services delivered by professionals from a variety of disciplines. These organizations will be characterized by 24-hour coverage, a rapid response time to referrals, and internal mechanisms to ensure practitioner competency and client satisfaction. Such practices will have a senior clinician, president, or CEO who serves as a practice administrator, marketing services and securing inclusion in provider networks; keeping abreast of changes that affect practice conditions, such as legal, regulatory, and financial trends; monitoring compliance; addressing personnel issues; and generally administering the practice. Although many current distinctions between private practice and agency-based work will be obscured in the future, one continuing difference is that clinicians in private practice will still determine the terms and conditions of their services. In the large group or adaptive practices, procedures will need to be in place to facilitate collective decision making.

The adaptive practice will be technologically advanced, utilizing automated systems directly linked to payers for verifying benefits, providing information for claims and reducing paperwork and record keeping. Advanced technology will also be used to aid clinical processes. Not only will computers be used for self-administered client assessments and scoring, but expert systems will assist in assigning diagnoses and formulating treatment plans based on the best available empirical data on effective interventions. Computers will also be used for the interventions themselves, for example, in guiding clients in biofeedback activities or providing assistance with cognitive and behavioral restructuring steps.

The adaptive practice will be acutely attuned to its market niche, selecting its location carefully for strategic advantage, structuring services according to unmet needs or payer interests, and selecting participating practitioners to complement its strategic mission. Likewise, the practice of the future will have built-in quality-assurance mechanisms to provide safety for clients and a market advantage with potential payers. Quality-assurance mechanisms include careful screening and selection of prospective partners; examination of clinicians' liability claims, licenses, and credentials; inquiries about impairments due to chemical dependence or other problems; requirements for ongoing professional education; regular peer review and evaluation; and periodic analyses of outcome data and client satisfaction, among other measures.

Funding for the adaptive practice will come from diverse sources, although payment for clinical services will likely come from a handful of managed care firms representing both insurers and government programs, such as Medicaid and Medicare. The contracts may range from prepaid capitated agreements to fee-for-service arrangements, and the reimbursement rates may vary widely among contracts. To the extent that a practice relies on prepaid capitated plans, its participating clinicians will be at some risk for financial loss, should utilization rates be poorly calculated or should an unexpected catastrophe drive up use of services.

As payers seek to have more and more control over the provision of services, some private practices will be wholly or partially owned subsidiaries of managed care companies. Through such arrangements the managed care firm brings administrative expertise to a (generally) large group practice with a well-established market niche and existing, profitable contracts on which it can build. Participating clinicians trade autonomy for security and a financial payoff for the enterprise they have helped to build.

The adaptive practice of the future will make itself attractive to mental health payers by marketing itself as one-stop mental health shopping—an organization that can provide the appropriate level and type of care needed by the insurance plan's subscribers. As such, services will cover crisis intervention, prevention, and enhancing family relations as well as treating major mental illnesses. Thus services will be diverse and flexible—offered at convenient hours, off-site if needed, and tailored to emerging needs. Interventions will include a more sophisticated use of medications and case management and the liberal use of homework, educational interventions, self-help, and natural helping networks.

Research on the biological bases of major mental illnesses and on outcome-oriented interventions will lead to increased use of clinical path models or practice guidelines, which will delineate the steps to be taken, for example, in treating depression or schizophrenia. Similarly, with the advent of technology and utilization management, as described earlier, the therapeutic efforts of the clinician will largely involve the provision of prescribed services as opposed to extensive assessment and problem analysis.

The orientation of services in the future will likely be toward alleviation of presenting problems or symptoms rather than addressing longer-term change. As such, brief targeted treatment approaches will be utilized, with the focus on restoration of previous functioning, not characterological change. Data on services rendered will be more widely available, contributing to the improved evaluation of practice approaches and to the evaluation of practitioners as well. Provider profiling will increase, as payers have ready access to information on clinicians' average number of treatment sessions, their "adverse outcomes" (hospital readmissions, suicides, substance abuse case relapses), and on their proclivity to use expensive services such as inpatient referrals. To the extent that clinicians associate certain services with a potential loss of business, the services may fall into disuse, although not because they are unnecessary or ineffective, only unfavorable.

Clientele

The clientele of a practice used to be those individuals who sought help from the practice in alleviating their problems—the patients or clients. The private practice's marketing was targeted toward this population or those who might possibly serve as referral sources. In the coming decades the funding source, be it the managed care concern or the government contract administrator, will become the primary client. Inasmuch as they buy services and decide who will be approved providers, *their* acceptance becomes the clinician's primary concern, and the patient will become the recipient of services rather than the purchaser of them.

Who will these *recipients* of private social work practice services be? That will depend on who has mental health coverage and which providers they are allowed to see under that coverage. As government programs move to managed care formats, and with the possible passage of national health care, the client population will become more diverse in terms of age, race, class, and presenting problems. Regardless of these changes, however, the population being seen in private practices will be older, by virtue of the nation's demographics, and concerns with life transitions and afflictions common to the elderly will be an increasing focus for treatment.

The clientele will be shaped somewhat by the services or niche developed by the particular private practice. Emerging service areas include those that help forestall more expensive services, such as forensic evaluations, alternatives to sentencing and jail time, pain management, and community case management for the severely mentally ill. Other emerging services will reflect growing social problems, such as addressing treatment needs resulting from urban violence and chaos or mediating between increasingly divided and combative segments of society. In response to technological advances, social workers may be active in the development of computerized forms of treatment, such as developing software to be used by clients in resolving marital or workplace conflicts or in carrying out task-centered treatment plans.

Assuming that they choose their range of services carefully, the adaptive practices of the future will find themselves with ample clientele, owing to capitated contracts. The issue for those practices will not be obtaining clients but being able to treat adequately those that they have contracts to cover. However, because customer satisfaction will be evaluated by payers through multiple methods during and after service delivery, practices will need to concern themselves with both quality and access. For example, clients may be asked how long it took to obtain an appointment, how convenient the office's location was, how promptly they were seen, how effective the services were, and how satisfied they were with their individual clinician. All of the foregoing changes bode a different way of life for the social worker in private practice.

Clinician Characteristics

To be successful in the adaptive practice model, a clinician will share the values of the managed care marketplace. That is, the clinician will be concerned with treatment outcomes and clinical efficiency, up to date on the treatment research in the field, conversant with the language of the evolving health care system, skilled in determining the appropriate level of care for a given diagnosis, and comfortable with use of technology to aid in diagnostic and therapeutic processes. The clinician will necessarily be comfortable with collaboration, the use of psychotropic medications, and the abridged clinical freedoms that will accompany team practice and outcome-oriented funding streams.

Its likely that such individuals will be less experienced, as they may be less expensive to employ and easier to mold into the models necessary for success in the practice. Schools of social work will be under great pressure to prepare students for the technical and outcome-dependent tasks required in the next century. Such a focus may work against the generalist orientation of many schools, and against the broad interpretation of social work as encompassing both large and small systems change. Conversely, the additional preparation required may add a third year to traditional MSW education as social workers attempt to affirm their competence in comparison with psychologists and psychiatrists.

Despite their limited experience, social workers should bring to the practice a facility with diverse tasks, along with a specialty, or market niche. Specialties make the individual marketable to the practice and the practice marketable for potential contracts. They can be as diverse as having expertise or programming in sports psychology, career counseling, parenting skills, or preadoption home assessments. Market niche can also refer to specialized populations, such as work with gay and lesbian clients, counseling infertile couples, or having bilingual skills or expertise with specific ethnic groups.

Thanks in part to the movement of women and minorities into the U.S. workforce, and to the fruition of affirmative action efforts by educational institutions, private practice workers in the coming decades will be more diverse racially and ethnically. The increased value placed on a racial or ethnic niche may also make private practice more attractive to diverse populations.

Although women have always constituted the larger proportion of social workers, private practice was traditionally attractive to men because of the higher earning power the setting offered. However, as the earning power in private practice decreases and the non-clinical tasks increase, the more men are expected to leave private practice or to assume administrative positions within their practices.

Finally, practitioners in the adaptive practice model are likely to work there full-time and to be paid and evaluated on an incentive basis. The social worker in the adaptive private practice will be rewarded for productivity, in that total pay, or a "commission" over base pay, will be determined by how many hours of direct client service are offered. Pay may also be differentially affected by the types of services rendered, which clients are seen, or which contracts are serviced. Practitioners' performance appraisals will involve a review of their activities in support of the fiscal health of the organization. For each clinician, reviewers will examine the particular clinician's cancellation or failure rate, how thoroughly records were kept, how quickly claims were filed, and how often claims were rejected or preapprovals denied. Clinical performance will also be assessed. The clinician's patterns of treatment should conform to practice guidelines both for form and length of services, and the clinician's caseload should indicate both positive outcomes and a high level of client satisfaction posttreatment.

Clearly the prevailing practice model for the future represents a consolidation of various forms of private practice and a significant departure from the type of practice many social workers originally chose to pursue. What option will exist for practitioners who do not want to work in an agency setting or in a "corporate" practice as described above?

The Orthodox Practice

Some social workers may prove unwilling or unable to adapt to market forces, and may maintain conventional or "boutique" practices into the next century. These practices will likely be fewer in number over time, as this model will not be a viable option for new private practitioners, and others, who may have traditionally operated in this manner, will find it difficult to stay in business without making concessions to the pressures of managed care.

The resulting practices under this model will be small, solo or two-person enterprises, in which services are offered on a part-time or (less likely) full-time basis. To survive, such practices must be well established and relatively stable over time, with a consistent cadre of clients and referral sources. Orthodox practices will be "low-tech" operations. Billing and records will likely not be computerized, nor will computers be used as adjuncts to therapy. Because the impetus is to avoid the encumbrances of agency and corporate practice, orthodox models will lack hierarchical structures, practice policies and guidelines, stringent record keeping and paperwork requirements, marketing initiatives, and liaisons to keep abreast of managed care panels and other contractual opportunities.

The funding for services in the orthodox setting will be primarily through client self-pay, perhaps with fees adjusted on a sliding scale, and with some clients receiving pro bono services. Decisions on fees will be made on a more individualized basis as they will not be tied to contracts or other larger obligations.

Practitioners will be clear that their market niche is narrow and that those who cannot afford the service or those who wish to use their mental health coverage to pay for services are not appropriately served in this setting. As such, they will be comfortable setting clear parameters about client payment and making referrals to other sources for those they choose not to treat.

Orthodox practices will specialize in offering those services that aren't covered by third parties. These may include family or conjoint counseling or long-term psychotherapy oriented to reparations or characterological change. The theoretical approaches employed will thus be less tied to brief, solution-focused models and more to psychodynamic approaches or long-term supportive services.

Clientele

Clearly, the clientele of the orthodox practice will include those who can afford to pay for their services out of pocket, those who eschew the third-party-paid system because of its complexity, and those who want services not covered by insurance. Clients who are concerned about the lack of confidentiality in third-party systems or the repercussions of having received mental health services for future benefits may choose to obtain their services outside the managed care system through a smaller, independent practice.

Given the economics of weekly out-of-pocket payments for therapy, it is likely that those seen for services will be well-to-do and much less diverse in race, age, and ethnicity than the general population. Should they have the financial means, it is possible that individuals with severe and prolonged mental illnesses will be able to access help through an orthodox practice. However, it is more likely that the clientele will be seeking less acute services, for example, ongoing support for recovery from substance dependence or childhood trauma or assistance with life transitions.

Clinician Characteristics

The clinicians who are able to maintain a private practice successfully while resisting market pressures will be highly experienced, both in their area(s) of clinical expertise and in private practice itself. Such experience is necessary to ensure the reputation and contacts required to keep self-paid referrals coming. As such, clinicians in a "boutique" practice may be less diverse in age and race than private practitioners overall and may be less responsive to trends in the profession, both in therapeutic approaches and emerging problem areas.

These social workers may also be less diverse socioeconomically. For example, in order to withstand the financial uncertainty of a small, self-paid clientele, such practitioners will likely have other means of financial support, such as a working spouse or income from other sources.

Whatever the influences shaping private practice over the coming decades, some practitioners will be able to maintain a practice that does not conform to those trends. They may be few in number, and more often part-time endeavors rather than full-time, but there will always be a client and practitioner niche supporting the orthodox practice.

Summary

Even with powerful and well-defined forces shaping private practice, the future is difficult to predict. Will the coming decades bring an epidemic that affects human needs or the shape of services the way the crack crisis and the disease of AIDS have? Will the economic concerns and a generally angry citizenry that characterized the 1994 elections continue or abate? If societal divisiveness continues, what unanticipated roles might social workers be required to play?

Specific to private practice concerns, will emerging health care financing consider allowing for services for all segments of society? Will coverage for "mental health problems" be broadly defined, confined to biologically based illnesses, or excluded entirely? Will social workers continue to be covered at reimbursable providers of mental health services? Can social workers ensure the requisite level of competency for autonomous practice if they are included? As private practices, some to resemble agencies, how will employment and services in nonprofit organizations change? Will the dichotomy between private and agency practice cease to exist?

Whereas the precise events of the future are difficult to foretell, the forces that will shape them are not. The nature of private practice and the history that has shaped it to date, evolving forms of health care financing, cost containment, and emerging human needs will all converge to create the practices of the twenty-first century. Whether they are adaptive, orthodox, or some unimagined hybrid remains to be seen.

References

Barker, R. L. (1992). *Social work in private practice: Principles, issues and dilemmas* (2nd ed.). Washington, DC: National Association of Social Workers.

Levenstein, S. (1964). *Private practice in social casework.* New York: Columbia University Press.

Specht, H., & Courtney, M. (1994). *Unfaithful angels.* New York: Free Press.

Chapter 11

The Future of the DSM-IV in Social Work Practice

GAYLE KLAYBOR, ACSW, LMSW-ACP

University of Houston

The use of the *Diagnostic and Statistical Manual of Mental Disorders* (DSM-IV) is a controversial topic in social work education. In the clinical practice of social work, however, it is not. The facility and efficacy with which social workers utilize the DSM in the future will have a great bearing on their successes in public or private practice mental health settings. Knowing and accurately applying diagnostic criteria will be necessary not only for third-party reimbursement but also for treatment plans, authorized assessments, and demonstrations of outcomes to further fund mental health programs and services.

Particularly in the last half of the twentieth century, the American Psychiatric Association sought to develop and implement a diagnostic system that would be used as a standard throughout the United States and one that would be compatible with international diagnostic systems for mental disorders.

Evolution of the DSM

DSM-I was the first official manual of mental disorders to contain a glossary of descriptions of diagnostic categories (American Psychiatric Association, 1994). Heavily influenced by psychodynamic and psychoanalytic practitioners including Adolph Meyer, mental disorders were described as reactions of the personality to psychological, social, and biological factors. In 1968 DSM-II was published; the number of disease categories substantially increased, and the authors largely dropped the term *reaction* to explain disorders (Kirk & Kutchins, 1992). DSM-III, published in 1980, was heralded as a major advance in the diagnosis of mental disorders and a significant reaffirmation of the medical identity and commitment to science for American psychiatry (Klerman, Vailliant, Spitzer, & Michels, 1984; Kutchins & Kirk, 1986). The DSM-III quickly became the standard reference for mental health professionals, and it functioned as a document of legal and economic consequence (Kutchins & Kirk, 1986; Schacht & Nathan, 1977).

A number of advantages were cited to support the exceptional advancement of DSM-III over previous versions (Klerman, Vailliant, Spitzer, & Michels, 1984; Kirk, Soporin, & Kutchins, 1989). It was considered a step toward clarifying communication in psychiatry (Adamson, 1989). To psychiatrists and other physicians, it moved diagnoses from a biopsychosocial model to a reaffirmation of the medical model (Wilson, 1993). It used a descriptive approach rather than one based on etiology or theoretical framework, thus attempting to broaden its appeal across clinical perspectives (Kirk et al., 1989). The guiding principle of the DSM-III was inclusion of diagnostic categories rather than exclusion so that the number of specific disorders grew to 265, with clinical relevance as a basic concern (Frances, Pincus, Widiger, Davis, & First, 1990). Another prominent addition to the DSM-III was its multiaxial system. In DSM-III the multiaxial system was an attempt to include aspects of psychosocial information, to acknowledge clinical experience, and to be sensitive to the uniqueness of the individual (Klerman, Vailliant, Spitzer, & Michels, 1984). On Axes I and II, mental disorders and mental retardation are listed. On Axis III physical conditions that may contribute to the psychological disorder is listed, and Axis IV is reserved for psychosocial stressors that may be contributing factors. Axis V represents the Global Assessment Functioning scale (GAF) on which a person's functioning level is scored. It has been suggested that the Axes IV and V most resemble the problem-person-situation model of social casework, and therefore the multiaxial system should be more easily adaptable to social work practice (Williams, 1981).

DSM-IV was published in May 1994 (American Psychiatric Association, 1994). According to Frances, Pincus, Widiger, Damis, & First (1990), the DSM-IV was an advance over DSM-III-R in that greater emphasis was placed on empirical evidence for disorders. It was meant to be simpler, clearer, and more clinically useful, and the threshold for including diagnoses in DSM-IV was much higher than in previous editions.

The disadvantages of previous DSM editions, according to Klerman, Vailliant, Spitzer, and Michels (1984), outweigh the advantages. The DSM is insensitive to value judgment, cross-cultural and cross-generational perspectives. In DSM-IV, however, cultural references are included. The diagnostic system does not interpret psychopathological disorders as dimensional or dynamically placed on a continuum but rather reduces disorders to static descriptions of behaviors. Many critics have argued that the DSM diagnostic system does not meet high standards for reliability (Kutchins & Kirk, 1986; Williams, 1985) and that the DSM has sacrificed validity for reliability (Klerman, Vailliant, Spitzer, & Michels, 1984).

Despite the criticisms, the DSM-III-R, which was published in 1987, was used extensively by psychiatrists, psychologists, and social workers in various settings. It was also used by insurance companies related to third-party payments, government agencies, and psychiatric researchers (Kutchins & Kirk, 1988). In fact, according to Kutchins and Kirk (1988), the DSM has become the most frequently consulted reference book in the practice of clinical social work.

Although the DSM classification system is widely used in social work practice, particularly in mental health, a controversy between social work theoreticians, academics, and clinicians has emerged. Debates continue between those social workers who view DSM diagnosis as a significant departure from the values and mission of social work and those who believe diagnostic assessment to be an evolutionary aspect of social work practice. To them, diagnosing is one way to validate social worker's clinical parity with other mental health professionals.

The emergence of clinical social work as a valuable expression of social work practice can be traced to two distinct forces within and outside social work beginning in the 1920s (Wasserman, 1982). There was first a diverging of approaches in the delivery of services to clients who had an array of psychosocial problems. Generally, social casework from the 1920s to the 1960s fell into two philosophical and practical approaches. Although most social workers accepted the idea that working with individuals might be an effective intervention, those from the diagnostic school were more likely to consider intervention treatment and incorporate a medical or Freudian model into their practice repertoire. Those practitioners from the functional school rejected that emphasis and instead focused on the helping process and, in that focus, emphasized agency structures as the aspect of the intervention process most effective.

Secondly, since World War II psychiatric social workers were placed in positions that reinforced their development as mental health professionals alongside psychiatry (Wasserman, 1982). By the late 1940s social workers filled positions in psychiatric hospitals, child guidance clinics, the VA, and other agencies specializing in marital and family relationship problems. Social workers developed expertise and found themselves doing work that was similar to, if not the same as, that of psychiatrists and psychologists.

An obvious problem arose. Social workers, psychologists, and psychiatrists were involved similarly in the psychotherapeutic arena, yet there were tremendous differences in esteem and prestige of these professions and even greater disparity in economic compensations (Wasserman, 1982). One response, especially for psychologists and socials workers, was to define professional specialties. Psychologists became expert in psychological testing and assessment, whereas social workers became known as specialists in marital and family therapy, psychosocial assessment, and community resources. Psychiatrists continued to be considered the "real experts" in mental health treatment because they alone had admitting privileges to hospitals and prescribed medications and very importantly were the only mental health professionals who could make diagnoses. A commonly heard warning in mental health facilities was, "Only doctors can diagnose."

As social workers attempted to extend themselves into the private practice arena, it became apparent that they needed legislative and organizational legitimacy in the form of licensing and certification. New laws and licenses gave social workers expectations of third-party reimbursements and increased professional status.

Social Work and the DSM

Also during the 1980s insurance companies, emerging managed care companies, Medicare, and Medicaid sought measures to decrease mental health treatment expenditures, which ultimately increased their own corporate profits. They realized that social workers who had won acceptance as competent psychotherapists charged considerable less for many of the same services as their psychological and psychiatric counterparts. Besides evaluating the costs per session, insurance companies and managed care companies looked at cost cutting through decreasing the number of sessions, utilizing stricter guidelines for accountability, and promoting brief, effective treatments. A logical solution to determine effective treatment was to identify disorders and monitor symptom reduction in clients. The obvious choice for an instrument to describe symptoms and define mental disorders was the *Diagnostic and Statistical Manual.* The DSM had been firmly embedded in the psychiatric world as the universally accepted reference for psychiatric disorders. Rather than duplicating services by having psychiatrists diagnose patients that social workers were seeing, social workers were expected to provide diagnoses in order to secure payment and justify the need for treatment. Payers made decisions regarding treatment based on the prognosis of certain diagnoses and often paid for only certain disorders, sometimes based on severity. Social workers more than ever learned to use the DSM in practice.

In a nationwide survey regarding social workers' attitudes toward the DSM-III (Kutchins & Kirk, 1988), findings indicated that practical reasons rather that clinical usefulness were the main motivators for social workers' utilization of the manual. Insurance reimbursement, agency requirements, Medicaid, and legal regulation were listed as the top four reasons for using the DSM. There was also an even split concerning whether or not the DSM serves the purposes of social work. Only one-third found the DSM helpful in treatment planning. Another alarming issue raised by Kirk and Kutchins (1988) is that social workers may be committing deliberate misdiagnosis, which becomes both an ethical and liability issue. In an effort to minimize the harmful effects of labeling and stigmatizing clients by reporting serious mental disorders, psychotherapists from all disciplines have given a more innocuous diagnosis, quite commonly an "adjustment disorder." Conversely, in order to obtain services for clients who might not qualify because of payer requirements, professionals have overdiagnosed, that is, given a more serious diagnosis in order to secure payments for services.

Kutchins and Kirk (1987) also question whether a social worker has the legal or ethical right to make a diagnosis using DSM. Compton and Galaway, in their book *Social Work Process* (1994), agree. They state that "DSM III may be useful for psychiatry, but social workers are not psychiatrists and have no business using terms and labels developed for a sister profession. We need to understand DSM III to be able to communicate with our psychiatric colleagues, but we do not need to use it as a guide to our own practice" (p. 223).

Raffoul and Holmes (1986) surveyed accredited graduate schools of social work to examine the position of the study of the DSM-III in social work curricula. On the basis of 57 completed questionnaires, findings suggested strong support for the inclusion of the DSM-III content in the social work curriculum, primarily for practical reasons. Philosophical and ethical concerns related to labeling clients remain.

Harry Specht (1990), a modern-day functionalist, is one of the most outspoken opponents not only of social workers in private practice but also of social work involvement in psychotherapy at all. He believes that social work's only true mission is one of developmental socialization through the expansion of social roles, information, social support, and social skill development. He is opposed to the focus on the individual and what he defines as a move from social work's original mission of working with the "poorest among us" to working with young, attractive, verbal, intelligent, successful clients (YAVIS) (Seiz & Schwab, 1992).

Others like Jerome Wakefield (1990) argue that Specht's perspective is too narrow and that if the profession of social work could achieve a conceptional clarity about its identity, there would be no difficulty in embracing multiple avenues of social work practice, including psychotherapy (see Chapter 10).

Whatever the philosophical debate, for those social workers practicing in mental health, using the DSM is a certainty. For all the dissent from social work educators and researchers about the harmful effects of labeling and a myopic view of clients through a medical-model lens, no system for assessing mental or emotional difficulties or dysfunction other that the DSM has been consistently utilized or accepted.

Predictions

For third-party payers including insurance and managed care companies, Medicare, and Medicaid, measurable dysfunction and improvement criteria will become more standardized than ever. In mental health treatment, those criteria will be based on the DSM.

In particular, treatment plans and outcome evaluations will primarily be focused on diagnostic criteria. Not only will treatment plans be required for all reimbursement, but clinicians from all disciplines will be required to diagnose on all five axes. Establishing the need for treatment will necessitate listing those DSM descriptions that qualify the symptoms as a disorder. For example, if a clinician believes that a client is very depressed, the clinician must be able to list the DSM characteristics of major depression, such as loss of pleasure, depressed mood, insomnia, significant weight gain or loss, fatigue, and suicidal feelings. Reports of previous traumas and family dynamics will be considered only if symptoms indicate some mental disorder resulting from those environmental factors.

Clinicians have previously diagnosed supposedly innocuous disorders such as adjustment disorder to protect clients from stigmatizing labels or because of their own lack of sophistication in the use of the DSM. In the future, mental health professionals will have to diagnose more carefully, because payers will reimburse only services that are considered serious enough to warrant mental health treatment or prognostically good enough to expect some significant success in short-term treatment.

Specific diagnoses will determine the number of sessions authorized and inevitably the specific treatments or services administered. A child diagnosed with attention deficit/hyperactivity disorder (ADHD) may be authorized to see a psychiatrist for medication evaluation and he and his family may have 10 sessions by a social worker to resolve his behavior problems and enhance their parenting for this child. Extending services will depend on how his symptoms (as listed in the DSM) have changed. If he has significantly improved, the provider may consider his need for further service unnecessary except for occasional medication checkups. Services may also be curtailed if the client has not improved because he is then considered a poor treatment candidate.

Each payer, including managed care companies and federally funded or state-funded revenue sources will have specific professional practice standards. These standards will determine what treatments and how many treatments will be approved for each diagnosis. If the client is diagnosed as schizophrenic, Medicaid may decide by looking at their approved protocol for schizophrenia that the client can receive five days' inpatient treatment including medication, five days in an outpatient day hospital, and then monthly medication visits with a psychiatrist. A social worker may also have monthly visits approved to follow up on housing and family support issues. Should a crisis occur such as an acute psychotic episode, Medicaid would then have to approve services from their professional practice standards for such an event.

Service providers including social workers will become much more competitive in an effort to be placed on and remain on specific referral lists. These lists of providers compiled by the various payers are used to make all referrals for mental health services. If a social worker or his or her group practice is not on the list, then that social worker will not receive clients.

Outcome studies are one method that social workers and other professionals are employing and that ultimately will be required to demonstrate their competence and efficiency to the payers. Again, the guidelines to show success in their clients will be a reduction in client symptoms according to DSM criteria. The GAF (Global Assessment Functioning scale), which is scored on Axis V, will also function as an instrument to measure client progress. Based on a 100-point system (the lower the score, the lower the functioning level), the GAF will be measured at intake, at completion of services, and at other intervals to determine functioning. Payers may have standardized policies about where and when particular services are provided, continued, or curtailed by GAF scores.

There will inevitably be computer and technological applications in diagnosing. Already there are programs such as D-Tree® which use decision tree systems listed in the DSM to assist clinicians in using the DSM. In the future, however, the DSM will be part of software packages and services that will connect mental health organizations; government agencies; and third-party payers including insurance companies, managed care companies, EAPs, Medicare, and Medicaid directly to social workers, psychologists, and psychiatrists. Agencies, hospitals, social workers, and other mental health practitioners will be directly linked together in a kind of "mental health internet." When services are requested, treatment plans utilizing DSM will be sent through the system to the potential payer. Part of the package may be a checklist of criteria from the DSM list of characteristic symptoms for each disorder. Through formulas for treatment incorporated within the program, an immediate response will appear. That response will indicate approved number of sessions and recommended treatment interventions. Follow-up modifications to the original treatment plan, progress reports, and requests for further services will all be handled through this interactive program. In the past four decades, social workers and other mental health professionals have had considerable flexibility in treatment planning, allowing for the choice to use diagnostic categories or other more intrapsychic or behavioral criteria. In the future, those options will be virtually eliminated in favor of specific diagnostic descriptions and interventions based on symptoms.

Imagine the cries from social workers about the inhumanity and lack of social work values in such practices. There certainly should be. If it sounds like the Big Brother of mental health, there is good reason. The potential for individual clinicians to lose therapeutic freedom and creativity is on the horizon. It is frightening to consider that critical decisions pertaining to client care will be determined by a computer program or a voice on the phone. Not only will decisions be made by people who do not have personal contact with your client, but they may not have clinical expertise themselves. It will certainly be the challenge for social workers in mental health practice in the future to know and utilize the DSM effectively and simultaneously keep the DSM classification system in its proper perspective. Even though the DSM has been widely adopted as a system in which client change can be measured, accepting the DSM as the only lens in which to view emotional and mental suffering and abnormality is an incredible oversimplification of the human condition. It is that very understanding of human complexity that social workers have prided themselves in addressing. Since the days of Mary Richmond, social workers have been interested in assessment of human problems. As a profession, however, social work has taken a passive role in instituting an assessment system that honors the person-in-environment focus. When placed in psychiatric settings in both the private and public sector, social workers have either adopted completely the standards set by the medical staff such as the DSM or avoided any commitment to a different assessment tool by denying the profession's ability to contribute to the development of the diagnostic assessment process. In the DSM-III and DSM-IV, additions were made to accommodate a more psychosocial perspective. In the DSM-III the multiaxial system was added to address environmental stressors and levels of functioning, and in the DSM-IV ethnic and cultural considerations are included. It remains the responsibility of the clinician using the DSM to bring both technically accurate and empathic, sound judgment to the process of diagnosis. As stated in the introduction of the DSM-IV, the manual is not meant to be a used as a cookbook without regard to clinical consideration. The real danger is that social workers and other mental health professionals may succumb to the pressures exerted by managed care providers and federal and state agencies to give diagnoses that are incongruent with the actual needs and conditions of clients to satisfy the demands for shorter-term and less costly mental health services. Conversely, it is in the best interest of our clients to be knowledgeable about psychopathology and the diagnostic system so that clients receive the best scientific, medical, and psychosocial intervention possible.

There will always be those social workers who choose not to adapt to changes in mental health care practice and the increased focus on the DSM. These practitioners will probably be found outside of agencies in an orthodox or more traditional private practice setting (see Chapter 10). They may choose to avoid using the DSM or third-party payments. These practices, however, will be dependent on clients who can pay out of pocket or who are seen at substantially reduced rates.

Considering the force and speed with which managed care companies, insurance companies, and public funded revenue sources are focusing on the DSM to determine mental health care, it seems that it will be even more important for schools of social work to properly educate students in the use of the DSM. Not only would it be professional suicide for social workers not to understand psychopathology and be able to use the DSM effectively, but it will be a disservice to clients to deprive them of any potentially useful intervention available.

In his 1994 workshop, "A Practitioner's Guide to DSM-IV," Allen Francis, the chair of the DSM-IV task force, described the future of the DSM. He stated that there will probably be no new editions to the DSM-IV for a number of years and that the focus will be on a deeper understanding of the individual disorders through empirical studies improving the validity of diagnosing. The future of the DSM is not in the changes in the manual but rather in the emphasis on diagnosis for treatment, assessment, and payment for services. It becomes fundamentally clear that in order for social workers to maintain the professional respect and esteem that they have certainly earned and come to expect, they must be both knowledgeable and skilled in the use of the DSM-IV. Equally important, however, is that social workers bring their sense of value for the individual and their differences to the diagnostic process.

References

Adamson, J. (1989). An appraisal of the DSM III system. *Canadian Journal of Psychiatry, 34,* 303–310.

American Psychiatric Association. (1994). *Diagnostic and statistical manual of mental disorders.* (4th ed., rev.). Washington, DC: Author.

Compton, B. R., & Galaway, B. (1994). *Social work processes.* (5th ed). Pacific Grove: Brooks/Cole.

Frances, A., Pincus, H. A., Widiger, T. A., Davis, W. W., & First, M. B. (1990). DSM IV: Work in progress. *American Journal of Psychiatry, 147*(11), 1439–1448.

Kirk, S. A., & Kutchins, H. (1988). Deliberate misdiagnosis in mental health practice. *Social Service Review, 62*(2), 225–237.

Kirk, S. A., & Kutchins, H. (1992). *The selling of the DSM.* New York: Aldine de Gruyter.

Kirk, S. A., Soporin, M., & Kutchins, H. (1989). The prognosis for social work diagnosis. *Social Casework: The Journal of Contemporary Social Work, 70*(5), 295–304.

Klerman, G. L., Vailliant, G. E., Spitzer, R. L., & Michels, R. (1984). A debate on the DSM III. *American Journal of Psychiatry, 141*(4), 539–553.

Kutchins, H., & Kirk, S. A. (1986). The reliability of DSM III: A critical review. *Social Work Research and Abstracts, 22*(4), 3–12.

Kutchins, H., & Kirk, S. A. (1987). DSM III in social work malpractice. *Social Work, 32*(3), 205–211.

Kutchins, H., & Kirk, S. A. (1988). The business of diagnosis: DSM III in clinical social work. *Social Work, 33,* 215–220.

Raffoul, P. R., & Holmes, K. A. (1986). DSM III content in social work curriculum: Results of a national survey. *Journal of Social Work Education, 22,* 24–31.

Schacht, T., & Nathan, P. E. (1977). But is it good for psychologists? Appraisal and status of the DSM-III. *American Psychologist, 32,* 1017–1025.

Seiz, R. C., & Schwab, A. J. (1992). Values orientations of clinical social work practitioners. *Clinical Social Work Journal, 20*(3), 323–335.

Specht, H. (1990). Social work and the popular psychotherapies. *Social Service Review, 64*(3), 335–357.

Wakefield, J. C. (1990). Debate with author. Why therapeutic social work don't get no re-specht. *Social Service Review, 64*(3), 141–151.

Wasserman, H. (1982). Reflections on clinical social work. *Smith College Studies in Social Work, 52*(3) 169–187.

Williams, J. B. W. (1981). DSM III: A comprehensive approach to diagnosis. *Social Work, 26,* 101–106.

Williams, J. B. W. (1985). The multiaxial system of DSM III: Where did it come from and where should it go? *Archives of General Psychiatry, 42,* 181–186.

Wilson, M. (1993). DSM III and the transformation of American psychiatry: A history. *American Journal of Psychiatry, 150*(3), 399–410.

Part *IV*

Gerontology

Part IV describes the field of gerontology, an important field of practice in the future of social work. With the demographic projections described in Chapter 1, this field of practice should be *the* place to be in the future of social work. Kennard Wellons begins this section with two scenarios of "older persons" to consider; then Rebecca Walker describes the implications of aging on families in terms of caregiver stress and the roles needed by social work to deal with this population in the future.

In Chapter 12, Kennard Wellons describes some aspects of aging in the next century of relevance for social work practice using a point-counterpoint approach. The reader can choose from an optimistic or pessimistic twenty-first-century scenario and answer the following queries:

1. Based on the information provided in this chapter, which description of an "older person" do you prefer? Describe the implications for social work practice of your choice.
2. What will be the role of gerontological social workers in working with older people in the next century? How does that differ from their role today?
3. What implications do you see for social work education both now and in the future?

"Caregiver Stress, Long-Term Care, and Future Social Work Practice" is the title of Chapter 13. Rebecca Walker describes current trends that suggest predictions about the needs of older people in the next century. Readers will want to ask the following questions after reading this chapter:

1. What are the current trends that will require increased resources for long-term care by families and will create a diminishing array of long-term care options from which to choose?

2. What will social workers do to assist families with declining personal resources to provide for the growing numbers of elders who will require care?

3. What can social workers do to prevent unnecessary institutionalization of dependent family members?

Chapter 12

Aspects of Aging in the Twenty-First Century

Opposing Viewpoints

KENNARD W. WELLONS, PhD

University of Kentucky

The volatility of the American political economy and the diversity of the aging baby boom generation make it extremely difficult to predict the shape of an aging society in the twenty-first century. This chapter will describe and assess the known numerous antecedent, current, and future variables that will influence the older population; predict outcomes based on these variables; and define the roles, functions, and locations of a greatly expanded social work profession that will provide a large portion of the services to older persons in the early years of the millennium (National Institute on Aging, 1987; Select Committee on Aging, 1988).

The stage was set for the twenty-first century by a complex set of rather ironic, dramatic population transitions—a progressive, occasionally striking drop in the death rate; a continual high birth rate until the mid-1960s, accelerated briefly by a phenomenon termed the *baby boom*. Following the baby boom period the birth rate underwent a radical and abiding decrease (University of Mississippi Medical Center, 1992). In 1900, 50 percent of the population survived to almost 60 years of age, whereas in 1990, 50 percent survived to almost 80 years of age. We have recently reached a period where the birth rate is no longer greater than the death rate; thus the population is no longer increasing but aging rapidly. The birth rate will continue to decrease until about 2030 when it will level off. During this same period the death rate will remain approximately at the level of the 1990s. The median age will increase from 32.6 years in 1989 to 38 years in 2010. It is clear that the percentage of the population greater than 65 years of age will continue to increase significantly through the year 2030 (Dychtwald, 1989; Grigsby, 1991).

An Optimistic or a Pessimistic Twenty-First-Century Scenario?

These population shifts will play out in one of at least two alternative scenarios—will the twenty-first-century society be that of an older and sicker elderly population or that of an older but healthier one? Will the older population reflect a lifetime disregard for health—a bored, socially isolated, intellectually unstimulating group never having learned the skill of making new friends—or one sensitized to the necessity and habits of exercising the mind and the body and to the development of social skills necessary for a reasonable quality of life? That decision is likely still being made, although there are a number of known antecedent factors, demographic and morbidity measures, and policy considerations that will inform and influence that determination. An assessment of the significant individual and systemwide social, cultural, environmental, technological, biological, and psychological changes that are likely to occur in the next three decades leads one to opt for the scenario of an older, healthier, more socially skilled modal twenty-first-century older person (University of Mississippi Medical Center, 1992).

The ingredients of this belief are numerous. Already the process of aging has begun to slow down. During the initial period of the twenty-first century the genetic aspects of aging shall be better controlled. Most cancers will be controlled as well as the debilitating hazards of vascular and bone diseases. Alzheimer's disease and other dementing, cognitive impairments will be controlled or eliminated. As the biological quality of life is elevated, older persons will move toward greater self-activity and self-reliance. The stereotypes of mental deterioration will disappear as older persons increase their capacity to develop and train mental capabilities and, more importantly, take on a self-perception of greatly expanded potential. The concept of old-age-based dependency will give way to a functional definition applied to all ages (Bass, 1989; Chen, 1987; Hudson, 1989; Simonton, 1994; Zedlewski et al., 1989).

Older persons themselves will be active participants in this optimistic scenario, demonstrating a strong and increasing commitment to elevating the quality of old age. This commitment results in a literal explosion of fitness/wellness activities, including attention to nutrition, exercise, and stress reduction. These changes will result in the compression of morbidity of the most seriously debilitating chronic illnesses into the final 2 to 3 years of life, a major factor in improving the quality of life of the older population (Kart, 1994; University of Mississippi Medical Center, 1992). The ages from 60 through the late 70s will become the most productive years. Life expectancy will reach 85 years (Grigsby, 1991).

A revolutionary cultural shift will occur in which the United States—from the traditional focus on youth to an emphasis on both the needs and the resources of the older segments of the population. There is a high likelihood that older persons beginning at the turn of the century will be a vital, vigorous, active, future-oriented, healthy, long-living, long-producing group. They will discover that they no longer are a minor cultural tapestry but *the* fabric of society, possessing the power to dominate, to control, and to mete out the resources of society to all. This form of power felt by the older population will be different from the organizational power such as that allocated to the AARP, but a more personal, prideful self-perceived prestige that will derive from a society that desperately needs older persons to fill meaningful roles in the social, cultural, and occupational arenas. The older population has not felt this power in such a personal manner since the agrarian era prior to the beginning of the Industrial Revolution. Although this realization will be surprising to some and frightening to others, it will very likely lead to the disappearance of the currently widening schism between old and young (Dychtwald, 1989; Kaye, 1994). Commensurate with this realization of the possibility of immense social and political control and a renewed self-respect, older persons, given the choice, will elect not to engage in an "age war" between generations fighting for the scant resources of the society. There will emerge a new commitment to the well-being of all people, with older persons playing the leading, not only the beneficiary, role. Older persons, advantaged and disadvantaged alike, possess a great need to give back some of what they believe they have been provided. This altruistic ideology will intensify with the realization of political power and control in the twenty-first century (Bass, 1989). Human service professionals will play a key, proactive role in this shift and will be discussed later in the chapter.

Services: Type, Numbers, and Needs

The large majority, likely greater than 80 percent, of the older population of the twenty-first century will need the direct assistance of no one in order to carry out their usual day-to-day activities. This group will be composed of those electing to work beyond the traditional retirement age. They will be the consumers of leisure services and provide a large cadre of community volunteers and participate in advocacy and professional organizations. The services they will need will relate to their caretaking role with older, more debilitated family members, primarily utilizing linkage services by which to connect their older family member with a variety of direct health and social environmental services. The direct human services they will seek will center primarily on family disjunctures incumbent in the newer forms of families and in an increasing divorce rate of the older population. Of that approximately 20 percent (approaching 10 million persons in the early 2000s) who will require more direct and more intensive health and human services, approximately 2.5 million will require the intensive services of institutions such as nursing homes and mental hospitals; another 2.5 million will be bedridden at home; and 5 million will be seriously at risk of either becoming homebound or requiring institutional services.

As 80 percent of the caretaking of older persons is provided by family members, the design of programs that make it possible for family members to provide this care without overwhelming themselves (Dychtwald, 1989) will become a particular challenge for the social work profession; social workers must deal with the resulting family disjunctures and stresses by participating in the provision of individual and family counseling, support groups, respite care, and intervention aimed at reduction of caretaker stress.

The nuclear family as it is known today will fade into the background. Lifetime monogamy will become increasingly exceptional as the divorce rate rapidly increases for the 60-plus generation. Eighty percent of divorcees remarry. Fifty percent of these second marriages end in divorce, and by the year 2000 approximately 4 million persons will have had three or more marriages. Multigenerational families will abound. Communities consisting of a wide age range of related and unrelated persons will form for mutual support. Older women will be firmly ensconced in the labor force, likely even more unwilling to retire than their male counterparts. They will continue to provide the primary caretaking for that group of 15 million older, frail, and at-risk persons residing in their homes. A preponderance of these women will be single through widowhood and increasingly through separation and divorce. They will increasingly gravitate to nontraditional relationships, including younger men and related and unrelated "families," and increasingly will conclude that their lives can be satisfying without the presence of a man (Dychtwald, 1989; Friedman, 1992).

The twenty-first-century social worker will be asked to deal with the fallout related to these issues of multiple marriages; multiple divorces; blended, extended, and unrelated families; and the stresses of being single.

The Elder Care Generalist

Finally, the long-predicted proliferation of occupational opportunities in the aging service field will come about. There will emerge a dramatic need for the professional elder care generalist who will provide the older client a single, coordinated entry point and access to a wide range of needed services (Dattalo, 1992; Kart, 1994; National Institute on Aging, 1987; Zedlewski et al., 1989). They will be attached to corporations, to universities, to agencies in the Area Agency on Aging network, to the senior center, and, indeed, in private practice. These generalists will perform functions not unlike those of workers in the 1960s and early 1970s, prior to the mass movement of the social work profession toward specialization:

- Understand the biological, psychological, and social needs of their older clients.
- Based on this understanding, steer the client through the maze of community health, social, and economic resources.
- Perform as a linkage agent to and advocate for needed services.
- Coordinate the client's participation in the service arena.
- Assist the client and the client's family in planning and decision making regarding future and imminent needs such as housing changes, companionship, respite care, and the possibility of a transition to some level of long-termcare.

The role of elder care generalist lends itself naturally to the training, knowledge, and skills of the generalist social worker. The education and training of the elder care generalist will require a broad range of gerontological knowledge and skills related to multiple ecological systems (Lowy, 1991), including the following:

- Knowledge of individual development, dynamics, and functioning—normal, patho-logical, and dysfunctional—cognitive, emotional, social, physical, and pharmaco-logical.
- Clinical intervention skills at the individual, family, and small group levels.
- Knowledge of aging social policy and programs: social policy analysis; policy development; organizational and community theory; ethnic/cultural diversity; dis-crimination and oppression; organizational dysfunction; and the aging service deliv-ery system.
- Intervention at the macro level: policy change strategies, community organization, advocacy, resource linkage, and intervention in the workplace.
- Knowledge of each of the micro and macro social systems in which older persons function and the interaction among these systems: family systems, small groups, orga-nizational systems, and community systems.

In spite of the national social work education movement toward specialization, a few schools of social work (such as the University of Kentucky) continue to focus on the gen-eralist practitioner.

Strange Bedmates: A New Partnership

As the pendulum of the political economy swings in a more conservative direction, the future is likely to realize a vast expansion of the participation of private enterprise in the aging services network in concert with public-sector agencies. The traditional animosity and mutual distrust between health and human service providers in the public sector and the private sector corporate world have already begun to diminish, and the diminution will accelerate if current trends continue. Numerous liaisons and collaborative efforts already exist and will proliferate in the foreseeable future. The traditional distrust notwithstanding, the eventual outcome is that public-sector human services will enter into this partnership (possibly kicking and screaming) and an exciting new and effective public–private coali-tion will emerge to the benefit of both (and, alas, the older population), although the tran-sition will be a stormy one (Dychtwald, 1989).

There are four potential leaders in this new partnership: the Area Agency on Aging network, the corporate structure, the university, and, locally, the senior citizens center.

Corporate Participation

Older workers will be very reluctant to bow out of the workplace. Retirement as it is now known will disappear. The overwhelming majority of older persons will be healthy and vital and will not be "worn out" but very ready to go on with their work-productive lives. These jobs will not likely be the those for which they were trained, but jobs performed in a much more flexible work arena. Retirement funds will become more transportable, and movement between corporations will become commonplace. It will be rare that people will spend their entire working lives in a single job with the single employer, and this more flexible work arena could well be more satisfying for the individual and more productive for the economy. As there will likely be a great increase in the number of middle-aged and older persons participating in the labor force who will be living in four- and possibly five-generation families, the service-providing corporate workplace will emerge (Chen, 1987; Easterlin, 1994; Hudson, 1989).

Social workers will work in corporate-sponsored elder care programs dealing clinically with the problems that employees encounter in their caretaking responsibilities of older parents, and they will also be involved in linking these employees' older relatives with needed community services. Industries will expand contract-based services to their employees with caretaking responsibilities, begun in the early 1990s, often in collaboration with universities, and these relationships will predictably expand greatly. Social workers will administer volunteer programs organized in the workplace (Dychtwald, 1989) to harness and focus the altruistic concerns of older workers.

Other than services to older persons located within other industries, there are a number of autonomous private businesses providing direct service to older persons, especially in the area of home care. A major increase has begun for private practitioners, particularly social workers, who are providing fee-based case management services—those of the elder care generalist discussed previously.

Role of the Area Agency on Aging

The Area Agency on Aging (AAA) currently does very little proactive planning for the provision of services to the older population but functions predominantly as a pipeline for funds for programs designed at the federal level. Little room is left for flexibility in designing of programs or the use of funds that fit with an area's particular needs. They are the implementers rather than the designers of programs—reactive rather than proactive.

The AAA network will begin to fulfill its mandate and expand the participation of private industry in the provision of services to older persons. To survive in the twenty-first century, the AAA must be willing to move toward becoming an active recruiter of private industry participants, coordinator of public–private efforts, and planner to define needs and design services. It will become the contact locus and coordinating partner with private industry, linking the industry, the senior center, the service provider, and the older client. The AAA can become the central local planning and coordinating body, allocating funding to programs based on real needs assessments. This role is more in tune with the original design of the purpose and functions of the AAA.

The AAAs will be a major employer of the professional social worker in the macro arena—researching, defining, planning, designing, and arranging for the most efficient provision of programs. Numerous social workers will be utilized by the AAAs in providing these macro services.

The function and, indeed, the survival of the AAA will depend to a great degree on the mechanism by which federal funding for aging programs is made available. If the present system of having program- or population-specific funding continues, the AAAs are in a perfect position to perform the vital brokering, contracting, and coordinating activities.

The possibility of modification of the funding mechanism for aging services is addressed in a final caveat of this chapter.

The Role of Institutions of Higher Education

Higher education institutions will become major players in the developing partnership with private industry. University-based gerontology centers will increasingly form contractual relationships with corporations to provide service to employees with caretaking responsibilities for older family members; to provide direct services to older persons, including day care, interdisciplinary assessment, and intervention; to continue to provide basic biomedical research; and to increase their participation with industry and the local planning body through the conduct of action research, including the determination of needs of the older population.

Universities will become major employers of social workers both as aging specialists providing end-line direct services and as elder care generalists providing linkage services for the person in need with the resource.

The Senior Center

The senior center, because it is much more visible than the AAA, will become a multiservice entry point for many older persons seeking service. This will greatly expand its function, as it will become a major employment base of the elder care generalist, ensuring the older client access to each of the community services that the client needs. These practice arenas will pose not only great opportunity but great challenge for the social worker of tomorrow.

A Caveat

The social, political, and economic conservatism begun in 1995 could very well portend the advent of an "age war," as some have predicted. There is a great hue and cry to provide federal human services funds to the states in the form of block grants to deal with the problems of all population groupings across many problem areas and to leave the allocation to each group to the discretion of the individual states and local communities. Such a move could very well dismantle the established effective aging services, particularly those within the Older Americans Act network, and risk a monumental increase in competition for resources between the young and the old, widening the schism to extraordinary proportions rather than diminishing the divisiveness as was previously predicted here. Aging services have not fared well when funding decisions were relegated to individual states and local communities. If such an age war comes about, the older population will win that war carte blanche, negating the healing that has already begun, an outcome not desirable to either group. Older persons are just now beginning, even with a clear awareness of their political power, to mend this hole in the fabric of the culture.

References

Bass, S. (1989). Symposium on tomorrow's able elderly: Implications for policy and practice. *Gerontologist, 27,* 403–412.

Chen, Y. (1987). Making assets out of tomorrow's elderly. *Gerontologist, 27,* 409–415.

Dattalo, P. (1992).Case management for geriatric social workers. In R. Schneider & N. Kropf (Eds.), *Gerontological social work* (pp. 138–170). Chicago: Nelson-Hall.

Dychtwald, K. (1989). *Age wave: The challenges and opportunities of an aging America.* Los Angeles: Tarcher.

Easterlin, R., et al. (1994). Retirement prospects for the baby boom generation. In R. Enright (Ed.), *Perspectives in social gerontology* (pp. 366–377). Needham Heights, MA: Allyn & Bacon.

Enright, R. (Ed.). (1994). *Perspectives in social gerontology.* Needham Heights, MA: Allyn & Bacon.

Friedman, E. (1992). Health care's changing face: The demographics of the 21st century. *Hospitals, 65,* 36–40.

Grigsby, J. (1991). Paths for future population aging. *Gerontologist, 31,* 195–204.

Hudson, R. (1989).Tomorrow's able elders: Implications for the state. *Gerontologist, 27,* 405–410.

Kart, C. (1994). *The realities of aging.* (4th ed.). Needham Heights, MA: Allyn & Bacon.

Kaye, L. (1994). Generational equity: Pitting young against old. In R. Enright (Ed.), *Perspectives in social gerontology* (pp. 343–347). Needham Heights, MA: Allyn & Bacon.

Lowy, L. (1991). *Social work with the aging.* Prospect Heights, IL: Waveland Press.

Martin, L. (1991). Population aging policies of the United States and East Asia. *Science, 251,* 527–531.

Moody, R. (1994). *Aging: Concepts and controversies.*Thousand Oaks, CA: Pine Forge Press.

National Institute on Aging. (1987). *Personnel for health needs of the elderly through the year 2020.*Washington, DC: U.S. Government Printing Office.

Schneider, R., & Kropf, N. (1992). *Gerontological social work: Knowledge, service settings and special populations.* Chicago: Nelson-Hall.

Select Committee on Aging: House of Representatives. (1988). *Planning for an aging America: The void in reliable data.* Washington, DC: U.S. Government Printing Office.

Simonton, D. (1994). Creativity in the later years: Optimistic prospects. In R. Enright (Ed.), *Perspectives in social gerontology* (pp. 132–139). Needham Heights, MA: Allyn & Bacon.

University of Mississippi Medical Center. (1992). *Age Quake XXIL: Preparing state governments for an "Age Quake" in the 21st century.* Jackson: University of Mississippi.

Zedlewski, S., et al. (1989). *The needs of the elderly in the 21st century.* Washington, DC: The Urban Institute.

Chapter *13*

Caregiver Stress, Long-Term Care, and Future Social Work Practice

REBECCA J. WALKER, PhD
University of Kentucky

The number of elderly persons who depend on family caregivers for assistance in coping with the wide-ranging physical and mental consequences of aging has increased dramatically during the last century. Due to a number of demographic and public health trends, these numbers will only continue to increase into the next century. Just as importantly, this burgeoning group of elders will find themselves dependent on a shrinking cohort of potential family caregivers, who are themselves rapidly growing older. If older adults cannot depend on declining family resources to provide the care they need, where can they turn? The answer today is to a narrow range of options provided by a society that too often has an equally limited view of the elderly, their unique needs, and their capabilities.

The number of elderly persons is growing faster than any other age group, with the group over 85 showing the most rapid increase. In 1980 there were approximately 25.7 million elderly persons, composing approximately 10 percent of the total population. By the turn of the century, it is projected that there will be approximately 34.8 million elders. By the year 2050 their numbers will have grown to 68.5 million, representing 22.9 percent of the total population (Atchley, 1994).

With each passing year the number of elderly increases, as does the likelihood of their dependence on others for supervision and care. The number of persons in the age group of

85 years or older (the frailest segment of the population) can be expected to be seven times as large in 2050 as it was in 1980. This population of the "oldest old" is most at risk for physical infirmity and dementing illnesses such as Alzheimer's disease (AD). For example, those persons between the ages of 65 and 74 exhibit a 1 in 25 chance of having AD, and those 85 and older have a staggering 1 in 2 chance of developing the disorder (National Institutes of Health, 1992).

In addition to dementia, this growing segment of the population is also more likely to experience other compounding physical, social, and economic difficulties. These conditions serve to increase the dependency of these older adults and their need for family supervision and support. For example, over the past several decades the incidence and distribution of illness have shifted from acute to chronic diseases because of advances in public health and medical care. There also has been a decline in the death rates from such illnesses as stroke and cancer and an increase in survival rates from accidents. These changes in the nature, course, and outcome of illness leave many individuals with activity and mobility restrictions, as well as an increased chance of living to an age when the risk of other chronic, debilitating mental and physical diseases greatly increases (Biegel, Sales, & Schulz, 1991).

Finally, certain groups of the elderly are particularly at risk of dependence on family caregivers. Women not only live longer than men but are also more likely to have outlived a spouse, to live alone, to be more economically disadvantaged, and to have more chronic physical and mental health problems (U.S. House of Representatives, 1988). All of these factors increase the chance of their being even more at risk for requiring supervision and support. In addition, the proportion of older African Americans, Hispanics, and Native Americans is growing at a faster rate than that of older White Americans. The rate of poverty among older minorities is far higher than it is among whites. Additionally, their health is on the average worse, and they have more limited access to health care. Helpful community programs and the financial resources of the extended family are also often less available (Dychtwald, 1989).

When elders require supervision and care, public policy and cultural values increase the likelihood that such caregiving will be provided by a family member. First of all, there has been an alarming increase in the total expenditures for nursing home care. Between 1970 and 1988 such expenditures increased from $4.7 billion to $47 billion, representing almost 11 percent of all health care expenditures. This increase in the cost of institutional care can only be expected to increase over the next several years unless radical changes occur in the way in which health care is delivered and financed. Considering the recent experience in making such changes at the national level, such reform appears unlikely in the next decade. Delaying institutionalization is one way to reduce the cost of such care. As a result, many states are now offering some type of economic support for family caregivers to assist them in maintaining their family members in the home. Medicare payment procedures and advances in medical technology have also increased the rapidity with which chronically ill patients are discharged from the hospital to family caregivers. Persons who might have remained hospitalized for protracted periods at one time are now discharged according to rigid guidelines (Biegel et al., 1991; Lubkin, 1990). Medicaid payment for nursing home care, furthermore, is not available until other resources are depleted. Families often have no other choice but to keep their elderly members in the community as long as possible to forestall such impoverishment.

Aside from such demographic trends and government policies, deeply ingrained social values continue to compel family members to play a primary role in providing care for this growing population of impaired older adults. Despite the perception that placement of those elderly persons with chronic mental and physical illness in nursing homes is a routine matter for family members as they move into the twenty-first century, current trends would suggest otherwise. Currently, the majority of persons with AD and other types of dementia, among the most difficult to manage of disorders, are cared for by family members (Brody, 1985; Given, Collins, & Given, 1988; Horowitz, 1985; Shanas, 1979). According to Lubkin (1990), studies have shown that family members provide 60 to 80 percent of all care received by elderly persons who are impaired.

Over the next several decades, therefore, it can be anticipated that the number of elderly persons who may require long-term care will increase. It can also be assumed that families will continue to consider it their responsibility to provide such care whenever possible. It can be predicted, however, that because of other demographic trends, families will have fewer internal resources to call on to meet this demand. Additionally, based on current trends in long-term care, families will have a diminishing array of affordable long-term care options from which to select when the family is no longer able to provide the required care.

The demands for caregiving will fall on families that are increasingly unable to bear such a burden. For example, because of the increase in life expectancy of the parents, the adult children looked to for care will be growing older themselves. Fully one-third of caregivers to older adults are currently 65 or older themselves; the average age is 57 (Dychtwald, 1989). Many of the young old (60 to 75) caring for their old-old parents (75 and up) will be experiencing their own decline in energy, finances, and health. They may be increasingly concerned about their own retirement, which may be delayed because of the projected crisis in the Social Security fund, resulting in the necessity of their working longer. Elders and their aging children also have often experienced financial reversals during what should have been their most productive years. Inflation, with its resulting lessened purchasing power and increased cost of living, downsizing of corporations, and other economic reversals have left many elderly more likely to need economic help and their adult children less able to provide it (Cicirelli, 1981).

Women's entry into the labor force in increasing numbers, along with the trend toward delaying childbirth, also affect the family's ability to provide care. The probability that child care and elder care will overlap will likely show an increase as women continue to delay childbearing. There has been a steady increase in the birth rate among women over 30 since 1976 (Atchley, 1994), and this appears likely to continue. Many caregivers, therefore, are caught in the middle, caring for aging parents while still raising children. Women, who continue to be the primary caregivers of both children and elderly parents, are likely to actually spend more time caring for their parents than their own dependent children (U.S. House of Representatives, 1988). In addition to caring for children while they are caring for their aging parents, many of these working women are also caught in the middle between family and career as well. In the past, family caregiving traditionally fell to the daughter or daughter-in-law who stayed at home. Although currently there appears to be a trend toward stay-at-home moms while children are young, most women either launch or restart a career when this phase of caregiving is completed, making them less available for the day-to-day care many elders require.

A third trend affecting the pool of potential caregivers is that toward having smaller families. The ratio of adults between 18 and 64 to people over 65 was 13.6 to 1 in 1900; by 1990 the ratio had dropped to 4.8 to 1. This dearth of available caregivers can be expected to grow worse; as the baby boomers age, the children they failed to have will not be there to care for them (Dychtwald, 1989).

A final trend that will further deplete the pool of potential caregivers for the growing number of elderly is the increasing divorce rate. Divorce can complicate family caregiving by limiting the number of spouses who can provide such care to their loved one and increasing the demands on adult children to provide care to parents who do not live together. Divorce among "blended families" may leave a stepparent with no support despite years spent in childrearing. Finally, divorce is often acrimonious, resulting in emotional barriers to providing care (U.S. House of Representatives, 1988).

If this fragile family support system cannot provide the kind of care the growing numbers of elders will require, what will families do in the future? If current trends continue, affordable long-term care in the numbers necessary to meet the need may simply not be available. With an increasing population of elders who are rapidly moving into the age group that has traditionally been cared for in nursing homes, a serious look must be taken at the resources that will be required to care for them. In 1990 approximately 500,000 elders in the 85-and-older age range were in long-term beds; by the year 2000 it is expected that 1 million long-term beds will be needed. By 2020 the number is expected to increase to 1.5 million, and by 2050 the required number of long-term beds is projected to be over 3 million, based on current utilization rates. That number represents a sixfold increase in long-term beds required in 2050 as compared with those needed in 1990 (Atchley, 1994). In light of all the competing social needs and the current political environment that are fueling the construction of prison beds, it seems likely that neither the public nor the private sector will be able to address the need adequately. This is, of course, not altogether undesirable. As U.S. society has moved away from congregate living for persons with disabilities, it must also view institutionalization of the elderly as the recourse of last resort. Just as others deserve to live in the least restrictive alternative, so do the elderly.

Even if such beds were available, the family's distress and guilt over the prospect of placing its loved one in an institution will continue to prevent many from making use of available resources. Institutional care can also quickly eradicate a lifetime of savings, leaving the loved one impoverished and dependent on government assistance, a prospect that many elderly and their families find unacceptable.

The result of these trends is that fewer and older caregivers must provide care for longer periods of time to a growing number of older, more impaired family members. Their ability to provide such care allows the elderly person to remain independent of expensive institutional care, which is of benefit to both the care recipient and society as a whole. But what about the caregiver? Research has consistently shown that although caregiving can have many positive effects on the caregiver, providing care to elderly family members is often highly stressful. There is ample evidence to indicate that the caregiving role can have deleterious emotional, physical, and financial consequences for the caregiver and can lead to feelings of depression, anxiety, and burden in those individuals who take the responsibility for the care of a spouse or other loved one (Gallagher, Rose, Rivera, Lovett, & Thompson, 1989; Haley, 1989). Not only do these effects have long-ranging consequences for the caregiver, but they may also affect the care recipient as well. For example, although the availability of family members is critical in the care recipient's ability to remain in the community, several studies have found that subjective feelings of distress and other negative effects experienced by the caregiver, rather than the actual demands of caregiving or the severity of the patient's symptoms, are the critical determinants of the caregiver's ability to continue to provide care to the patient in the community (Colerick & George, 1986; Morycz, 1985; Zarit, Todd, & Zarit, 1986). As the caregiver's distress and burden increases, so too does the elder's risk of being placed in an institution.

To realize the benefits of family care to forestall the institutionalization of elderly persons while preventing the negative impact of such care on family caregivers, two approaches should be taken simultaneously by social work practitioners in the future. First, social workers must direct their intervention toward preventing the premature dependence of elderly family members on their potential caregivers for as long as possible. This approach will help to ensure that the family and other resources necessary to support the dependent family members will be there when required. Secondly, when such dependence is necessary, practice efforts should be directed at mitigating the negative impact of caregiving on those who provide care. This strategy not only will assist the caregiver in maintaining their physical and mental health but may further prevent the necessity of the older adult's taking that final step into a nursing home. Although it is advantageous to the elders, their family, and society to prevent unnecessary institutionalization, the caregivers and their families must not be sacrificed. The remainder of this chapter will be directed toward these two approaches, followed by a description of the specific roles that social work practitioners and educators must play to meet the challenge of the twenty-first century.

Forestalling Dependence

Advances in medical science and public health initiatives have resulted in the "compression of morbidity," which means that people tend to stay healthy for much of their lives, becoming impaired only when their lives are approaching an end (Fries, 1990). The first effort of social work practitioners should be directed toward the "compression of dependency" so that elders retain their full independence as long as possible, lose aspects of their independence incrementally over a period of time, and become dependent only during a brief time prior to their death. By delaying such dependence, the chances that the family and financial resources needed to maintain them will be there, and will be enhanced. Social workers should be in the forefront of the social and public policy debate on what constitutes an appropriate retirement age, when one is "too old to work." It can be expected that within the next decade the age of eligibility for Social Security benefits will increase to 70 or, possibly, 75. This may be required to fund the system adequately and adjust for the current drain caused by too many retirees supported by too few workers. Expanding the expectation of people's ability to contribute is also consistent with both what our health care system has accomplished and what we now know about people's ability to learn and adjust over the life span. Extending the age at which most people come to consider themselves ready for retirement means that more resources will be available when they do retire. Just as importantly, the sense of purpose that meaningful work provides to older people can contribute to their sense of well-being and perception of themselves as independent, self-directed adults. Social workers should not only participate in and direct this debate but also be active participants in the extended job readiness and placement process. As the resource that older workers represent becomes more apparent—and as our ability to prosper without their contribution becomes more in doubt—social workers must assist older workers in finding new ways to apply existing or new skills in ways that are commensurate with their physical and mental changes. They must also deal with those barriers within the older worker and within the work setting that may prevent their utilization.

A second area where social workers can contribute to the increased independence that additional work years will provide is in helping older workers to accept the necessity of such a shift. Older workers not only will face additional work years but may also likely feel that the rules have been changed and experience considerable anger. Social workers can be important links to the older worker's ability to maintain proficiency in current jobs, to develop the skills needed to shift to another career, or to reenter the job market. Just as importantly, social work practitioners can assist these older workers in dealing with the anger and fears that may be associated with such a move.

A second way that social workers can assist older adults in remaining independent is through the provision of mental health services. Too often, older adults are viewed as being unable to benefit from psychotherapy. We have a long tradition of not expecting old dogs to learn new tricks. Thus many social workers view the elderly in a most pessimistic manner, feeling that all they can accomplish with such a client is preparation for death. Just as with retirement, social workers must give more than lip service to the expectation that development continues throughout the life cycle. There are at least two areas in which social work intervention can positively affect the older adult's ability to remain independent as long as possible and to transition toward dependence as smoothly as possible. Long before they lose their independence, the elderly experience numerous other losses (such as spouse, friends, health, and physical and mental abilities) (Conway, 1988). Many of these losses are not recognized by either the older adults or their families. Social workers should direct their interventions to assisting elderly people in identifying these losses and grieving them. If these multiple losses are not grieved, the chances of "bereavement overload" (Lehman & Russell, 1985) increase as the losses pile up. "With accumulated losses, the grieving process becomes more complex, and physical, emotional, and environmental resources for moving through that process are rapidly depleted" (Conway, 1988, p. 543). A particularly painful loss that elders must grieve is that of their own life, which is brought into sharp focus if a diagnosis of a terminal illness is made. Social work intervention during this time will allow dying patients to exercise whatever amount of control they can through the remainder of their lives.

A second area in which therapeutic intervention may be beneficial to the older adult is to encourage and support them to make use of the time prior to dependence as an opportunity to take care of business with friends and family members. Not only should social workers encourage older adults to address such issues as establishing wills, trusts, powers of attorney, and advanced directives, but they should also assist them in dealing with the emotional business left over from a lifetime. Helping older adults to engage in the final psychosocial stage of integrity versus despair (Erickson, 1950) may necessitate the confrontation of issues that have been long left unresolved or that become an issue again as impending shifts in roles, power, and the structure of the family become apparent. Dealing with such issues prior to the onset of debilitating mental or physical illness and the resulting dependence may allow such transitions to be effected with greater ease.

A final focus of direct social work intervention directed toward enhancing older adults' ability to remain independent is the area of health care. There will be an increasing need for medical social workers to assist the elderly in returning home following discharge from medical facilities. A thoughtful, comprehensive, and carefully monitored discharge and after-care plan may mean the difference between a successful return home and institutionalization. Medical social workers must also be involved in other aspects of the health care delivery system. Just as we have had well-baby clinics, we must also promote well-elder clinics, which stress prevention, early intervention, and the teaching and training required to maintain healthy practices throughout the life cycle and to participate in a personal home health program.

On a policy level, social workers must also become effective advocates for clients in the increasingly strident health care debate. In the future, older adults will require access to costly long-term care through a federally supported insurance system that does not require their depleting every dollar earned over their lifetime. Just as importantly, they will also need the financial and technological supports required to remain in their homes. An array of services from telephone check-ins to daily chore, homemaker, and home health services would serve to prevent the premature use of family caregivers. Funding must be provided for the renovation of existing residences to make them useable by those with emerging physical and sensory disabilities. Money must be directed toward these services that are at once more cost-effective, consistent with our values of family responsibility and autonomy, and more feasible than constructing institutions.

A second area that would benefit from the advocacy of social work practitioners is that of housing alternatives for the elderly. Too often there are three choices for the elderly: to live totally on their own, to live with relatives, or to reside in an institution. The first alternative may be unavailable to many elders as declining health and limited support conspire to prevent their continued independence. The other alternatives imply total dependence. An array of housing options must be developed in response to the various degrees of dependence that elders exhibit. Like all other people, elders deserve to exercise self-determination to the extent possible. To be self-determining, however, elders must have options from which to choose. Furthermore, not only should options be available, but they should be configured in a variety of ways and locations. For example, elders should not be required to live in "elderly ghettos." For some, living among their peers is desirable; for others, living in communities of residents of all ages is preferred.

Of particular concern in the future must be the growing number of elders who have neither children nor spouses to support them. Useful ideas must be borrowed from other age groups and earlier times to prevent the isolation that often results in institutionalization. For example, workers must promote older adults' having roommates, taking in boarders, renting out rooms in their homes, and utilizing dating services. Elders should be offered such options as boarding houses and cooperative houses. Just as such co-ops on college campuses are organized around interests (such as foreign languages), elder co-ops could also be organized around such interests as hobbies, prior careers, or travel. Even more basically, they may be organized around skills and abilities, with some of the elders preparing meals while others attend to maintenance and cleaning responsibilities. Such arrangements would compensate for the individual's deficits, further extending his or her independence.

The result of such efforts would be both the expectation and realization of more people remaining independent longer. In addition, their lives would continue to be richer, filled with meaningful work and expanding relationships. Furthermore, making good use of this time would more adequately prepare the older adult and his or her family for increasing dependence, making such changes more palatable for all concerned. Finally, as the ability to remain totally independent declined, additional options would be available to further extend the sense of control and autonomy.

Mitigating the Effects of Dependence

When these supports are no longer successful in maintaining the older adult in an independent residence without significant amounts of family support, the focus of social work intervention must shift to assisting the caregiver. By focusing on the caregiver, not only can the debilitating physical and emotional problems that they may experience be prevented, but the final step toward long-term care of the loved one may also be forestalled.

The families that social workers will be working with in the future are increasingly likely to include three or four generations. Just as we must expand our appreciation of elders' ability to benefit from psychotherapy before they become more dependent, so too must we understand that family therapy of the future may include grandparents. Social workers will see more older families on their caseloads in the next decade. As more families take over the care of their aging parents, new types of problems will also emerge. For example, sibling rivalry among adult children may reemerge when one sibling feels that he or she is having to assume a disproportionate share of the caregiving; when others feel they are being "bossed" by a sibling; when it is felt that "mother always liked you best" despite the fact that one is devoting his or her life to the parent's care while the other simply comes in for a visit.

In the future, all social workers must develop expertise in working with older adults and multigenerational families; it can no longer remain a specialty area for the few. All agencies that provide services to families should provide additional training to their staff on working with the elderly, their caregivers, and multigenerational families. This is particularly important in rural and more isolated areas, as such specialized services as local chapters of the Alzheimer's Disease and Related Disorders Association may not be available. Even when this is not the case, family members may not recognize that their problems are related to their loved one and may appear at a family agency. Being tuned in to the special problems of this population is especially important, as many people have great difficulty expressing the often unacceptable feelings they may have toward an ill and dependent family member.

It is also critically important that we develop additional support systems for the caregivers. Family and individual therapy, support groups, psychoeducational groups, and skills training must all be readily available to the growing number of family caregivers. We must recognize, however, that the empirical support for the effectiveness of most such programs is equivocal (Biegel et al., 1991; Gallagher, 1985; Toseland & Rossiter, 1989). We must, therefore, be creative in the development and evaluation of additional programs.

A lot has been learned about caregivers over the last decade. Considerable research has focused on the characteristics of caregivers, the demands and stressors of the caregiving process, and the impact of this process on the caregiver. One of the most perplexing and consistent findings of numerous research studies, however, is that there is only a weak to moderate relationship between objective caregiving stressors, such as patient impairment and duration of caregiving, and feelings of subjective distress and other negative effects of caregiving (Biegel et al., 1991; Haley, Levine, Brown, & Bartolucci, 1987). Both clinical impressions and empirical research have shown that there is wide variability in the manner that caregivers respond to providing care to a relative with dementia. Some caregivers seem unable to cope with even the mildest demands. Other caregivers not only endure but actually appear to flourish and gain satisfaction from what appears to be more demanding care (Pearlin, Mullan, Semple, & Skaff, 1990; Stephens & Zarit, 1989; Townsend, Noelker, Deimling, & Bass, 1989). Recent research suggests that anticipatory grief of the caregiver of AD patients may contribute to their unique response to the demands of caregiving (Walker, 1994).

Family caregivers will also need material support to effectively provide the care to their family member at minimal cost to their physical and emotional health. As with forestalling dependence, public funds must be provided to support the family in maintaining the older adult in the community. As more and more families are dependent on two wage earners, family members will be unable to interrupt their careers for substantial periods of time without financial support. Family members must be compensated for what that effort means not only to their loved one but to society as a whole.

Support must also be increasingly available for routine in-home support and respite care, as well as for adult day care and drop-in centers. The caregivers not only must have regular assistance with the care of their loved one but must be able to leave their responsibilities for a few hours or a few weeks. Relief in the form of respite care and drop-in centers needs to be available not only for the errands and chores or the planned vacation but as a way to escape the daily hassles and frustrations of providing care. Such a break from caregiving duties can have a tremendous impact on the caregiver's ability to regain perspective, to refresh and renew. It has been shown that feeling tied down and unable to control time is very stressful for caregivers (Montgomery, Gonyea, & Hooyman, 1985). It must be recognized that caregiving does not follow a predictable course, and the demands of caregiving vary on a day-to-day basis, as do the emotional and physical resources of the caregiver. As a result, caregivers may need relief unexpectedly and quickly. Red tape should be kept to a minimum; service caps should be minimal; and justification should not be required.

In addition to government programs and funding, corporate support for and provision of elder care will be an increasingly common trend. As the primary family caregiver is still the wife or daughter, and she is increasingly likely to be engaged in a career, the need for dependable, affordable, and convenient day care for aging parents will be viewed by corporations as being in their best interest. Corporations will also increasingly offer long-term care insurance to employees as a part of their benefits package. Such insurance must be available to families who want to plan responsibly for their loved one. Finally, those family members who elect to interrupt their careers for substantial periods of time to care for a family member must be allowed to reenter the job market without penalty.

When maintaining the older adult in the community, even with the support of the family, is no longer feasible, social workers must be prepared to help families to place their loved one in institutional care with minimal guilt and regret. This is more likely if the kind of assistance outlined above has been provided to both the older adult and the family. Social workers must also recognize that placement of the family member in a nursing home does not eliminate the family's need for support. The burden of care does not automatically stop at the nursing home door. Adult children are often racked by guilt and remorse; they continue to grieve for their parent and for their own childhood; they continue to demand of themselves that they supervise and monitor their loved one's care. Nursing homes of the future must acknowledge the need for this ongoing involvement of the family and provide them with more than the opportunity to visit or to receive answers to specific questions. Support services, grief groups, and multigenerational family counseling must all be available for the families of nursing home residents.

As a nation, as a society, and as a profession we must also come face to face with the impact of the final step that older adults must take. Elderly persons use a disproportionate share of health care resources, utilizing more expensive options for longer periods of time. Death is often preceded by the most expensive of life-sustaining efforts (Kart, Metress, & Metress, 1988). It can be argued that a substantial portion of the health care crisis could be mitigated if the cost of such efforts were redirected to preventative measures among the young, such as adequate prenatal care for all expectant mothers. Social work practitioners must serve as articulate advocates for older clients so that they are not "triaged" out of the impending rationed health care simply because they belong to a less appealing group. At the same time, we may find ourselves advocating for our clients' ability to remain self-determining as they deal with the health care system. We emphasize the right of people to be self-determining, except when a person's life is at risk. The fact that one value overrides the other is certainly defensible in most cases. However, it would appear that, just as people are allowed the right to dictate that no heroic measures should be taken to sustain their life, it is likewise defensible to allow aged persons with certain types of chronic illnesses to make the decision to voluntarily end their lives, so that the family is not placed in the position of enduring their agonizing and painful decline or making the desperate choice to end their loved one's life and suffer the legal and emotional consequences. Social workers must not sit on the sidelines of this debate but must be active participants, advocating both for their clients' right to equal access to services and their ability to make choices and maintain some measure of control over their final task in life.

The Role of Social Work

What are the roles that social workers will play with this growing population of older adults and their caregiving spouses and children? What are the skills they will need to effectively meet the needs of the elderly to remain as independent as possible for as long as possible? When elders are no longer independent, what are the skills social workers will need to assist caregivers to deal with the stress of caregiving and, thus, delay institutionalization? Social workers must first become aware of their own prejudices and biases against the elderly. Just as it is expected that all social workers be accepting of other forms of diversity, so must they be willing to accept the elderly where they are, to recognize their strengths as well as their weaknesses, and to approach them with optimism. Only after dealing with their own issues involving the aging process and the elderly, death, and their own mortality will they be effective practitioners with older adults. Social work practitioners must also become more effective advocates for their older clients and the elderly as a whole. Ageism is still pervasive in our society. Ageism can be expected to diminish as the baby boomers, who "never trusted anyone over 30" become the older generation. The sheer number of elders will redefine what it means to be old. As this definition changes, our notions about the role of the elderly in the family and the expectations of families to provide care may also change. But work will still need to be done.

To prevent unnecessary dependence and to mitigate the demands when such dependence is unavoidable, practitioners must become proficient in direct practice skills with the elderly, their children and spouses, and multigenerational families. Practitioners should view the time prior to dependence and death as therapeutic opportunities, as times to engage in preventative intervention. Such interventions will allow for the taking care of old business, for the discussion of important matters when the elder can still fully engage in the process; and for the making of decisions and plans when the family has the benefit of their loved one's counsel and input. Such timely intervention can result in future benefits for the family when dependence is a reality, when debilitating illness renders the elder "psychosocially dead," or when death occurs. In addition to individual counseling with elders and their caregivers and family counseling, workers will also need to become more proficient and creative in group work services. Workers will have to continually seek out new approaches with this population and be willing to engage in the evaluation of such services.

Older adults typically require more services and assistance to remain independent. When family members, who typically provide assistance in accessing and coordinating these services, either work or are unavailable for geographic or other reasons, families may determine that a change in the living situation of the older adult is the only way to effectively provide the supervision and assistance that is required. This is the point at which the independent case manager may bridge the gap, providing everything from simple information to coordination of a comprehensive service plan. They may provide information about community resources to adult children who must make decisions with their parent even though they live in a distant community. They may assess the need for and coordinate acceptance into the array of services required by the parent. An independent case manager may serve as advocate for the elder, may assist them in cutting through the bureaucratic maze that is often so perplexing to them and their relatives, and may provide such additional services as simply checking in to combat loneliness and despair or providing the elder with a trusted resource to assist in the evaluation of potential exploitation.

Social work educators must, of course, prepare students for the roles and interventions described above. Even more basically, however, is the need to attract, recruit, and retain students into the medical and gerontological fields of social work practice in order to fill the explosion of jobs that will be available. Too often younger students seem to find these fields of practice less glamorous than working with adults and children in private agencies or independent practice. Too many feel that the aged are hopeless and that working with them is therefore pointless. Scholarship support for undergraduate and graduate education for students who commit to working with the elderly after graduation should be available. Exciting field placements must be developed in places other than nursing homes, so that students receive a broader view of working with the elderly. Finally, social work educators must take the lead in developing and evaluating the effectiveness of interventions designed specifically for the elderly, their caregivers, and the multigenerational family.

Conclusion

As a society, we will become increasingly dependent on the labor of family caregivers, due to both the number of elders and our intolerance of creating another system to "warehouse" a dependent population. Currently, we receive much of this care at no cost. However, as more families are dependent on two wage earners, this may not continue in the future. If suddenly there were no informal, unpaid caregivers, the needs of the elderly simply could not be met, either now or in the future. Despite the family's expected continuing commitment to care for its own, this is unrealistic in light of the prolonged period of dependency that may result from the increasing life expectancy and the limitations of all forms of family resources. As social workers, we must take all measures possible to forestall premature dependency and assist families and their elder members in making the best use of the time to prepare for the future. When dependency becomes unavoidable, we must support the family to limit the victims of the aging process.

References

Atchley, R. C. (1994). *Social forces and aging: An introduction to social gerontology.* (7th ed.). Belmont, CA: Wadsworth.

Biegel, D. E., Sales, E., & Schulz, R. (1991). *Family caregiving in chronic illness: Alzheimer's disease, cancer, heart disease, mental illness, and stroke.* Newbury Park, CA: Sage Publications.

Brody, E. M. (1985). Parent care as a normative family stress. *Gerontologist, 25,* 19–29.

Cicirelli, V. G. (1981). *Helping elderly parents: The role of adult children.* Boston, MA: Auburn House.

Colerick, E. J., & George, L. K. (1986). Predictors of institutionalization among caregivers of patients with Alzheimer's disease. *Journal of the American Geriatric Society, 34,* 493–498.

Conway, P. (1988). Losses and grief in old age. *Social Casework: The Journal of Contemporary Social Work, 69*(8), 541–549.

Dychtwald, K. (1989). *Age wave: The challenges and opportunities of an aging America.* Los Angeles, CA: Jeremy P. Tarcher

Erickson, E. H. (1950). *Childhood and society.* New York: W. W. Norton.

Fries, J. F. (1990). Medical perspectives upon successful aging. In P. B. Baltes & M. M. Baltes (Eds.), *Successful aging: Perspectives from the behavioral sciences* (pp. 35–49). Cambridge: Cambridge University Press.

Gallagher, D. E. (1985). Intervention strategies to assist caregivers of frail elders: Current research status and future research directions. In C. Eisdorfer (Ed.), *Annual review of gerontology and geriatrics: Vol. 5* (pp. 249–282). New York: Springer.

Gallagher, D., Rose, J., Rivera, P., Lovett, S., & Thompson, L. W. (1989). Prevalence of depression in family caregivers. *Gerontologist, 29*(4), 449–456.

Given, C. W., Collins, C. E., & Given, B. A. (1988). Sources of stress among families caring for relatives with Alzheimer's disease. *Nursing Clinics of North America, 23*(1), 69–81.

Haley, W. E. (1989). Group intervention for dementia family caregivers: A longitudinal perspective. *Gerontologist, 29*(4), 478–480.

Haley, W. E., Levine, E. G., Brown, S. L., & Bartolucci, A. A. (1987). Stress, appraisal, coping, and social support as predictors of adaptational outcome among dementia caregivers. *Psychology and Aging, 2,* 323–330.

Horowitz, A. (1985). Family caregiving to the frail elderly. In C. Eisdorfer (Ed.), *Annual review of gerontology and geriatrics: Vol. 5* (pp. 194–246). New York: Springer.

Kart, C. S., Metress, E. K., & Metress, S. P. (1988). *Aging, health and society.* Boston: Jones and Bartlett.

Lehman, V., & Russell, N. (1985). Psychological and social issues of AIDS. In V. Gong (Ed.), *Understanding AIDS* (pp. 177–182). New Brunswick, NJ: Rutgers University Press.

Lubkin, I. M. (1990). Chronic illness. In I. M. Lubkin (Ed.), *Chronic illness: Impact and interventions* (pp. 200–216). Boston: Jones and Bartlett.

Montgomery, R. J. V., Gonyea, J. G., & Hooyman, N. R. (1985). Caregiving and the experience of subjective and objective burden. *Family Relations, 34,* 19–25.

Morycz, R. K. (1985). Caregiving strain and the desire to institutionalize family members with Alzheimer's disease. *Research on Aging, 7*(3), 329–361.

National Institutes of Health. (1992). Progress report on Alzheimer's disease 1992. (NIH Publication No. 92-3409). Washington, DC: U.S. Government Printing Office.

Pearlin, L. I., Mullan, J. T., Semple, S. J., & Skaff, M. M. (1990). Caregiving and the stress process: An overview of concepts and their measures. *The Gerontologist, 30*(5), 583–594.

Shanas, E. (1979). The family as a social support system in old age. *Gerontologist, 19*(2), 169–174.

Stephens, M. A. P., & Zarit, S. H. (1989). Family caregiving to dependent older adults: Stress, appraisal, and coping. *Psychology and Aging, 4*(4), 387–388.

Toseland, R. W., & Rossiter, C. M. (1989). Group intervention to support family caregivers: A review and analysis. *Gerontologist, 29*(4), 430–448.

Townsend, A., Noelker, L., Deimling, G., & Bass, D. (1989). Longitudinal impact of interhousehold caregiving on adult children's mental health. *Psychology and Aging, 4*(4), 393–401.

U.S. House of Representatives. (1988). Exploding the myth: Caregiving in America. Select Committee on Aging Publication No. 100-665. Washington, DC: U.S. Government Printing Office.

Walker, R. J. (1994). *The impact of anticipatory grief on caregivers of patients with Alzheimer's disease.* Unpublished doctoral dissertation, The University of Texas at Austin.

Zarit, S. H., Todd, P. A., & Zarit, J. M. (1986). Subjective burden of husbands and wives as caregivers: Longitudinal study. *Gerontologist, 26*(3), 260–266.

Part *V*

Women, Children, and Families

The opening chapter in this section (Chapter 14) was written by Rosemary C. Sarri, who paints a bleak picture in her overview of the current status of services for children and youth. She documents an undeniable need for our renewed commitment to improving the status of the nation's children, and she suggests a developmental approach as the best way for us to proceed. She suggests some answers to important questions such as the following:

1. What are the trends and future directions for services for children and youth?
2. What are the policy and program alternatives that will benefit our youth?

Creasie Hairston follows in Chapter 15 with an equally stark description of trends and future issues in foster care. The system has failed to effectively serve the most vulnerable families and children, and it is plagued by insufficient foster care facilities, inadequate funding, and an expanding foster care population. There is no way to accommodate even those children in families where there is documented abuse or neglect, or children defined as being at risk. Given these constraints,

1. What are the *realistic* prospects for improvement?
2. What alternatives to current forms of foster care may allow us to better serve a higher proportion of clients?

In Chapter 16 Paula Nurius, Marian Hilfrink, and Rosemary Rifino deal with the violence against women, the single greatest cause of injury to reproductive-age women in the United States. In the midst of this epidemic, it is ironic that there are three times as many animal shelters as women's shelters. The contributors link this problem to substance abuse, economic inequalities, and discrimination, and they present an alternative model for delivering services at the community level. The most compelling questions are the following:

1. How could such a significant problem be virtually ignored for so long?
2. How can individual social workers become personally involved in developing solutions to this problem?

Karen Holmes bursts the myths surrounding the American family in Chapter 17 and explains how families are changing. She presents an *inclusive* view and definition of the family and explains how that differs from the traditional view. Also included is an assessment of the impact of technology on the family. The author herself asks several interesting questions:

1. What is your vision of the ideal family?
2. What do you see as the major problems facing families in the twenty-first century?
3. What kinds of knowledge and skills will you need to work with families in the twenty-first century?

Finally, Epstein and Smith examine the growing problem of teen pregnancy in the next century in Chapter 18. They point out that sexual intercourse today no longer requires an antecedent promise of engagement or marriage, and that this has widespread implications for our social structure. Implications of recently proposed policy changes in the AFDC program are also examined. We must ask the following questions:

1. What impact will teen pregnancy have on the changing shape of the American family?
2. If the problem continues to grow at its current rate, will *family* even be a meaningful term beyond the twenty-first century? Or will it be synonymous with *mother and children?*
3. What degree of stigmatization of teen parents is necessary, justified, or effective in dealing with the problem?

Chapter *14*

An Agenda for Child and Youth Well-Being

ROSEMARY C. SARRI, PhD
University of Michigan

> *Many things we need can wait, the child cannot. Now is the time his bones are being formed, his blood is being made, his mind is being developed. To him we cannot say tomorrow, his name is today.*
> —*GABRIELA MISTRAL, Chilean poet*

A healthy, vigorous, enthusiastic, and well-educated youth population is essential to the vitality of any society, for today's children are the parents of tomorrow's families. But the myth of being a child-oriented society is only a myth. The social and economic policies implemented in the last two decades have had a profoundly negative effect on America's children. Today,

- One child in four lives in poverty and in a single-parent household.
- One in six lacks access to health care, while the rates of infant mortality and morbidity rates exceed those of other developed countries.
- School dropout and failure rates remain at crisis levels.
- Homicide and suicide are the leading causes of death among teenagers.
- A half million children are born to teen mothers annually.
- Youth experience the highest rates of unemployment.

- Crime, violence, homelessness, and substance abuse are continue to escalate in this population.

It is not surprising that young people manifest general attitudes of pessimism about the future. The costs of our negligence with respect to their needs are likely to be greater than those that might have resulted from a stock market crash, a major earthquake, or any similar event. Unfortunately, this society has permitted the status and well-being of children and adolescents to suffer significantly in recent years, and very few voices have been raised in opposition (National Commission on Children, 1991).

Now is an excellent time for action to change negligence into commitment. Federal and state legislatures are considering numerous proposals for significant social policy reform that, as written, will result in further deterioration of the well-being of our children. Bringing together interested citizens, practitioners, policy makers, academics, and youth to discuss those proposals is an excellent vehicle for developing an action agenda for the future. The achievement of positive results will require our best knowledge, skill, fortitude, perseverance and creativity, as well as cooperation with all other interested groups because resources are limited. Unless action is taken now, children tomorrow will experience a future with less opportunity and security than that which youth faced just two decades ago. Perhaps Jane Addams and Grace Abbott felt the same way at the beginning of the twentieth century when they undertook and successfully implemented major reforms such as the establishment of the child welfare system, the juvenile court, and the community center.

The Need for Change

There is growing interest in changing our present child and youth policies because most agree that they are not working and that the plight of young people is deteriorating (Dryfoos, 1990; Wollins, 1993). Not only are social workers and other human services personnel recommending change, but employers also have become concerned and fear that future workers, consumers, and taxpayers will be in jeopardy because they are undereducated and ill-prepared to participate effectively in a society that demands high levels of competence and training (U.S. Committee on Economic Development, 1987). (See Chapters 2 and 27.) Others recognize that the rapidly growing aged population will not be cared for adequately in the future unless children are prepared to become productive adults (See Chapters 12 and 13).

Increasingly, the federal government and other national bodies are arguing that state and local governments have the primary responsibility for child well-being. Such recommendations ignore the significant regional inequality of resources. Only the national government has the ability to effect major changes across the United States that will result in reduced inequality for all children. It is a responsibility that the nation must bear as a whole.

Public opinion surveys indicate that three out of four people think that problems affecting children and youth have gotten worse and that poverty, education, health care, neglect, and substance abuse all need to be addressed directly in our communities. What remains unclear today is what the public wants done about the problems because people are now unwilling to pay for the programs to improve the situation. The public needs to understand that improving our children's lives is a key element in a viable future.

Sociodemographic Trends

Major sociodemographic changes are underway in the United States and throughout the world that have significance for children's and youth policy (See Chapter 1). A UNICEF report (1994) identified the following major social issues affecting youth on a worldwide basis: poverty and lack of employment, rapid urbanization and migration in developing nations, the growth of diseases such as AIDS and tuberculosis, changes in life expectancy, health status, adolescent childbearing, marriage, the roles of women and family structure, and cross-national media that provide rapid communication of ideas, information, music, arts, and lifestyles to youth in various countries. Many of the youth problems of concern here are global concerns, thus requiring international cooperation.

In 1991 there were 63.6 million children living in 31 million households, or about half of all family households in the United States. Although this ratio is somewhat less than the 60 percent of families with children in 1970, the downward trend does not hold for African American, Hispanic, and Native American families, where nearly three out of four families have children. The latter families are likely to be somewhat larger and to have more preschool-aged children. This is reflected in the differences in median age groups among these groups, in immigration, and in different childbearing patterns (Anna Casey Foundation, 1994).

One in four children lives in single-parent households, with 97 percent of those households headed by women. Among white children 15 percent live in single-parent households, but among African American one in two children lives in a single-mother household. One in two marriages ends in divorce, and although divorces have declined slightly, the majority occur in families with children, and following divorce most children live with their mothers in lower standards of living and financial security than prior to the divorce. Nearly half (43 percent) of all children in single-mother families live below the poverty level versus 7 percent of children in two-parent households (U.S. Bureau of the Census, 1992). Eight out of ten of these women are in the labor force, and therefore their children require special supports merely because of fewer parental resources. However, these families are least likely to be able to pay for the supports that they require because of the low income of their mothers. The majority of all children 5 years of age or older live in a household in which both parents work, and that is nearly the case for families with infants (Hernandez, 1993).

Children are the poorest of all Americans, and what is particularly disturbing is that the depth of their poverty is becoming greater each year. Income inequality in the United States was at an all-time high in 1992 and is most evident in families with children compared with the other households (Shapiro & Barancik, 1992). From 1968 to 1990 increases in poverty progressively declined with age—increasing numbers of children and youth became poor, while poverty for those over 55 declined both absolutely and relatively, largely because of the Social Security benefits. As a maturing society there are increasing numbers of elderly persons requiring care by family members, usually women. (See

Chapter 13.) Caregiving of the dependent (both young and old) as a societal responsibility remains largely unexamined, in contrast to the attention that this problem is receiving in other industrial and postindustrial countries. Compared with other countries of the Western world, we have the highest child poverty rate, 80 percent higher than Canada and double the rate in Germany, Norway, and Sweden. Although we have Aid to Families with Dependent Children (AFDC) to alleviate the poverty of poor children, inflation-adjusted benefits have declined since 1970 and are so low that families are not brought up to the poverty level. Moreover, one-third of all poor families receive no welfare even when they areeligible.

Children are the group least likely to have health insurance. Declines in Medicaid coverage for poor children have left fewer than half with any care. (See Chapter 4.) The lack of immunization of children from infectious diseases exceeds that of many developing countries, and yet this problem is very easily resolved. Adolescent pregnancy is recognized as a serious problem, but the draconian punitive measures and abstinence-only programs that are being implemented in many states will not solve this problem. (See Chapter 18.) Adequate education on reproduction and sexuality is urgently needed along with school clinics if we are to achieve the low rates of adolescent childbearing found in most Western countries (Jones, 1986).

Youth are more likely to be victimized by violent crime and are also more likely to commit violent crime than other age groups. Homicide is the major cause of death among youth between the ages of 15 and 24, and it is far higher for minority than for white youth. Prothrow-Stith (1993) argues that it is destroying our teenage population in many cities. Youth gangs are found in large urban centers as well as in small towns throughout the country. Violent crime is nearly 16 times as high for persons under 25 as for those over 65 years. Youth are also abused in their own homes, both physically and sexually, at far higher rates than was thought possible a few decades ago.

The population of children under 18 years will not grow rapidly between 1995 and 2020, but the growth rate will vary substantially among minority children of color and whites. The United States is changing rapidly to a country in which minority-group children will constitute the majority child population early in the twenty-first century. (See Chapter 1.) This shift results from differences in the median age among the several groups, from immigration and differential childbearing. This social change is problematic because so many minority children are being reared today in serious poverty and therefore can be expected to face problems as adults. Particularly problematic is the educational experience of these youth. Present rates of functional illiteracy, expulsions, premature school leaving, and lack of adequate occupational training are unacceptable and continue to grow disproportionately for minority youth (Haveman, Wolfe, & Spaulding, 1991; Wilson, 1987). Because of the cost of postsecondary education and the decline in student loans, fewer of these youth enter college today than two decades ago.

What are the consequences of growing up poor for health, education, and a productive, satisfying adulthood? Being raised in poverty affects one's health, school performance, future employment, and emotional and family well-being. Poor children have more problems from infancy throughout their lives. Poverty is associated with family stress, violence, and abuse. The unemployment rate of high school dropouts is twice that of graduates. Between 1973 and 1980 earnings of young African-American males who had not finished high school fell by 62 percent, and it continues to decline.

Since 1970 there have been fundamental changes in the U.S. economy that have reduced traditional job opportunities and earnings, especially for young workers and in manufacturing. Six million new jobs are forecast for highly skilled occupations for the next decade, compared with only about 1 million in low-skill occupations. Job losses in manufacturing are likely to continue, and even service industries will experience slow growth or stability. It is expected that 50 percent of adult workers today will change their occupations in the next 10 years with much of the shift downward from the worker's perspective.

The decline in the postsecondary education of minorities will have negative consequences for many occupations but especially in social work and other helping professions who desire to provide role models for students and clientele. It is unlikely that existing affirmative action policies will be effective in resolving this problem.

Lastly, the conditions and communities in which children and youth reside today need to be addressed. Lack of affordable housing is a major problem for families with children, and it is increasingly the major cause of their homelessness. The 1994 Kids Count Report documents that 4 million children live in severely distressed neighborhoods characterized by high poverty, single-mother households, high rates of school dropping out, unemployment, violence, and reliance on welfare as a major source of income (Anna Casey Foundation, 1994).

The picture of the sociodemographic characteristics of children and youth at the end of the twentieth century is not a happy one, but we can solve these problems if we wish to do so. Another major policy area needs to be addressed before we consider our agenda for the social transformation that is necessary to resolve the problems facing our children today: care outside the family in institutions and foster care. These are rapidly growing problems with long-term consequences.

Out-of-Home Care of Children and Youth

More than 600,000 children and youth reside in institutions or in foster care in the United States (Lindsey, 1994). The majority are poor, male, and minority youth, and most are under the age of 5 or between 13 and 18 years of age. Reports of abuse and neglect of children continue to mushroom, but little is done to attempt to resolve the problems that bring children into care. (See Chapter 15.) These numbers have increased quite dramatically in recent years despite federal and state legislation that was supposed to reduce the numbers in care. Children often drift in care for years because there is little effort directed toward helping parents or other kin to be able to have their children return home. When youth reach older adolescence, foster care and transition to independent living may be particularly problematic. The difficulty arises from the inadequacy of the transition programs and failure to recognize how difficult it is to live in this society with no family or resources. There are reports from homeless shelters and substance abuse programs that many of their clients are youth for whom the foster care system has failed or is failing.

Nearly 360,000 youth are institutionalized in the United States on any given day in all types of correctional residential facilities (Barton, 1995). Approximately five out of six are young men, the vast majority of whom are in prisons, jails, or juvenile correctional facilities. Two-thirds of the young men are minority youth, often incarcerated with lower risk scores than white youth. Many young persons convicted of violent crimes find themselves committed to prison for the rest of their natural lives.

About 90,000 young persons are in mental hospitals, and here too African Americans and Hispanics, especially males, are disproportionately represented among all the institutionalized. There continues to be a remarkable growth in the number of youth in private residential facilities, especially those providing long-term secure care for substance abuse and incorrigibility from the parents' perspective. There is minimal monitoring or evaluation of the latter types of programs, which primarily serve middle-class families who can afford this very expensive care or have insurance coverage for it.

A Framework for Conceptualizing Youth and Social Policy Responses

There is a tendency today to view social policy for youth only in terms of problems that need to be corrected, or as a means to demonstrate that something is being done to alleviate problematic behavior as defined by adults. Drury and Jamrozik (1985) identified six perceptions of youth, each of which generates different policy responses. A modified version of their framework, adapted to the United States, will now be described.

First, there is a widespread perception of youth as a self-contained social group with homogeneous needs and interests. Along with this perception is the view that they exist outside the mainstream society. Such a perception leads to universalistic policy solutions as in public education, health care, income support, and so forth. However, as is well known today, even public education is not offered universally at the same level, because not all students have the same needs and interests. In the past decade, there has been a decline in support for universalistic policies and programs as a part of the more conservative approach toward governmental intervention. (See Chapter 24.)

Second, if youth are perceived only as in a time of transition, then policy and programs facilitate a smooth transition to adult social roles. It is assumed that all youth will have essentially the same normal developmental pattern with minor fluctuations during adolescence. Again, this assumption is highly questionable, given the knowledge that we have about major inequalities among youth and about the differences in transition from youth to adulthood.

The third perception of youth—that it is a problem group—is undoubtedly the most common perception today. In the perceptions of adults, youth are a problem not only to and for themselves but also for the society generally. The current responses to youth unemployment, substance abuse, and school failure all reflect this perspective. We tend to have ad hoc short-term solutions in order to minimize up-front costs to the "angry taxpayer."

Youth are also viewed as a threat to the social stability of the society. Current concerns about delinquency, youth violence, teen pregnancy, and dropping out of school all reflect this perspective (National Research Council, 1993). The policy responses are defined in terms of social control through the juvenile court and corrections system and in supervised "socially useful" activities such as community restitution or service.

When youth are perceived as a disadvantaged group because of poverty, physical or mental disabilities, or racism, policy solutions in the form of remedial measures to improve their equal opportunity or competitive strength are enacted. However, today strong support for affirmative action or the achievement of equality in outcomes for youth is lacking throughout the country.

Lastly, youth can be viewed as a vehicle for social change—a perspective that has been flirted with at times but never taken seriously. If it were, then policy measures to increase the involvement of young people in all levels of decision making would be required (Medoff & Sklar, 1994). This type of involvement would include youths' participation in decisions that affect them and their communities. The current situation, in which children and youth are the population in the society at greatest risk for poverty, illness, and lack of opportunity, may well be a reflection of their lack of participation in decisions affecting their basic well-being.

This framework does not propose any one solution to the situations facing youth today; it provides a way of thinking about social issues and policy that is more differentiated and specific. Given current demographic trends it would appear that the framework could be useful now and in the future. However, it appears that the main thrust of social policy affecting children, youth, and their families today is one of minimal intervention—the family is a private institution that is best left alone. Using this rationale as a disguise, government can ignore its societal responsibility for children. The only purpose for governmental intervention then is social control when there are basic problems threatening the society. The Children Act in Britain was passed in 1989 and is already demonstrating that far more can be achieved when the state and the family collaborate in the rearing of children (Packman & Jordan, 1991).

Systems of Social Control

Rather than functioning as systems to enhance the well-being and opportunity structures for youth, our systems of child welfare, juvenile justice, and mental health emphasize social control, the allocation of blame or fault on parents, and the punishment of parties rather than the provision of material and nonmaterial support and assistance. Control of critical decision making has moved to judicial and administrative bodies rather than remaining with the family and community (Mason & Gambrill, 1994). Intervention technologies emphasize individual rather than communal solutions. Many youth problems are those of growing up in a complex urban society, but we are increasingly criminalizing these problems with negative consequences. States are routinely passing legislation to permit the waiver of youth as young as 12 years for trial as adults and commitment to prison for life. The rate of waivers is also increasing twice as fast for minority youth as for others (McNeece, 1994).

How can we break out of the system of more and more elaborate systems of social control even when they are said to be in the interests of treatment? A developmental perspective can be the basis for more constructive policy and practice. The developmental approach regards much crime and deviance of young people as transient and inextricably part of the process of growing up. Instead of *exclusion,* the developmental approach seeks *absorption* and fortifies the role of the home and the school. If either or both of those are inadequate or unsatisfactory to change and improve them as is needed, an institutional approach may be required.

The developmental approach has remained largely unarticulated because it rarely is considered in policy terms. There are four basic elements to the developmental approach:

1. The principal sources of support and control for young people are invested in the home and the school.
2. When formal intervention is invoked this should, to every possible extent, be focused primarily on enhancing the strengths of home and school; the length of that intervention should be definite, not indeterminate.
3. Only in the most exceptional cases should formal intervention separate a young person from developmental institutions such as the family, and any period of separation should be kept to the minimum required for other purposes.
4. Formal interventions, especially in the case of incarceration, are disruptive in two crucial senses. First, the normal growth and development of the young person is threatened. Second, the capacity for developmental institutions to be effective is weakened.

The developmental approach does not recommend ignoring or taking no action. Instead, it insists that intervention seek to be primarily the responsibility of those institutions with a commitment to normalization and mainstreaming for youth.

What Can We Do?

There are many policy and program alternatives that will enhance the well-being of all our youth. Moreover, these alternatives will be far more effective and less costly than present strategies of large-scale institutionalization and other forms of out-of-home care.

1. Community services, education, primary prevention and care, and enhanced youth opportunity for access to legitimate adult roles deserve greater priority and resources. "Nurturing the natural" supports the strength of the youth, their family, and the community but does not overwhelm them. It means championing the social links of family, neighborhood, church, school, clubs, and other associations (Carnegie Council on Adolescent Development, 1993).

2. Advocate for universal programs of health care, child care, children's allowances, low-cost postsecondary education, youth employment, and service. Such programs must be primarily federally funded if inequality is to be reduced and efficiency achieved. Year-round elementary and secondary education programs are overdue, given the fact that both women and men are expected to be employed outside the home.

3. A comprehensive program to reduce poverty is also long overdue. We have the resources and simply cannot afford not to do so. It is time for a much more objective rather than ideological analysis of how this goal can be accomplished. We cannot afford to lose one-third of our youth population.

4. Coalitions of churches, service clubs, social agencies, and professional organizations must play leadership roles to see that conditions of children's well-being prevail. Youth themselves need to be invited, encouraged, and supported to participate in these community organization efforts. We see how effective older Americans are today, so we might well adopt their strategy. The proposal for a Younger Americans Act is an step toward this goal.

5. Work toward the closing of all large, closed institutions and utilize those resources for community-based care and education, youth employment, health care, and related programs. It is not a question of more resources but rather the redistribution of resources. Far more is spent on out-of-home care than for care of children by parents in their own homes.

6. The United States is a multicultural society strengthened by the variety of its people. We must create a moral climate in which children can develop in this society, one that includes self-respect and respect for others, caring for self and others, rejection of violence, and valuation of citizenship in a democratic society.

7. Strengthen developmental institutions for youth, especially the family, school, community services, and employment. The creation of a AmeriCorps and work apprenticeship programs are clearly in the national interest if the majority of adolescent youth are to be helped to become effective adults in a democratic society. The models of the founder of the Children's Bureau, Grace Abbott, were not to remove children from the community but rather to try to improve their well-being in their families in the community.

The groundwork for child welfare in this country was laid by great reformers such as Jane Addams, Florence Kelly, and Grace Abbott. Youth workers today might follow the admonition in Abbott's book, *The Spirit of Youth and the City Streets:*

> We may either smother the divine fire of youth or we may feed it. We may either stand stupidly staring as it sinks into a murky fire of crime and flares into the intermittent blaze of folly, or we may tend it into a lambent flame with power to make clean and bright our dingy city streets. (1909, p. 211)

References

Abbott, G. (1909). *The spirit of youth.* Chicago: University of Chicago Press.

Anna Casey Foundation. (1994). *Kids count data book: State profiles of child well-being.* Greenwich, CT: Author.

Barton, W. (1995). Juvenile corrections. In R. Edwards (Ed.), *Encyclopedia of social work* (pp. 1563–1577). Washington, DC: National Association of Social Work.

Carnegie Council on Adolescent Development. (1993). *A matter of time: Risk and opportunity in non-school hours.* New York: Carnegie Foundation.

Drury, S., & Jamrozik, A. (1985). Conceptual issues of relevance to social policy and services for young people. In A. Jamrozik (Ed.), *Issues in social welfare* (pp. 22–39). Kensington, NSW, Australia: Social Welfare Research Centre, University of New South Wales.

Dryfoos, J. (1990). *Adolescents at risk: Prevalence and prevention.* New York: Oxford University Press.

Haveman, R., Wolfe, E., & Spaulding, J. (1991). Child based events and circumstances influencing high school completion, *Demography, 28*(1), 133–157

Hernandez, D. (1993). *America's children: Resources from family, government and the economy.* New York: Russell Sage Foundation.

Jones, E. F. (1986). *Teenage pregnancy in industrialized countries.* New Haven, CT: Yale University Press.

Lindsey, D. (1994). *The welfare of children.* New York: Oxford University Press.

Mason, M., & Gambrill, E. (1994). *Debating children's lives: Current controversies on children and adolescents.* Thousand Oaks, CA: Sage.

McNeece, C. (1994). National trends in offenses and case dispositions. In A. Roberts (Ed.), *Critical issues in crime and justice* (pp. 157–170). Thousand Oaks, CA: Sage.

Medoff, P., & Sklar, H. (1994). *Streets of hope: The fall and rise of an urban neighborhood.* Boston: South End Press.

National Commission on Children. (1991). *Beyond rhetoric: A new American agenda for children and families.* Washington, DC: U.S. Government Printing Office.

National Research Council. (1993). *Losing generation: Adolescents in high-risk settings.* Washington, DC: National Academy Press.

Packman, J., & Jordan, B. (1991). The Children Act: Looking forward, looking back. *British Journal of Social Work. 21,* 315–327.

Prothrow-Stith, D. (1993). *Deadly consequences.* New York:Harper.

Shapiro, I., & Barancik, S. (1992). *Where have all the dollars gone? A state-by-state analysis of income disparities over the 1980s.* Washington, DC: Center on Budget and Policy Priorities.

UNICEF. (1994). *Status of the world's children.* New York: Oxford University Press.

U.S. Bureau of the Census. (1992). *Money income and poverty status of persons and families in the United States.* Current Population Reports, Series P-60, No.160, 1993. Washington, DC: U.S. Government Printing Office.

U.S. Committee on Economic Development. (1987). *Youth and the future.* New York: Author.

Wilson, W. J. (1987). *The truly disadvantaged.* Chicago: University of Chicago Press.

Wollins, R. (Ed.). (1993). *Children at risk in America: History, concepts and public policy.* Albany, NY: SUNY Press.

Chapter *15*

Foster Care Trends and Issues

CREASIE FINNEY HAIRSTON, PhD
University of Illinois

Current Trends

The number of children living outside their own homes and under the protective custody of the state is large and has grown continuously since the mid-1980s. At the end of the 1992 fiscal year there were 442,000 children in foster care, also called substitute care, with an estimated 659,000 who had spent some time in care during the year (Lewit, 1993). This large and growing population exists despite the 1980 Child Welfare and Adoption Assistance Act, which was enacted to prevent the removal of children from their homes except when absolutely necessary and to ensure permanent living arrangements for children in foster care.

Child welfare officials note that a mix of social, economic, and cultural forces have affected the number of children in foster care. Among these are rising rates of family and child poverty, transformations in the domestic labor market, numerous health care crises, greater numbers of teen pregnancies, and the AIDS and substance abuse epidemics (*Federal Register,* June 27, 1994).

Increased reporting of suspected cases of child abuse and neglect and administrative policies and procedures governing child welfare day-to-day decisions and practices have also contributed to the growing foster care population. Federal-level funding streams, for example, provide open-ended matching funds for out-of-home placements for children but more restrictive funding for services to prevent placement and reunify separated families. Consequently, services to help parents who are at risk of abuse and neglect to keep chil-

151

dren safely in their own homes are minimal, and a family orientation that supports family reunification and empowerment is noticeably absent. Also not highly visible in public child welfare agencies are significant numbers of professionally trained social work staff to design, direct, and implement a conceptually sound and empirically validated system of family-focused child welfare services.

The growth in the number of families who are unable or unwilling to protect and nurture their children without support can be expected to continue beyond the year 2000. The social, health, and economic problems that were at the root of the tremendous influx of children into foster care in the late 1980s and early 1990s have not abated and in some instances will become more intense. The increase in HIV/AIDS among poor women of color, many of whom are young mothers of dependent children, for example, will increase the number of children who need care during the illness of their mother and who will be orphaned upon her death. Similar increases in the number of HIV and drug-exposed infants and young children will increase the number of children requiring special care outside their homes and protective child welfare services.

New problems and changing social norms and societal expectations will also affect child welfare caseloads in the year 2000 and beyond. Criminal justice legislation passed in the 1990s, including mandatory sentences for drug-related crimes, life sentences for criminals convicted for a third offense, and harsher punishment for women offenders, will lead not only to a prison population in the millions but also to record numbers of children entering the child welfare system. The majority of men and women entering the prison population are poor persons of color who are parents of dependent children (Harlow, 1994), and many of their children will grow up while their parents are in prison. Most of the women, who are and will be incarcerated under these new laws and stricter penalties, are the sole caretakers of their children at the time of their arrest (Bloom & Steinhart, 1993; Hairston, 1991), and many of their children will become wards of the state.

Punitive welfare policies will also affect the number of children in the child welfare system. For example, families that have used up their 2 years of eligibility for welfare benefits and have no source of income will be homeless and have no means of supporting their children. They will be placed in the position of abandoning their children, voluntarily surrendering their parental rights, or facing charges of child neglect. The laws that reduce already inadequate welfare benefits for families on welfare who have more children or fail to increase welfare benefits to support additional children will also render many families unable to provide adequate care for their children.

By the year 2000 experiments proposed in 1995 and 1996 to address other societal problems such as teenage pregnancy, maternal drug abuse, and youth violence by taking children from their mothers or denying mothers welfare benefits will have been enacted, thereby bringing more children into substitute care. Changing societal norms about children's exposure to family violence as a form of endangerment or neglect will also bring many children who witness violence into the child welfare system, although they may not have been physically abused themselves. Because poor families experiencing violence are the ones more likely to be involved in criminal justice processing, they are the ones more likely to have their children removed from their homes as well.

Current Initiatives

In response to the growing foster care population and service demands, the limited success in achieving the goals and objectives of the Child Welfare Adoption and Assistance Act, and the child welfare systems' failure in effectively serving the most vulnerable families, several federal initiatives have been undertaken to reform the child welfare system. Foremost among these is the passage of legislation and the allocation of funding beginning in fiscal year 1994 for states and Native American tribes to develop and carry out a comprehensive 5-year plan for providing a continuum of integrated, culturally relevant, family-focused services to children and their families. This family support and preservation legislation provides modest funding to expand community-based prevention and early intervention activities, and to make changes in the child welfare system and the way services are delivered.

A second initiative is the funding in 1995 of several national child welfare resource centers for up to 5 years to strengthen publicly administered or supported child welfare agencies' capacity to develop and improve the quality and effectiveness of child welfare services. One of these centers, the National Resource Center for Permanency Planning, is charged specifically with helping agencies develop and implement high-quality foster family and residential care for children who must be removed from their families. One of the center's major tasks is to promote agencies' reconceptualization of foster care as a family-focused, community-based service through services to birth and foster care families, and collaboration with community educational, health, and social services agencies.

The third initiative is the development of the Adoption and Foster Care Analysis and Reporting System and the Automated Child Welfare Information System. Expected to be operative by fiscal year 1995, these information systems will make it possible to track and manage the placement of individual children and will provide uniform aggregate data on foster care from state to state. Currently, information as basic as how many children are in foster care must be estimated. Performance and outcome measures are seldom available, and the database to guide policy and practice is woefully inadequate.

The fourth initiative involves partnerships between schools of social work and public child welfare agencies. The purpose of these partnerships is to create interest among social work students in public social services careers and encourage and provide incentives for child welfare agency staff to return to school to obtain BSW and MSW degrees. They also focus on providing inservice training for child welfare staff and revising social work curricula to reflect the needs of families and children served by public agencies and contemporary child welfare policies and services. Some limited attention is also given to research on foster care and the evaluation of permanency planning programs. Funding for these different efforts is provided primarily by federal training and curriculum development grants. Private foundation grants and state monies also provide some support.

These federal initiatives are important strategies for addressing issues of quality and provide a strong context for change and for shaping the future direction of child welfare practice well into the next century. They do not, however, mandate or prescribe the future structural arrangements for providing out-of-home care for children. There are emerging developments, however, that provide strong indications for what these structural arrangements will be.

Future Foster Care Models

First of all, we can expect family foster care homes to continue to be considered a desirable living arrangement for children who must be removed from their own homes. However, foster care by nonrelatives, particularly for children of color, will not be the dominant form of substitute care. Recruitment and retention of family foster homes will continue to be difficult and will be exacerbated by new demands and requirements of foster parents. Continuing problems for recruitment will be low pay, licensure standards (such as apartment size and physical condition), and the more complex health and behavioral problems of children and youth in foster care and the subsequent need for foster parents with more specialized training. New expectations involving foster families' relationships with birth parents and provision of more than custodial care for children in foster homes will cause some foster parents to resign as caregivers and some potential parents to choose not to apply. Some persons who have sympathy for abused or neglected children, for instance, would be uncomfortable if they had to have contact or be involved with mothers known to have criminal histories or to be drug addicts. In other cases racial and religious differences, cultural bias and insensitivity, or geographical location of the foster parents' home (for example, having a home in a rural county when the need is in big cities) will mitigate against placement of children.

Increasingly, nonrelative family foster care homes will be reserved for special intensive short-term use or for children with specific needs, such as drug-exposed infants. Respite care, day care, support groups, and orientation and training will be provided as basic services to help retain these foster parents and to help them carry out their demanding roles. In addition, innovations involving incentives to retain experienced and valued foster parents, such as hiring foster parents as salaried agency staff and providing career ladders with differential job expectations and pay, will be implemented.

In some areas of the country, primarily large cities, relative foster care, also known as kinship care, will be the major form of family foster care. This trend is already in evidence, as most of the recent growth in foster care in cities, such as New York and Chicago, can be accounted for by the rise in the number of relative foster care homes, particularly among African Americans (Lewit, 1993). Reconceptualization of foster care as a family-oriented service and efforts to minimize disruptions in children's lives will result in expanded use of placements with relatives. Formal agency placements of children with relatives will be driven primarily by the limited number of available nonrelative foster parents and by relatives' reluctance to take on the state's protective responsibility without financial support. Both economic factors and increased sophistication about foster care benefits have led poor African American families who might have previously cared for kin as a moral obligation to refuse to do so when monies are being paid readily to more financially able nonrelatives for the same services.

Kinship care is different, however, from nonrelative foster care, and it is not clear that foster care policies are relevant to kinship care. Questions have been raised about whether kinship care is a form of family preservation designed to keep children within their extended family network, and whether "return home" or "adoption" are appropriate goals of service, because a child in kinship care is "already home" (Gleeson & Philbin, 1994). The response to these pertinent policy issues will affect the level of benefits, the focus and goals of service for individual families, and the type of needed and required social work intervention for a significant portion of the foster care caseload. Concerns about costs will also direct kinship care. Children remain in kinship care for longer periods of time than in nonrelative foster care (Government Accounting Office, 1993), and many relative caregivers will be poor and unable to meet licensure standards. Future policies and agency practices will therefore address cost containment. Different (lower) benefit levels or pay for relative foster homes than nonrelative homes will be provided. The fact that foster care payments are for the care of the children and that care may be the same in relative and nonrelative homes will be overlooked. Lower benefits will be rationalized on the basis of relatives' lack of formal foster parent training, lower licensure standards, and different job or care requirements. Some states will also argue that relatives have a legal obligation to take care of dependent kin.

Orphanages will be reinstituted as a standard part of the substitute care system for children. They will be used primarily for children whose parents are dead or incarcerated, children whose parents are deemed permanently unfit, and children and youth at risk of social behavior that would be too unruly for families to handle. Orphanages will become widespread, even given the family-focused orientation of the family support and family preservation legislation and social work support for maintaining children in their own homes, when this can be done safely. Highly visible cases of poor children who are abused or neglected, of young mothers on welfare having more children while on welfare, and of behavioral problems (such as delinquency, drug use, and gangs) among youth residing in poor families have been instrumental in helping vocal and powerful politicians and, in some instances, child advocates gain public support for the termination of parental rights of certain groups of parents and the placement of their children in orphanages.

Justifications for orphanages vary. Some people believe that orphanages located in rural areas will provide more wholesome and healthy environments for children than their rat-infested inner-city apartments and neighborhoods. Others are more focused on ways to punish parents even if it means also punishing children. Still others believe that family preservation and attempts to reunify children with parents who have abused or neglected them is a misguided notion being pushed by social workers and that orphanages, in contrast to these families, at least, offer children a stable, safe living arrangement.

Because residential care is expensive, federal and state funding to support services beyond basic custodial care for the children placed in orphanages is highly improbable. It is also not likely, given all the other pressing priorities, that state child welfare offices will establish, without concerted effort and tremendous external pressure, the necessary monitoring, compliance, child placement, and service support systems to ensure that these new forms of substitute care provide high-quality care. Under these situations many poor, inner-city children of color will grow up in substandard, custodial institutions far removed from their families and, in some cases, communities. Although these facilities may provide a place for a child to live for a prolonged period of time, their high turnover in staff and bureaucratic policies and operating procedures will hardly constitute a stable, wholesome living environment.

It is clear that a strong cultural identity; warm, stable adult relationships; and a supportive family environment and family connections are important to the healthy development of children. It is also clear that, historically, orphanages in the United States have failed to provide these critical elements and have also often been harsh and work-focused, rather then child-oriented, environments (Costin & Rapp, 1984). Given these factors, social workers should seek through lobbying and public education to slow the growth of orphanages as homes and early jails for poor, dependent children and youth.

Future Problems

Problems facing the child welfare system and its use of foster care in the 2000s will be similar to those found in the criminal justice system in the 1990s. Just as the correctional system does not have enough prison beds to accommodate all the persons charged with crimes, the child welfare system will not have sufficient foster care facilities to accommodate all the children in families where there is substantiated neglect or abuse or children defined by public policy to be at risk. Nor will it be possible to remove all maltreated children from their parents' homes, even with the building of orphanages, the conversion of public housing units to boarding schools for youth in care, and the use of licensed relative homes.

Priority and funding must be given to finding alternatives to foster care that ensure the physical safety and emotional security of children. Neither poverty, incarceration, nor bearing children out of wedlock deems mothers or fathers to be unfit parents. Public policies that make villains out of parents in these situations will punish parents, but they will just as surely punish children. In the absence of safe, nurturing, and individualized placements for children, many children will be worse off as wards of the state. The needless separation of parents and children can be averted by enacting measures that enable many parents to take care of their own children while engaging in activities to improve their life chances and their children's well-being. In some instances this will mean providing community-based residential facilities wherein parents and children live together in supervised situations. This option might be the case for nonviolent criminal offenders. In others, teaming young parents with older neighborhood mentors or helpers who are available on an on-call basis to provide time-outs from the children, involvement in family activities, and guidance in childrearing will present an effective, less intrusive option. In still others, concrete assistance such as permanent housing, jobs that pay above the poverty level and have benefits, and financial subsidies will prevent placement.

Providing all children who must be removed from their homes because of serious abuse or neglect and their families the individualized attention, intensive case management, high-quality treatment intervention, and supportive services needed to attain and sustain reunification and healthy child development and family empowerment will, likewise, be extremely difficult. Within foster care the highest priority will, therefore, be given to developing and testing model service protocols that provide different levels of social work intervention for children and their fathers and mothers in different situations. The preferred service model for families more at risk of foster care recidivism may be intensive casework intervention involving birth mothers and fathers, foster parents, and children. In stable, relative foster care homes, periodic, planned monitoring, with caseworker help available as requested, may be an appropriate service approach.

Limited resources, the expanding foster care population, and the more difficult problems of families and children will dictate that attention be directed toward determining what interventions work best with what types of children and families, and how to use those interventions differentially. Accordingly, classification systems that define levels of monitoring and types of intervention will be used to place children and to group children and families for service programs. Recruitment of professionally trained graduate-level social work staff and the involvement of social work education programs in training and research will facilitate the design and management of these case classification systems and program models. Retention of graduate-level social workers in any great numbers will not occur, however, if the goal of striking a balance between large caseloads, complex cases, and high-quality services is not achieved. Retention will also be threatened if social workers are constantly subjected to harsh criticism with no defense and little recognition of their accomplishments. These social workers, having other more gratifying and supportive options for employment, will choose to exit the system, thereby rendering the professionalization efforts of the 1990s null and void.

Future Vision of Foster Care

Achievement of a vision of foster care as one component of a continuum of high-quality, effective, and caring services for children and their families will require a tremendous infusion of resources and new ideas into the child welfare system. It will also require a highly educated and trained cadre of experienced staff at all levels of child welfare organizations; stability of leadership and clearness of vision at the highest federal and state administrative and policy-making levels; and serious, focused national research and evaluation programs to guide policies and service programs.

Social workers must provide leadership for this vision even in the midst of public leaders who push in another direction. Highly visible, organized programs of advocacy for humane federal and state public policies that strengthen rather than punish families with problems and mobilization of voter support for compassionate and competent public officials are important strategies in this endeavor. Social workers should be involved in all aspects of child welfare and should be at the forefront in defining the situations wherein different forms of care such as orphanages represent the most appropriate homes for children. They should be key actors in setting the standards and principles to guide the operations of the full range of foster care options, and in educating and training agency administrators and service providers. The efforts to promote a high-quality foster care system through legislation and standards need to be as strong and as focused as the work undertaken to promote social work certification for clinical practice in the 1980s.

Fundamental to the achievement of this vision, as well, is the need for social workers to take ownership of and responsibility for workplace reform in public social services. Although future structural arrangements may include significant private agency involvement, the care of children who are wards of the state remains a public responsibility. Administrative regulations, agency policies and procedures, worker knowledge and skill, and workplace practices are among the major determinants of foster care outcomes. In the absence of conceptually sound and empirically validated service models and a commitment to excellence, a system that works for children in need of protection and their families is not likely to develop. Foster care can be different and better in the year 2000 and beyond if those who care enough work to make it better.

References

Bloom, B., & Steinhart, D. (1993). *Why punish the children? A reappraisal of the children of incarcerated mothers in America.* California: National Council on Crime and Delinquency.

Costin, L.B., & Rapp, C.A. (1984). *Child welfare policies and practices.* New York: McGraw-Hill.

Federal Register (June 27, 1994), *59*(122), 32964–32990. Washington, DC: U.S. Department of Health and Human Services.

Gleeson, J.P., & Philbin, C. (1994). *Current practice in kinship care: Supervisors' perspectives.* Chicago: Jane Addams Center for Social Policy and Research and Jane Addams College of Social Work.

Government Accounting Office. (1993). *Foster care: Services to prevent out-of-home placements are limited by funding barriers.* Report to the Chairman, Subcommittee on Oversight of Government Management, Committee on Governmental Affairs, U.S. Senate. Washington, DC: U.S. General Accounting Office.

Hairston, C.F. (1991, Summer). Mothers in jail: Parent-child separation and jail visitation. *AFFILIA: Journal of Women and Social Work, 6*(2), 9–27.

Harlow, C. (1994). *Comparing federal and state prison Inmates, 1991.* Washington, DC: Bureau of Justice Statistics.

Lewit, E. (1993). Children in foster care. *The Future of Children: Home Visiting, 3*(3), 192–199.

Chapter 16

The Single Greatest Health Threat to Women

Their Partners

PAULA S. NURIUS, PhD, MARIAN HILFRINK, MSW,
and ROSEMARY RIFINO, MSW
University of Washington

Partner violence continues to be the single biggest cause of injury to reproductive-age women in the United States (Novello, Rosenberg, Saltzman, & Shosky, 1992). Each year millions of women are beaten or terrorized by their husbands or lovers (Straus & Gelles, 1990; U.S. Department of Justice, 1994); more women are injured by partner abuse than the total from accidents, muggings, and cancer deaths *combined* (U.S. Senate Judiciary Committee, 1992; Stark & Flitcraft, 1988). Prevalence studies indicate that between 14 and 25 percent of adult women experience rape or sexual assault (Koss, 1993, for a review) and that up to 80 percent of women experience some form of sexual aggression, perpetrated primarily by someone they know such as a dating partner (Koss, 1988; Muehlenhard & Linton, 1987). The incidence of violence against women by their partners is so huge that as a disease it would be recognized as constituting epidemic proportions; as a war it would galvanize a state of national alarm. Yet, as Senator Joseph Biden noted, "when it comes to the 3 to 4 million women who are victimized by violence each year, the alarm bells ring

The authors would like to acknowledge the highly interactive collaborative process among us as a writing team and the helpful contributions of both field and academic colleagues Carole Antoncich, Nancy Ashley, Leslie Asplund, Judith Clegg, Sheila Hargesheimer, Valli Kanuha, and Jill Morton.

softly" (Biden, 1993, p. 1059). It is pathetic but true that U.S. society maintains three times as many animal shelters as it does battered women's shelters (McCarthy, 1991); that high school and college females see sexual harassment, coercion, and possible assault as one of the costs of obtaining an education.

Evidence has repeatedly revealed that there is no typical woman who will be the victim of partner violence: It doesn't only happen to women different from those you know. Although some women may be particularly vulnerable due to personal or social conditions that marginalize or isolate them (such as not speaking English, homelessness, prostitution, or connection to the military), the risk crosses virtually all lines of race/ethnicity, socioeconomic status, region, religion, abledness, and sexual orientation.

Ironically, worry about *random* societal violence has moved to the forefront of public attention. The media informs us daily of the increase in assaults, robberies, gang violence, and murders. Some individuals respond by choosing to carry weapons or to purchase alarm systems; others become more acutely aware of safety in planning their activities. Our payroll tax deductions are used to pay for hospitals, police, prisons and correctional centers, to mention only a few monetary costs related to societal violence.

But is arbitrary violence truly the looming danger to us all that it seems to be? Not if you are a child or a woman. Women and children are certainly well represented among those killed and injured in the senseless acts of violence seen on the evening news (drive-by shootings, dramatic assault weapon attacks in public settings, and the like). But the bitter truth—one rarely seen in political speeches or funding rationales—is that it is not the stranger in the shadows that represents the greatest threat to women's physical and mental health and safety, but those (predominantly men) with whom she has formed relationships. Current evidence suggests that the risk of random violence is on the decline and is lower than the public's perception of their risk. Unfortunately, the opposite appears to be true about partner violence: women are at far greater risk than the public believes, and we have yet to come anywhere close to curbing this risk adequately.

Given the limits of space, attention here will be limited to partner violence. Given the magnitude of threat, damage, problems related to entrapment, and the sociopolitical realities of society today (and tomorrow), the focus here is on the endemic problem of women as the targets of control, derision, and violence by those most intimately related to them—their dates, boyfriends/courtship partners, lovers, husbands/life partners—and on future issues that social work needs to prepare itself to address. However, many of the scenarios and suggestions offered here can be usefully applied to social work's role in curbing all societal violence, and in starting where the client is—whatever the age, gender, race, religion, sexual orientation, or ability status of the client.

Brokers, Bridgers, Advocates, Organizers—Social Workers' Many Opportunities to Be Part of the Solution

Whose responsibility is all this? Aren't there now legions of specialists in areas such as domestic violence, date rape, and sexual harassment that are taking care of this problem? Yes and no. There have indeed been important and significant strides made in the past three decades toward better understanding and countering such forms of violence against women. Yet, given the magnitude of the need, the impediments and controversies that must be grappled with, and the largely hidden nature of the problem, the simple reality is that the majority of women in this country continue to experience one or more forms of violence by a partner. It is important to keep in mind that the picture that typically comes to mind of partner abuse is that of physical violence between a married couple. In reality, partner violence and control is manifest across the developmental life span of relationships (among teens and elders as well as young and middle-aged adults) and in wide-ranging forms. For many women, the scars from sexual violation, from the emotional trauma of repeated betrayal and terrorization, and from the psychological consequences of derision and assaults on one's basic worth by a partner who knows how to personalize this abuse for maximum pain are as injurious as the beatings, if not more so.

In addition, violence by a partner is still experienced by many as confusing, demoralizing, and shameful. Few women immediately and decisively recognize the problem for what it is and seek out help from service providers with specialized training related to partner violence. Moreover, most social service systems and individual workers are ill-prepared to offer the kind of assistance needed. Consider the many places and ways in which endangered and abused women are likely to reach out for help—to medical and dental services for routine as well as injury-related care; to school or family service counselors to help with their children's problems; to religious institutions; to housing, vocational, or public assistance workers to meet economic needs; to police and criminal justice services for protection—virtually the whole spectrum of human services. The good news is that social workers' presence across this spectrum of service providers and fields of practice provides a vast array of conduits and opportunities in which to seek out and extend assistance. All social workers are encountering endangered and abused women in their work worlds whether they realize it or not. Some may acquire the preparation needed to serve as advocates, organizers, and specialized service providers. Others may play less intensive but no less important roles as brokers and bridgers—assisting women in recognizing their need and connecting up with the local resources that would be most helpful to them.

We are not saying that this is easy. This is an intensely personal, complex, and politicized social problem, and one with limited and conflicting legal mandates and protections (contrast this with the legal requirements of social workers to intervene on the behalf of abused or endangered children and elders; similar behaviors against wives often carry no such mandates—including marital rape). If nothing else, we hope you end this chapter understanding the vital opportunity that you as a social worker have to make a significant difference, and take with you a spirit of creative commitment to find ways to actualize this opportunity. Following is a look at the impact and presence of partner violence across several domains of social welfare, followed by attention to future directions for practice, policy, and research.

Impact of the Problem: Today and Tomorrow

So you are not a violence specialist and you wonder how much partner violence will really affect you as a citizen and a social work practitioner. That is a reasonable question. Everyone has limited time and energy and must prioritize. Thus, before moving to considering future *responses,* we will draw on current realities to lay out a picture of the challenges and costs that lay ahead.

The costs and effects of violence against women are not borne solely by the individual victims. If you are in health/medical social work, it's your problem. It is estimated that 20 to 25 percent of all hospital emergency room visits, 50 percent of all injuries presented by women, and 25 percent of suicide attempts stem from domestic violence (and this does not take into account dating and courtship aggression). The high medical costs associated with treating such injuries is growing steadily and poses serious questions in the face of health care reform and the availability of health care personnel who are equipped to recognize and respond to partner abuse *and* who will be permitted within cost containment guidelines to do anything about it (see the American Medical Association citations for further reading). Consider also that women of color and poor women are more likely to use emergency rooms for treatment and, due to their overrepresentation, may be at even higher risk of their endangerment or abuse remaining unattended.

A host of troubling societal problems are intertwined with partner violence. A woman may be coming to you for help with any one of a range of secondary problems in living. For example, homelessness is one result of the attempts of women to flee violent living situations. Data indicate that about half the homeless population are women and that a significant proportion of these women trace their circumstances to family conflict and dissolution (Hagen & Ivanoff, 1988; Roth, Toomey, & First, 1985, Slavinsky & Cousins, 1982). Women with children who do not have resources to buy themselves into a new, safer situation risk homelessness or shelter housing that, in the long run, imposes serious questions about the adequacy of nutrition, health care, education, and developmental opportunities. Women who are forced to cope with assaults and terrorization by their partners also suffer psychological and physical impairment that results in work absenteeism or diminished performance (see Shepard & Pence, 1988). This causes an estimated loss of $3 billion to $5 billion annually to businesses and jeopardizes her job security and advancement.

Substance abuse and dependency and domestic violence are societal problems that are frequently interlinked. By contrast, service providers in these realms have tended to function quite independently, often with conflicting priorities and adversarial relations. Efforts are under way to develop better means of communication, education, understanding, and service coordination among these service providers and advocates. However, problems of considerable concern do exist related to reliance on domestic violence myths and fundamental differences in service models. Examples of domestic violence myths include the following: alcohol and drug abuse cause domestic violence; domestic violence is anger out of control; and victims of domestic violence are codependent and share in the responsibility for the perpetrator's violence. Substance abuse treatment that does not include explicit attention to violence runs a high risk of continued and potentially less observable forms of violence that further endanger women (for example, a decrease in physical forms followed by an increase in threats, manipulation, isolation, and terrorization; *OPDV Bulletin,* 1993).

Particularly worrisome is the codependency component of many forms of substance abuse treatments. The codependency model was formulated from a systems perspective of family dysfunction (Wegscheider-Cruse, 1989) and was not conceptualized to account for the dynamics of violence or of gender power differentials. As a consequence, codependency formulations do not assess endangerment or trauma factors relative to violence. Practice based on a view of the woman as codependent risks collusion with the perpetrator that she is responsible for his abusive behavior. If issues of abuse and accountability are not explicitly incorporated, many of the actions a substance abuse counselor may expect of a domestic violence victim (such as setting boundaries, greater assertiveness, and self-focus) are quite likely to be perceived as a threat by the abuser and increase the risk of escalating violence (Frank & Kadison-Golden, 1992). In a similar vein, intervening with victims of partner violence who themselves are in need of substance abuse treatment without active intervention for their safety leaves them at high risk for relapse and greater immersion into the hopelessness of an abuser's control.

Economic inequities and discrimination serve as potent pressures that can keep women in abusive situations and indirectly reinforce inappropriate forms of control over women by coercive or abusive partners. For example, a woman who believes she would be unable to secure or maintain adequate housing for herself and her children, afford transportation, or pay for child care, health care, food, and clothing for her children may stay in or return to an abusive relationship to avoid impoverishing her family. Women are inherently at a disadvantage in regard to salaries and secure employment, facing societal inequities such as the dual labor market and issues of comparable worth. Women with abusive partners have added obstacles to work, training, and financial self-sufficiency. In light of an increasing press by Congress to reduce the budget by cutting social programs ("to get the federal government out of the welfare business"), future endangered women may find little or no federal sources of aid for them or their children—suggesting that local sources of help will become more important than ever (an issue that becomes crucial as we consider locally coordinated systems response efforts later in the chapter).

At present, there are few alternatives. Although there are some innovative grassroots and community-based developments, there are also some very frightening portents of the future as well. Consider, for example, the attitudes behind policy recommendations such as those of Speaker Newt Gingrich's that young, single mothers be prohibited from receiving welfare support and that children whose parents are not able to adequately care for them be placed in orphanages. In such a future scenario, what options does an impoverished mother have (whether she is a poor woman who is seeking escape from a violent home or one who has recently lost resources as a function of leaving a job, home, and relationship)? Should she dare reveal her economic hardship, which may be interpreted as lack of sufficient stability or fitness to retain and raise her child? Add to such scenarios the double and triple jeopardy faced by women of color, women in lesbian relationships, women with disabilities, women in remote or highly conservative communities, women with stigmatizing problems (such as chronic mental illness or chemical dependency) and the scope and complexity of need becomes evident.

In short, violence by partners can have a wide range of social welfare implications (related to health, housing, employment, education, child welfare, and the capacity to achieve independence and self-determination). Also profoundly evident are the deeply personal emotional and psychological costs. Partner violence, for many, is traumatizing. Initial reactions, similar to other types of personal threat, include shock, fear, confusion, withdrawal, denial or minimization, and numbing. Survivors of rape and physical abuse by male partners evidence higher levels of depression, suicide ideation and attempts, chronic fatigue and tension, disturbed eating and sleep patterns, and startle reactions. Ongoing victimization may produce protracted fear, emotional numbing, passivity and feelings of help-lessness, intrusive memories, abuse of substances, constricted affect, hypervigilance to danger cues, and impaired concentration and decision-making capacity (see Browne, 1993, for an overview).

One approach to organizing some of the emotional and psychological effects of abuse observed in some women victims of partner violence is the diagnostic concept and category of posttraumatic stress disorder (PTSD), a construct used in association with a broad range of traumatic experiences including combat, natural disaster, and a variety of criminal assaultive experiences (Davidson & Foa, 1993). Battered women's syndrome and rape trauma syndrome have been identified as two subsets of PTSD, in addition to other subcategories such as combat veteran's syndrome and battered child syndrome. For the social work practitioner, the PTSD construct holds a number of advantages: (1) It builds on a broad spectrum of evidence regarding human response to and aftereffects of severe and disruptive external stress, (2) it provides a framework for assessing effects of stress as well as environmental factors likely to increase or reduce negative effects (as one would following any traumatic experiences) and for developing appropriate and effective interventions, and (3) it is consistent with an ecological perspective that recognizes combined contributions of and interaction among structural or environmental variables and intrapersonal factors.

However, use of PTSD or any other psychological diagnostic category should be approached with caution. There is a critical balance between appropriate use of guidelines for assessing and assisting abused women who do have clinically significant needs and inappropriate use of guidelines that result in stereotyping what in reality is a heterogeneous population of women with various sets of life circumstances, in characterizing victims' needs wholly in intrapsychic terms, and in translating a societal problem rooted in socialization and reinforcement of gender bias into a defect view of the victim. For example, use of PTSD as a DSM-IV diagnosis is easily only a few steps from "syndromizing" victims, of using it as a clinical tool to understand why women stay; of victim blaming that may be unintended but is nonetheless seriously misleading and damaging. Part of what is fundamental to social work practice is attention to the multiple levels of any social problem and the diverse needs of those that the problem touches most directly.

Before turning to practice priorities for the future, the single most important step that everyone can take must be pointed out: *asking the question*. The real Achilles' heel of a future where we better meet the challenge of violence is knowing that it is there—in the behavior and life of the person(s) in front of us. As seemingly obvious as this sounds, we are nowhere close to achieving this simple goal. For example, in spite of the high percentages of partner abuse victims among those seeking medical services, victimization history and risk are typically neither assessed nor documented (American Medical Association's Council on Scientific Affairs, 1992; DeLaTorre, 1990). Similarly, Koss (1990) reports that mainstream agencies providing psychological services often do not include questions about sexual, emotional, or physical aggression by partners in routine assessments. The lack of such potentially important information seriously increases risk of misdiagnosis and resultant inappropriate or insufficient intervention (Browne, 1993).

Practice Priorities for the Future

The picture being painted here is not one of every social worker becoming a violence specialist or participating in rallies and policy changes. This will be appropriate for some social workers who are prepared to make the commitment. Rather, the metaphorical image that we see as part of the future of practice is one of a web. This web is based on a network of contacts, communications, and coordination—a web that begins with communities and works to expand outward to link counties, states, regions, the nation, and beyond as part of a global commitment to safer societies.

Aside from increasing awareness and understanding, the single most important element for the future is coordinated action. No one agency or system can prevent or redress violence against women. It will take integrative community-based approaches that strive to operate at multiple levels of prevention and change as well as a commitment to coordination and cooperation among service providers, policy-setting groups, and funding sources (see Davis & Hagen, 1988, 1992; Edleson & Tolman, 1992; Peled, Jaffe, & Edleson, 1995; and Schechter, 1988, for discussions). Obviously, this is a tall order and an achievement that can be accomplished only by concerted effort over time. Having a clear vision, sense of shared purpose, and evidence that supports the achievability and utility of any given action plan is extremely important. Thus the remainder of this section will draw on efforts of innovative experts in the field who are in the midst of developing and implementing coordinated action agendas.

Seldom is there any single, "right" or complete answer, and the future-oriented practice recommendations identified here are no exception. Part of what makes any solution work is the process of developing the relationships and shared commitments that are the real glue of any team effort. Thus part of your challenge is to review some of the available models as possible starting points and determine what would work for you, your agency, your professional network, your community, and your region. Although space limitations do not permit the detailing of current models, we can provide guidance in locating in-depth information.[1] In these integrative community-based coalitions, considerable attention is often given to the expansion of services (for example, to victims, children, and batterers) with an eye to future needs and coalition building among services, government, and community groups that are necessary to providing such services (Human Services Roundtable, 1993; see also Peled et al., 1995, for other examples and Hanson & Harway, 1993, for perspectives regarding family-oriented approaches). Collaboration with self-help and grass-roots organizations is another vital component. One example of a self-help effort for perpetrators is Men Working Against Violence; an agency founded and sustained by formerly abusive men working to foster abuse-free lives for themselves and others.[2]

Equally important, however, is attention to factors associated with leadership (that is, ensuring that those with the power to change laws, channel resources, and influence attitudes have adequate understanding of and concern for the problem) and the training, education, and system coordination that are essential to building and sustaining a shared vision and a web of effective services and responses. (For an overview of different approaches to coordinated response as well as progressive state codes defining prevention, treatment, child safety, civil orders for protection, and criminal penalties and procedures associated with domestic violence, see *Family Violence: A Model State Code,* 1994; and *Family Violence: Coordinating Councils,* 1994).[3]

Given the presence of social workers across a wide range of service systems, as well as the multilevel roles that they fulfill (such as policy, advocacy, organizing, administrative, direct service provider, educator, researcher/evaluator), social workers have special opportunities and responsibilities to provide productive contributions within integrative frameworks (see Nurius & Asplund, 1994). Social workers have historically been crucially important in keeping social activism alive. Violence against women, particularly by intimates, fits squarely within social work's historic mandate to fight against social injustice, disempowerment, and the disabling effects that these induce. The specific models that we have drawn on here for illustration by no means represent the only options. Each set of approaches will have strengths and limitations (see the notes at the end of this chapter for contact information related to other models). As a social worker, your mission is to find ways of working productively to prevent and effectively respond to violence against women (and others that are affected) within the context of your community, your field of practice, and in respectful collaboration with the grassroots activists and service providers who have been so important to galvanizing societal attention and action.

The future practice agenda for addressing aggression and violence in dating and courtship relationships is not yet defined as sharply as the agenda for domestic violence. However, there is clearly considerable overlap among various forms of violence against women by intimates, particularly in relation to prevention and problem assessment (Levy, 1991). The following set of recommendations set forth as policy, practice, and research priorities in response to rape (Koss, 1993) can be generalized for use in family violence and other forms of aggression in social relationships: (1) expanded education of providers (inclusion in professional training curriculum; provision of victim-sensitive care), (2) greater support for grassroots and community-based services (technical support of prevention and treatment programs; funding mechanisms that encourage collaboration; increased funding for crisis centers and capacity to serve diverse populations), (3) expanded treatment capability (leadership in identifying and responding to violence by intimates; commitment to multilevel intervention; strengthening assessment and measurement—particularly key variables such as social cognitions; encouragement of treatment innovation appropriate to diverse age, cultural, and functioning-level groups), and (4) improving information bases (monitoring and strengthening information sources such as the National Crime Victimization Survey; resolving fundamental measurement controversies and improving the sensitivity, reliability, and validity of measures; fostering information sharing across sites and systems; building bridges between practitioners and researchers so that advances in each domain can support the other; expansion of our knowledge base beyond mainstream women to understand the differential needs of diverse women, families, and communities).

Given safety as a predominant concern, many practice issues will focus on social work contact with victims of partner violence. However, to successfully achieve the ultimate goal of the cessation and prevention of violence, social workers must be prepared to recognize and effectively intervene with perpetrators and others who witness and are touched by partner violence (such as children and other family members). This section has detailed a continuum of practice issues for the future, including specialized intensive treatment and system-level response. This sketches a big picture based on a locally coordinated systems approach. Equally important is the immediate-picture question: What can each of us do as individuals today, or next week?

The following core capacities that *all* social workers in the year 2000 and beyond will need to have mastered provide important starting points for today (Browne, 1993): (1) routine screening for evidence or history of violence (as victim and perpetrator); (2) identification and consideration of trauma symptomatology in assessment, diagnosis, and service planning; (3) sufficient understanding of the dynamics of coercion and violence to provide accurate explanations of endangerment and of perpetrator behavioral accountability; (4) safety planning with victims and contracting with perpetrators regarding alternatives to violence and control; (5) familiarity with appropriate local resources and vigorous referral and brokerage efforts; (6) thorough documentation (of assault histories, observed sequelae, and responses to victims' efforts to obtain help or leave relationship); (7) incremental efforts toward consciousness-raising with colleagues, supervisors, and administrators; and (8) incorporation of agency protocols to systematize and strengthen an agency's responsiveness. Needless to say, there are many unanswered questions. Continued research and theory development are integral parts of social work activities for the future, as is an ongoing commitment to remaining ongoing learners and contributors to a strong and balanced knowledge base.

Visions of the Future: Paralysis or Catalyst?

Thus far we have described a challenging vision of the future, but one with promising and encouraging practice possibilities. There are, of course, other possibilities. One very possible scenario is that the social work profession will spin its wheels and be essentially paralyzed by the layers upon layers of complexity, controversy, and conflicts. We see, for example, considerable time and energy spent debating what to call the problem, whose purview intervention rightly belongs within, whether a real problem even exists, and the merits of various ideological perspectives. Many of these concerns are legitimate and meaningful issues (see Gelles & Loseke, 1993, for a look at current controversies). However, if most social service providers simply do not ask women about potential risk for or experience of partner abuse, are not engaged in outreach or prevention efforts, or are expressing conservative attitudes and biases toward endangered or abused women (all of which have been documented: Davis, 1984; Davis & Carlson, 1981; Koss, 1993; Ross & Glisson, 1991), we are at risk of generating the illusion that we are responding professionally and adequately without truly taking the actions that make this a meaningful reality. Another worrisome factor is the splintering evident in specialization of and competition among services. This splintering is felt most acutely by the woman who must go from one social service provider to another to obtain the various "pieces" of her needs attended to (physical injuries; stress and emotional trauma; training or employment; food, housing, and transportation; children's needs; and possibly other problems in living such as substance use, disability, chronic mental health problems, immigration-related needs, or issues related to lesbian couplehood or community); a process that can be inordinately onerous and, at times, revictimizing.

In addition to fragmentation, institutional response can also involve competing and conflicting values, priorities, and organizational cultures (Nurius & Asplund, 1994). Child welfare and domestic violence providers, for example, often find themselves in a tug-of-war over priorities and intervention philosophies when family violence is present, potentially setting them at cross purposes in their respective efforts. Future practice, however, has the opportunity to learn from this history and to build on policy, practice, and research findings regarding common purposes (such as McKernan-McKay's 1994 review findings of linkages between the two sets of problems and advocacy for research and intervention in both arenas that takes these relationships into account).

In short, one fear for the future is that social workers will intellectually acknowledge a professional responsibility to women who are endangered and abused by their partners but will not take the individual concrete steps necessary to do something about it. A more optimistic vision is that, as the profession increases its recognition and understanding of this social problem, motivation and energy will be unleashed that will produce creative, highly innovative, and effective results. Such efforts will then carry us through a transition from awareness to action and take form in our own everyday consciousness and practice, in the protocols and commitment of our organizations, in how we manage professional parochialism and political infighting, and in how we innovate and persevere in the face of challenges and cutbacks that will undoubtedly be a part of social work practice in the twenty-first century.

The Future Starts Today

As this chapter concludes, there are three themes that bear repeating. The first is that abuse and endangerment of women by their partners is a social welfare issue that touches and concerns us all. Future practice will clearly require service providers with appropriate specialized training to work most intensively in this arena. However, the complexity and enormity of the need will require that all social workers embrace a professional responsibility to support justice, quality of life, and self-determination by preparing to be alert to and effectively respond to abuse and endangerment, including those who may well be seeking assistance for problems in living other than violence.

A second theme builds on the first. It has to do with the future's need for coordinated, multisystem-response approaches in communities. This notion of an interlocking web of communication, relationships, and services is particularly germane to social workers given their presence across many systems and levels of human service. Thus, even though many social workers will specialize in practice areas other than partner violence per se, representation across such a wide spectrum of helping services offers a special opportunity to facilitate and foster integrative, consensus-building efforts.

A third theme is that of "three steps forward, two steps back." The constancy of challenge and impediments to change are neither new to social work nor unique to the area of violence against women. Yet it is important to prepare for future practice issues with a realistic perspective that fundamental change in the root causes of problems (such as sex role socialization, legislation, and cultural norms and attitudes that reinforce domination and abuse) comes in increments and as a function of innovative, persistent, and broad-based reform efforts.

So, if the future starts today, what are some of the steps that you can take today, and tomorrow? Broadly, we offer the personal challenge of thoughtfully examining your current practice setting and habits and considering the ways to work with your colleagues toward picking up a strand of the web. The detailed models and guidelines presented in the chapter are intended to aid you in such efforts. Even more immediately and incrementally, consider undertaking one or more of the following before the week's end: (1) Call a local agency that specializes in partner violence services and ask for a community resource listing, tools to assist in assessing and documenting abuse and endangerment, educational materials that can be shared with clients, speakers list, and so forth; (2) read journal articles, book chapters, or other relevant material to update and expand your personal and professional understanding of the dynamics of partner violence and how best to take effective first steps; (3) make a point of raising the question of how to strengthen your organization's understanding of and capacity to respond to abused and endangered women (for example, with a coworker, at a staff meeting, or during a supervisory or case consultation session); (4) work with colleagues and local consultants to develop assessment, intervention, and referral protocols and materials for use within your agency; and (5) stimulate interagency dialogue—perhaps invite speakers for inservice training, for discussion about service coordination possibilities, or for ways to reach out to local leadership to help organize and sustain a planning process.

We were clear in the introduction of our need to delimit our focus, in this case to violence against women by their dating, courtship, and domestic partners. We noted that this form of violence is but one aspect of larger societal violence. It is also important to note that partner violence is but one aspect of a broader social context of women as targets of domination including but not limited to workplace harassment, marketplace sex discrimination and inequities, various forms of exploitation and endangerment of women working in the sex trades, sexism related to reproductive rights and childrearing, use of women in media and sales as sex objects to be owned and controlled, and stereotypic and unhealthy depictions of gender roles and attitudes presented as socially acceptable.

Part of the point of moving toward the future with these broader perspectives in mind is that through acceptance that we are each part of the problem, we therefore have the opportunity to become part of the solution. We have offered a vision that moves toward the creation of more cost-effective, comprehensive, and community-based approaches that not only maintains the safety of victims but simultaneously functions to change societal attitudes and institutions that create and support learned violent behavior and conditions that undermine individual dignity, security, and self-determination.

Notes

1. For more information, contact the Human Services Roundtable, 811 First Avenue, Suite 200, Seattle, WA 98104 (phone: 206-623-7134). It is important to note that there are a number of innovative and important models and contributors to draw on. The Human Services Roundtable is part of the authors' own community and provides a useful beginning point. We urge readers to investigate coordinated, community-based efforts in your own communities. Although it is beyond the scope of this chapter to provide an exhaustive listing of all such efforts or models, contact with the following groups should provide a sense about vari-

ations in how these efforts are being undertaken and what might work best in your own community: Domestic Abuse Intervention Project (and National Training Project), 206 W. Fourth St., Duluth, MN 55806 (phone: 218-722-2781); and the Domestic Abuse Project, Inc., 204 W. Franklin Ave., Minneapolis, MN 55404 (phone: 612-874-7063; fax: 612-874-8445).

2. Men Working Against Abuse, 428 Pioneer Building, 600 First Avenue, Seattle, WA 98104 (phone: 206-461-7824). This nonprofit organization,

founded in 1986, maintains a public information and referral service and a referral network for professional and public education programs, in addition to ongoing support services for abusive men. A recent book (Paymar, 1993) provides a useful national list of resource hotlines and organizations regarding services for batterers.

3. National Council of Juvenile and Family Court Judges, PO Box 8970, Reno, NV 89507 (phone: 702-784-4463).

References

American Medical Association's Council on Scientific Affairs. (1992). Violence against women—Relevance for medical practitioners. *Journal of American Medical Association, 267,* 3184–3189.

Biden, J. R., Jr. (1993). Violence against women: The Congressional response. *American Psychologist, 48,* 1059–1060.

Browne, A. (1993). Violence against women by male partners: Prevalence, outcomes, and policy implications. *American Psychologist, 48,* 1077–1087.

Davidson, J. R., & Foa, E. B. (1993). *Posttraumatic stress disorder: DSM-IV and beyond.* Washington, DC: American Psychiatric Press.

Davis, L. V. (1984). Beliefs of service providers about abused women and abusing men. *Social Work, 29,* 243–250.

Davis, L. V., & Carlson, B. (1981). Attitudes of service providers toward domestic violence. *Social Work Research and Abstracts, 17,* 34–39.

Davis, L. V., & Hagen, J. L. (1988). Services for battered women: The public policy response. *Social Service Review, 62,* 649–667.

Davis, L. V., & Hagen, J. L. (1992). The problem of wife abuse: The interrelationship of social policy and social work practice. *Social Work, 37,* 15–20.

DeLaTorre, A. (1990). Abuse statistics comunique. Lincoln Shelter and Services.

Edleson, J. L., & Tolman, R. M. (1992). *Intervention for men who batter: An ecological approach.* Newbury Park, CA: Sage.

Family violence: Coordinating councils. (1994). Reno, NV: National Council of Juvenile and Family Court Judges.

Family violence: A model state code. (1994). Reno, NV: National Council of Juvenile and Family Court Judges.

Frank, P. B., & Kadison-Golden, G. (1992). Blaming by naming: Battered women and the epidemic of codependence. *Social Work, 37,* 5–6.

Gelles, R. J., & Loseke, D. R. (Eds.). (1993). *Current controversies on family violence.* Newbury Park, CA: Sage.

Hagen, J. L., & Ivanoff, A. (1988). Homeless women: A high risk population. *Affilia, 3,* 19–33.

Hamberger, L. K. (Ed.).(1994). Domestic partner abuse: Expanding paradigms for understanding and intervention [Special issue]. *Violence and Victims, 9*(2).

Hansen, M., & Harway, M. (Eds.). (1993). *Battering and family therapy: A feminist perspective.* Newbury Park, CA: Sage.

Human Services Roundtable. (1993). *A regional plan to help children affected by domestic violence.* Seattle, WA: Author.

Koss, M. P. (1988). Hidden rape: Sexual aggression and victimization in a national sample of students in higher education. In A. W. Burgess (Ed.), *Rape and sexual assault* (vol. 2, pp. 3–26). New York: Garland.

Koss, M. P. (1990). The women's mental health research agenda: Violence against women. *American Psychologist, 45,* 374–379.

Koss, M. P. (1993). Rape: Scope, impact, interventions, and public policy responses. *American Psychologist, 48,* 1062–1069.

Levy, B. (1991). *Dating violence: Young women in danger.* Seattle, WA: Seal Press.

McCarthy, C. (1991, July 23). Countering violence at home. *Washington Post*, p. 13.

McKernan-McKay, M. (1994). The link between domestic violence and child abuse: Assessment and treatment considerations. *Child Welfare League of America, 73,* 29–39.

Muehlenhard, C. L., & Linton, M. A. (1987). Date rape and sexual aggression in dating situations: Incidence and risk factors. *Journal of Counseling Psychology, 34,* 186–196.

Novello, A., Rosenberg, M., Saltzman, L., & Shosky, J. (1992). From the Surgeon General, U.S. Public Health Service. *The Journal of the American Medical Association, 267,* 3132.

Nurius, P. S., & Asplund, L. M. (1994). Community responses to partner abuse: Challenges and opportunities for social work and feminists. *Social Policy and Social Work Practice, 18,* 17–29.

OPDV Bulletin (1993, Winter/Spring). Adult domestic violence: The alcohol connection. New York State Office for the Prevention of Domestic Violence, Troy, NY.

Paymar, M. (1993). *Violent no more: Helping men end domestic violence.* Alameda, CA: Hunter House.

Peled, E., Jaffe, P. G., & Edleson, J. L. (Eds.). (1995). *Ending the cycle of violence: Community responses to children of battered women.* Thousand Oaks, CA: Sage.

Roth, Toomey, B., & First, R. (1985). *Homeless women: Characteristics and service needs of one of society's most vulnerable populations.* Columbus, OH: Ohio Department of Mental Health.

Ross, M., & Glisson, C. (1991). Bias in social work intervention with battered women. *Journal of Social Service Research, 14,* 79–105.

Schechter, S. (1988). Building bridges between activists, professionals, and researchers. In K. Yllo & M. Bograd (Eds.), *Feminist perspectives on wife abuse* (pp. 299–312). Newbury Park, CA: Sage.

Shepard. M., & Pence, E. (1988).The effect of battering on the employment status of women. *Affilia, 3,* 55–61.

Slavinsky, A.T., & Cousins, A. (1982). Homeless women. *Nursing Outlook, 30,* 358–362.

Stark, E., & Flitcraft, A. (1988). Violence among intimates: An epidemiological review. In V. N. Hasselt et al. (Eds.), *Handbook of family violence* (pp. 293–318). New York: Plenum.

Straus, M. A., & Gelles, R. J. (Eds.). (1990). *Physical violence in American families: Risk factors and adaptations to violence in 8,145 families.* New Brunswick, NJ: Transaction.

U.S. Department of Justice, Bureau of Justice Statistics. (1994). *Report to the national on crime and justice: The data.* Washington, DC: U.S. Government Printing Office.

U.S. Senate Judiciary Committee (1992, October). *Violence against women: A week in the life of America* (prepared by the majority staff of the Senate Judiciary Committee). (Available from Hart Office Building, Room B04, Washington, DC 20510).

Wegsheider-Cruse, S. (1989). *Another chance—Hope and health for the alcoholic family.* Palo Alto, CA: Science and Behavior Books.

Chapter *17*

Headed for the Future

Families in the Twenty-First Century

KAREN A. HOLMES, *PhD, ACSW, LMSW-ACP*
University of Houston

Back to the Future?

The decade is the 1950s. The medium is revolutionary: It is called television. The show is "Father Knows Best." Insurance salesman Jim Anderson, his homemaker wife, Margaret, and their three children, Betty (also known as "Princess"), Bud, and Kathy (also known as "Kitten"), find their way into our homes weekly. Joining them are other "all-American" families such as the Cleavers and the Stones. Ward and June Cleaver have two sons, Wally and Theodore, better known as "the Beave." "Leave It to Beaver" enjoys several successful seasons and still runs in syndication for yet another generation's role model confusion. Ward—like his counterpart, Jim Anderson—puts on his suit and tie each morning and goes to work in an office. Both Margaret and June toil away at the household chores, smiling as they clean and vacuum. They wear the media-defined uniform of the era: a shirtwaist dress, heels, and, on occasion, a tasteful set of pearls. Perhaps they were modeling themselves after Donna Stone, the picture-perfect representation of both mother and womanhood, a role model for women of the era. Donna had married well, had a lovely home, and belonged to a variety of women's clubs. Her husband Alex was the kind and patient pediatrician, and they had produced (magically, considering that they slept in twin beds) two very cute, high-energy, always-bickering offspring, Mary and Jeff.

What would an inquiring extraterrestrial have noted from observing these television programs? Our data-gathering ET might well have returned home to report that earthlings were all very pale-skinned humans who entered and exited square or rectangular-shaped dwellings at various time intervals. The taller ones with the shorter head fur placed dark, two-piece cloth units over their bodies with a long, pointed cloth that hung around their necks. They carried with them rectangular brown boxes, except for one who had a smaller, rounder black carrying device. The humans with longer head fur remained within the square or rectangular dwellings most of the time, watching over and tending to smaller human units who appeared to have no particular function. At the close of each of these discrete viewing segments, our ET would note that all of the human units smiled broadly at one another, achieved perfect empathic attunement with each other, and went on to another week of happy and contented family life.

This model of family, of course, was a myth, the media's version of an ideal type. Much like the perennial warmth and wisdom of the Walton elders in later years, these families never existed in such pure, ideal form. These models did create expectations, however. Like our ET data gatherer, television viewers were given the message that *the family* is, or should be,

A man and a woman who are married, and who after marrying produce 2.25 children

A unit living together in a single dwelling on a street called Maple or Oak

A husband/father who goes to work in a suit and tie

A wife/mother who takes care of all the domestic in-house chores (cooking, vacuuming, and baking cookies seem to be particular favorites), tends to the children's emotional needs, and sometimes attends various women's gardening club or PTA meetings

Children who are well groomed, clever, and respectful of their elders

Family crises that consist of sibling squabbles, teenage angst (typically about boyfriends or girlfriends, or making the cheerleading squad), or "boys will be boys" behavior (this was a particular specialty of the Beave, naively well intended but always ending up in a "mess" or a "pickle").

And, in case it went unnoticed, this vision of the family was white and solidly middle class. Even the Anderson's Hispanic gardener was named Frank Smith.

What Is Family?

A recent dictionary defines family as "parents and their children; a group of persons related by blood or marriage; members of one household" (*American Heritage Electronic Dictionary,* 1990). According to the *Random House Encyclopedia* (1992), the family is an "institutionalized bio-social group made up of adults and children. It forms a unit that deals with both economic and affective needs and provides a sociocultural context for the procreation, care, and socialization of offspring. It can consist of a nuclear or extended network." Duvall (1971) states that the family is "a unity of interacting persons related by ties of marriage, birth, or adoption, whose central purpose is to create and maintain a common culture which promotes the physical, mental, emotional, and social development of each of its members" (p. 5). These definitions actually bear a close resemblance to the pre–Industrial Revolution family of the nineteenth century.

Pre-Industrial Era

Prior to the Industrial Revolution, extended family structure was common. The family included a father—the head of the household—his wife, children, and assorted relatives living in the same dwelling in a rural area. Family size was related to economics; children were useful and necessary contributors. All members, to the extent of their abilities, worked to produce what the family needed to survive. To a large extent, the family unit consumed what it produced and produced what it consumed as a self-sufficient unit. Family members were viewed less as individuals than as part of the total unit. Educating children was seen as necessary insofar as the emphasis was on practical learning and skill acquisition. Home was a haven from intruders, both human and animal: Husbands protected wives, and both protected the children. Religion was a focal point that met several needs. The Bible was read aloud as a means of teaching reading, and it served as the repository of genealogical history. The family Bible was the singular place in which all significant family events were recorded. Recreation was either church affiliated through socials, or it was home based. Affective ties in the family were often strong, although sexual relations were viewed primarily as a means of procreation. This description of the pre–Industrial Revolution family paints a picture of a tightly knit group with common bonds and shared purpose. That does not, mean, however, that life was wonderful, nor that families of that era were necessarily better. They were what they needed to be at that time and place.

Post-Industrial Era

The vast majority of families in the United States now live in cities or large urban centers. There are fewer family units with both original biological parents present, and there are increasing numbers of single-parent households. There are family units that, contrary to traditional definitions, do not include children. Status is as likely tied to an individual as to the family itself or to the family name. Few families produce their own consumable goods. What is produced at home is likely done as a hobby or as a means of generating additional income. Families have become oriented to consuming rather than producing goods. Food, clothing, and other consumables are purchased outside the home. Formal education is now mandatory for children. School systems are required to teach an array of curricular areas, many of which are not related to pragmatic skill acquisition. Children are now seen as major economic investments rather than as direct contributors to family maintenance. The family is protected by sanctioned, organized groups such as law enforcement personnel, social service agencies, and the military. Recreation, once centered at home or in the immediate community, has become an open set of choices limited only by access to a car or to mass transportation. Distance is no longer measured by miles but by time. Ironically, it was the advent of television (and subsequently VCRs and video games) that has helped to return some measure of recreation to the home. Many families have reached out to organized religion as a focal point of family maintenance and stability. For others, organized religion has lost its significance. Even affection and procreation are no longer the exclusive domain of the family. Interestingly, high divorce rates are being followed by high rates of remarriage. This likely suggests that the needs for affection remain strong, and that people attempt to meet them as they can, whether through a series of significant relationships or in a single, life-long commitment. Sex, once primarily viewed in terms of procreation, has taken on new meaning as recreation or, in some cases, as a substitute source of nurturing outside the family unit.

Has *the family* as a social institution disintegrated? Have we witnessed the decline and fall of *the American family*? If the only viable definition of the family is one that includes a white, middle-class, heterosexual couple who produce 2.2 children and rear them through the course of various stages of family development, then the answer is yes. A better question to ask is this: To what extent was this *ever* an accurate description of family? Certainly there have been and there are still such families, but why should they be viewed as *the family* model against which all other models are measured?

As the close of the twentieth century approaches, 50 percent of all marriages in the United States end in divorce, and women are less likely to remarry than men. In 1992 married couples with children under the age of 18 constituted 25 percent of all U.S. households; how many of these were first and only marriages is not known. That leaves some 75 percent of U.S. households falling outside of the traditional definition of family. There have always been variations in what is simplistically called *the family.*

There are many persons—not the least of whom are politicians—who are telling us that a return to family values is the solution to a wide range of social problems. Soaring divorce rates; out-of-wedlock births; alcohol and other drug abuse; teen suicide, crime, and delinquency; incest and child abuse; spousal abuse; and school dropouts are all laid at the feet of "failed" families. Would a return to traditional family values reverse the situation? The religious right and the political conservatives who court that segment of the voting population would quickly say "Yes!" Their solution is a return to basic family values as reflected in the structure and form of families somewhere around the nineteenth century. The social, demographic, and technological changes of the twentieth century make such a return to yesteryear quite impossible.

As a society and as a profession, our challenge is not to go back but to look ahead, to envision new possibilities that are congruent with the changes that have occurred in the world. Schriver (1995) presents a new conceptualization called *familiness,* which broadens the traditional vision of family:

> Familiness includes the traditional functions and responsibilities assigned by societies to families, such as childbearing, child rearing, intimacy, and security. It also recognizes the great diversity in structures, values and contexts that define family for different people. In addition to traditional concerns . . . familiness includes consideration of culture, gender, sexual orientation, age, disabling conditions, income, and spirituality. (p. 220)

A significant element of this vision is the reference to great diversity. In my earlier descriptions of the all-American family as reflected in various television programs and in the discussions of pre– and post–Industrial Revolution families, conformity rather than diversity was evident. The television depictions, in particular, reflected a sameness, a unidimensional, homogenized picture of family that reflected only one vision—and a highly suspect vision at that—of *the family.*

Schriver's view of familiness does not do away with the traditional functions and responsibilities given to the family as a social institution. This concept addresses differences in structure, form, and inclusiveness. This concept reminds us that families are not all white, middle-class, physically able, two-biological-parent heterosexual units. Familiness allows for a vision of same-gender couples, with or without children; for persons of various ages sharing the traditional functions and responsibilities of the family; and for persons of different cultural backgrounds or differing physical and mental abilities creating and maintaining families.

Schriver's view is an inclusive one, a view that emanates from an implicit comfort with and appreciation of difference. It is not, however, a radical or visionary view. It is a view that acknowledges what already exists. It is radical or visionary only when juxtaposed with a traditional model that has been deemed the "right" or the "ideal type." To some, Schriver's concept of familiness may seem radical because it is different; it is a departure from tenaciously held beliefs, desires, and myths about *the family.* Most humans resist change. Change is unsettling; it disturbs our *illusion* of control, it upsets our equilibrium, and it thwarts our need for predictability in the world. We talk about the family as if it is a universally determined, commonly understood, never-changing entity. A possible explanation for this definitional inertia may lie in our knowledge base, including the knowledge base of social work education.

A quick review of most human behavior texts, particularly those that include content on various life-cycle theorists, reflects a knowledge base that continues to rely on certain fundamental assumptions. One of those fundamental assumptions is that the world is conceptualized around a white, middle-class, heterosexual perspective. This is the foundation for what is viewed as normal and is the yardstick by which everything is measured. It has been so normalized throughout history that one hardly notices it is there, but it is. Texts that are used to teach about families or working with families reflect the same fundamental worldview with white, middle-class, heterosexual persons at the center. Although the family is a social institution, it—like other social institutions—is neither impervious nor immune to the stresses, pressures, and inevitable changes of the social contexts in which it exists. The family, in terms of structure, form, and function, has always been more varied and far more complex than the literature would seem to indicate. As a social institution, it has changed over time and it will continue to do so.

Two Future Scenarios

The year is 2006. Promptly at 7:00 A.M., CARA (your Computer Automated Robot Assistant) awakens you by playing your favorite digitally synthesized musical score. After your preprogrammed, perfect-temperature shower or bath, you open your closet, press a button, and step into your Thursday clothing. In the nourishment-acquisition area, at the push of a button, your preferred breakfast selection is delivered to you. At various intervals over the next half hour, you are joined by other members of the household. Amid the usual raucous noise and interchange, you put on the headset connected to your laptop and you listen to the global headline news via NERD (News Editing Retriever Daily). CARA efficiently reminds each household member to check their personal computer screens to review their day's plans. A few of the children select individually tailored learning lessons from the massive database, and others opt for extended virtual reality lessons, but most are eager to meet with their master teachers via global satellite interactive television. Some of the adults will travel to their work sites on their solar-powered vehicles, whereas others will do their business at home via teleconferencing and e-mail. The elders, many of whom are well into their 90s, will pursue their various interests: Some continue with their wisdom writing, others focus on their rainforest replication projects, and some work with the children on their learning lessons.

This particular household includes several adults (ranging in age from their 20s into their 90s) and several children of various ages. Some are biologically related to one another; others have joined this household by choice. Some were conceived *in vitro*. The household is one of many in the MADET community (Mega-Affluent Disciples of Education and Technology), a gathering of like-minded persons who have come together in relationship. They live together cooperatively and in connection with one another, whether or not they are biologically related. They view their living arrangement as a family. They are among the fortunate ones, having enjoyed the benefits of higher education and affluence throughout the latter part of the twentieth century. Having come from homes where family incomes were over $75,000 per year, they came of age technologically in the 1980s and 1990s. Their homes included one or more personal computers. They surfed the net and explored cyberspace by the hour. They located and downloaded information never before accessible to them. They were on the cutting edge of the new technology that now routinely offers up instant global information at the click of a mouse.

Is this just an idyllic, futuristic fantasy? Idyllic, yes. A fantasy? Perhaps not, if you are among the fortunates of the latter half of the twentieth century. But what of the others, the less fortunate ones?

The year is 2006. The place is the community of HAVNOT (Highly Alienated Voiceless Nadir of Technology). You are awakened by the cacophony of shrill voices, too many to identify, but of all ages, men, women, and children. The sun has risen but you can barely appreciate its warm rays in the chilled, dank air. Another day of scrounging for a meal. Another day of hanging out until you find shelter from the cold. You stink. And you hate that you stink. You think back to the old days in the 1980s and 1990s. Back then you could get a hot meal at the soup kitchen and, if you got there early enough, you could get a shower and bed at the shelter. No more. You belong to the family of the have-nots, those who were left behind when the new technology redefined society. You're part of a growing extended family.

You look around at the faces. They mirror your own. You see despair, rage, and resignation. The faces are ancient, even the children's. How did I get here? What could I have done differently? You think to yourself for the millionth time, "It wasn't *my* fault I was born poor! I wanted to make something of my life like those people in the MADET community living up there behind those huge walls. I wanted to make a good life. I wanted to work. I wanted to have nice things. I wanted my part of the American Dream. How did I end up here?"

Families in the New Millennium

These two scenarios are only extensions of current reality. Changing definitions of the family cannot be separated from the economic status of family units, however they are structured. There can be little argument that economics are inextricably interwoven with education and success in life. To the extent that the new technology becomes yet another line of demarcation between the haves and have-nots, the two scenarios of family life presented here may be realities in the new millennium. Support for children's services is under attack. Decreasing support for early education programs, school lunch programs, and aid to dependent children is a current, not a future, political reality. If such attacks are successful, we will see a greater exacerbation of the divisions between rich and poor. Social workers will be increasingly called on to engage in social and political activism to meet basic human needs.

Among the MADET family forms, I believe we will see more of the diversity Schriver describes as familiness. Many diverse or nontraditional families already exist but are not visible. For example, no one knows how many gay or lesbian couples there are. Unlike those who are single, married, or POSSLQs (persons of the opposite sex sharing living quarters), the U.S. Census Bureau has no category for same-gender couples in committed relationships. Many gay and lesbian parents remain hidden for fear of custody battles. Diversity will be evident in form and structure, in mixed racial and ethnic heritage, in same-gender relationships, and in arrangements with and without children. Changing demographics, instability in the economic structure, and rapidly expanding technologies will yield greater diversity throughout all facets of our society and perhaps across the globe.

Implications for Practice

What does all this mean for social work practitioners in the twenty-first century? Nothing new, really, except that we will likely be forced rather than reminded or encouraged to be flexible and expansive in our thinking and attitudes. Social work educators have always challenged students to examine their personal values and attitudes. We teach the professional values of acceptance, the inherent dignity and worth of all persons, and the right of client self-determination. These values will take on even greater importance. Ethnocentric assumptions and myopic thinking will be challenged by the visibility of more diverse family forms and structures.

Social work practice in the twenty-first century will be characterized by a renewed professional commitment to social and economic justice. As the gap between the haves and have-nots widens, we will be challenged to move more assertively toward achieving a just and equitable society. Our work will cross the spectrum of all client groups, as it always has. We will be challenged to more fully embrace the high-tech age, utilizing the vast resources of cyberspace in the service of our clients. In our work with families of all kinds, we will be challenged to accept and appreciate diversity in its many forms.

Headed for the Future

A decade from now, we might look at this collection of articles and chuckle at how far off we were in our projections of the future. Then again, we may look back and find ourselves thankful that, here and there, someone had the foresight to identify something important.

Our accuracy in predicting the future is less important than our success in having stimulated your thinking. Rather than leave you with a summary of my thoughts, I leave you with questions and dilemmas. You are the ones headed for the future.

- What is your vision of the ideal family? Why?
- What do you see as the major problems facing families in the twenty-first century?
- What kinds of knowledge and skills will you need to work with families in the twenty-first century?
- Human needs for connection and relationship are likely to increase, not decrease, as everything becomes more technologically advanced. What are some possible implications for diverse family forms?
- If the second scenario presented here moves toward becoming a reality, how would you suggest that the gap between the haves and have-nots be addressed? Would your intervention be at the micro level, working with individuals, groups, and families? At the macro level, with our social institutions? Would you propose major legislative changes, and, if so, what would this be?
- The face of America is aging. The baby boomers are the largest generational group in history. They are now reaching middle age and will be retiring in the early part of the twenty-first century. What do you see as some implications for families? For the health care system? For Social Security and employment-based retirement programs?
- In addition to demographic changes based on age, there are clear indications that the demographics of ethnicity are changing as well. How do you think social services might be affected?
- Computer technology continues to create new possibilities vis-a-vis information exchange and global communication. Issues and concerns about confidentiality are already being raised among social workers (and others). What do you see as some of the benefits of this new technology, and what do you see as concerns?

References

Duvall, E. M. (1971). *Family development.* (4th ed.). Philadelphia, PA: J.B. Lippincott.

Schriver, J. M. (1995). *Human behavior and the social environment: Shifting paradigms in essential knowledge for social work practice.* Needham Heights, MA: Allyn & Bacon.

Chapter 18

Teen Pregnancy in the Twenty-First Century

MAXINE L. WEINMAN, DrPH
University of Houston

PEGGY B. SMITH, PhD
Baylor College of Medicine

In spite of medical, social, and educational interventions targeted at U.S. inner-city youth, adolescent pregnancy persists as an important social and health concern in the late 1990s. For the fifth consecutive year, the birth rate among U.S. teens has increased. In 1991 approximately 532,000 teenagers under the age of 19 had delivered babies. Historically, the birth rate is highest among African-American teens; however, for a variety of reasons the recent increase in the teen birth rate has been particularly large among Hispanic teens (Child Trends, 1994). It is puzzling that science can decipher complicated genetic patterns and codes, but various professionals have been unsuccessful in the prevention of teen pregnancy.

Among U.S. females 15 to 44 years of age, one-quarter of African-American adolescents had a child by 18.7 years of age, a quarter of Hispanic adolescents had a child by 19.6 years of age, and a quarter of non-Hispanic White adolescents had a child by 22.1 years of age. Teenage mothers are more likely to have daughters who have babies as teens themselves. According to the National Survey of Children, among women who were 19 or younger when they first became mothers, half their daughters became a teen parent, compared with 25 percent of daughters whose mothers were at least 20 when they had their first child (Child Trends, 1994). The problem is quickly exacerbated in that an estimated 60 percent of teen parents who have children will conceive again prior to reaching their twentieth birthday.

Teen Pregnancy and the Supreme Court Abortion Decision

Adolescent childbearing usually means adolescent childrearing. About 95 percent of teens will parent their infants. This is a dramatic departure from the 1950s and 1960s, when adoption was the most frequent parenting choice for single adolescents. In 1970, 80 percent of single teen mothers made an adoption plan. By 1976 as a result of changing social attitudes and abortion service accessibility, only 10 to 20 percent of teen mothers were planning adoption (Baldwin, 1976).

Most of the research through the 1970s supported the view that unwed mothers who decided to parent were more deviant and of lower socioeconomic status than those who made an adoption plan. Investigations initiated by many professional disciplines reinforced this perception of social and emotional misconduct. In the years following the Supreme Court decision legalizing abortion, attention focused on examining the consequences of teen pregnancy such as personality characteristics of those who used contraceptives, those who become pregnant, and those who choose to abort their pregnancy (Blum & Resnick, 1982). It was suggested that personal reproductive health choices rather than psychopathology influenced pregnancy decisions. By the late 1980s it was recognized that single mothers could no longer be considered deviant because they constituted 21 percent of the nations's 30.6 million families with children.

Furstenberg (1988) suggests that major cultural shifts may have driven the changing profile of pregnant teens, especially in regard to marital status. These cultural shifts found their roots in the post–World War II era and in factors associated with the baby boom. Between 1955 and 1970 large numbers of adolescents reached puberty and increased the proportion of births to teenagers. These trends may have gone unnoticed, except that a growing number of teenage births occurred to single women. The relatively early marriages characteristic of the late 1940s and early 1950s had concealed a high rate of premarital sexual activity. In the late 1950s close to one-half of all women married before they reached 20, and perhaps as many as half of these women were already pregnant at the time. During the 1960s and 1970s as the age when women married increased, the consequences of sexual activity and the resulting conceptions became more visible. Some sociologists conjectured that such behaviors reflected a very subtle cultural shift concerning the role of intercourse and marriage, which affected the adolescent female cohort. Culturally, intercourse was part of the courtship process as a precursor to marriage for many couples. However, the prevailing culture prescribed that such an action required an interpersonal commitment so that if a conception occurred, the wedding date was just moved up. Beginning in the 1970s large numbers of adolescents engaged in sexual intercourse with no prospects for marriage. As an activity, sexual intercourse today no longer requires an antecedent promise of engagement or marriage (Furstenberg, 1988).

The Emergence of Psychosocial Issues

Driven by subtle changes in social values as well as sexual behaviors, the number of nonmarital births to teens has quadrupled since 1960, whereas the number of marital teen births has declined substantially. In 1991, 69 percent of the births to mothers 19 or younger occurred to unmarried mothers, compared with 30 percent in 1970 (Child Trends, 1994). The consequences of these births became more severe as the age of the mother declined. Research has shown that the younger the age of first pregnancy, the greater is the likelihood that the teen will experience school dropout, welfare dependency, repeat pregnancy, and poor health outcome. At-risk adolescents also demonstrate various negative behaviors. Studies have documented that teens do not use birth control consistently, are engaging in sexual intercourse at earlier ages, and self-report heavy use of cigarettes and alcohol.

In addition to psychological risks, it has been suggested that young teenage mothers have a greater risk of having preterm deliveries, stillbirths, and neonatal deaths than postadolescent mothers. It is not clear whether these adverse medical outcomes are due to biological immaturity and inadequacy or to confounding factors such as low socioeconomic status, multiple sex partners, poor nutrition, personal behaviors and lifestyles such as smoking and drug use, and inadequate prenatal care (Lawrence & Merritt, 1981).

Postnatal care has also been shown to be problematic by parenting adolescents, despite the fact that postpartum services emphasize the importance of health care for both the teen and the infant (Beck & Davies, 1987). Studies on postpartum compliance suggest that even with incentives, adolescent mothers do not return for family planning services following delivery. Family planning services offer both pregnancy protection, treatment and identification of STDs, and an entry to health services.

Because of their immaturity and lack of financial and emotional support systems, teenage parents have been identified as at high risk for being child abusers (Bolton, Laner, & Kane, 1980). Teenage motherhood has long-term adverse effects on the social and psychological aspects of the mother's life. The availability and use of social supports is limited, and low socioeconomic status results from early and continuous welfare dependence coupled with school dropout. Recent literature on the consequences of teen pregnancy have been especially concerned about intergenerational patterns such as intrafamily propensity for early childbearing and repeat pregnancy leading to cycles of child abuse, teen childbearing, and poverty within families (Hoffman, Foster, & Furstenberg, 1993). Data gathered over the last 30 years suggest that poverty and pregnancy are intertwined, especially for this age group. Without hope and without a future, early sexual intercourse forces the adolescent into welfare and the entitlement system. Younger teens fare much worse than their older sisters who might have finished high school.

Cultural factors associated with ethnicity, the roles of women, and the value of children may also affect reproductive health care. Weinman and Smith (1994), in a recent examination of Hispanic teens, found that neither first- nor second-generation teens were likely to return for postpartum services. They postulated that cultural notions about childbearing, lack of access to culturally compatible health care, and language barriers all contribute to poor health compliance. It is not surprising that the Hispanic teen birth rate is almost twice as high as that for non-Hispanic teens (Council on Scientific Affairs, 1991). Economic and educational factors may compound these problems in that studies have found that Hispanic teens are more likely to experience school dropout, economic hardship, and lack of birth control services than other adolescents.

Finally, recent data indicate that adolescents, particularly minority adolescents, are a significant high-risk group for acquiring HIV infections. The Center for Population Options (1989) has recently reported that each year 2.5 million teenagers contract a sexually transmitted disease, less that 25 percent use contraceptives consistently, and one in six high school girls have had at least four different sexual partners. The factors that contribute to high-risk status among adolescents include the presence of a sexually transmitted disease, multiple sexual partners, and experimentation with drugs and alcohol, which impairs the willingness or ability to use condoms or to take other precautions. Inner-city adolescents are especially high risk because of the presence of these multiple risk factors. In addition, the research literature on knowledge and behavioral risks of AIDS in teenagers suggests that knowledge about AIDS has not led to behavior changes (DiClemente, Zorn, & Temoshok, 1986). Minority adolescents have been identified as less knowledgeable about the protective value of condoms and as having more misconceptions about the routes of viral transmission.

Social Work Intervention and Teen Pregnancy: Into the Twenty-First Century

In attempting to project and forecast the trends that impact the way social work will intervene in the area of teenage pregnancy in the twenty-first century, it is probably useful to acknowledge the way that a variety of social forces beyond the control of many human interventions may dictate these trends. Previous programmatic interventions often did not consider those factors that reflect more global events. Although slow-moving, these macro forces have social power equivalent to that of the physical force of glaciers.

Geographical

As suggested in the emerging research, the impact of immigration from Mexico and parts of South America and Central America has gradually altered the cultural fabric of teen pregnancy. The increasing numbers of undocumented Hispanic workers especially in the southern and western segments of the country harbinger the gradual migration of these groups. Whether seeking economic security or freedom from political oppression, most of those women who migrate to the United States are poorly educated, young, and separated from the social infrastructure present in their native countries. Working for substandard wages often without health benefits, these young women resort to public perinatal programs. In addition to needing maternity and pediatric services, they also need but may not receive basic primary health care services. Immunizations and routine screening for orthopedic and congenital defects often does not occur. To exacerbate the situation, their clouded or illegal immigration status makes it difficult for them to qualify for public health assistance. Whereas their infants may qualify for medical care, having been born in the United States, the mother may not be able to receive preventive medical services through her pregnancy or the case management referral system provided as routine social services through the Medicaid program.

The trends continues to worsen when cultural issues are factored into the health system. Decisions associated with contraception and medical care are often influenced by the male partner or husband. Their absence or unfamiliarity with the system can become a stumbling block to a young woman's receipt of effective maternity or family planning services. In addition, religiosity and the influence of the Catholic church can be reinforced by

Hispanic males who adhere to the traditional roles of women. Social service providers must have a very special understanding and appreciation of this culture and of the importance of the male in the Hispanic couple. To deal effectively with the Hispanic adolescent mother these trends require that the professional must acquire a unique understanding of the way to provide services to both the male and his adolescent female partner in a non-threatening and culturally sensitive way.

Linked with the challenges of dealing with growing numbers of nonacculturated migrating adolescents are the barriers generated by limited mastery of the English language. As the majority of the Hispanic adolescents who migrate to the United States have not finished high school, the opportunity to develop a working knowledge of English usually has not been available. Even if some rudimentary English language skills have been obtained, familiarity with medical and social terminology has not been mastered. These possible trends in the twenty-first century dictate that providers of medical and social services to this cohort of teenagers must also possess some proficiency in Spanish. When the counselor or practitioner is unable to communicate with the Hispanic patient, the staff often must resort to using professional translators or other family members of the teenage mother to develop an accurate social and medical history. The ethical issue of confidentiality must be addressed, not to mention the concern that the information has been accurately reported through a second person. Sexuality and sexual activity in the Hispanic culture is considered to be a very private topic. Reporting intimate information through a family member is a very difficult thing for a teenage mother to do (Stunzer-Gibson, 1990).

Political

With the ebb and flow of political forces, recent swings in political philosophy have forced elected politicians to reevaluate how they assess the merits and perceived incentives associated with public subsidy of adolescent mothers. Although the validity of the point can be argued from both sides of the political fence, a growing groundswell suggests that conservative forces interpret adolescent pregnancy as a functional way to receive monetary and social support. During the twenty-first century this perception may be implemented in a variety of policy changes. One of the most controversial proposals that may be acted on during this new century is to eliminate any financial subsidy for adolescents who find themselves pregnant. The conservative corner continues to argue that as long as adolescents are paid to have babies, the incentives to stay in school and delay childbearing are minimized. The deleterious consequences to the newborn can be addressed by encouraging these young mothers to relinquish custody of the children and place them in orphanages. This is probably not a realistic alternative for a variety of developmental and social reasons, but this position may provide leverage for other, less dramatic, but equally conservative, options. A compromise to this position is the belief that all welfare benefits should be limited to two years with a few exceptions for true disability or advanced age. In addition, these benefits will be limited to two children per household. Such a trend may not be effective in encouraging family planning but may force families with other siblings to share resources designed for only two children.

Another policy change that could fall in this category could involve the male and a political move to retrench responsibility into his role in the teen pregnancy equation. Previous social policy did not require that the adolescent identify the putative father either to the hospital or to public agencies interested in establishing paternity. Garnishment of wages and the public acknowledgment of paternity could perhaps provide a subtle encouragement to the male to be more responsible in his sexual behavior, but social pressure to document fatherhood has historically been unsuccessful. Many pregnant teens when queried on the identity of the father choose to keep his identity anonymous because of the teenager's and her family's wish as well the wish to terminate all contact with him. The relinquishment of any financial benefits for the baby seems in the teenage mothers' minds a fair price to pay in exchange for the severing of all ties to the father. In addition, these mothers may intuitively know that the possibility that an adolescent father could provide adequate child support is small. Another group of adolescent mothers does not reveal the identity of the baby's father because he is either older and provides material support in exchange for sexual favors or is currently married and unable to publicly acknowledge his offspring. A significant policy change that could affect family formation in the twenty-first century is the legal mandate for young mothers to identify their children's father to the Child Support Office prior to the receipt of any financial or medical subsidy such as Aid to Families with Dependent Children or Medicaid. The consequences of this trend to acknowledge both parents are difficult to forecast. It is probably accurate to say that such a mandate will have repercussions on how families are formed and maintained. Once paternity is established, a further elaboration of this policy can also be predicted. Certain conservative groups suggest not only that wages should be garnered but that any state or federal licenses be revoked for a father who is delinquent in child support payments. Mandating male responsibility with economic consequences will change the way single families with dependent children support themselves.

Educational

In the twenty-first century pregnant teenagers may face several educational initiatives either to reduce first or subsequent pregnancies or to provide educational training to reenter the marketplace. Following the mindset that adolescent sexuality and pregnancy can probably be avoided through the teaching of various assertive skills, educational efforts will probably shift from sex education and its associated controversies to abstinence education, which will emphasize the risks of early sexual involvement. Such efforts, however, may miss adolescents who are not enrolled in school or who are involved in a sexual relationship to receive financial support, or teenage girls who have been involved in date rape or sexual assault. Social service providers will be challenged to be realistic about the feasibility of these efforts and keep the service alternatives broad enough to accommodate all teenagers, including those who are sexually active.

Following this trend a variety of bootstrap educational services targeting teenage mothers can probably be anticipated. This would include the mandate for the adolescent to participate in a variety of job training or educational services in order to receive any public assistance. Associated with this mandate is the requirement that a conservative lifestyle while on subsidy is espoused. This would include perhaps the signing of some type of work contract that would stipulate that the adolescent mother agree to accept a job to continue some type of benefits and maintain a drug-free household. For those individuals who are unable for whatever reason to obtain a job, the teenager must agree to participate in some sort of community service to qualify for public assistance. Such trends, although consistent with a more conservative mindset, may in fact be in conflict with a variety of constitutional amendments. The compromises that may be hammered out in terms of the educational obligations required of pregnant teenagers will probably reflect a stronger work ethic than present social educational and social programs. Social service providers will be challenged to synthesize traditional social work values with this changing educational climate.

Conclusion

To prepare for the twenty-first century, social service providers need to be conversant with the multifaceted nature of the problem both from a programmatic and global perspective. Crucial in this ability is the flexibility of the social services provider to effectively address and implement the programmatic needs while taking into consideration the prevailing changes in the political and social climate. It is worthwhile to remember that individuals receiving help from the public sector are vulnerable to these forces. Teenage pregnancy will not receive much public sympathy in the twenty-first century. Teenaged motherhood, and especially single motherhood, will not be glamorized in the movies as it has been in the past. It will carry with it a severe social stigma akin to conditions such as homelessness, yet it will still be among us, as close to half a million teenagers each year will deliver and/or parent their infants.

The most important areas social service providers will be concerned with are the comorbidity of teen pregnancy with poor physical and emotional health, the emergence of AIDS and other sexually transmitted diseases, and family-of-origin issues such as generational violence and poor nurturing. Traditional program interventions have met with limited success. All across the nation, professionals who have been working with teens have reported difficulties in reaching them. New and innovative strategies are required. However, new strategies cannot be implemented without public support. This means that government should provide a minimum benefit to all children, including universal health care and subsidized child care to all working parents regardless of their marital status. The goal of any public policy must be not just to reduce welfare dependence but to increase family stability and the well-being of children. Before we can impact personal responsibility and initiative, we must reduce poverty. We have cut poverty rates among the elderly by two-thirds from 1967 to 1993; it is time to do the same for children.

Therefore programs in the twenty-first century must consider an approach that emphasizes moving from hopelessness to personal responsibility. A central component of this is to emphasize the strengths of teenage mothers and their families, to acknowledge and work with their cultural heritage and their family supports, and to have a committed public policy that reduces poverty. These programs should view the family as being socially responsible and deemphasize dysfunctional behaviors and problems in pregnancy.

We then suggest that social workers who are trained in a systems approach develop programs that do the following:

- Support comprehensive home health services for families in need of primary prevention
- Coordinate medical, behavioral, social, family, and community resources through case management services that are located at one site
- Provide multiorganizational collaboration in the delivery of basic services to pregnant and parenting teens
- Emphasize the importance of cultural heritage and cultural compatibility in the delivery of services
- Involve natural support groups such as schools, health and recreation centers, churches, stores, and other built-in community resources that people use in their everyday lives

In sum, new programs will need to address a variety of interpersonal, social, cultural, and community concerns. Teenage pregnancy does not exist in isolation. It does not appear to be fruitful to pursue the prevention and intervention of teen pregnancy from a model of dysfunctional behaviors. Rather, we believe that social workers who use a person-in-environment approach can enhance the well-being of the teen and her family and at the same time support community efforts in the prevention of teenage pregnancy.

References

Baldwin, W. H. (1976). Adolescent pregnancy and childbearing—Growing concerns for Americans. *Population Bulletin, 31*(2), 2–34.

Beck, J. G., & Davies, D. (1987). Teen contraception: A review of perspectives on compliance. *Archives of Sexual Behavior, 16,* 337–368.

Blum, R. W., & Resnick, M. D. (1982). Adolescent sexual decision-making: Contraception, pregnancy, abortion, motherhood. *Pediatric Annals, 11*(10), 797–805.

Bolton, F. G., Laner, R. H., and Kane, S. P. (1980). Child maltreatment risk among adolescent mothers: A study of reported cases. *American Journal of Orthopsychiatry, 50,* 489–504.

Center for Population Options. (1989). *Adolescents, AIDS, and the human immunodeficiency virus.* Washington, DC: Author.

Child Trends, Inc. (1994). *Facts at a glance.* Washington, DC: Author.

Council on Scientific Affairs. (1991). Hispanic health in the United States. *Journal of the American Medical Association, 265*(2), 248–252.

DiClemente, R. J., Zorn, J., & Temoshok, L. (1986). Adolescents and AIDS: A survey of knowledge, attitudes, and beliefs about AIDS in San Francisco. *American Journal of Public Health, 76*(12), 1443–1445.

Furstenberg, F. F. (1988). *Adolescent mothers in later life.* New York: Cambridge University Press.

Hoffman, S. D., Foster, E. M., & Furstenberg, F. F. (1993). Reevaluating the costs of teenage childbearing. *Demography,30*(1), 1–11.

Lawrence, R. A., & Merritt, T. A. (1981). Infants of adolescent mothers: Perinatal, neonatal, and infancy outcome. *Semin Perinatol, 5*(1), 19–32.

Stunzer-Gibson, D. (1990).Women and HIV disease: An emergency social crisis. *Social Work, 36,* 22–28.

Weinman, M. L., and Smith, P. B. (1994). Characteristics of U.S.-born and Mexico-born Hispanic teens attending a county maternity hospital: Factors that relate to post-partum compliance. *Journal of Hispanic Behavioral Sciences, 16*(2), 186–194.

Administration

Part VI concerns administration in social work practice. A traditional field of practice, administration in teh future will likely be very different. Zeke Hasenfeld begins this section with a chapter on the key forces that will shape the future of human service organizations and the consequences for administrative practices. Beginning with changes in the environment, he then describes the administrative challenges and new strategies that must be identified in the new administration of human services. Readers of this chapter will want to answer the following questions:

1. How will the changing social environment affect human service organizations in ways that portend the future administrative changes outlined?

2. How will changing human needs in our society today affect human service organizations in ways that will require future daministrative changes?

3. What are the implications of these current changes on the administration of human service agencies? Which one(s) do you think are likely to occur first?

As outlined in Chapter 1 of this book, ethnic diversity will be the hallmark of the next generation of U.S. citizens. Lorraine Gutiérrez and her colleague Biren Nagda describe what the multicultural human service organization (MCOD) of the future might look like and why. Jean Latting ends this section with a historical review of human service organizations (HSOs) and where they are likely to be going in the next century.

In chapter 20 Gutiérrez and Nagda describe the implication of this demographic change and social work's ethnically sensitive services response by going one step further and speculating about the need for structural changes in human service organizations within the framework of multicultural organizational development. From reading this provocative chapter, one should be able to address the following questions:

1. What are the characteristics of multicultural human service organizations as outlined by the authors of this chapter? Which one(s) do you think will be the most difficult to implement? Why?

2. What will be the paradigm shift between clients and society required in implementing a multicultural human service organization?

3. What are the two strategies for developing a multicultural human service organization described in this chapter?

Jean K. Latting begins Chapter 21 with a review of the historical development of human service organizations (HSOs) and then predicts, in elaborate detail, how current trends will create future human service organizations in the new community. After you read this chapter, the following questions should be answerable:

1. What are the changes that have occurred in our society relative to the management of HSOs with the explosion of information, new technology, and accompanying societal change?

2. Which unique features of HSOs will make implementing continuous quality improvement processes difficult?

3. What will be the future changes in HSOs that are predicted to occur in the next century? Which one(s) are more likely to happen? Why?

Chapter 19

The Administration of Human Services—What Lies Ahead?

YEHESKEL HASENFELD, PhD
University of California at Los Angeles

Human service organizations are highly dependent on their environment for legitimation, clients, service technologies, and resources. The dependence on the environment goes beyond the need for resources; it also reflects the essential role that human services play in upholding important social norms and values. In the case of public assistance, for example, values about work ethic, family structure, gender, and sexual behavior are manifested in the policies that welfare agencies must implement (Handler & Hasenfeld, 1991). Similarly, mental health agencies uphold social norms concerning normalcy and deviance. In this sense human service organizations are said to be *institutionalized* rather than *technical* organizations (Meyer & Rowan, 1977); that is, their success is measured less by their technical competence than by the moral systems they affirm. Thus dominant moral systems (that is, the institutional environment) influence and play a central role in justifying human service organizations. The dependence on the institutional environment is further magnified by the fact that the environment is turbulent because human services cannot easily buffer themselves from cultural, political, demographic, economic, and technological changes that affect dominant social values. Hence these environmental changes have a direct impact on the services and their administration.

A Changing Environment

The Decline of the Welfare State and the Rise of Inequality

I begin with a key normative change facing human service organizations, namely, the decline in the legitimacy of the welfare state and the triumph of individualism over collective responsibility (Mishra, 1990). The decline is fueled, in part, by economic pressures such as low economic growth and global competition coupled with demographic changes such as the aging of the population that have made the costs of the welfare state increasingly burdensome. The welfare state is also jeopardized by the increase in social inequality, which has threatened the social consensus on which it rests.

The rise in income inequality, often attributed to the restructuring of the economy and the declining power of labor unions, has been quite pronounced in the past decade and is likely to continue into the next decade (Gottschalk, 1993). From 1979 to 1989 the bottom tenth and twenty-fifth percentiles experienced a significant decline in their income relative to the median, whereas the top seventy-fifth and ninetieth percentiles saw a significant increase (Karoly, 1993). Inequality has increased not only across occupations and industries but also within education and experience groups. Moreover, the inequality accentuates gender, ethnic, and racial inequalities as members of oppressed social groups tend to concentrate in low-income occupations. Inequality is, of course, further reinforced by the opposition of upper- and middle-income groups to income redistribution policies.

One consequence is the retreat from the idea of entitlement to the idea of charity. The second consequence is the increasing social bifurcation in the client population human services encounter. Several implications emanate from these trends. First, reliance on government for funding is and will become more precarious, while the dependence on the whims of donors will increase. Second, there is greater normative pressure on agencies, especially those dependent on government contracts, to differentiate between deserving and undeserving clients and to deny services to the latter. Third, services are becoming more segmented between the haves and the have-nots. That is, clients with means are able to seek out high-quality services they can afford, whereas poor clients are relegated to low-quality services that are specifically targeted to serve them.

The Privatization and Commercialization of Human Services

The retreat from the welfare state also results in the privatization and commercialization of human services, especially in the nonprofit sector (Salamon, 1993). The delivery of publicly mandated services is being shifted to both voluntary and for-profit service providers. On one hand, such a shift increases the decentralization of services, organizational flexibility and innovation, and the promotion of new organizational forms such as self-help groups and community-based organizations. On the other hand, it is also accompanied by a significant reduction in state resources, and agencies are forced to commercialize, that is, to sell their services in order to raise needed revenues. Indeed, the distinctions between voluntary and for-profit organizations are becoming more and more blurred in such sectors as child care, home care, and mental health (for example, see Clark & Estes, 1992). The commercialization of services reinforces the bifurcation and segmentation of services along income lines.

The privatization of human services also alters the relationship between citizens and welfare state programs. Specifically, the responsibility is being shifted from the state to the citizens to mobilize the services they need. That is, increasingly citizens needing human services are expected to assume the role of buyers, shopping around in the marketplace for the best services they can obtain with the resources they have. These resources include both the entitlements they receive from the state for certain services and their own personal means. Thus citizens will be expected to be far more active in getting and managing the services they need. Becoming a buyer creates the advantage of having choices and having the right to select the service provider most compatible with one's needs. Yet to be a successful buyer the person must have considerable knowledge of the service marketplace, not to mention information about the effectiveness of its constituent elements. Yet such knowledge is difficult to attain and is unevenly distributed. There is, as a result, greater potential for misinformation and abuse. Consequently, vulnerable populations might become even more victimized in the human services marketplace.

Focusing more specifically on changing funding patterns, there is a shift toward a highly mixed model of government contracts, charitable contributions, and market-oriented payment mechanisms. Agencies, public and private, must compete for resources via the market while facing pressures to contain costs. In the case of mental health services, for example, the introduction of competition and cost containment has resulted in managed care and utilization review that are no longer controlled by mental health professionals (Dorwart & Epstein, 1993). The introduction of market forces has led to the purchase of services for public-care patients with private providers (see Chapter 4); to the rise of specialization and diversification (see Chapter 7); and, most importantly, to the medicalization of psychiatric care. As competition sets in, for-profit and even nonprofit facilities begin to shy away from services to the chronically mentally ill, Medicaid patients, and the uninsured (see Chapter 9).

Indeed, the creation of a private system of care that caters mostly to those who can purchase its services further erodes the principle of universality, which is so fundamental to the welfare state. It increases and reinforces the bifurcation of the service delivery system. In particular, the introduction of market forces increases the fiscal stratification among the agencies. That is, agencies with highly successful market strategies are able to garner considerable resources, whereas those that fail or cannot appeal to market forces experience serious fiscal deprivations. The latter are, of course, the very agencies that serve the most vulnerable, who also become the victims of these market forces.

Changing Human Needs

Economic and technological changes will also affect the type and nature of the needs human service organizations will encounter. Two important forces can be identified. First, technological advances, especially in medicine, are enabling people to live longer and to survive with more serious disabilities. As a result, human service organizations are called on to serve an ever-increasing client population that suffers from serious physical and mental disabilities. There will be an increasing demand for personal care from clients with a high degree of chronicity. The provision of services to such a population will require different service modalities than those developed for clients with acute problems.

Second, the restructuring of the economy—shifting from a manufacturing economy to a knowledge and service economy—is also creating a significant class of people who become marginalized in the new economy. They experience severe economic deprivation because they lack the skills to become integrated in the new economy and earn a decent wage. Especially at risk are young people, both men and women, with limited education and training who consequently experience a very high unemployment rate. Not surprisingly, ethnic minorities are overrepresented in this high-risk population (Wilson, 1987). Yet the state does not provide them with any adequate economic protection. Indeed, state income security policies are likely to be even less responsive to their plight. Severe economic deprivation is highly correlated with serious social pathologies such as crime, mental illness, child abuse, teen pregnancy, and addiction (see Chapter 18). Increasingly, publicly mandated human service organizations are asked to serve a population that present serious social problems for whom the typical service technologies seem ineffective. At the same time, private agencies, not dependent on public funds, shy away from such clients because of the high costs of serving them and the limited prospect for success. Thus we are witnessing a distinct trend in which publicly mandated human services will be inundated with clients with serious and severe service needs. Yet the current practices and service technologies may prove ineffective in responding to their needs.

Ethnic Diversity

Human services are also experiencing significant demographic changes in their client population as well as their future staff. As we look toward the twenty-first century our population, especially in the large urban centers, is becoming increasingly culturally and ethnically diverse (see Chapter 1). The past decade has witnessed a surge in immigration from non-European countries, especially Latin America and Asia. The rate of immigration doubled from 1.5 per thousand U.S. population in 1951–1960 to 3.1 in 1981–1990 (Statistical Abstract of the United States, 1992). Over 43 percent of the immigrants arrive from Asia, and 36 percent arrive from Mexico, Central America, and the Caribbean Islands.

The implications to human services are profound. The dominant Anglocentric service ideologies and practices in most human service agencies are often in conflict with the values, norms, and expectations of the clients. In particular, the service technologies that embody these ideologies may be unresponsive and possibly ineffective when applied to clients whose cultural and behavioral patterns are alien to the technology. Moreover, relations between staff and clients become strained when they fail to share a common communication system. The clients become alienated and view the agency as a hostile environment. One consequence of this trend is the disengagement of ethnic minorities from mainstream human service organizations and the resurgence of ethnically based social service agencies.

The Information Revolution

Human service organizations must also respond to the rapidly changing information technologies that will dramatically alter the ways these organizations assemble, manage, and disseminate their information. There will be enormous pressures on human service organizations to gather, process, and produce more information about their clients and services; to link up with other human services information systems; and to make information about their services more accessible to the public via new computer technologies (see Chapter 2). The emerging information technologies will also push for radical changes in the service technologies by affecting how staff use information to make service decisions and how they monitor the progress of their clients. It will also affect the nature of the relations between staff and clients as these relations will be mediated by new communication systems.

Coupled with the information revolution, human service organizations will encounter far greater pressures to demonstrate effectiveness and efficiency. The ease by which information about clients and services can be assembled and manipulated will also provide the means, as well as raise the expectations, for agencies to demonstrate their effectiveness and the cost benefit of their services. Indeed, the availability of public funding is going to be made contingent on demonstration of effectiveness. It will also stimulate considerably more sophisticated research on the efficacy of the service technologies as can be seen, for example, in the controlled experiments on the effectiveness of work programs for welfare recipients (Gueron & Pauly, 1991) or the research on the effectiveness of family preservation strategies for abusive parents (Rzepnicki et al., 1994).

The development of highly sophisticated knowledge systems will stimulate considerable innovation in service technologies. Research and development in social interventions will become far more sophisticated. As a result, many current service technologies will be discarded for failure to demonstrate effectiveness (see Chapter 8). More research-based service technologies will replace them, and agencies will be pressed to implement newer and more effective technologies.

The New Administration of Human Services

What are the implications of these trends on the administration of human service agencies? What administrative challenges will they face? And what new administrative strategies should we expect to see?

Emergence of New Organizational Forms

The environmental changes will stimulate new organizational forms in the provision of services (see Chapter 21). The impetus for these new forms will come from the search for greater efficiency, cost reduction, and enhanced competitiveness. The introduction of competition and market mechanisms will encourage the formation of human service conglomerates, alliances, and chains, as is already happening in the health and mental health sectors (Dorwart & Epstein, 1993). What is common to these organizational forms is the pooling together of resources and services to provide for a competitive advantage. Consolidation of service organizations generates economies of scale, centralization of common administrative tasks, and thus reduction in administrative costs. These conglomerates and alliances will push for uniformity and standardization in the basic services their constituent units provide (that is, the "McDonaldization" phenomenon). At the same time, they will also encourage the development of multiple tiers of services to accommodate different groups of clients on the basis of their ability to pay for services. The mental health sector, for example, is witnessing the rise of conglomerate structures that incorporate under one umbrella publicly mandated services to the chronically mentally ill, employee assistance programs, and managed care services to insured clients (see Chapter 9). Other emerging examples are national chains providing home care services to frail elderly where the amount and quality of the services are differentiated by the economic status of the clients (see Chapter 13).

Thus, as the privatization process of human services continues, it will lead to greater concentration and consolidation of service providers within the same sector. At the same time, however, the increased competition and the expanding contractual market will also spawn many new small agencies searching for a specific service niche. These agencies will be marked by a high degree of innovation, lean and flat administrative structure, and a capacity to respond quickly to market opportunities. Some will be community-based or ethnically oriented agencies capitalizing on their superior knowledge of local conditions and relations with the targeted client population. Others will be driven by professional entrepreneurs who offer new and promising service technologies. However, these organizations will also experience a high mortality rate, as the market will become crowded with such service providers.

Social movement agencies such as feminist service organizations, self-help associations, and grassroots agencies whose success depends on their ability to mobilize resources are likely to find the changing environment less hospitable (Hyde, 1992). On the one hand, the decline in a collective orientation coupled with the retreat of the welfare state will make the mobilization of resources more difficult. On the other hand, the increased competition will force many of them to adapt to the new market conditions by taking on the structural attributes of their competitors.

The Ascendancy of Fiscal Management and the Decline of Professionalism

The rise of these new organizational forms suggests that a fundamental process of structural isomorphism will occur in the human services, whereby agencies will increasingly emulate the organizational practices of for-profit business organizations. First and foremost, fiscal management will ascend to dominate and control many service decisions. Service components will be reorganized as revenue centers, and programmatic decisions will be driven by revenue-cost calculations. That is, decisions to provide, expand, or reduce services will be based to a great extent on the capacity of such services to generate revenues and to show "profit," that is, excess of revenues over costs. Tight cost-control mechanisms will be established that will curb the autonomy of the professional staff. Managed care is one such mechanism. It prescribes the scope and amount of services professionals can provide, requiring preauthorization that is based on standards established to contain costs that may be in conflict with professional standards of care (Schreter, Sharfstein, & Schreter, 1994). Moreover, being accountable to revenue centers, professional staff will be evaluated by measures of "productivity," that is, the extent to which they generate units of service or revenues and minimize costs.

Undoubtedly, these trends will curb the autonomy and discretion of the professional staff. At the same time they will create a push toward deprofessionalization as a means to contain costs. That is, whenever possible nonprofessional or semiprofessional staff will replace highly paid professional staff. To some extent this will be made possible because the new information technology will make highly technical knowledge, previously controlled by professionals only, accessible to the semiprofessionals. In addition, agencies will rely on contract and casual staff, namely, staff who are hired on a contractual, temporary, or part-time basis, in order to avoid the costs of employee benefits.

Marketing and Public Relations

A feature of the new human service administration will be greater emphasis on marketing and public relations. These strategies are designed to secure the agency a market and to ensure a steady flow of external resources. Considerable efforts will be made to advertise and publicize the agency's services and to engage in highly visible marketing and fundraising campaigns using mass media technologies. Agencies will be in a constant search of new promising markets, developing and repackaging their services to respond to new service opportunities. The search for new contractual opportunities and playing the "funding game," that is, searching for new funding opportunities and tailoring services to compete for these opportunities will dominate strategic planning (Gronbjerg, 1993). Considerable resources will be devoted to environmental scanning, gathering intelligence and information on new developments in policies, funding patterns, and service demands, and to actions by competing organizations. Agencies with more effective environmental scanning capabilities are more likely to have a competitive advantage. Hence boundary-spanning roles will assume greater importance in the agency.

In addition, agencies will spend considerable energy and resources to develop extensive interorganizational linkages. One way to manage the turbulent environment is to forge linkages with providers of clients, funding agencies, legitimating organizations, and providers of complementary services. A key administrative strategy will be to link the agency to a broad network of organizations and to develop interdependent relations through exchange relations, coalitions, and alliances.

Transformational Leadership and Network Structure

The survival of human service agencies in the turbulent environment will require new forms of leadership, often referred to as *transformational* rather than *transactional* (Bargal & Schmid, 1989). The earmark of transformational leadership is a commitment to entrepreneurship and a willingness to cast away old organizational practices and to restructure the agency and its services to meet the exigencies of the new environment. It is a form of leadership that is externally rather than internally oriented, constantly seeking new opportunities and new ways to enhance the competitive advantage of the agency. Transformational leaders have little patience with established agency conventions and traditions if those are seen as hindering innovation. It would mean that increasingly leadership would be recruited external to the organization. Moreover, the tenure of leaders will be shorter because of the need to adjust to rapidly changing conditions, precipitating periodic succession crises.

Transformational leadership will be accompanied by nonbureaucratic structures. These will be characterized by a "flat" administrative structure with few managerial layers; the grouping of staff positions into flexible work teams rather than permanent units; and the contracting out of many organizational functions. Thus the permanent organizational core will be small but densely connected to a network consisting of work teams, task groups, and subcontractors (Miles & Snow, 1986). Such a structure enables the organization to reduce capital outlay and shift to new activities and services without excessive delays or transition costs. Such a structure, on the one hand, centralizes strategic decisions in the organizational core. On the other hand, it decentralizes operational decisions to the constituent elements of the network. The organizational core sets objectives and strategies, allocates resources, and determines performance standards. The network units are given considerable autonomy to decide how they will accomplish their tasks, but they are held accountable to strict performance criteria.

Innovative Service Technologies

Agencies are likely to face daunting technological challenges. First, the rate of innovation in service technologies is likely to increase rapidly as knowledge about the efficacy of various service approaches expands. Second, agencies will need to acquire new technologies that focus on the personal care of clients with serious chronic problems. Third, publicly mandated agencies will need to find effective technologies in handling clients with severe personal and social problems. All of these pressures will take place in a context of increasing demands to demonstrate both effectiveness and efficiency. Under these conditions one would expect a high rate of both technological innovations and failures, and agencies will need to devise administrative strategies to cope with both.

A network structure will enable human service organizations to develop the flexibility needed to adopt new technologies and to alter and modify existing ones. The environmental changes will dictate that the organization be able to modify its service technologies as it develops and adapts its services to new market conditions. Seeking new markets and clients will require agencies to import new service technologies to meet their service needs. Therefore we are likely to see agencies with multiple service technologies that are loosely coupled with each other. That is, agencies will be configured around internal "technological clusters," each consisting of a distinct client population with a defined set of needs that are met by a specific service technology. These technological clusters will be weakly tied to each other so that changes or problems in one will not affect the others.

The rapid obsolescence of many service technologies will require agencies to retool themselves fairly rapidly. In a turbulent environment, high premium will be given to agencies that can implement innovative technologies, especially those that can reduce costs.

The organization of the service technologies into clusters will enable agencies to discard old technologies and adopt new ones without major restructuring.

Internal Monitoring and Control

A related administrative development will be the increasing use of computer technologies for internal monitoring and control and for assessment of performance. Agencies will adopt highly sophisticated computerized information systems that will closely record and monitor staff activities, patterns of service delivery, and assessment of performance. These new technologies will alter administrative practices in important ways. First, accountability and performance measures will increasingly become commonplace. Second, considerable information on the clients and services will be available for administrative planning. Administrators will have readily accessible data on the performance of various programs, such as volume of services provided, characteristics of the clients served, and the results attained. Administrative decisions will increasingly be informed by data, thus increasing the capacity of the organization to learn from its past performance and to take corrective actions more rapidly. Third, the staff themselves will have access to a complex and rich client database that will greatly facilitate their ability to monitor their clients and to make appropriate service decisions.

The new information technologies will greatly expand the capacity of human service organizations to evaluate their services. No longer will agencies be able to use testimonials and anecdotal information to justify their services. Agencies will be expected to develop fairly sophisticated program evaluation systems. These evaluation systems will enable staff to assess the effects of their intervention and the organization to assess the impact of its various service programs. Such an ongoing evaluation system will also enable the organization to make rapid yet informed adjustments and changes to improve its effectiveness. This is a central feature of the *self-learning* organization. The idea of a self-learning organization will be a dominant theme in future administrative practices (March, 1991). It would mean that for agencies to survive and remain effective, they will have to develop the capacity to learn what works and what does not. They will be able to do so only if they develop an extensive information system that provides them with the necessary feedback to assess their performance and learn from their experiences.

Diverse Workforce and a Multicultural Organization

Human service organizations will have to contend with a very diverse workforce reflecting the broader demographic changes mentioned earlier. Diversity by gender, age, and ethnicity will be commonplace and essential if the agency is to be responsive to the cultural diversity of its clients (Gutiérrez, 1992). Yet the diversity of the workforce is also a potential source of conflict and internal divisions unless the agency transforms itself into a multicultural organization (Cox, 1991). A multicultural organization not only eradicates gender and ethnic inequities and prejudices among its staff but also actively promotes the diverse cultural values in the organization of its work and the delivery of its services. This will be one of the great administrative challenges as agencies face the next century, because the effectiveness of the agency will hinge on its ability to be responsive to the cultural differences among its staff and clients. As a first step, agencies will need to eliminate inequities in salaries, promotion opportunities, and representation at all levels of the organization. Such inequities produce conflict, dissension, alienation, morale problems, and high staff turnover that wreck the ability of the agency to be effective and efficient. Second, the agency will need to purge all forms of communication that are culturally biased and degrading. Biased and prejudiced communication not only denigrate minority staff members but also hinder effective relations with the culturally diverse client population. Third, and most importantly, the agency must grant legitimacy to the different cultural values its members bring with them and enable their appropriate expression in its service delivery system. For example, a feminist perspective that reinforces the sharing of power and democratization of the workplace may be built into the decision-making system of the agency. An African American celebration of narratives as a form of discourse may be incorporated into the transactions between staff and clients. This will happen when cultural diversity is represented at all levels of decision making within the organization. To do so, the organization must promote a climate that acknowledges and appreciates the cultural differences among its members without imposing the hegemony of one particular culture. Thus, by transforming itself to a multicultural organization, the agency, simultaneously, is far more effective in utilizing the talents of its diverse workforce and is far more competent in reaching out and responding to its diverse client population.

Client-Centered Relations

As human service organizations encounter an increasingly culturally and ethnically diverse client population, conventional patterns of worker–client relations will have to give way to new forms (Pinderhughes, 1989). These will have to be informed by and be sensitive to the cultural background of the clients and will require the establishment of new communication strategies that incorporate traditional patterns of communication in each particular cultural or ethnic group. These may include using bilingual workers, relying on indigenous members as liaisons, and shifting the place of contact from the agency's premises to the client's home or local ethnic associations.

Human service organizations will also look to restructure their relations with their clients. The typical pattern of clients being highly dependent on the staff, lacking an active voice in their own treatment, and abdicating responsibility for their course of treatment is likely to change because it will no longer be viable in the new environment. In a market-oriented service delivery system, clients will have to assume a far more active role in securing services. More importantly, agencies will no longer find it efficient or effective to foster dependency. Clients will be expected to become active participants in the management of their own care, thus relieving the staff from extensive case management functions. Put differently, agencies will increasingly search and use whatever resources clients can contribute to the service delivery process.

Moreover, a new practice ideology is emerging in the name of empowerment. It posits that the well-being of clients will be greatly enhanced if they take an active role in making decisions about their treatment and in assuming greater responsibility for their own actions. An increasingly common empowerment strategy is the facilitation of self-help and peer support groups. An empowerment strategy can ennoble the clients when the agency shares power with its clients and can provide them with concrete resources and adequate knowledge and support to become true partners in the decisions about their care (Handler, 1992). It is under such circumstances that it is fair to expect clients to assume greater responsibility about their actions in the service trajectory. However, empowerment becomes a hollow slogan when clients are given the responsibility but not the wherewithal to assume it.

Conclusion

The next decade will witness profound changes in the organization of human services. These will be driven by important changes in the environment in which these organizations operate. To survive, adapt, and be effective, human service organizations will adopt new administrative strategies. As we have seen, some of these strategies will benefit their clients, but others are likely to harm them, especially highly vulnerable clients. One of the tasks of the social work profession is to carefully assess these strategies and their impact on the clients. Ultimately, the only justifiable administrative strategies are those that promote fairness and justice and enhance the well-being of all clients.

References

Bargal, D., & Schmid, H. (1989). Recent themes in theory and research on leadership and their implications for management of the human services. *Administration in Social Work, 13,* 37–54.

Clarke, L., & Estes, C. L. (1992). Sociological and economic theories of markets and nonprofits: Evidence from home health organizations. *American Journal of Sociology, 97,* 945–969.

Cox, T. (1991). The multicultural organization. *Academy of Management Executive, 5,* 34–47.

Dorwart, R. A., & Epstein, S. S. (1993). *Privatization and mental health care.* Westport, CT: Auburn House.

Gottschalk, P. (1993). Changes in inequality of family income in seven industrialized countries. *American Economic Review, 83,* 136–142.

Gronbjerg, K. (1993). *Understanding nonprofit funding.* San Francisco: Jossey-Bass.

Gueron, J. M., & Pauly, E. (1991). *From welfare to work.* New York: Russell Sage Foundation.

Gutiérrez, L. M. (1992). Empowering ethnic minorities in the twenty-first century: The role of human service organization. In Y. Hasenfeld (Ed.), *Human services as complex organizations* (pp. 301–319). Newbury Park, CA: Sage.

Handler, J. (1992). Dependency and discretion. In Y. Hasenfeld (Ed.), *Human services as complex organizations* (pp. 276–298). Newbury Park, CA: Sage.

Handler, J., & Hasenfeld, Y. (1991). *The moral construction of poverty.* Newbury Park, CA: Sage.

Hyde, S. (1992).The ideational system of social movement agencies. In Y. Hasenfeld (Ed.), *Human services as complex organizations* (pp. 121–144). Newbury Park, CA: Sage.

Karoly, L. A. (1993). The trend in inequality among families, individuals, and workers in the United States: A twenty-five year perspective. In P. Gottschalk & S. Danziger (Eds.), *Uneven tides: Rising inequality in America* (pp. 19–98). New York: Russell Sage Foundation.

March, J. (1991). Exploration and exploitation in organizational learning. *Organization Science, 2,* 71–87.

Meyer, J., & Rowan, R. (1977). Institutionalized organizations: Formal structure as myth and ceremony. *American Journal of Sociology, 83,* 340–363.

Miles, R., & Snow, C. C. (1986). Network organizations: New concepts for new forms. *California Management Review, 28,* 62–73.

Mishra, R. (1990). *The welfare state in capitalist society.* Toronto: University of Toronto Press.

Pinderhughes, E. (1989). *Understanding race, ethnicity, and power.* New York: The Free Press.

Rzepnicki, T., Schuerman, J., Littell, J., Chak, A., et al. (1994). An experimental study of family preservation services. In R. Barth, J. Duerr Derick, & N. Gilbert (Eds.), *Child welfare research review, vol. 1* (pp. 60–82). New York: Columbia University Press.

Salamon, L. (1993). The marketization of welfare: Changing nonprofit and for-profit roles in the American welfare state. *Social Service Review, 67,* 16–39.

Schreter, R., Sharfstein, S., & Schreter, C. (Eds.). (1994). *Allies and adversaries: The impact of managed care on mental health services.* Washington, DC: American Psychiatric Press.

Wilson, W. J. (1987). *The truly disadvantaged: The inner city, the underclass, and public policy.* Chicago: University of Chicago Press.

Chapter *20*

The Multicultural Imperative in Human Services Organizations

Issues for the Twenty-First Century

LORRAINE GUTIÉRREZ, PhD and BIREN A. NAGDA, MSW
University of Michigan

The Problem

The growing ethnic diversity of the coming millennium will present many challenges to our profession. It is projected that within the next 50 years immigration and fertility patterns will lead to an increasingly multiracial, multicultural, and multiethnic society (Gutiérrez, 1992). At the same time, conditions of economic inequality and economic stratification by gender and race have not abated (Dressel, 1994; Simon, 1994). Because both women and people of color continue to experience economic and social disadvantage, these demographic projections have led to concerns that the United States could become a nation of poor children and youth of color and older European Americans, with neither group being capable of producing the economic resources necessary for supporting existing social services or other social goods (Ozawa, 1986; Sarri, 1986; Williams, 1990). These trends in the substance and structure of our society challenge our profession to evaluate how it can best address these demographic shifts (Gutiérrez, 1992).

Although social work has a history of working in communities of color, it has not adequately explored ways to respond to the increasing need for services by people of color or nor has it been successful in working with them to achieve greater equity. Yet social service and community organizations could play a particularly crucial role in creating a society in which diversity can contribute to our strength as a nation by improving the human capital potential of all people through improved access to quality health care, education, and support services. As we look to the future we must consider ways in which our work can support greater equity and social justice.

How has our profession traditionally dealt with racial and ethnic diversity? The roots of social work practice reflect a monocultural or *ethnocentric perspective* that considers, either explicitly or implicitly, the norms, values, and needs of the majority culture to be the most desirable (Gallegos, 1982; Chau, 1991; Morales, 1981). This perspective places little or no value on the unique experiences of people of color and may approach their cultures as the source of many of the problems they face.

The ethnocentric perspective has been the dominant orientation of social services. It was reflected in the development of the social services by predominantly upper-class men and women who created programs that often reflected classist, racist, and nativist social mores (Wenocur & Reisch, 1989). In response, immigrant, Native American, and African American communities developed their own systems of self-help and mutual aid (Mankiller, 1993; Wenocur & Reisch, 1989).

Ethnocentrism has manifested itself in social service organizations as the provision of segregated services (Stehno, 1982), in the deportation of aliens (Guerin-Gonzales, 1994), or in Americanization programs that resulted in the loss of culture and community (Carpenter, 1980). The presence of some ethnic groups, such as Asian Americans, has been ignored by service planners and providers (Lee, 1986). Some ethnic groups and their needs have been overlooked based on the notion that they "take care of their own" or may not respond well to the treatments offered at agencies (Land, Nishimoto, & Chau, 1988; Lee, 1986; Starret, Mindel, & Wright, 1983). In its more subtle form, ethnocentrism has led to client typification and tracking within the human services (Gutiérrez, 1992). Rather than looking at ways in which existing agency procedures, structures, or treatments can be altered to better respond to the needs of ethnic minorities, the ethnocentric approach assumes that the problem in accessing and using services exists in the client group and that it is their responsibility to change.

Organizing within communities of color has led to the development of *ethnic-sensitive* and culturally competent approaches to social service organizations and programs (Chau, 1991; Devore & Schlesinger, 1987; Gallegos, 1982; Scott & Delgado, 1979). The goal of the ethnic-sensitive or ethnic-competent approach is to create or recreate programs and organizations that will be more responsive and responsible to the culture of people of color. Training for cultural competence and the delivery of ethnic-sensitive services requires understanding of one's own personal attributes and values, gaining knowledge about the culture of different groups, and developing skills for cross-cultural work (Chau, 1991; Gallegos, 1982). It is based on the notion that our society is multicultural and that positive gains can result from learning about different cultural groups and incorporating culture into agency procedures, structures, and services (Devore & Schlesinger, 1987; Gallegos, 1982).

Although the development of the ethnic-sensitive approach to social services has led to changes in the training and thinking of individual service providers and the creation of new programs, it is not an adequate response to the challenges related to the low status and power of people of color. These methods are limited by their focus on individual change and cultural factors. It ignores the role of power in the social order and social work practice (McMahon & Allen-Meares, 1992), is more concerned with individual change at the expense of maintaining an institutional status quo (McMahon & Allen-Meares, 1992), equates ethnicity to culture with the danger of stereotyping and typifying clients (Green, 1982; Jayasuriya, 1992; Longres, 1991), is more suited for working with refugees than with ethnic minorities who have been in the United States for more generations (Longres, 1991), and lacks a social development agenda (Midgley, 1991). The question arises as to how the profession can respond to societal changes in more comprehensive and effective ways.

Research suggests that if ethnic-sensitive services do not lead to structural changes in organizations and a greater participation of people of color in the governance of the agency, efforts toward change can be mostly symbolic and marginal (Gutiérrez, 1992; Mizio, 1981; Morales, 1981; Solomon, 1976; Washington, 1982). The *ethnoconscious* approach, which combines an ethnic-sensitive orientation and an empowerment perspective on practice, holds promise for creating empowering services, programs, and organizations.

The ethnoconscious approach is based in an appreciation and celebration of the strengths existing in communities of color (Gutiérrez, 1992, Pinderhughes, 1989; Solomon, 1976). At its center is a concern with power and confronting social inequality through work with individuals, families, groups, organizations, and communities. The process of helping is that of partnership, participation, and advocacy. In all work, people of color are active agents in individual and social transformation.

At the center of the ethnoconscious approach is empowerment: the process of gaining personal, interpersonal, and political power (Gutiérrez, DeLois, & GlenMaye, in press; Pinderhughes, 1989; Simon, 1994; Solmon, 1978). The empowerment perspective on practice is not new; it reflects a tradition that challenges the conceptualization of social workers as benefactors or liberators of the less fortunate (Simon, 1994). The first two traditions, with their paternalistic assumptions, have most often been tools for social control. The empowerment tradition is identified as one that can most effectively work for both social and individual change through active engagement of community members in change efforts at all levels (Simon, 1994).

This brief review of this history of our profession concerning communities of color suggests that if we are to have a positive impact in the twenty-first century, then we must examine ways to develop and support an ethnoconscious approach to practice. Elsewhere in this volume, similar approaches to work with small systems are described and discussed (see Chapter 19). However, these services can not exist in a vacuum: In order for them to be effective they must operate within supportive institutions. Therefore we contend that through the development of multicultural human services organizations, we can meet the challenges of this demographic shift and begin to work toward greater equity in our society. In this way the human service organization itself can become a vehicle for positive social change. In this chapter we begin to identify what we mean by multicultural organizations, what challenges we face in their development, and what we can do to achieve thisgoal.

The Multicultural Human Service Organization

Multicultural organizational development (MCOD) has grown from a desire for organizational efforts to impact on social conditions. MCOD provides a framework for planned, large-scale, and long-term organizational transformation approaches to systems change that is informed by social justice concerns (Chesler, 1993; Jackson & Holvino, 1988; Katz, 1988; Pope, 1993). MCOD efforts have primarily occurred within business, industry (Jackson & Holvino, 1988; Cox, 1993), and higher education (Katz, 1988, McEwen & Roper, 1994). Only recently have the human services been a focus of this work (Nixon & Spearmon, 1991; Nagda, 1994).

The work on MCOD identifies two dimensions of the organization to be particularly crucial. The first is the representation and contributions of diverse social groups in the organizational culture, mission, and outputs. These groups should be involved at all levels of the organization, including decision-making bodies. The second is a concerted effort to eliminate social injustices and oppression. In these ways the mission of a multicultural organization is not limited to the workplace but extends to the larger community in which it is situated (Jackson & Holvino, 1988; Nagda, 1994)

What would a multicultural *human services* organization look like? It would place the focus on social justice for communities of color into a human services framework. These organizations would have the following characteristics:

- **A multicultural human service organization is dually focused on bringing about social change and providing empowering programs and services to its clientele.** It is committed to transformational efforts to eliminate all forms of social oppression that discriminate, disempower, and alienate its clientele. It aims to provide services to a wide range of clients who have been socially, politically, and economically disenfranchised. Its ideology, goals, and practices are strategically aligned to create socially just conditions for its clients and society at large.
- **A multicultural human service organization is committed to an empowerment perspective that appreciates, celebrates, and values clients strengths, resources, needs, and cultural backgrounds.** It aims to provide accessible and convenient services that contribute to individual, family, group, community, or organizational empowerment. It achieves these goals by providing a wide range of preventive and ameliorative services across the life span. These services are provided in multiple contexts and using multiple methods.
- **A multicultural human service organization aims to create workplace conditions that are modeled on its multicultural ideology and goals.** It is committed to an equitable and diverse social and cultural representation among its workforce not only in numbers but also in structures, norms, styles, and values. It values difference by nurturing the participation and learning of all of its members. It strives for the workplace to be an endeavor in multicultural learning, supporting, challenging, and growing for its members. It recognizes the potential for conflict and uses these conflicts as opportunities for learning and growth.

- **A multicultural human service organization is horizontally linked to client communities through its programs and services and involvement in community networks.** It encourages and facilitates client collaboration and partnerships in organizational governance, program development, staffing and evaluation.
- **A multicultural human service organization sees itself as an active participant in the larger environment.** It is vertically linked to professional, legislative, and funding sources. When necessary it advocates for client rights, changes in regulations, educational reform, or other changes that will support social justice.
- **A multicultural human service organization is also linked in local, national, and international networks.** It strives to build coalitions with other community groups and social movement organizations. It plays an important role in encouraging, pressuring, and facilitating the multicultural mission of other coalition members.
- **A multicultural human service organization is a praxis-oriented, learning organization that is in a dialectical relationship with its internal and external environment.** It embodies and models praxis, a process of reflection and action, in its dealings with external and internal environments. It aims to be a learning organization that is reflective about its processes, structures, policies, practice, and membership.

The multicultural organization, therefore, involves a paradigm shift in existing conceptions of human services organizations. It differs from other approaches to diversity by calling for second-order change (Bargal & Schmid, 1992; Porras & Robertson, 1992). Previous attempts by organizations to work with diverse populations have included increasing worker sensitivity through education, tailoring interventions to cultural beliefs and practices, and increasing access to services (Gutiérrez, 1992). These developmental efforts have required only first-order changes in that they involve alteration in characteristics of programs without questioning basic paradigms (Nagda, 1994; Porras & Robertson, 1992). Second-order changes, such as the one we are proposing, require dramatic shifts in organizational paradigms and a critical examination of existing practice. As described here, multicultural organizations need to change the traditional nature and configuration of relationships with constituencies outside and within the organization (Jackson & Holvino, 1988; Katz, 1988).

This task of creating multicultural human service organizations is complicated by the nature of human service organizations. Human service organizations are situated in a heterogeneous and unpredictable environment made up of multiple constituencies (Hasenfeld, 1992; Martin, 1990). External constituencies include funding sources, regulatory agencies, professional schools, and training programs and the communities in which they are located. Internal constituencies include administrators, staff, and advisory or governing boards. Much of the work of human service administrators involves finding ways to create a positive organizational culture that can encourage productivity while answering to these constituencies.

One way in which an organization interacts with its constituencies is through its ideational system consisting of organizational ideology and organizational goals (Hyde, 1992). Both ideology and goals may be explicit or implicit, public or private. The duality of the internal–external environments is reflected by reflexive and transitive goals, respectively. Reflexive goals guide intraorganizational maintenance activities such as personnel development and governance. Transitive goals guide extraorganizational relations through its services, actions, and products (Hyde, 1992).

Creating multicultural service organizations means changing transitive goals by developing ethnoconscious services for clients but also creating new reflexive goals and organizational ideology. By placing social justice at the center of its internal and external processes, the multicultural human service organizations becomes a crucial participant in the social environment, with dialectic relationships with the client, workers, profession, and society. Rather than mediating between clients and society, the role of the multicultural human service organizations is to become an advocate for communities of color with its many constituencies.

Strategies for Developing Multicultural Human Service Organizations

By calling for a paradigm shift, this model for organizational practice requires a radical change in our profession and its relationships with external and internal constituencies. It calls for an alliance with communities of color and a careful distancing from external groups that would like to use human services to control them. Within our current, and perhaps future, political context that has become less tolerant of communities of color (Dressel, 1994; Simon, 1994), this strategy can involve considerable risk. Traditionally, human services have derived their legitimacy from their support of dominant cultural systems. By challenging dominant values, and the organizations that represent them, multicultural human service organizations can jeopardize their own existence. How can we create multicultural human service organizations that work for social justice during the next decades?

Current research on organizations operating from this perspective provides some insights into this dilemma. These organizations have had to make conscious and sometimes difficult choices to maintain their social justice mission while attending to organizational maintenance. The experiences of these organizations suggest the following strategies.

1. Tight Coupling of Ideology/Culture/Practice

One way in which organizations can avoid threatening institutional legitimacy is to have public and private faces: Its ideology and mission are more consistent with dominant social values. This implies that the ideology and transitive goals in the organization's ideational system need not be aligned. This notion of "loose coupling" states that the ideology of the organization should conform to the values of its resource agents. Although this strategy could be effective, it would create organizations susceptible to co-optation and goal displacement.

An alternative would be "tight coupling" that strategically aligns organizational ideology, culture, and practices. This strategy would place ideology at the center of administrative decisions and make the organization more accountable to the community at large (Nagda, 1994). Research on empowerment practice in organizations suggests that this work is best supported when organizational leaders are able create a vision that guides organizational work (Gutiérrez, GlenMaye, & DeLois, 1995). This lends support to the hope that the hard decisions that are involved in this work can pay off in longer-term survival and effectiveness.

2. Coalition with Similar/Allied Organizations

Organizations can gain legitimacy and power through coalitions with client interest groups, other human service agencies, and social movement organizations. Such coalitions have the potential to increase the collective resource power within the community of clients and its member organizations. As such, there is a resource interdependence among clients and organizations and a resource independence from legislative and funding sources that may be opposed to the organization's multicultural or social justice ideologies. Coalitions can create their own niche through collaboration.

Strong coalitions can be viewed as another source of organizational power. Multicultural organizations need to take a creative and expansive view of coalition building. Coalitions can involve community leaders, businesses, religious institutions, and educational programs. In this way it reflects the ecosystem of communities of color. Diversity within coalition building is crucial for organizational maintenance and growth. It can become the bases of economic development or other community-based activities.

3. Diversification of Programs and Resources

Building on resource independence and interdependence, a range of programs and resources can increase the power of individuals and organizations. In addition to providing more resources for the community, the organization also creates service flexibility for itself. In today's environment of uncertainty and heterogeneity, this strategy can maximize organizational survival. As described by Schmid (1992),

> organizations operating in stable environments, where certainty is high, will prefer specialist and domain defensive strategies, whereas those operating in unstable, uncertain environments will tend to adopt generalist and domain offensive strategies. (p. 170)

Tourigny and Miller's (1981) analysis of how neighborhood-based community organizations are affected by vertical and horizontal systems of influence reinforces these assertions. They observed that organizations that receive large amounts of state or federal funding experience vertical control and therefore must put effort into developing good local, or horizontal, linkages. Conversely, organizations that receive local funding are horizontally controlled and are often limited in setting goals for local social change. Organizations that have mixed funding sources can be affected by both systems but also may have more autonomy and more sensitivity to local needs (Tourigny & Miller, 1981). Therefore multicultural human service organizations may function best when receiving funding from sources that share their organizational goals or when mixing funding sources so that no one source can control the organization. In addition, horizontal support, and organizational team building, may be crucial so that programs are directly responsive to community and staff needs and priorities.

4. Changes in Social Work Education

In order for these strategies to be effective, changes will need to occur within our profession with respect to professional education. As currently structured, the focus is on direct practice, specialization, and work with small systems (Sarri, 1986). Although accreditation standards call for a focus on social justice and human diversity (CSWE Curriculum Policy Statement, 1994), efforts to teach this content are uneven and at times unfocused. Only a handful of schools teach practice from a social justice framework.

Work from an ethnoconscious perspective calls for learning different methods of practice. Group work, organizational change, and administrative practice each call for a different set of skills than specialized individual work: an awareness of group processes, interpersonal interaction, organizational theory, and power dynamics. As a form of intervention, empowerment also requires a sharing of information, control, and resources that does not usually occur in individual work (Garvin, 1985; Gutiérrez, DeLois, & GlenMaye, in press; Hirayama & Hirayama, 1985; Longres & McLeod, 1980). If we are to support the development of ethnoconscious services and multicultural organizations, it will be necessary to train social workers in the skills necessary to work with groups, organizations, and communities effectively. The educational process will also need to focus on developing within students a commitment to the principles of democracy, equality, and noncompetitive and nonviolent forms of power. Through working in partnership with community members social workers will develop a different form of "expert knowledge" (Adams & Krauth, 1994).

Conclusion

We have titled this chapter the "Multicultural Imperative" because we believe that our profession stands at a critical juncture. The demographic changes in our society will proceed regardless of how our profession responds. We now stand at a choice point between working for social justice and equality in an increasingly diverse world or working to reinforce current calls for social control. Taken to what we hope is an extreme, will our role be focused on the development of "ethnic-sensitive" detention facilities for youth of color who slip from the "safety net" or will we work to create more economic opportunity for all? The path we take will be affected by our professional mission as well as our ability to create multicultural organizations.

In some respects current social conditions mirror those experienced in large cities 100 years ago. Our profession was founded with the goal of controlling and preventing the problems associated with capitalist development (Simon, 1994; Dressel, 1994; Wenocur & Reisch, 1989). During the final two decades of the nineteenth century social conditions such as the concentration of wealth, large-scale immigration, and an economic recession led to a crisis in the nascent welfare state. One response to these conditions was the development of the progressive movement that contributed to social reform and the creation of the social sciences (Simon, 1994; Wenocur & Reisch, 1989).

How well did these efforts address the problems of the nineteenth-century city? Charity organizations, sectarian services, settlements, social legislation, and other efforts created mechanisms for improving the lives of the poor and working classes. However, the spirit and intent of these efforts were more often to contain and control the behaviors of those served than to change social conditions (Simon, 1994; Wenocur & Reisch, 1989).

In its development throughout the twentieth century our profession has at times lost its empowerment tradition (Resich & Wenocur, 1986; Simon, 1994; Specht & Courtney, 1994). In an effort to gain legitimacy, we have focused primarily on issues of individual functioning, coping, and social control. Although social workers participated in the poverty programs of the New Deal and Great Society, they have been relatively quiet in recent debates over welfare reform. Some have argued that in the past nine decades our profession has lost its way (Specht & Courtney, 1994).

In some respects, these models of practice that are based on a professional and expert role are embraced by social workers in an attempt to counteract the feelings of powerlessness they experience in their work. By seeing themselves a capable and expert, and the client as deficient and ineffectual, social workers can feel a sense of personal control and power (Pinderhughes, 1989; Weick, 1982). The ethnoconscious model, which requires a sharing of power and control between worker and client, can occur only when social workers not only will *not* be threatened by the collaborative role but will be assisted and supported by managers and educators in this radical restructuring of power and control. Recent work on organizational empowerment suggests that with effective support and leadership, workers need not gain feelings of power at the expense of the communities with which they work (Adams & Krauth, 1994; Bailey, 1994; Gutiérrez, GlenMaye, & DeLois, 1995).

In order for our profession to contribute to the empowerment of communities of color, we need to recognize our role within the society and engage in a process of political education of ourselves and others (Frumkin & O'Connor, 1985; Resich & Wenocur, 1986). Through this exploration we can identify ways in which we can work more effectively as allies to the people and the communities that we serve. We need to maintain a positive focus both on the strengths and possibilities that exist in our world, but also on our own strengths and possibilities as a profession. The order of change we are proposing here requires both transformational leadership and optimism regarding our endeavor. As stated by Simon (1994),

> Only practitioners who have believed deeply that people can change and that environments can be transformed have been able to work from an empowerment perspective in a sustained fashion. (p. 3)

This brief discussion has highlighted issues involved in the implementation of multicultural organizational practice. An important element is the interrelationship of systems within the profession. Although this model could enhance current practice and effectively impact many of the problems facing our society, without concurrent changes in the structure of social work and the education of practitioners, they cannot be implemented effectively. As we enter the twenty-first century it is imperative that we take a hard look at our roles and mission and find ways to work together for a more equitable society.

References

Adams, P., & Krauth, K. (1994). Empowering workers for empowerment based practice. In L. Gutiérrez & P. Nurius (Eds.), *Education and research for empowerment practice* (pp. 183–194). Center for Social Policy and Practice, School of Social Work, University of Washington, Seattle, WA.

Bailey, D. (1994). Organizational empowerment: From self to interbeing. In L. Gutiérrez & P. Nurius (Eds.), *Education and research for empowerment practice* (pp. 37–42). Seattle: University of Washington Press.

Bargal, D., & Schmid, H. (1992). Organizational change and development: A prefatory essay. *Administration in Social Work, 16*(3/4), 1–13.

Carpenter, E. (1980). Social services, policies, and issues. *Social Casework, 61,* 455–461.

Chau, K. L. (1991). Social work with ethnic minorities: Practice issues and potentials. *Journal of Multicultural Social Work, 1*(1), 23–39.

Chesler, M. (1993). *O. D. ≠ M. C. O. D.* PCMA Working Paper Series #42. Ann Arbor: University of Michigan, Program on Conflict Management Alternatives.

Council on Social Work Education. (1994). *Curriculum policy statement.* Alexandria, VA: Author.

Cox, T. (1993). *Cultural diversity in organizations: Theory, research and practice.* San Francisco, CA: Berrett-Koehler.

Devore, W., & Schlesinger, E. G. (1987). Ethnic-sensitive social work practice. St. Louis, MO: C. V. Mosby.

Dressel, P. L. (1994). . . . And we keep on building prisons: Racism, poverty and challenges to the welfare state. *Journal of Sociology and Social Welfare, 21,*7–30.

Frumkin, M., & O'Connor, G. (1985). Where has the profession gone? Where is it going? Social work's search for identity. *The Urban and Social Change Review, 18*(1), 12–19.

Gallegos, J. (1982). The ethnic competence model for social work education. In B. White (Ed), *Color in a white society* (pp. 1–9). Silver Spring, MD: National Association of Social Workers.

Garvin, C. (1985). Work with disadvantaged and oppressed groups. In Sundel, M., Glasser, P., Sarri, R., & Vinter, R. (Eds.), *Individual change through small groups* (2nd ed.; pp. 461–472). New York: The Free Press.

Green, J. W. (1982). *Cultural awareness in the human services.* Englewood Cliffs, NJ: Prentice Hall.

Guerin-Gonzales, C. (1994). *Mexican workers and American dreams.* New Brunswick, NJ: Rutgers Press.

Gutiérrez, L. (1992). Empowering clients in the twenty-first century: The role of human service organizations. In Y. Hasenfeld (Ed.), *Human service organizations as complex organizations* (pp. 320–338). Newbury Park, CA: Sage.

Gutiérrez, L., DeLois, K., & GlenMaye, L. (in press). Understanding empowerment practice: Building on practitioner based knowledge. *Families in Society.*

Gutiérrez, L., GlenMaye, L., & DeLois, K. (1995). The organizational context of empowerment practice: Implications for social work administration. *Social Work, 40*(2), 249–258.

Hasenfeld, Y. (1992). The nature of human service organizations. In Y. Hasenfeld (Ed.), *Human services as complex organizations* (pp. 3–23). Newbury Park, CA: Sage.

Hirayama, H., & Hirayama, K. (1985). Empowerment through group participation: Process and goal. In M. Parenes (Ed.), *Innovations in social group work: Feedback from practice to theory* (pp. 119–131). New York: Haworth Press.

Hyde, C. (1992). The ideational system of social movement agencies: An examination of feminist health centers. In Y. Hasenfeld (Ed.), *Human services as complex organizations* (pp. 121–144). Newbury Park, CA: Sage.

Jackson, B. W., & Holvino, E. (1988). *Multi-cultural organizational development.* PCMA Working Paper Series #11. Ann Arbor: University of Michigan, Program on Conflict Management Alternatives.

Jayasuriya, L. (1992). The problematic of culture and identity in social functioning. *Journal of Multicultural Social Work, 2*(4), 37–58.

Katz, J. H. (1988). *Facing the challenge of diversity and multi-culturalism.* PCMA Working Paper Series #13. Ann Arbor: University of Michigan, Program on Conflict Management Alternatives.

Land, H., Nishimoto, R., & Chau, K. (1988). Interventive and preventive services for Vietnamese Chinese refugees. *Social Service Review, 62,* 568–484.

Lee, J. (1986). Asian-American elderly: A neglected minority group. *Journal of Gerontological Social Work, 9*(4), 103–116.

Longres, J. (1991). Toward a status model of ethnic sensitive practice. *Journal of Multi-cultural Social Work, 1*(1), 41–56.

Longres, J., & McLeod, E. (1980). Consciousness raising and social work practice. *Social Casework, 61,* 267–277.

Mankiller, W. (1993). *Mankiller: A chief and her people.* New York: St. Martin's Press.

Martin, P. (1990). Rethinking feminist organizations. *Gender & Society, 4(2),* 182–206.

McEwen, M., & Roper, L. (1994). Incorporating multiculturalism into student affairs preparation programs: Suggestions from the literature. *Journal of College Student Development, 35,* 46–53.

McMahon, A., & Allen-Meares, P. (1992). Is social work racist? A content analysis of the recent literature. *Social Work, 37*(6), 533–539.

Midgley, J. (1991). Social development and multi-cultural social work. *Journal of Multi-cultural Social Work, 1*(1), 85–100.

Mizio, E. (1981). Training for work with minority groups. In E. Mizio & A. Delaney (Eds.), *Training for service delivery to minority clients* (pp. 7–20). New York: Family Service Association of America.

Morales, A. (1981) Social work with third world people. *Social Work, 26,* 48–51.

Nagda, B. (1994). *Toward a vision of a multi-cultural human service organization: A confluence of ideologies, missions, goals and praxis.* Preliminary Examination Paper. School of Social Work, University of Michigan, Ann Arbor, MI.

Nixon, R., & Spearmon, M. (1991). Building a pluralistic workplace. In R. L. Edwards & J. Yankey (Eds.), *Skills for effective human services management* (pp. 155–170). Silver Springs, MD: National Association of Social Workers.

Ozawa, M. (1986). Nonwhites and the demographic imperative in social welfare spending. *Social Work, 31,* 440–445.

Pinderhughes, E. (1989). *Understanding race, ethnicity, and power: The key to efficacy in clinical practice.* New York: The Free Press.

Pope, R. (1993). Multi-cultural organization development in student affairs: An introduction. *Journal of College Student Development, 34,* 201–205.

Porras, J. I., & Robertson, P. J. (1992). Organizational development: Theory, practice, and research. In M. D. Dunnette & L. M. Hough (Eds.), *Handbook of industrial and organizational psychology, vol. 3* (2nd ed.; pp. 719–822). Palo Alto, CA: Consulting Psychologists Press.

Resich, M., & Wenocur, S. (1986). The future of community organization in social work: Social activism and the politics of profession building. *Social Service Review. 60,* 70–93.

Sarri, R. (1986). Organizational and policy practice in social work: Challenges for the future. *Urban and Social Change Review, 19,* 14–19.

Schmid, H. (1992). Strategic and structural change in human service organizations: The role of the environment. *Administration in Social Work, 16*(3/4), 167–186.

Scott, J., & Delgado, M. (1979). Planning mental health programs for Hispanic communities. *Social Casework, 60,* 451–456.

Simon, B. L. (1994). *The empowerment tradition in American social work.* New York: Columbia University Press.

Solomon, B. (1976). *Black empowerment.* New York: Columbia University Press.

Specht, H., & Courtney, M. E. (1994). *Unfaithful angels: How social work has abandoned its mission.* New York: The Free Press.

Starret, R., Mindel, C., & Wright, R. (1983). Influence of support systems on the use of social services by the Hispanic elderly. *Social Work Research and Abstracts, 19*(4), 35–40.

Stehno, S. (1982). Differential treatment of minority children in service systems. *Social Work, 27,* 39–45.

Tourigny, A. W., & Miller, J. A. (1981). Community based service organizations. *Administration in Social Work, 5*(1), 79–86.

Washington, R. (1982). Social development: A focus for practice and education. *Social Work, 27*(1), 104–109.

Weick, A. (1982). Issues of power in social work practice. In A. Weick & S. Vandiver (Eds.), *Women, power, and change.* Silver Springs, MD: National Association of Social Workers.

Wenocur, S., & Reisch, M. (1989). *From charity to enterprise: The development of American social work in a market economy.* Chicago: University of Illinois Press.

Williams, L. (1990). The challenge of education to social work: The case of minority children. *Social Work, 35,* 236–242.

Chapter *21*

===

Human Service Organizations of the Future

JEAN KANTAMBU LATTING, Dr PH, LMSW
University of Houston

Every few hundred years throughout Western history, a sharp
transformation has occurred. In a matter of decades, society altogether
rearranges itself—its world view, its basic values, its social and
political structures, its arts, its key institutions. Fifty years later a
new world exists. . . . Our age is in such a period of transformation.
                                            —PETER DRUCKER (1992)

It has become commonplace to speak of dizzying change in the world of work. Rapid technological change—particularly in the information technologies—the globalization of economic activities, and changes in the expectations of today's workers have all fueled widespread organizational restructuring in the for-profit sector and increasingly in the public and nonprofit sectors as well. This chapter will briefly review historical factors that led to current trends in how companies are organized and managed. Based on this review, I will offer several predictions of likely future developments.

Where We Came From

At the beginning of the twentieth century, massive numbers of people began leaving their farms and flooding the cities seeking more lucrative work in the burgeoning smokestack industries and factories. To ensure that these formerly autonomous employees conformed to the tedium of factory work and were maximally productive, organizational theorists advocated a hierarchical organizational structure. Several features that characterized these organizations still prevail in today's human service bureaucracies: (1) specialization and division of labor—the more narrowly defined the job, the greater the expected expertise; (2) unity of command (one man, one boss) so that lines of authority and communication remained clear; (3) hierarchy of authority, so that decision making was centralized increasingly as one moved to the top; (4) formalization, or clearly specified rules and procedures to ensure continuity and uniformity of operations; and (5) administrative impersonality—managers and employees alike were expected to maintain a social distance from one another and to maintain objective neutrality in their interactions with one another.

In a time when the environment was relatively stable, work was boring, and employees were mostly illiterate, this form of design made sense. Managers were able to anticipate most problems and had time to resolve them, they strictly enforced rules and procedures as needed to ensure uniform production, and they closely monitored the activities of their employees who likely would not have chosen to screw in the same bolt 1,000 times a day without threat of job loss or promise of adequate pay.

In the 1920s and 1930s the famous Hawthorne studies led to the discovery of the "informal organization"—the informal groupings of employees who communicated among themselves outside of formal organizational channels. With this discovery, theorists began to explore how to motivate employees intrinsically by "arrang[ing] organizational conditions and methods . . . so that people can achieve *their own* goals best by directing their own efforts toward organizational objectives [italics in the original]" (McGregor, 1957/1989, p. 18).

In 1956 the number of white-collar workers (professionals, teachers, clerical and sales personnel, and the like) outnumbered blue-collar workers for the first time, reflecting the growth of service organizations. Correspondingly, management approaches changed as theorists and practitioners alike began to recognize that organizations were open, not closed, systems (Kast & Rosenzweig, 1972/1987), the informal organization had as much a influence on what actually happened within an organization as did the formal structure, and the needs of a service organization required an investment of the whole person, not just the automated movements of uninterested employees. By the 1970s and 1980s new approaches to managing employees in the context of bureaucracy were actively promoted, including decentralization, participatory management, and job enrichment.

Where We Are

Witness the dawn of the information age, made possible by mind-boggling technological breakthroughs. Television cable channels broadcast information—pictures and words—directly to viewers around the globe simultaneously. Those with access to a fax machine and telephone are capable of transmitting information to each other from any point on the globe. The awesome Internet has allowed more than 3,000,000 people worldwide to have direct access to one another via electronic mail (e-mail), spawning new work relationships—and new forms of romancing.

With the explosion of information, new technology, and accompanying societal changes have come new problems and new opportunities. These include (1) the elimination of whole classes of jobs and creation of a two-tier society—those with access to the information technologies and those without, (2) the emergence of the "knowledge industry" as a new employment sector, (3) overwork and the decline of leisure time, and (4) transformational approaches to management and organization.

The Two-Tier Society

New technologies have virtually eliminated whole classifications of jobs. Typing pools, shorthand stenographers, elevator operators, and baggage handlers have all been drastically decreased or curtailed by automation and new technologies. Robotics have automated many industrial jobs. Within the professional classes, companies downsize or "rightsize" by laying off or providing incentives for early retirement to middle managers whose role as controllers of employees is no longer needed.

Unfortunately, most of the new jobs in the knowledge sector require formal education and skills that the displaced industrial, clerical, and manual worker do not possess. In fact, during the 1980s the earnings differential sharply increased between workers with a college education and those without (Riche & Merrick, 1992/1993). Some experts direfully predict that as innovations in information technology continue, we will literally engineer a world without jobs for the masses. In this view, we are headed for a two-tier society with the employed technical or professional knowledge elite on the one hand and the deskilled, unemployed, or underemployed underclass on the other (Aronowitz & DiFazio, 1994; Rifkin, 1995).

Emergence of Knowledge Work

In 1959 Drucker coined the term *knowledge workers* to describe those whose primary jobs entail processing, developing, or transmitting information (Drucker, 1994; Pasmore, 1993). Unlike their industrial predecessors who worked at repetitive, definable tasks in relatively stable sociopolitical environments, today's knowledge workers perform indeterminate tasks in organic environments. As Drucker notes, the new capital in the knowledge industry is no longer machines and equipment. Rather, capital is the years of training and learning that knowledge workers obtain—capital that they may take with them when they leave the organization. Also, many knowledge workers have greater allegiance to their professions (for example, social work or teaching) than to the organizations in which they work. This poses an interesting dilemma for organizational leaders. Whereas the machine-based industrial worker needed the organization more than it needed him, organizations need their knowledge workers more than their knowledge workers need them. Those who attempt to supervise knowledge workers by production-line methods quickly learn the difficulties of this approach. As Pasmore (1993) explained, "knowledge workers are highly sensitive to top-down interventions that threaten to impose methods of working upon them" (p. 79).

Overwork and the Decline of Leisure

Contrary to predictions during the 1950s that the four-day workweek was imminent, between 1969 and 1987 the average paid work year in the United States increased by 163 hours (Schor, 1991). The result is less time for family life and childrearing, less time for personal growth, and less time for leisure and social activities outside the workplace. The resulting increase in stress and stress-related diseases is probably well known to the readers of this chapter. According to Schor's (1991) research, current patterns of overwork stem from the massive level of consumption that now occurs in this society. As she describes the "work-and-spend" cycle, relatively high pay creates a high level of consumption and greater debt. Work is then rewarded by even more pay and longer hours rather than time off. Information overload compounds the problem for knowledge workers who have to spend even more hours just to manage the volumes of information that they may now access.

Organizational Transformation

As many researchers and theorists have noted, traditional management methods that were successful in an industrial economy no longer work with today's knowledge workers. Global competition, the decline in U.S. productivity, and the demands of today's knowledge workers for meaningful, challenging work in humanistic work environments have created a groundswell of interest in new forms of organizations and management. Various labels have been applied to describe the attempted changes, including total quality management (TQM), continuous quality improvement (CQI), reengineering, organizational transformation, and, most recently, organizational learning. Regardless of the label chosen, four interrelated concepts are commonly emphasized: (1) a focus on customer service as a primary goal—organizations are urged to go beyond meeting customer expectations to "delighting" them; (2) a focus on improving work processes rather than overseeing task accomplishment; (3) employee empowerment via self-managing and cross-departmental teams; and (4) use of data-based decision-making tools, including statistical process control, root cause analysis, and benchmarking the processes of "world class" organizations.

As a management approach, however, CQI (by whatever label) can be time-consuming. Defining one's customers and determining their preferences, process reworking, retraining organizational leaders, and continuous measurement can be daunting undertakings. Also, because TQM has been poorly applied in some organizations, it has become equated with downsizing, cutback management, and expectations that more will be done with less (Hyde, 1992). Nevertheless, 60 percent of federal executives responding to a 1989 survey indicated that they were in the process of planning or initiating a TQM initiative (Hyde, 1992), and nearly all of the Fortune 500 have undertaken organizational reform.

Status of Human Service Organizations

Traditionally, human service organizations have been structured according to the same bureaucratic principles that dominated the industrial age. Unfortunately, because human service work is often performed autonomously or semiautonomously, requires considerable judgment, and entails an emotional investment, bureaucratic approaches to management are often counterproductive. The effects of attempting to enact bureaucratic procedures within HSOs are legion: burnout among staff and undue emphasis on regulations and procedural requirements to the neglect of individual client needs. In recent years, however, greater emphasis has been placed on participatory management, although still within the strictures of the pyramidal (hierarchical) form of organization (Toch & Grant, 1982).

Even more recently, some nonprofit and government HSOs have sought to implement continuous quality improvement processes into their organizations with various degrees of success. Several unique features of HSOs make implementing quality improvements difficult:

1. HSOs have multiple categories of customers. These include recipients of service, funders, volunteers including board members, and the often skeptical public. Faced with the need to meet the often conflicting expectations of diverse stakeholders, "delighting" customers is a difficult undertaking.

2. As explained below, management of processes and tasks using data-based techniques requires a different perspective toward supervision and leadership than is the norm. Those who wish to use these approaches must be willing to invest the time and resources to learn, often at the cost of "letting go" of lesser projects during the retraining. Because most HSOs must keep administrative costs low and may even lack a training budget, only a few can arrange to receive such services at affordable prices or on a volunteer basis.

3. Contractual funding requirements provide powerful disincentives for nonprofit organizations to experiment with true employee empowerment. The incentives to tell and direct rather than guide and support are strong. Mistakes can be costly and, in this current political environment, may cost an organization its funding base. Even managers who attempt to establish a participatory environment find themselves overriding these principles when confronted with mandates from their boards or directors.

4. Civil service and other requirements make it difficult to remove marginal or even below-marginal performers. The admonition given by many quality advocates to hire and retain only those who can function in an empowered environment is difficult to heed in organizations in which hirings are beyond the administrator's control and firings require copious paperwork.

5. Many HSOs have a history of collecting meaningless (to them) data to satisfy funding requirements. The additional requirement of CQI to collect even more data for process improvement measures is often perceived as burdensome.

Where We Are Going

Despite these disincentives, change is in the air. Several mavericks in HSOs are now experimenting with various forms of organizational transformation (see Bargal & Schmid, 1992, for a review). Their efforts are motivated by their own need for improvement, increased competition for philanthropic dollars, and the example of board members who have successfully used CQI approaches in their corporate environments. I predict that these few experiments will eventually become the norm as employees have unprecedented access to information about their organization, each other, and the world at large through computerized networks. As explained below, I also predict that this unprecedented access to information will lead to a reframing of the organization's relationship to its environment, redesign of the organization's structure and reward systems, greater employee empowerment, increased demand from employees for organizations to perform community functions, and a redefinition of the role of manager.

Reframing the Organization's Relationship to Its Environment

Focus on Core Competencies

The current orientation of human service organizations to be all things to all people so as to attract any possible funding will change to an orientation toward developing a unique market niche and to partner with other organizations for related services. Establishing a market niche in the interorganizational network will become increasingly important as funders demand to know that HSOs are not duplicating each other's services. In addition, HSOs will be forced to identify their own unique "core competencies" (Prahalad & Hamel, 1990)—those strategic capabilities in which the organization excels and that form the foundation for their service responses to emerging client needs.

Demonstrated Outcomes and Public Image

No longer content with do-good messages only, funders driven by the cynical public will increase their demands for visibly demonstrated effectiveness, explained in lay terms. As evaluation technologies become more sophisticated and data-gathering and data-analyzing procedures are facilitated by computerized scan sheets, HSOs will find it easier to monitor service delivery and to demonstrate outcomes. At the very least, regular customer satisfaction surveys will become the minimum standard for demonstrating effectiveness.

Even more so than now, HSOs will need to portray effectiveness via a positive public image. With the rise of cable television and the prospect of having more than 100 cable channels and numerous local access channels, HSOs will have ample opportunity to deliver their message to the funding public. Satisfying a diverse public, however, is no easy task, making it again important for organizations to hone their own particular market niche and to tailor their message to that group.

Collaborative Partnerships

Collaborative partnerships across organizations will be facilitated by electronic communications and decisional tools that allow small HSOs to consult and coordinate with one another from remote locations. Attempts will be made to formalize these relationships, although formal procedures and agreements will prove to be not nearly as effective as informal cross-organizational connections among individuals who are internally motivated to collaborate together. E-mail, the Internet, and community electronic bulletin boards will greatly enhance the ease of these individual and small group collaborative efforts.

Organizational Redesign

New Organizational Designs

As a result of changes in information technologies and customer needs, the typical pyramidal organization with fixed job descriptions, production-line approaches to supervision, and unity of command ("one man, one boss") will prove to be unworkable, particularly in smaller HSOs. Rigid boundaries between departments and units will need to be dissolved as new opportunities develop, rapid communication across the organization becomes an imperative, and work that needs to be done in real time cannot wait for requests to go through channels.

Current trends toward increased experimentation with nonpyramidal forms of organizational design will increase and expand into the nonprofit sectors. Examples of these are the matrix organization, the hub or circle, and the networked organization. In the matrix organization, project leadership of specific assignments is overlaid on the traditional pyramidal structure. In the hub, the organizational leader(s) are placed in the center and branches or teams are linked around them or to each other. In the networked organization, employees are grouped based on the skills needed to accomplish the goal, not their positional rank within the hierarchy.

Self-Contained Units

Traditionally, larger HSOs are organized to reflect the specialized function to be performed. Unfortunately, functional departmentalization also fosters disagreements and conflicts among those in different workgroups. Waste occurs, then, through failed and exhausting attempts at coordination. For example, I have consulted in organizations in which foster care and adoption care workers were at loggerheads, hospital nurses and social workers competed for primacy in discharge planning, and social services staff complained that they could not get meaningful help from the computer or finance departments.

In contrast, a self-contained approach to departmentalization combines several functions into one work unit and encourages workgroup members to learn about each other's skills. A self-contained approach would combine foster and adoption care workers, for example, into one unit or work team and departmentalize the workers by client type (such as service to the physically challenged) rather than by functional area (adoption versus foster care). Rather than bouncing clients from worker to worker, staff would be able to support each other's efforts as they pool their skills and knowledge to provide the best possible service to the client Staff would also experience greatly enriched jobs as they contribute more to each other's work.

Increased Self-Managing Teams

Because much will rest on the ability of individuals to collaborate with one another and on an organization's ability to form collaborative partnerships, a shift will occur from a focus on the individual to a focus on the team as the building block of the organization. Teams will hire and fire, determine salary increments, select their managers, and determine promotions. As organizations grow more culturally diverse, work teams will be challenged to forge consensus among competing viewpoints on emotionally charged issues. They will be aided in this challenge by new informational technologies such as groupware, decisional support systems, laptops, and distributed processing and networks. These resources will speed up and improve the quality of decisions even among teams who are located in different sites.

Skill-Based Approach to Work Design and Pay

Skill-based approaches to work design emphasize "person descriptions" (Lawler & Ledford, 1992) rather than job descriptions. Rather than shape individuals to fit jobs, jobs will be shaped to fit the unique abilities of individuals to contribute to the organization's success. By shaping jobs around individuals' abilities, individuals will be free to go beyond the boundaries of a fixed job description to develop new skills and to use those skills to create opportunities for future endeavors. This will require salary banding—collapsing job titles and salary ranges into a few, meaningful broad salary bands—so that teamwork, lateral movement, and skill development, rather than climbing through the hierarchy, are rewarded (Wilkinson, 1993).

Strategic Staffing

Establishing core competencies, staying lean and mean, and increasing use of self-managing teams will require a strategic staffing approach (Messmer, 1992). Human service organizations will find it cost-effective to outsource services that are not central to their mission (such as janitorial services and some data management services). Also, instead of hiring permanent staff outright, the trend will be toward hiring professional staff on a contract basis first—or even testing them out first as volunteers—and then, following satisfactory performance and team approval, hiring them as paid, permanent professionals.

More Flexible Reward and Compensation Systems

A greater move toward skill-based rather than merit pay will occur concurrently. Traditional approaches reward performance via vertical promotion into supervisory ranks. The result is that excellent clinical workers often become less effective clinical supervisors, master teachers often may become mediocre administrators, and superb nurses become frustrated nursing supervisors. As organizations reduce their hierarchies and become flatter, alternative ways of rewarding performance other than vertical promotions become important. Instead of paying individuals based on the jobs they hold, skill-based pay systems will reward people for the skills and new knowledge that they acquire (O'Neill & Lander, 1993/1994). This approach deemphasizes job status and seniority in the hierarchy as individuals have a means of gaining additional incomes without climbing the hierarchical ladder. In addition, organizational flexibility is increased and burnout decreased as employees acquire breadth and depth of skills and knowledge and develop new challenges and skills. A local organization, for example, created the position of "caseworker mentor" for a very skillful worker at a higher level of pay. In this person's new role, he carries a caseload, orients all new caseworkers, and goes on field visits with other caseworkers to provide them direct feedback on their performance and to help them troubleshoot problem cases.

Current population projections indicate that the workforce will increasingly become more culturally diverse, older, female, and living in nontraditional families well into the twenty-first century (Riche & Merrick, 1992/1993). By the year 2020 all working age groups will contain roughly similar numbers of workers, in contrast to previous decades in which larger numbers of workers were found in the younger age groups. Increasingly, these employees will demand that HSOs formally support themselves and their nontraditional families via flextime, cafeteria benefits packages to include nontraditional families (such as same-sex partners and aging parents), dependent-care spending accounts, paid time off for participation in education activities (such as PTAs and parent-teacher conferences), and provisions for children to be brought to work for after-hour meetings—or for staff to work at home so that they might care for sick children or aging parents.

Employee Empowerment

New Bases for Power

Ronfeldt (1992) has coined the term *cyberocracy* to describe the emerging form of organization that he predicts will replace both bureaucracy and technocracy. Whereas bureaucracy requires that information flows through formally designed lines of authority, cyberocracy places a premium on gathering information from any source, public or private. Because knowledge will no longer be the province of managers, and information about all aspects of the organization will be readily available to those who care to find out via computerized database systems and e-mail communications, the bases of power will shift from one's position within the organization to one's ability to acquire information and expertise and to mobilize others in the use of that knowledge. Consequently, a major determinant of power and influence will be the ability to share what one knows with others effectively.

Some authors have wondered whether the new technologies will increase the power of managers and executives to monitor and control employees via electronic monitoring. I believe not. Rather, as recent history has demonstrated, a more plausible scenario is not that Big Brother (organizational leaders) will monitor the people (employees), but that the people will be able to monitor Big Brother through their many sources of information.

Focus on Intrinsic Motivation

Much of human service work already occurs beyond the direct purview of the supervisor. Youth workers, counselors, and others do their work in the field and report back in the form of case notes or supervisory conferences, if they report back at all. As teleconferencing, e-mail, and conference calls enable people to link together without ever meeting together face to face, autonomy that traditionally has been granted only to professional or field workers may now be extended to others with desk jobs. Consequently, greater reliance will be placed on hiring trustworthy employees, establishing a common values base for decision making, and ensuring their intrinsic motivation to get the job done according to those values.

As Bowen and Lawler (1992) observe, however, this will require greater selection and training costs. Employees who are not good candidates for empowered, flexible job descriptions will need to deselected. Those who make it past the initial screening will need sufficient training so that they have the requisite information and decision-making skills to exercise judgment, work together in teams with others, and perform in environments in which chaos, complexity, and change are an everyday occurrence (Pascale, 1994).

Pushback

An empowered, knowledgeable, and culturally diverse staff will inevitably confront the discrepancy between social work values and human resource practices. Our values promote respect for the dignity and uniqueness of the individual, client self-determination, and an examination of person–situation interactions in problem situations. Unfortunately, the human resource practices of too many organizations tolerate demeaning of employees, an orientation toward artificially treating all employees equally despite unique individual circumstances, and a propensity to blame the individual staff member (manager or worker) as problems occur rather than examining lack of fit between individual expectations and organizational constraints. As employees are encouraged to use their discretion in dealing with rapid environmental changes and immediate customer needs, they will become more emboldened to "push back" (Waterman, 1994) against managerial imperatives or initiatives that they deem contrary to the values of the profession. They will also encourage managers to investigate systemic rather than person-blaming approaches to work breakdowns.

Organizations as the New Community

Organizations as the Social Hub

Human service organizations will become the social hub for those who work within them. As people become increasingly mobile and separated from their own extended families, increased demands will be placed on HSOs to serve as the extended family. This is not necessarily new. I have known many HSO staff members who refer to themselves as a family. The extent to which this occurs will increase as these families form bowling teams, care for each other's children when they are sick, provide each other with emotional support during times of personal difficulty, serve as the basis for romantic connections, and provide answers to questions about the worth and meaning of their own life and each other's lives through service to others.

Changing Definitions of Privacy

Many aspects of our lives that are now considered private will become open knowledge, particularly among our organizational family members. First, data once stored under lock and key will become accessible to many. Second, the informality of e-mail communications often encourages personal sharing beyond professional boundaries. Many a person's private lives (including my own), for example, are now known to thousands of subscribers to computer bulletin board discussion groups. Third, as employees become empowered and involved in all aspects of the organizations' performance, previously private matters such as salary amounts, previous work references, and health matters will be shared so that the collectivity may make equitable personnel decisions affecting the whole team. More importantly—and perhaps dangerously—as skills in team building are developed and people are expected to contribute as team members, previously personal matters such as one's family of origin issues, personality strengths, and areas of growth are all subject to scrutiny and discussion by the team to improve performance and to build team cohesion.

Demand for Healthy Organizations

Human service organizations commonly attract those who seek meaning, personal fulfillment, and personal growth in their lives. To achieve this, many are willing to sacrifice the higher pay available in the for-profit sector for the opportunity to help improve the quality of life of others. However, meaning and fulfillment often are contraindicated by long work hours. Organizational leaders will be confronted with the split between their emphasis on improving the quality of life of their clients and failing to support the quality of home life of their employees. An emphasis on healthy organizations supporting personal development and family cohesion will occur, giving increased impetus for teleworking, flextime, and spreading the 40-hour work week over a range from 4 or 4.5 to 6 days, according to the organizational member's choice.

Redefinition of Managerial Roles

Ship Navigator, not Captain

As Senge (1990) explained, the roles of organizational leaders will shift from overseeing, monitoring, and coordinating (the ship's captain) to facilitating, mobilizing, and setting a strategic vision (the ship's navigator). This change will not occur easily, particularly among those who believe that they already are participatory in their approaches to staff but whose staff experience them otherwise. Rather than considering decision making to be their sole province, managers will find it necessary to create conditions under which others may make intelligent decisions and form needed alliances.

Process Management

Collaborative arrangements and a team approach to management will require increased leadership skills in process rather than task management. Typically, managers or supervisors (sometimes together with staff members) specify the tasks that need to be done and the desired end product and then oversee each step. This approach to management is often experienced by intrinsically motivated staff as micromanagement. Breakdowns in task accomplishment are likely to be blamed on the individual to the neglect of looking at the system of events or processes that led to the breakdown. Task managers also often ignore the "white space" between organizational units and instead focus on each box to determine who did or did not do a required task. On the other hand, process managers look at the entire process of getting a job done across work units. For example, in my own organization, seven staff members and volunteers recently flow-charted the entire process of getting a newsletter produced and the flow of paper (initial drafts, spell checking, production of final draft) from one person to another. More than 15 steps were delineated involving us all. In so doing, we discovered several flaws in our initial conceptualization of how the newsletter should be produced, the basis for controversy among us was resolved, and the time for production of the newsletter was shortened considerably.

Demise of Strategic Planning

Strategic planning normally requires that organizations or individuals set goals, gather information pertaining to those goals, determine the parameters of the action to be taken, and then engage in that action. Because of the rapid pace of change, we may no longer be able to afford to study and learn before acting. Rather, organizational members will become more sophisticated in making leaps of faith, committing to some action and then learning from their failures or successes. Strategic planning as we once knew it, with tedious data collection, resource assessments, and specific action plans, will give way to strategic visioning—deciding on a course of action—and then determining how to accomplish it as the vision is implemented.

Conclusion

These changes will not come easily. They may be especially difficult to implement in human service organizations that have involuntary clients or are monopolies (such as probation departments and public schools). My major point is that information technologies will literally revolutionize the way we think, our conceptions of authority, and our self-perceptions of who we are and what we are capable of becoming. At the same time, the public, who is also privy to that same information, will increase its demands for accountable, effective services. Organizations that can harvest those new perceptions and adjust to the demands of public scrutiny and open-book management will be the most successful. Those that won't or don't, I predict, will function at a drastically curtailed level of effectiveness—if they continue to exist at all.

References

Aronowitz, S., & DiFazio, W. (1994). *The jobless future: Sci-tech and the dogma of work.* Minneapolis: University of Minnesota Press.

Bargal, D., & Schmid, H. (1992). Organizational change and development in human service organizations: A prefatory essay. *Administration in Social Work, 16*(3/4), 1–13.

Bowen, D. E., & Lawler, E. E. I. (1992, Spring). The empowerment of service workers: What, why, how and when. *Sloan Management Review, 33*(3), 31–39.

Drucker, P. F. (1992). The new society of organizations. *Harvard Business Review, 70*(5), 95–104.

Drucker, P. F. (1994). The age of social transformation. *Atlantic Monthly, 274*(5), 53n.

Hyde, A. C. (1992). The proverbs of total quality management: Recharting the path to quality improvement in the public sector. *Public Productivity and Management Review, 16*(1), 25–37.

Kast, F. E., & Rosenzweig, J. E. (1972/1987). General systems theory: Applications for organization and management. In J. M. Shafritz & J. S. Ott (Eds.), *Classics of organizational theory* (pp. 278–293). Chicago: The Dorsey Press.

Lawler, E., & Ledford, G. (1992). A skill-based approach to human resource management. *European Management Journal, 10*(4), 383–391.

McGregor, D. M. (1957/1989). The human side of enterprise. In W. Natemeyer & J. Gilberg (Eds.),

Classics of organizational behavior (pp. 14–20). Danville, IL: Interstate Printers & Publishers.

Messmer, M. (1992). Practice management in the year 2000: Strategies to think about now. *The Practical Accountant, 25*(12), 48–57.

O'Neill, G. L., & Lander, D. (1993/1994). Linking employee skills to pay: A framework for skill-based pay plans. *ACA Journal, 2*(3), 14–26.

Pascale, R. T. (1994). Intentional breakdowns and conflict by design. *Planning Review, 22*(3), 12–16.

Pasmore, W. A. (1993). Designing work systems for knowledge workers. *Journal for Quality and Participation, 16*(4), 78–84.

Prahalad, C. K., & Hamel, G. (1990, May). The core competence of the corporation. *Harvard Business Journal, 3,* 79–91.

Riche, M. F., & Merrick, T. W. (1992/1993). Work force and compensation in the 21st century: A demographic perspective. *ACA Journal, 2*(2), 48–59.

Rifkin, J. (1995). *The end of work: The decline of the global labor force and the dawn of the post-market era.* New York: Putnam.

Ronfeldt, D. (1992). Cyberocracy is coming. *Information Society Journal, 8*(4), 243–296.

Schor, J. B. (1991). *The overworked American: The unexpected decline of leisure.* New York: Basic Books.

Senge, P. M. (1990). *The fifth discipline: The art and practice of the learning organization.* New York: Doubleday/Currency.

Toch, H., & Grant, J. D. (1982). *Reforming human services: Change through participation.* Beverly Hills: Sage.

Waterman, R. H. J. (1994). P&G, Lima—A learning organization. *At Work: Stories of Tomorrow's Workplace, 3*(4), 1, 10–13.

Wilkinson, J. G. (1993). Duke Power integrates employee rewards with its business vision of excellence. *National Productivity Review, 12*(3), 325–335.

P a r t **VII**

Policy, Politics, and Activism

Part VII deals with those social work functions that, although deeply embedded in our history, tradition, and mission, are not likely to be perceived by most modern social workers as part of the *essence* of the profession.

In Chapter 22 John Longres revisits radical social work, a subject on which he has been writing for over two decades. Although he doesn't see a resurgence of the more pure forms of radical thought, he does believe that progressive thinking always has been and continues to be important to the profession. He also proposes that the struggle for material equality should be "the glue that holds us together as a profession." These are quite different concerns, indeed, than have been discussed in most of the earlier chapters. Perhaps we may be moved to ask the following:

1. How can one profession embrace such a wide array of roles and functions, especially when many of them seem to be at odds with each other?

2. How did the profession drift so far away from concerns about altering social circumstances?

3. Is it possible to attract white, working-class, heterosexual men and women into a unified working-class movement in order to counter the current conservative trend?

In Chapter 23 Linda Reeser considers whether professionalism may be antithetical to activism on behalf of clients. Essential to answering this question is an understanding of both the nature of professions and the purposes of activism. Reeser examines these issues in the context of changing practice contexts and changing political environments. She concludes that social work must maintain a dual focus on both the individual in need and on the social, economic, and political forces that contribute to individual misery. This may discourage those students who choose social work because they regard it as the quickest route to private practice. Her discussion of these issues may provoke us to ask the following:

1. How do we overcome the inherent conflict between attaining the status and power of traditional professions and social activism?

2. Has social work changed so drastically over the past two decades that it may be impossible to renew our interest in social justice?

Diana DiNitto presents us, in Chapter 24, with the vision of a widening gap between what she views as the ideal and what she predicts the situation will be in the year 2000. According to DiNitto, social welfare will be more residual and less universal, more like workfare than welfare, and heading rapidly toward privatization. There are no easy answers here to these questions:

1. How do we reform welfare without penalizing those clients who are most in need of assistance?

2. What is the quality of life likely to be in the next century for those persons who are dependent on social welfare programs?

3. Are there any realistic expectations that these conservative trends could be reversed?

Finally, in Chapter 25 Karen Haynes reminds us that there are still a few social workers who believe that all social work is political. She also reminds us that both NASW and CSWE have adopted standards that are intended to encourage and promote political social work. Haynes states that political activism is crucial to the profession because it legitimizes our role in policy formulation. She sees some hope that political social work has recently achieved *professional* legitimacy and denies any inherent conflict between clinical (including private) practice and political activism. Here are some interesting questions:

1. Why have our professional associations been so concerned with political activism, changing social conditions, and social justice, when those concerns do not appear to be similarly reflected among practitioners, educators, and students?

2. Can we effectively teach such widely disparate skills in the same curriculum as those associated with clinical practice and those needed for political activism? (If we add courses on political social work, doesn't that mean less attention to clinical practice?)

3. Is there a sufficiently large potential market for a professional social work curriculum designed to teach political activism?

Chapter 22

Radical Social Work

Is There a Future?

JOHN F. LONGRES, PhD
University of Washington

Somewhere in the 1980s the term *radical social work* disappeared from the social work lexicon. An entry on radical social work appeared in the eighteenth edition of the *Encyclopedia of Social Work,* but by then the large gatherings of self-defined radical social workers so common at the annual NASW and CSWE meetings of the 1970s were a thing of the past. *Catalyst: A Socialist Journal of the Social Services* became *The Journal of Progressive Human Services* and, in keeping with this, the nineteenth edition of the *Encyclopedia* has an entry on progressive rather than radical social work. Not all is lost; *progressive* may indeed be a better word than *radical.* British, Canadian, and Australian social workers still write a good deal about radical issues; and in the United States the progressive forces in social work keep the spirit alive through their involvement with ethnic-sensitive, feminist, empowerment, strengths, and other more current alternatives to mainstream social work practice. Nevertheless, it is clear that radical voices are relatively muted in today's social work and it is not clear that we will hear their return any time soon.

Historical Background

Radical thinking in social work has a long history. Although present in every generation, it has been more prevalent in some periods than in others. Historians point to the Progressive Era as a time when social work radicals captured the attention of the budding profession and the nation (Davis, 1964a, 1964b; Osofsky, 1964) . The Progressive Era coincided with efforts to deal with the immigration from southern and central Europe, and the movement of African Americans from the rural South into the large industrial areas of the North. Settlement house workers who were interested in changing the circumstances of the urban poor challenged charity workers who were more interested in changing their character. Group work and community organization became important social work methods and the use of demonstrations to gain political and economic reform was common. When the Progressive Party was defeated in the elections of 1912, many progressive social workers shifted into mainstream democratic politics.

Radical thinking burst on the scene again during the 1930s as part of the rank and file movement and its quest for a welfare state (Fisher, 1990; Leighninger & Knickmeyer, 1976). The practitioners' movement, as it was often called, grew out of the Depression, disenchantment with capitalist institutions, idealism over apparent successes in the Soviet Union, and the influx of many new, untrained workers into the social services as relief programs expanded. The movement took two main forms: the development of discussion groups and professional organizations and the development of protective associations including all social service employees, not just professional social workers. The movement was responsible for the first widely based analysis of the antiwelfare goals of welfare agencies, and the first affirmation of social service workers' common interests with the clients they served. It was also responsible for the publication of the journal *Social Work Today,* which was published between 1934 and 1941. The rank and file movement was a casualty of World War II when unemployment sharply declined in the face of a war economy. It was also a casualty of a right-wing backlash that became increasingly stronger through the late 1930s and 1940s, culminating in the McCarthy era of the 1950s.

As a result of the upheavals provoked by the Civil Rights Movement and the Anti-Vietnam War Movement, radical thinking reemerged. Social and especially community mental health services proliferated. The new untrained workers, many of whom were activists stressing "maximum feasible participation," emphasized the concepts of institutionalized poverty and racism and influenced educators to alter the content of their courses. The proliferation of services helped appease the poor sufficiently to quiet the urban rioting that was then common. As the nation went into recession in the 1970s and as conservatives took control of the presidency in the 1980s, the voices of radical social workers were once again in the minority. An era of cutbacks aimed at undoing the welfare state was ushered in. Services that were not eliminated often underwent redefinition. The Community Mental Health centers that were established under the progressive War on Poverty, for instance, were repackaged as the conservative "war on drugs." The "Just Say No" campaign that promoted this change reflected the view that substance abuse is caused by psychological defects in the abuser (Humphreys & Rappaport, 1993).

Radical Social Work

Radical thinkers hold in common a series of underlying principles (Longres, 1981). They believe that the private troubles of clients are fundamentally provoked by problems in the structure of our social, political, and, above all, economic institutions. The basic underlying concern in radical social work is that of the economic or material well-being of people. Radical social workers are concerned about the material want and insecurity experienced by those at the lower end of the socioeconomic continuum; individuals and families in the working class or blue- and pink-collar occupations, the working or unemployed poor, the underclass, and the homeless. Radical social workers believe that economic inequality is the fundamental problem confronting society and the basic issue out of which the need for social services emerge. Capitalism encourages self-interest and competition and places individuals and families in situations of chronic economic insecurity and risk. Working-class people, regardless of race or gender, can not be assured that they will have a job, that their job will pay them a livable wage, or that they will be able to obtain adequate housing, medical benefits, and other basic necessities. Other problems for which people require services are directly or indirectly related to material want or insecurity. Problems such as health and mental health, family violence and dissolution, educational failure, crime and delinquency, drugs, and alcohol are caused or exacerbated by material insecurity.

Radical social workers also assert that social welfare agencies, while manifestly aimed at the elimination of private troubles, operate latently to stigmatize, control, or appease clients. Radicals aim therefore to change the nature of social services. In particular, they believe that the principle task of social workers should be to reform societal institutions by acting as change agents on behalf of the poor and working classes. Toward this aim they advocate human behavior content that focuses on macro issues and social work methods content that prepares social work students for advocacy, group work, community organization, social development, and social action.

Although primarily concerned about altering social circumstances, radical social workers recognize that oppressive arrangements can be internalized. Although theories of human development postulate a society in harmony and consensus, socialization in fact encourages people to compete against one another and choose sides in the gender, racial, and other cultural wars that mark society. As a result, radical social workers accept the need to work for personal or intrapsychic change that protects clients from recreating oppressive circumstances (Lichtenberg & Roman, 1990).

Although there are points of agreement among radical social workers, there are also many points of disagreement (Mullaly & Keating, 1991). Beyond an underlying concern about the role of economic institutions in fostering inequality, radical social workers differ a great deal in the way they understand the problems of capitalism and in their social change or reform objectives.

The various approaches to radical social work may be described along a continuum from the least to the most revolutionary positions. Most espouse some form of socialism, yet no single socialist vision unifies radical practice alternatives. For some, socialism simply represents a set of ideals to guide practice, ideals that stress the elimination of social classes and promote cooperation and solidarity among races, genders, and other divisions in society. For others, socialism represents a more concrete set of rules for generating social policies: distribution of resources based on need, universal (available to all) and comprehensive (covering all contingencies) state financing of services, and participation by the working and lower classes in determining the nature of policy and services. Although radical practice is a left-of-center alternative to what might be called mainstream practice, in its least revolutionary forms it merges imperceptibly with mainstream forms of practice. According to Mullaly and Keating (1991), four variations may be described.

Revolutionary Marxists

The most radical approach to practice is seen in the writings of revolutionary Marxists (Buchbinder, 1981). They espouse that capitalism, and the resultant conflict between worker and management, is the fundamental, if not only, cause of social problems. Although they recognize the existence of gender, race, ethnic, and religious-based conflict, these are seen as secondary to class conflict. A socialist solution will, they believe, lead to the more or less automatic elimination of these secondary sources of conflict. They also believe that social workers ought to abandon the services provided through public and private social welfare agencies and departments. Instead, social workers should attach themselves to grassroots services such as welfare rights groups, self-help groups, trade unions, and other organizations developed and controlled by working and lower-class people.

Social Democrats

The least radical approach to radical practice is seen in the writings of social democrats in Great Britain and Sweden (Titmuss, 1968; Himmelstrand, 1981). Although they recognize the limitations of capitalism, they do not see it as the only or the most important source of human misery. Equal weight is given to conflict surrounding race, gender, age, religion, and so on. Similarly, although the social democrats espouse socialism they are more willing to recognize the positive contributions made by state-owned, public social services. The welfare state is seen as a stepping stone toward a socialist society. It represents a progressive institution that supplies a safety net without which the life of subordinated people would be far worse. Social workers thus are encouraged to work within the public services to provide basic human services.

Evolutionary Marxists

Most writings fall between these two endpoints of radical practice into what may be called evolutionary Marxist practice (Corrigan & Leonard, 1978; Galper, 1980). These tend to believe that capitalism is the fundamental source of social and personal problems but that the conflicts associated with race, ethnicity, religion, and gender should not be overlooked. Similarly, they tend to view social welfare services as both propping up capitalism and representing the needs of working-class and poor people. They encourage social workers to continue to work in the public services as a way of promoting the interests of subordinated groups against those of the more affluent.

Clinical Practice and Social Activism

Radical social workers of any political stripe may also differ in their relative emphasis on clinical practice and social activism. Although this is not strictly a separate category of radical practice, it does reflect an ongoing internal debate among radicals. Some ask social workers to completely shun all forms of clinical intervention in favor of social activist strategies or other environmentally focused interventions. Others emphasize the need to focus on clinical interventions either as a way for raising consciousness about public issues or as a way of rooting out those forms of internalized oppression that help keep people subordinated (Leonard, 1984). The debate here is on the relative merits of clinical versus activist interventions. However, many radical practitioners recognize the need for both kinds of interventions and see them as interrelated so long as practitioners are clear that they are working ultimately to overcome economic and social inequality.

Changes in the Thrust of Social Work Practice

Throughout its short history mainstream social workers have debated their role in the amelioration of inequality. Some have argued that our task is to become reformers and activists concerned with larger public issues. Others argued that our job is to work at the personal level, to help people function adequately by strengthening their capacity to cope and adapt. The debate has been referred to in many ways: cause versus function, wholesale versus retail, diagnosis versus evaluation, and, more recently, content versus process (Meyer, 1987).

As a result of these debates, social work practitioners have come to believe that both are important and that the uniqueness of social work is its commitment to both public and private troubles. Through the metaphor of person in environment, we believe that individuals are inseparable from their environments and that intervention is required at both levels to ensure goodness of fit. Although this metaphor binds us as a profession, it means different things to different social workers, and the debate simmers just below the surface of apparent unanimity. At times, the debate boils over and social workers become polarized around their visions of practice. During these periods radical thinking flourishes.

Franklin (1990) describes such shifts in social work's relative attention to the private and the public as "cycles of social work practice." She identifies three periods in which practice focused largely on the troubles of individuals and their interpersonal milieus. The first was in the earliest days of social work, when "friendly visitors" sought to instill moral character in their otherwise irredeemable poor and unemployed clients. The second was during the 1920s, when social casework techniques, heavily influenced by ideas from the then-new science of psychoanalysis, gained prominence. The third was during the 1950s, when McCarthyism and anticommunism campaigns were in full force and social workers began to enter private practice and do psychotherapy.

She also identifies three in-between periods in which practice was clearly more radical. The first of these was during the Progressive Era (1907 to 1915) as hundreds of thousands of southern and eastern European immigrants poured into the United States and threatened not only the economy but the dominance of White American cultural traditions. The second was during the 1930s, when the United States was suffering through the Great Depression, and the third was during the 1960s and 1970s, when the Civil Rights Movement and the Anti-Vietnam War Movement were at their peak.

Wagner (1989) has also called attention to shifts in the relative emphasis that social workers have placed on the public versus the private. His work, however, suggests that these are not real cycles. Regardless of historical era, the great majority of social workers have always been dedicated to working exclusively with private troubles. Similarly, the periods in which social workers appear to turn their attention to public issues have always been of relatively short duration. Wagner notes that a concern for equity and justice emerges during certain periods of crisis and is expressed only by some segments of practitioners, administrators, and policy makers. As a result of their efforts, a concern for social reform becomes incorporated into practice models on an official or theoretical level. No sooner is it incorporated, however, than it is shunted to the sidelines. Wagner argues that this is what happened during the Progressive Era, during the Great Depression, and more recently during the Civil Rights Movement. Wagner's work underscores the idea that commitment to equity and justice is a secondary concern in social work practice, a relatively minor theme that periodically intrudes into the conscience of professionals who are otherwise caught up in activities that are inclined to ignore the public issue of inequality.

Since the late 1970s social workers have once again found themselves disconnected from the struggle against economic inequality. Social workers today are increasingly guided by the *Diagnostic and Statistical Manual* of the American Psychiatric Association (see Chapter 11). They focus on mental disorders such as drug and alcohol use, depression and low self-esteem, hyperactivity, borderline personality, eating and conduct disorders, and the like. The environment is not altogether ignored, but its use is limited to the resolution of private troubles outside the context of the public issues that create and exacerbate them. In this atmosphere the desire to enter private practice and do psychotherapy flourishes just as the drive for change and reform-oriented profession diminishes.

To be sure, progressive issues are kept alive through feminist and ethnic-sensitive models, but even these, in keeping with the conservative times, seem more involved in subjective, clinical issues than justice and equity. In particular, the search for ways to alter the structural sources of inequality and discrimination has been replaced with a search to recognize and appreciate cultural and gender differences in values, beliefs, and worldviews. Disempowerment, once thought of primarily as a political and economic issue, is increasingly thought of as a personal difficulty; powerlessness is described as a feeling that anyone may have rather than a situation that accrues to those suffering economic and political privation. The strengths approach, the latest form of progressive practice, goes one step further to caution us against a critical evaluation of the social environment; environments, we are told, should not be problematized, as they are full of resources (Sullivan, 1992). The intellectual distance of these progressive alternatives from mainstream practice seems extremely narrow.

Is There a Future?

Social work programs and the way services are delivered in them continually change; they have a past, a present, and a future. Such change is sometimes believed to follow a path, that is, an orderly sequence of ever-progressive, developmental stages—brought about through painstaking research—that make professionals increasingly effective. As has been shown, this is assuredly not the case. Social work rocks back and forth between a relative emphasis on the public and the private.

Corrigan (1977) rightfully contends that the shape of practice is a function of the state of class conflict at any one period in history. Class consciousness has never been strong in the United States, but it does rise and fall. During the Progressive Era, during the Great Depression, and during the War on Poverty of the 1960s the working classes became more aware of their precarious circumstances, and social workers, following their lead, became more concerned with inequality and social justice.

Today class consciousness, especially among the working classes, is at a very low point, and this has enabled mainstream social workers to drift away from structural concerns. Yet the relative lack of class consciousness is perplexing given that since 1973 the real income of working-class people has remained stagnant, the real income of working-class White men has actually shrunk, and high levels of unemployment and marginalization from the economy have continued to haunt the African and Latino American working classes. The economy has been in a continuing process of downsizing and restructuring that has weakened the percentage of income and wealth controlled by the working classes while increasing the percentage controlled by the professional middle classes and corporate elites (Phillips, 1990; Oliver & Shapiro, 1990; Ryscavage, Green, & Welmiak, 1992).

Given these circumstances we should expect relatively high levels of consciousness among the working classes. Yet over the past 20 years sufficient numbers have consistently shifted their allegiance from the quasi–labor-oriented Democratic party to the clearly anti–welfare-state, pro-capital Republican party. Working-class people have either opted out of the political process by not exercising their right to vote or have tended to side with capital, believing that their poor economic circumstances are caused by such things as overregulation of capital, higher levels of taxation, affirmative action, entitlements for the poor, and government waste in general. The welfare state, brought to life by the clamor of the working classes, is now seen as the enemy of the people. So long as this remains, the working classes will not make their voices sufficiently heard to enable social workers to rally behind them.

Can the Situation Be Changed and Can Social Work Help?

These are difficult times for progressives. Within the United States those espousing progressive causes are attacked as "tax and spenders" and accused of being out of touch with middle America. *Liberal* has become the "L word," and liberals themselves are in disarray, without a vision that commands sufficient attention among working- and lower-middle-class people. The international support that enabled us to promote a socialist alternative has weakened considerably. The welfare state is on the defensive worldwide, and even the democratic socialist societies of western Europe are struggling against the push to privatize. The collapse of the Soviet Union and the other communist nations of Eastern Europe has appeared to put the nail in the coffin of a socialist vision. Indeed, the paucity of an alternative to laissez-faire capitalism does suggest that the end of history (Fukuyama, 1992) is upon us, and the working and lower middle classes must inure themselves to trickle-down economics.

We should not paint too bleak a picture. It is clear that even as working-class people side with capital, they support those entitlements, subsidies, taxes, and other government interventions that directly affect their socioeconomic well-being. The apparent conservative majority stands ready to erupt in a number of internal battles as its various constituencies begin to recognize their own competing interests. It is always the "other guy's" welfare state that they (we) most want to cut. For progressives to regain the momentum, the working and lower middle classes must once again come to believe that the welfare state represents their interests.

Social work as a profession cannot lead working- and lower-middle-class people, our natural constituencies, back into the fold. Social workers themselves exist somewhere between the working and professional classes. Our own jobs are often on the line and our professional autonomy is increasingly compromised (Fabricant & Burghardt, 1992). Yet there is something I believe that social workers can do to help change the course of history.

Whom Do Social Workers Serve?

Bertha Capen Reynolds (1935), one of the leading progressive figures in social work history, wrote that the role of social work, and by extension social welfare institutions, was to mediate between people receiving services and their social environment. Ideally, social workers are neutral mediators, standing where they can see both sides, understanding both and working with both. Yet for such neutral mediation to occur, certain preconditions must be met. The mediation function, based as it is on individual adaptive capacities, is possible only when there is a fairly stable, well-functioning, healthy social order. Social work practice presupposes the existence of basic necessities for survival and opportunities for advancement through individual initiative. If the social order can not supply the resources for subsistence, health, work, the development of personality, and a sense of community, social work can never supply them in any adequate quantity.

Capen Reynolds, like all progressives, did not see a healthy environment. She saw instead class struggle. She saw an economic oligarchy controlling the political process and a clash of interests between the working-class majority and the elite few who controlled productive resources. She saw a situation in which

> a man without a chance to work to provide for his family is deprived of employment . . . because it is to the interest of some other man, or group of men, to keep him out of the opportunity. (Reynolds, 1935, p. 6)

Under such circumstances social workers cannot be neutral mediators. When caught between armies in battle, she wrote, there was no "middle of the road." But whose side should social workers be on? She believed, as I do, that three alternatives are possible. Social workers can serve the larger community, that is, the citizens of the United States as a whole. The citizenry gives legitimacy to the services we provide, for services are paid through their tax dollars and charitable contributions. Yet there is no consensus, as the larger community is too full of conflicting interests and values, too full of what we call today *culture wars,* to give any real direction to practice. A second possibility is that social workers can serve the economic oligarchy. Capen Reynolds rejects this outright, as all progressives should, because to serve them is to legitimate the very exploitation we so much wish to eliminate. If social workers did the bidding of the professional middle classes and the corporate elites, they would "find themselves paid to enforce acceptance of starvation and misery, not to contribute to health and well-being." She concludes that in spite of the origin of our salaries and the power of elites, we must stand firmly on the side of those who voluntarily and involuntarily come to us because of the troubles they are experiencing. The third alternative is that we enter the class struggle on the side of the working and lower classes, seeking to mobilize their coping capacities and create an environment conducive to their well-being.

Reynolds was writing during the Great Depression of the 1930s, and her remarks are clearly directed at the problem of economic inequality, those inequalities rooted in social class divisions. Being a person of her time, she believed that economic inequality was central to all other forms of inequality. As a result she has nothing directly to say of inequalities based on race, gender, age, sexual orientation, and the like except insofar as these overlap with issues of economic inequality.

Since the 1960s we have become aware that these other forms of inequality must also be recognized and given their due. This is a good and needed correction to an overly narrow economic vision. A singular focus on class structure and conflict is insufficient for understanding the dilemmas of contemporary society. It appears too simple today to say, as Capen Reynolds did, that our clients are the working classes against the economic elites. Through the new focus on diversity social workers understand that they must also give attention to issues of race, ethnicity, and gender and to special populations such as the disabled, gays and lesbians, children, and the aged.

In making this needed correction, however, it has become much more difficult to define the client. Following Capen Reynolds, the client starts to resemble the larger community with all its contradictory and divergent interests. Depending on our practice interests, our clients may be the poor against the rich, people of color against whites, women against men, homosexuals and bisexuals against heterosexuals, the able bodied against people with disabilities, or children and the elderly against adults. The categories of class conflict today are not separate but overlapping, and therefore they produce contradictory constituencies. One may be an oppressed person of color but a man, heterosexual, affluent, and able bodied. Similarly, one might be an oppressed woman, but white, heterosexual, affluent, and able bodied. When categories overlap, solving one oppression may inadvertently lead to reinforcing others. Can we promote the aspirations of men of color as a class without somehow infringing on the aspirations of white women as a class?

What Now?

We live at a time when conservative ideas have gained the ascendancy and it seems, from the vantage point of this social worker, that there is no immediate hope for a return to liberal, let alone radical, ideas. This reality is affecting the policies we work under, the practice models we are designing, and the research we are doing. This is the context of practice today, the context out of which we must move forward.

I have indicated that progressive thinking has always been a part, however subdued, of social work. This is still the case today, and it is this voice that needs to be nurtured and kept alive. There are, as I have noted throughout, social workers who continue to keep alive the progressive tradition, although most of them write from a British, Canadian, or Australian context. In the United States, however, many of our finest progressive thinkers are writing within a multicultural, diversity, or feminist framework. This reflects our special heritage and our special American reality and also should be nurtured and kept alive.

As we move forward, however, the study of economic inequality should not be an afterthought. It often appears that we are interested in the poor and working classes only insofar as they may be of color, disabled, female, or gay or lesbian. In my opinion, progressive social workers in the United States need to refocus on economic class conflict. The struggle for material equality should be the glue that holds us together as a profession. I submit that Bertha Capen Reynolds was not wrong, nor is her position outdated. Our clients should be those poor and working-class men and woman of all colors, ages, orientations, and abilities. By having shifted our focus to the wider range of social inequities, seemingly without regard to economic conditions, we have helped divide the working classes and thereby made it easier for conservatives to pick up or politically immobilize those who feel left out, namely, white working- and lower-middle-class, heterosexual men, women, and their families. We would help the progressive cause by making this group feel more at home in the welfare state. They must once again come to see that their advancement depends on a unified working class rather than on an alliance with economic elites and social conservatives.

References

Buchbinder, H. (1981). Inequality and the social services. In A. Moscovitch & G. Drover (Eds.), *Inequality: Essays on the political economy of social welfare* (pp. 348–369). Toronto: University of Toronto Press.

Corrigan, P. (1977). The welfare state as an arena of class struggle. *Marxism Today, 21*(3), 87–93.

Corrigan, P., & Leonard, P. (1978). *Social work practice under capitalism: A Marxist approach.* London: Macmillan.

Davis, A. F. (1964a). Settlement workers in politics: 1890–1914. *Review of Politics, 26*(4), 505–517.

Davis, A. F. (1964b). Social workers and the Progressive Party, 1912–1916. *American Historical Review,69*(3), 671–688.

Fabricant, M. B., & Burghardt, S. (1992) *The welfare state crisis and the transformation of social service work.* Armonk, NY: M.E. Sharpe.

Fisher, J. (1990). The rank and file movement: 1930–1936. *Journal of Progressive Human Services,1*(1). 95–99.

Franklin, D. L. (1990). The cycles of social work practice: Social action vs. individual interest. *Journal of Progressive Human Services, 1*(2), 59–80.

Fukuyama, F. (1992). *The end of history and the last man.* New York: Free Press.

Galper, J. (1980). *Social work practice: A radical perspective.* Englewood Cliffs, NJ: Prentice Hall.

Himmelstrand, U. (1981). *Beyond welfare capitalism.* London: Heinemann.

Humphreys, K., & Rappaport, J. (1993). From the community mental health movement to the war on drugs. *American Psychologist, 48*(8), 892–901.

Leighninger, L., & Knickmeyer, R. (1976). The rank and file movement: The relevance of racial social work traditions to modern social work practice. *Journal of Sociology and Social Welfare, 4*(2), 166–177.

Leonard, P. (1984). *Personality and ideology: Toward a materialist understanding of the individual.* London: Macmillan.

Lichtenberg, P., & Roman, C. (1990). Psychological contributions to social struggle. *Journal of Progressive Human Services, 1*(2), 1–16.

Longres, J. (1981). Reaction to working statement on purpose. *Social Work, 26* (1), 85–87.

Meyer, C. H. (1987). Content and process in social work practice: A new look at old issues. *Social Work, 32*(5), 401–404.

Mullaly, R. P., & Keating, E. F. (1991). Similarities, differences and dialectics of radical social work. *Journal of Progressive Human Services, 2*(2), 49–78.

Oliver, M. L., & Shapiro, J. M. (1990). Wealth of a nation: A reassessment of asset inequality in America shows at least one third of households are asset-poor. *American Journal of Economics and Sociology, 49*(2), 129–130.

Osofsky, G. (1964). Progressivism and the Negro: New York, 1900–1915. *American Quarterly, 16*(2), 153–168.

Phillips, K. (1990). *The politics of rich and poor: Wealth and the American electorate in the Reagan aftermath.* New York: Harper Perennial.

Reynolds, B. (1935, May). Whom do social workers serve? *Social Work Today, 2*(8), 5–8.

Ryscavage, G., Green, E., & Welmiak, W. (1992). The impact of demographic, social and economic changes on the distribution of income. In *U.S. Bureau of the Census,* CPR. Series P60-183. Studies in the Distribution of Income. Washington, DC: U.S. Government Printing Office.

Sullivan, D. P. (1992). Reconsidering the environment as a helping resource. In D. Saleeby (Ed.), *The strengths perspective in social work practice* (pp. 148–158). New York: Longman.

Titmuss, R. (1968). *Commitment to welfare.* London: Allen & Unwin.

Wagner, D. (1989) Radical movements in the social services: A theoretical framework. *Social Service Review, 63*(2), 264–284.

Chapter 23

The Future of Professionalism and Activism in Social Work

LINDA REESER, PhD
Western Michigan University

It is difficult but necessary to try to predict the future for social work. We act according to our beliefs about what the future may hold. Our options are to shape the future and prepare for it, to react to it once it occurs, or to ignore it. Each of these responses will influence the future. Thinking about the future is valuable even if our speculations are inaccurate, because it involves making judgments about what must be done today to prepare for the future being sought. Social work professional organizations have primarily taken a reactive stance to events as they occur, and yet workers in practice have a future orientation with their clients. The expectation is that change is possible and interventions will enhance the quality of life for clients in the future.

Where is social work today in regard to professionalism and activism? What are its visions for the future and the barriers and opportunities for attaining them? What are the implications for the profession, for clients, and for society?

There are very different visions of what professionalism should be about, as illustrated by two influential past leaders in social work (Leighninger, 1986). Edith Abbott desired that social work emulate the traditional professions of medicine and law. Her image of professionalism emphasized a scientific basis of practice. The professional organization would serve as gatekeeper, imposing restrictive standards for entry into social work, and would work on improving the quality of training and the image of social work. She argued for an expert nonpartisan role for social workers in the development of social policy (such as providing expert testimony and lobbying). Like Abbott, Bertha Reynolds stressed a scientific base for social work practice, but differed in advocating for including the untrained and unskilled in the professional organization and for unions to improve work conditions and protect the rights of clients (see Chapter 22). The role of the professional association would be to improve the quality of education and training. She argued that it is the obligation of social workers to take a partisan political role and work for structural changes in the socioeconomic system.

These alternative images of professionalism have had a significant impact on the debate within social work. Social workers today seem to have taken up Edith Abbott's vision regarding professionalism and Reynolds' vision regarding partisanship. However, there is by no means consensus about the vision. There continues to be a struggle between those social workers who view social work as a function and strive for professionalization and those who view social work as a cause and social movement first and an occupation or profession second.

The Nature of Professions

The move to attain professional status has focused on working to obtain the attributes of the traditional professions and gaining control over practice. Although social scientists have not achieved consensus on these attributes, there are a number that seem to be common to most definitions of profession. Wilensky (1964) stated that "any occupation wishing to exercise professional authority must find a technical basis for it, assert an exclusive jurisdiction, link both skill and jurisdiction to standards of training, and convince the public that its services are uniquely trustworthy" (p. 138). Social work has had much difficulty with claims to exclusive competence because its knowledge base is "broad and vague" (p. 149), there are a number of other occupations making claims to the same knowledge base and skills, and the public does not view dealing with the problems of living as technical expertise. Flexner (1915, pp. 585–588), in the first systematic attempt to determine whether social work is a profession, concluded that the attributes of a scientific knowledge base, altruism, and "professional self-consciousness" are present, but the field was too broad in its boundaries to have the specialization needed for professional training. Many of those technical occupations that have the aforementioned attributes and that adhere to professional norms have obtained the much-sought-after attribute of autonomy. Social work has had difficulty also because of the expectations to conform to bureaucratic, political, and financial sponsors in the arenas in which they work. This vulnerability to sponsorship lowers its status as a profession.

A number of different approaches have been used to understand professions. The aforementioned attribute approach assumes that professions are beneficial for society. It focuses on a set of attributes that are assumed to represent the essence of professional occupations to distinguish them from nonprofessional occupations. In the functional model, professions are viewed as a natural result of modernization and the industrialization process. Occupations become specialized, develop distinctive scientifically based expertise and an ethics code, and obtain community sanction to gain professional status. It describes what essential societal needs professions fulfill. Functionalists assume that professions are "liberating for society, an integrative force that brings the wisdom of science to the service of the public interest" (Wenocur & Reisch, 1983, p. 722). The process approach is distinguished from these two approaches by its focus on how occupations achieve the status of professions. Attribute and functional theorists emphasize the service orientation of professions and often plead that certain occupations possess this character- istic and thus deserve the morally worthy status of profession. They do not discuss com- petition over status and benefits or the inequality that results from professionals' advanc- ing their economic interests.

The political–economic approach takes a very different perspective. These theorists focus on the significance of power relations, environment, and history in the development of occupational hegemony. They view a profession as a "quasi-corporate entity or enter- prise whose members have obtained a substantial degree of control over the production, distribution, and consumption of a needed commodity" (Wenocur & Reisch, 1983, p. 648). The control that some occupations are able to obtain is based on rationalizations to con- vince the public about the esoteric nature of their knowledge base and affinity with the dominant societal ideology.

Regulation and Control

The perspectives on professions one holds will influence one's response to social work's efforts to attain autonomy. Social work is using a number of strategies to attain a higher professional status by protecting its domain against competitors. One of these strategies is to attain autonomy via self-regulation and vendorship of the profession. This strategy is also justified by a desire to protect the public against practitioners without appropriate qualifications. It intends to ensure consistent standards across settings and give clients recourse if those standards are not met. The professional practice association, the Nation- al Association of Social Workers (NASW), has obtained legal regulation of the title of social work in all states and territories. There are some states with certification, which is a weaker form of regulation than licensing. In 27 states and Washington, DC, social workers are eligible to receive third-party payments. The future trend is to obtain licensing and ven- dorship in all states and to continue to make more stringent practice requirements, such as continuing education, periodic recertification, and periodic reviews of practice.

There are critics within social work who believe that licensing is elitist and sets up an inegalitarian relationship with clients. It is also argued that it restricts entry to social work inappropriately and serves primarily to protect and enhance the economic status of some social workers. For example, a number of states only license clinical social workers and exclude public employees. (This view is congruent with the political–economic perspec- tive of professions.)

There is also a barrier to obtaining autonomy through the regulation of social work in that competing occupations and professions cannot be legislated out of existence. They are competing for some of the same domains that social work wants to claim as its exclusive areas of practice. Some are older professions that discover new opportunities in what social workers are doing, and others are newly emerging occupations seeking professional status. Goode (1960) states that "if a new occupation claims that right to solve a problem which formerly was solved by another, that claim is an accusation of incompetence". The counter charge is likely to be "that its rivals are either charlatans, that is, not properly trained, or encroachers, that is, illegal competitors" (p. 904). For example, marriage and family therapy is a newly emerging profession that social work regards as encroaching on its territory. Addictions counselor certification is on the horizon, and its requirements may make it difficult for social workers to practice without more additional training. Nurses are competing with social workers to do discharge planning in hospital settings, and they have the edge with their medical background (see Chapter 7). Persons with MBAs and MPAs are winning in the struggle over who will administer human service agencies. There are a number of undergraduate degree programs (such as human service, family and child services, and gerontology) that indicate they are preparing students for what have been regarded as traditional social work jobs.

Whence and Wither Social Work's Commitment to the Poor and Working Class?

Social work seems stuck in reacting to these developments by chasing the illusive butterfly of exclusive domain and fighting off competitors. Political efforts seem to be too unbalanced in favor of professional protection as opposed to advocating for change in behalf of and with the poor and oppressed. Social work needs to examine to what extent its efforts to professionalize are detrimental to the interests of poor and working-class people. Bertha Reynolds' vision of unionization has not been the direction of social work. However, her notion of bringing in the untrained and unskilled has been partially realized by the bold move taken in the 1970s to include baccalaureate social workers (BSW) in NASW and to accredit BSW programs. This action was opposed for many years because of the belief that it would lower the status of social work. It has turned out to be a wise move in the sense that it has given the profession more control over the education and training of persons who practice social work. Nearly half of the 400,000 jobs that the Bureau of Labor statistics identifies as social work jobs are now filled with persons who have social work degrees. This is a definite increase over the pre-BSW era. Whether social work has increased its status as a result is a moot point, especially in light of the large numbers of persons still practicing social work without professional credentials. The supply of professional social workers cannot keep up with the demand for social work in the social welfare sector.

Unionization may be a future alternative to bring in these workers, improve working conditions for social workers, and realize common interests with other workers. Unionization may enable social workers to gain more political power and support for social services. There need not be incompatibility between unionization and professionalization. The unions of professionals are quite different from blue-collar unions. For example, the former tend to favor arbitration and mediation over strikes and merit over seniority for promotion.

There are barriers to unionization. Unions have become weakened, are under attack, and are losing members. Unions are seen as primarily serving the self-interest of members, whereas professionalism conveys a priority on serving the needs of clients. This need not be the case, as unions may include bread-and-butter issues in their goals as well as improvement of service to clients and involvement in social change. The interests of the less trained, lower-paid, nondegreed members may clash with the interests of the degreed social workers on such issues as civil service reclassification and licensing. Social work aspirations to attain the power, prestige, and financial status of the established professions encourages emphasis of the differences between degreed and nondegreed workers. NASW's strategic plan (1991) for the twenty-first century states that activities will be selected and evaluated "for their potential to advance the standing of the profession in the larger community and the professional development of NASW members" (p. 7). It is probable that NASW would regard unionization as inimical to advancing the status of the profession. It may be that some other form of organization is needed to support collective efforts to safeguard the interests of degreed and nondegreed workers.

Private Visions versus Public Agendas

Social work eclecticism is both a strength and a weakness. There is an appropriate array of responses to diverse problems and issues, such as casework, group work, community organization, psychotherapy, and crisis intervention. There are so many fields of practice that social workers cover, for example, child welfare, schools, mental health, and medical practice. Does the specialized competency required allow for professional education to provide this to students along with a common knowledge base, skills, and values? Flexner (1915, p. 588) criticized social work for its lack of an educationally communicable technique and believed that "the occupations of social workers are so numerous and diverse that no compact, purposely organized educational discipline is possible."

Social work has responded to this criticism by emphasizing psychiatrically oriented casework because it is believed that it offers an educationally communicable technique that is scientific and thus offers greater professional status. There have been periods in social work history when it has reacted to changing social and economic conditions by engaging in social reform as well as interventions such as group work, community organization, and resource mobilization. Currently the private practice of psychotherapy and employment in private for-profit businesses (such as drug and alcohol treatment programs and nursing homes) is an increasing trend in social work. Employment as a psychotherapist in a private fee-for-service setting may enable the income, autonomy, and status afforded the traditional professions (see Chapter 10). There continues to be an ongoing debate within social work whether this is what the profession should be about. There is not consensus about the central purpose of the profession. Some view private practice as a sign of attaining full professionalization and gaining recognition of social work expertise from all social classes. Others view it as abandonment of services to the poor and oppressed and social reform (Specht & Courtney, 1994; McNeece, 1995).

Social work's success in gaining licensing and vendorship status has attracted students into the profession who are interested in becoming private practitioners. Social work provides a shortcut in contrast to some other professions. Research has shown that students may be highly committed to working with disadvantaged clients and performing traditional social work interventions (Butler, 1990; Abell & McDonnell, 1990) but may choose to go into private practice because of the high level of autonomy, flexibility, challenge, status, and salary expected. The challenge is for the profession to do something about how organizations are structured and run and to create jobs for social workers in public and private nonprofit settings that would have these opportunities and more adequate compensation.

The future holds opportunities for working with low-income and oppressed clients, utilizing such methods and interventions as advocacy, case management, community organization, and resource mobilization. Child welfare is one arena that holds promise for the future. State social service departments and schools of social work have begun to work on professionalizing child welfare by developing curriculum materials and making arrangements for welfare workers to obtain professional social work degrees. Another possibility is the reconceptualization of case management as a position that will attract professional social workers and result in inclusion of appropriate curriculum content in schools of social work. This would also enable students to be competitive in gaining employment in managed care settings. A probable scenario for the future is that resources will become more scarce and social pressures such as the increase in the aged population and the growing AIDS epidemic will increase the demand for resources. There will be a need for case managers to coordinate services; facilitate interactions between consumers, their extended kin, and service systems; assess client needs; and design service packages.

Values, Ethics, and Professional Standards

One of the defining characteristics of professions is that they have a code of ethics that defines professional norms and a recognizable core set of values that undergirds the code. The professional adheres to a "service ideal." This means that "devotion to the client's interests more than personal or commercial profit should guide decisions when the two are in conflict" (Wilensky, 1964, p. 148).

Social work has a code of ethics and a mechanism for enforcing violations of the code. One of the primary ways students are socialized into the profession is by learning about its values, ethics, and practice standards. There are national and state Committees on Inquiry that process complaints lodged against social workers for allegedly violating the Social Work Code of Ethics. They have the power to accept complaints only against social workers who are members of NASW, so there are a large number of social workers who escape the sanctions of the professional association. However, state licensing boards and courts may sanction them for ethical violations. The Code of Ethics has had two revisions since its inception. The most recent revisions were in 1994, and they concerned dual relationships between clients and workers and mechanisms for dealing with impaired social workers. The concern that dual relationships may possibly harm or exploit clients seems to stem from the recognition that more social workers are going into private practice. There is less visibility of their practice, particularly if they are not receiving supervision; less organizational and collegial guidance; and potential for the profit motive to conflict with the service ideal. In their desire to please their customers they may subvert professional norms (as in massage therapy, bartering services, accepting gifts). The new norm that social workers have the responsibility for taking action regarding impaired colleagues is congruent with the profession's desire to be self-regulating and to increase the public trust in social work.

The future outlook for the code is that there will be continuing revisions. Not surprisingly, NASW has appointed a committee to review and revise the code and is soliciting suggestions from schools of social work and social workers. It seems likely that new provisions will have to be added to cover the changes entailed by "computerization" of the profession (see Chapter 2). Ethics will increasingly frame the debate about alternatives of choice and boundaries of acceptability for social work in this litigious society. Also, social workers have taken on more comprehensive roles in some areas of practice, such as mental health, where they provide the majority of services. They are also entering newer fields of practice such as industrial social work and divorce and custody mediation that have great potential for competing interests, tasks, and goals. Professional practice standards in these fields maybe evolving, unclear, or nonexistent. Thus the potential for moral dilemmas and ethical violations is high.

Social workers must be attuned to the ethical and legal responsibilities that they assume when establishing relationships with clients, supervising workers, or administering programs, or they will be vulnerable to malpractice suits, ethical complaints, and poor practice. It is predicted that the number of suits and complaints will increase in the future, especially because of the scrutiny of licensing bureaus and the demands for accountability of third-party payers and agencies that contract out services. The defensive social work practice that may be the result of these changes is likely to be inimical to social work values such as precedence of professional responsibility over personal self-interest and client self-determination.

Opportunities exist to improve the quality, consistency, and moral base of practice, as well as to decrease lawsuits and complaints against social workers. The Code of Ethics is very general; it has no historical references, no guidelines to interpret its principles, no opinions on previous cases, and no case examples. There are also few practice standards published, and the ones that are published are very general and concern only some of the fields and settings in which social workers function. This hinders Committees on Inquiry and state licensing boards, as they are often left to their own subjective interpretations of cases before them. There is not enough direction provided for the professional to prevent unacceptable conduct. This may result in extremely cautious behavior because of the fear of possible risks incurred. Thus the quality of practice may be lowered. Except for some of the most blatant offenses, such as sexual relations with clients, an alleged violator of the code may or may not be found in violation depending on the interpretations of the members of the particular ethics panel hearing the case. Even in cases where there are possible sexual violations, there is a need for more specificity. For example, are sexual relationships with ex-clients a violation? If not, is there a certain time period after therapy is terminated that must be observed for a sexual relationship to be considered ethically acceptable? The American Psychological Association has addressed these specific issues as well as others in its code and its standards. The Code of Professional Conduct in the legal profession contains actual cases and their outcomes, both official and advisory opinions, and practice guidelines.

Social work cannot totally emulate the legal profession with its many volumes of details about standards, because the nature of practice is much less clear-cut, less visible, and more diverse. However, it can work toward more specificity, like psychology, and like law, provide access to case summaries, opinions, and other information that might enable better decision making (Croxton, Jayaratne, Mattison, & Metzger, 1994). Much attention needs to be paid to respecting confidentiality in the cases provided. Because the Code of Ethics is periodically under revision, those are opportune times for historians and ethics, grievance, and professional standards committees to write up cases, opinions, guidelines, and standards. Establishment of clear ethical principles and standards is of the utmost importance not just for the protection of social workers in lawsuits and hearings but for the purpose of raising the esteem in which social work is held and gaining the public's trust.

A possible scenario for the future is that the accrediting body, CSWE, will upgrade its requirements for ethical content, and schools will require entire courses on values and ethics. NASW will require ethics in its continuing education requirements for licensing. This is most important because students and practitioners need not only to have understanding of standards of care but also of philosophical theories and guidelines for making decisions about moral dilemmas. No matter how the code and standards of practice are revised, there will always be cases that are unique, cases in which there is not enough information, or cases that involve conflicts between ethical principles. It is often likely that no matter which option is chosen, there will be harm. Also, professional standards may not be synonymous with ethical practice. Thus social workers need to study ethics and gain skills in ethical decision-making.

There are barriers to social work professionalization efforts, because there is dispute about its mission and whether it can claim a common base of values and ethics. The tradition of social work includes a belief that there is a foundation of common stable values. The question is whether this is a myth or a reality. If one believes that there is consensus about the meaning of values and assumes that values are employed to guide social workers across a number of different situations, then it is not a myth. However, there does not seem to be constancy, as the meaning of such values as self-determination and social justice seems to vary across persons, contexts, and situations. It is likely that social workers have a teleological orientation, that acts are neither good nor bad but become so depending on their consequences, rather than deontological, that people can determine that some acts are either inherently good or bad. A theory that is currently being taught as important for social workers to adopt is postmodernism. In this theory, values and knowledge are regarded as having meaning only in the interpretations put on them established through interactions that occur among the participants.

These theories have their strengths, but if values are seen as constantly changing, then social work cannot lay claim to a "shared and enduring value base" or to a stable knowledge base that can be imparted to those entering the profession (Meinert et al., 1994, p. 12). Social workers will need to decide the implications of these theories for professionalization and the mission of social work. It may be that postmodernism helps social workers abandon the role of expert and "enter into a collaborative search for meaning" with their clients (Hartman, 1992, p. 484).

There is a radical critique (see Chapter 22) of social work values and ethics that would support this debunking of the expert role. It assumes that the social worker's role has been to mediate established values and to work for individual solutions to problems. It rejects social work involvement in social control. It is suspicious of the professionalism enterprise and provides a lens for social work to see whether there are contradictions between its claimed values and ethics and its quest to attain professional legitimacy.

Social Work Education's Responses
to the Demands of the Environment

Changing Practice Contexts

As long as social work responds to the predominant values and assumptions of professionalism, it will react to the demands of the marketplace, emphasize individual status aspirations, and focus on providing those services that are most satisfying to the egos and class interests of social workers. The ascendancy of neoliberal and neoconservative ideologies and calls for deficit reduction and tax cuts seem to support a continuing trend toward the privatization of the social welfare sector, the decimation of public funding for social services, and hostility toward the public sector. The employment of social workers in private practice, proprietary businesses, and employee assistance programs reflects this trend. The push for results-oriented outcomes for money spent, cost containment, and the vendorship status often required for reimbursement of services affect the entire social service system, including the nonprofit sector.

How should schools of social work respond? Practice and education are integrally connected. One has no future without the other. Social work educators need to help students understand these changing practice contexts and the impact that payment systems and policies will have on limiting who is seen for services, what services will be provided, and what interventions are used. They have to decide whether to train students to be skilled in using the medical model and short-term interventions to adapt to the changing marketplace, or focus on asset-based and other models that are not marketplace driven. For example, in the clinical activist model, the social worker serves the most oppressed and poor clients and functions as clinician, data gatherer, and analyst to discover the types of social reforms needed, and as change agent to address the social casual factors (Walz & Groze, 1991). They have to debate the place in social work of private practice and practice in proprietary settings and the possibilities for alternative practice arenas. By ignoring the privatization that is occurring, educators abdicate their responsibility to address current issues, and they may appear to be irrelevant to students.

Educators need to use the changes in the marketplace as opportunities to teach students how to negotiate and advocate in behalf of their clients; to influence funding and service configurations; to develop, test, and adopt creative and cost-effective practice methods; and to work for structural change.

Changing Political Contexts

Social workers could play a critical role in responding to a change that is occurring in our political culture (see Chapter 25). There is national disillusionment with politics and the government, especially at the federal level. People believe that the government represents special interests and is not representative of the citizenry. Thus Washington is not trusted to do what is right. Social work educators need to seize the moment to prepare students to do grassroots community organizing. It is a part of the heritage of social work that has been jettisoned to pursue other, more "professional," interventions (such as therapy).

People have lost their political selves—the belief in their ability to participate in public life and impact the decisions that affect their lives. Many have turned to self-help to bring about change. An approach is emerging (the strengths approach) that regards poor neighborhoods as places with unrecognized assets, filled with individuals who have talents, abilities, and gifts. The concept of encouraging residents to recognize their power and be the force for change in their community is endorsed by both liberals and conservatives (Kretzmann & McKnight, 1993). Social workers have an opportunity to assist people in gaining political skills, realizing their strengths, and creating "community-based institutions of economic and political power" (Reisch & Wenocur, 1986, p. 86). There are grassroots citizens' movements throughout the United States that hold opportunities for employment. Career tracks need to be developed for social workers in those areas. The work will be done with or without the participation of social workers, because training institutions for community organizers (such as ACORN) and sponsors already exist and are not tied to the social work profession.

Social work needs to decide whether it can survive without responding to the pain and malaise of the disenfranchised. There is a poor match now between what is being taught in schools of social work about advocacy and social change, service to minorities and the poor, the political commitments of social workers to social justice, and the nature of social work practice. Social work students are primarily engaged in individual problem-solving and clinical work in their field placements. The challenge for the future is to work on resolving this serious dilemma. Grassroots community organizing and community development would provide one option for a better fit. Schools should consider requiring students to have two methods, one micro and one macro, so that they will have a range of interventions in their repertoire.

Diversity

Social work today requires the inclusion of minority content in its curriculum and at least pays lip service to the provision of services to minorities and other oppressed groups (see Chapter 20). Services to the poor and to persons of color have been drastically reduced, and social workers are now less likely to be employed in the public and voluntary sector. At some point in the twenty-first century, African Americans, Asians, and Hispanics together will constitute 50 percent of the U.S. population (see Chapter 1). By the year 2020 immigration will become the most important source of U.S. population growth. Persistent homelessness, poverty amidst affluence, and racism will rapidly increase social problems and create employment opportunities for social workers. Social work schools need to provide the knowledge, skills, and field placement experiences to prepare students for the upcoming "mosaic" society. The aforementioned theory of postmodernism may be especially helpful in enabling social workers to work with these populations. The theory calls for taking a position of uncertainty with clients in order to gain awareness and respect for how culture is part of every aspect of working with clients. Clients "supply the interpretive context that is required for determining the nature of a presenting problem, a proper intervention, or a successful treatment outcome" (Pardek, Murphy, & Choi, 1994, p. 345).

Global Influences

The global changes in the economy, telecommunications, trade, and increased numbers of immigrants in the United States require that schools of social work revise their curriculum. The basic curriculum for social work approved by CSWE has changed very little in 50 years. There needs to be an international perspective in the curriculum. Social work has tended to assume that other countries can benefit from American theories and practice methods but that the reverse is not true. Social work has been ethnocentric and parochial, although attitudes seem to be changing gradually. More social workers are visiting other countries, professional associations have strengthened their relationships with foreign organizations, and opportunities for international collaboration have increased. There needs to be reciprocal exchanges of theories and practice methods and an identification of what is useful in diverse social, economic, and cultural conditions. This can be especially helpful to Americans in learning more about cross-cultural practice. The human behavior in the social environment (HBSE) component of the curriculum needs to expand to include the global environment and future trends. Most importantly for social workers to partici-pate effectively in the twenty-first century, there is a necessity for major shifts in attitudes and values that transcend "domestic attachments and that facilitate modes of thinking that are instinctively cognizant of global realities" (Midgley, 1994, p. 178).

The shift to an international perspective may be helpful in enabling social workers not to be so localistic in their thinking so that they can see the drastic changes in the global physical environment and its impact on future generations. Due to population size, con-sumption patterns, and technology choices we are surpassing the earth's capacity to sup-port humans. Social work education is in need of new paradigms to respond to the demand for using resources more efficiently, more equitable distribution of resources, reduced pop-ulation growth, and reduced levels of consumption. The prediction is that without a rapid transition there will be more hunger and conflict over increasingly scarce resources. The social work person-in-environment paradigm must be enlarged to include the physical environment. New paradigms must be based on the ecological principle of sustainability—satisfying peoples' needs without jeopardizing the prospects of future generations. The present paradigms are based on a belief in unlimited continuous growth and extraction of nonrenewable resources. Schools need to reexamine what progress, optimal human devel-opment, and quality of life mean, and to provide students with the knowledge and skills that will enable them to be advocates for environmental justice (for example, to oppose unjust patterns of toxic waste management) (Hoff & McNutt, 1994). The study of social movements for justice, particularly the green movement, will provide case examples to inspire visions and hope for social reform.

Social Work Mission for the Twenty-First Century

As was mentioned at the beginning of this chapter, the visions of Edith Abbott and Bertha Reynolds have very different notions about the mission of social work. Edith Abbott saw social work as a profession, and Bertha Reynolds saw it both as a profession and a move-ment. The question as to whether social work is only a profession or both a profession and a movement continues to be raised. A related issue is whether social work should focus its resources on the poor and oppressed or work with all social classes. The ambivalence and tension generated by these issues is particular to social work because of its historical roots in social reform and service to the poor, and social workers' livelihoods are tied to conflicts over social and economic entitlements. The dual focus on professionalizing and social reform is not detrimental in that it allows for the simultaneous support of efforts in both directions.

Research in the 1960s and the 1980s has shown that there is little empirical support for the idea that professionalization is associated with greater conservatism and lesser activism among social workers. Individual involvement in social work was positively associated with participation in institutionalized forms of activism, such as visiting public officials and lobbying. However, social workers were more supportive of consensus approaches than conflict approaches for change (Reeser & Epstein, 1990).

Research on social work activism in the 1990s comes to some similar conclusions. NASW chapters are likely to be involved in traditional political activities rather than protests. Their goals seemed to be more concerned with promoting the profession than with social justice for the disenfranchised. Nonetheless, they did lobby for legislation on behalf of the poor (Salcido & Seck, 1992). In a recent survey of NASW members undertaken as part of strategic planning for the association, the first priority of members was to advance the profession, the second was to influence public policy, and the third was advocacy and activism on behalf of clients to enhance social justice and welfare. The balance of social work activism seems to be currently tipped in favor of consensus approaches to preserve and protect the turf, income, and status of social work. This is not to say that promoting and advancing social policies and programs aimed at meeting human need and improving the quality of life are not goals pursued by the profession. The NASW Delegate Assembly includes this as one of its program priority goals. The dual focus in social work remains and will continue into the future. The methods and goals of social work activism for the future will depend greatly on the mission of the profession.

It is likely that a key to social work commitment to bring about structural change in society is to revisit, renew, and do consciousness-raising about its mission. There is tension between the political context and professional culture. There is rapid movement to incarcerate the poor and decimate the welfare state (see Chapter 24). The choices that social workers make in response will determine whether they sell out in order to fit into the political culture. If social work is to be responsive to the crises of the next century it must respond to rebuilding the political culture and finding solutions to a host of social, economic, and physical ills (such as degradation of the environment and the growing inequality between social classes).

Social workers need to be able to operate under a variety of conditions in complex practice environments using a variety of responses. The mission needed for the next century is that social workers should work with individuals, groups, and communities, especially those on the margins of society, to alleviate and prevent pain, deprivation, and inequality. There must be a better fit between the purpose of social work, which deals with the intersection of private and public issues, and what most social workers do, which is deal with individual problems (private issues). Social workers need to work both sides of the road. The profession needs to prepare students to carry out this mission and to develop appropriate job opportunities. Bertha Reynolds believed that social work must maintain a dual focus on the individual in need and on the social, economic, and political forces in society that contribute to individual misery.

Social work needs to convey its mission clearly to the public. The purpose and goals of social work will have a definitive influence on the nature of students attracted to the profession. This renewed purpose may discourage those students who choose social work because they regard it as the quickest route to private practice. Differences in social work specialization (such as casework, group work, and community organization) and the background characteristics of social workers (such as race, religion, and political party) have been shown to have a significant impact on the activism of social workers (Reeser & Epstein, 1990). Thus, if social work develops itself as a profession and a social movement for justice and sustainability, it will likely recruit a more activist student group, people who view themselves as committed to social change. The future of social work will continue to be positively associated with professionalization. The nature of this activism will be determined by the mission of social work, the background characteristics and career interests of future social workers, and whether there will be a new period of social protest in society.

References

Abell, N., & McDonnell, J. R. (1990). Preparing for practice: Motivations, expectations and aspirations of the MSW class of 1990. *Journal of Social Work Education, 26*(1), 57–64.

Butler, A. S. (1990). A reevaluation of social work students' career interests: Grounds for optimism. *Journal of Social Work Education, 26*(1), 45–56.

Croxton, T., Jayaratne, S., Mattison, D., & Metzger, K. (1994). *A study of social work practice in the State of Michigan: Standards of practice and professional ethics.* Unpublished report, National Association of Social Workers, Michigan Chapter, and University of Michigan School of Social Work.

Flexner, A. (1915). Is social work a profession? In *Proceedings—National Conference of Charities and Corrections* (pp. 576–590). Baltimore: MD: Russell Sage Foundation.

Goode, W. (1960). Encroachment, charlatanism, and the emerging profession: Psychology, sociology, and medicine. *American Sociological Review, 25,* 902–914.

Hartman, A. (1992). In search of subjugated knowledge. *Social Work, 37*(6), 483–484.

Hoff, M. D., & McNutt, J. G. (1994). *The global environmental crisis: Implications for social welfare and social work.* England: Avebury.

Kretzmann, J. P., & McKnight, J. L. (1993). *Building communities from the inside out.* Evanston, IL: Center for Urban Affairs and Policy Research, Northwestern University.

Leighninger, L. (1986). Bertha Reynolds and Edith Abbott: Contrasting images of professionalism in social work. *Smith College Studies in Social Work, 56,* 111–121.

McNeece, C. A. (1995). Family social work practice: From therapy to policy. *Journal of Family Social Work, 1*(1), 3–17.

Meinert, R. G., Pardek, J. T., & Sullivan, W. P. (Eds.). (1994). *Issues in social work: A critical analysis.* Westport, CT: Auburn House.

Midgley, J. (1994). Transnational strategies for social work: Toward effective reciprocal exchanges. In R. G. Meinert, J. T. Pardek, & W. P. Sullivan (Eds.), *Issues in social work: A critical analysis* (pp. 165–180). Westport, CT: Auburn House.

National Association of Social Workers. (1991). *NASW Strategic Plan 1991–1996.* Washington, DC: Author.

Pardek, J. T., Murphy, J. W., & Choi, J. M. (1994). Some implications of postmodernism for social work practice. *Social Work, 39*(4), 343–346.

Reeser, L. C., & Epstein, I. (1990). *Professionalization and activism in social work: The sixties, the eight-*

ies and the future. New York: Columbia University Press.

Reisch, M., & Wenocur, S. (1986). The future of community organization in social work: Social activism and the politics of profession building. *Social Service Review, 60*(1), 70–93.

Salcido, R. M., & Seck, E. T. (1992). Political participation among social work chapters. *Social Work, 37*(6), 563–564.

Specht, H., & Courtney, M. E. (1994). *Unfaithful angels: How social work has abandoned its mission.* New York: The Free Press.

Walz, T., & Groze, V. (1991). The mission of social work revisited: An agenda for the 1990s. *Social Work, 36*(6), 500–504.

Wenocur, S., & Reisch, M. (1983). The social work profession and the ideology of professionalization. *Journal of Sociology and Social Welfare, 10,* 684–732.

Wilensky, H. L. (1964). The professionalization of everyone? *American Journal of Sociology, 70,* 137–158.

Chapter *24*

The Future of Social Welfare Policy

DIANA M. DINITTO, PhD
University of Texas at Austin

The scope of social welfare policy is difficult to define. Broadly conceived, "social welfare policy is anything a government chooses to do, or not to do, that affects the quality of life of its people" (DiNitto, 1995, p. 2), but for practical purposes I confine this discussion to the types of programs most closely identified with the concerns of the profession of social work: social insurance, public assistance, and social services. In speculating about the future of social welfare policy, I see a widening gap between what many social workers in the United States probably view as the ideal and what I suspect will be the situation in the year 2000 and beyond.

More Residual, Less Universal

Among the first concepts social workers learn in social welfare policy courses are *universal* or *institutional* and *selective* or *residual*. Universal or institutional provisions are available to most members of society and are considered preventive in nature. The major program that comes to mind when this term is used in the United States is Social Security. These social insurance programs help to prevent poverty. Nearly all working persons participate in these programs and their spouses and dependents are also entitled to benefits. The term *residual* refers to programs that serve a select group of people, generally those with an identified need; these programs are remedial or ameliorative because they tend to be available only after a problem such as poverty has become severe. In the United States

254

the program most likely to come to mind that fits this category is Aid to Families with Dependent Children (AFDC), the most reviled of social welfare programs. Social workers generally believe that universal programs are preferable to those that are residual. Universal programs address common human needs (Towle, 1965), normalize participation in the social welfare system, and do not carry the stigma associated with residual programs.

If current trends prevail, however, most social welfare programs in the United States will become increasingly residual—targeted to narrower categories of people and designed to address very specific types of problems for limited periods of time. The social safety net will become more tattered, and the United States will become less kind and less gentle to those in need.

There is ample evidence to suggest that this trend toward residualism will be more than a passing phenomenon. For example, the states of Arkansas, Georgia, Wisconsin, and New Jersey have already been granted permission (called waivers) from the federal government to deny additional payments to AFDC recipients who have more children while in the program (National Association of Social Workers, December 1994). Other examples of the move toward greater residualism in AFDC are plans to limit the amount of time a family can remain in the program. Some proposals, such as the Clinton administration's, would require recipients to work in public service jobs if they did not secure employment in the private sector within two years, but more conservative proposals would cut off assistance altogether. The two-year moratorium has also been suggested for receipt of public housing benefits, and the idea could spread like wildfire into food stamps and other programs.

Residualism in public welfare is also reflected in General Assistance (GA) programs (also called General Relief or similar names). GA programs are solely funded and operated by state and local governments, generally to assist people who are in need but who do not meet the criteria for federally supported public assistance programs. GA programs are needed because of the gaps in social welfare assistance. For example, there is no long-term, federally supported income maintenance program for poor people unless they are aged, disabled, or have dependent children. However, many communities have no GA program (Nichols, Dunlap, & Barkan, 1992). In locations that do, GA acts as a program of last resort (Handler & Sosin, 1983). Now, faced with increasing financial difficulties, many states and communities have cut back on this last hope for many needy individuals. This trend is likely to continue.

With the 1994 elections that brought a new Republican-controlled and more conservative Congress, there are new fears that block grants will be used to consolidate programs and reduce funding—even in programs once thought to be relatively tamper-proof. In the fall of 1994, newspapers began reporting on a Republican plan to consolidate the country's major nutrition programs (the Food Stamp Program; the Special Supplemental Food Program for Women, Infants, and Children, known as WIC; the school lunch and breakfast programs; and other nutrition programs of the U.S. Department of Agriculture) into a single block grant. Under the plan, the Food Stamp Program and school lunches and breakfasts would no longer be treated as entitlements. A ceiling would be set on nutrition benefits, and when reached, there would be no guarantee of food assistance for those who meet program requirements as there is today.

Nutrition programs have generally withstood conservative onslaughts, but with popular perceptions of rampant food stamp fraud and with weakened ties of the Food Stamp Program to agricultural interests, attempts to whittle away at the program may become more successful.

In the social services arena, the target populations of publicly supported state and community-based services have increasingly become those with the most severe needs. Certainly, individuals with serious problems deserve assistance, but in focusing on them in a time of budget cuts, less attention has been paid to prevention and to serving those with situational problems.

In the field of child welfare, as reports of abuse and neglect mount each year, protective services workers must allocate their time to children in greatest danger, leaving other cases unattended or to the hope that the family will voluntarily make use of referrals to other programs. Without the personnel to do follow-up, there is little assurance that families have availed themselves of any preventive services their communities might have to offer. Increased residualism in the child welfare system causes the public to become outraged when protective service workers fail to intervene more aggressively and a child later suffers severe injury or dies. Protective service workers are also at increased risk of civil and criminal penalties in such a residual system of care. Even as funding for family preservation grows, the increased demand for services suggests that only the most severe cases will be the targets of intervention; there will not be enough resources to provide more preventive and universal programs for parental assistance.

Residualism is most striking in the social insurance arena because it reverses long-standing trends toward more generous benefits. Because employees and their employers pay taxes earmarked for these programs, employees continue to feel strongly that they deserve these benefits regardless of their income and assets, and for years, politicians were afraid to suggest reining in payments or taxing benefits. These ideas were considered political suicide (Stockman, 1975, p. 9). Since the 1983 amendments to the Social Security Act, however, the rate of increase of Social Security payments has been subject to greater controls, and a portion of the benefits of those in even middle-income brackets is subject to regular income taxes. Additionally, the full retirement age, which is now age 65, will rise gradually, reaching age 67 in the year 2027 and affecting those born in 1938 and later. Younger generations will likely be faced with an even higher full retirement age. Whether it is fair to delay payments or not, the size of the older population is putting more strains on Social Security, and projections regarding the actuarial soundness of the retirement program have become more gloomy.

The trend toward residualism in social insurance has become especially pronounced in the Medicare program where all wages are now subject to the 1.45 percent hospital insurance (Medicare Part A) tax and where deductibles and other out-of-pocket costs for all but the very poorest older Americans will continue to rise.

Another social insurance program that may become more residual is unemployment compensation (UC). Today, individuals whose job history qualifies them for unemployment compensation are entitled to benefits regardless of their assets and previous earnings. Tomorrow it is likely that a second eligibility criterion—means testing—will be added to determine who qualifies for UC benefits. Under such a system, those who earned more than a given amount in the past months may be denied benefits. Or another approach might be to levy a higher tax on unemployment benefits at income tax time depending on an individual's total income at the end of the year. Although social welfare scholars have warned of the dangers in converting social insurance programs to public assistance because public support for the programs is likely to be weakened (Kingson & Berkowitz, 1993), all signs suggest that the United States is moving in that direction.

Why More Residualism?

Why will this trend toward residualism continue to prevail? Because increasing caseloads in social insurance and public assistance programs translate into greater costs and greater federal debt. AFDC is only a small fraction of the social welfare system; nevertheless, the size of its caseloads are impressive. Since 1950 the number of recipient families has grown from 1.5 percent of the total U.S. population (U.S. Bureau of the Census, 1975) to just under 5 percent in 1992 (Department of Health and Human Services, cited in *Congressional Quarterly,* 1994, p. 121). Projections are that by 1998, 5.2 million families, or 14.7 million individuals, will be receiving AFDC (Committee on Ways and Means, 1993, p. 685). Total costs of AFDC were $5 billion in 1970 and $24.9 billion in 1992; by 1998 they are expected to reach $29.6 billion (Committee on Ways and Means, 1993, p. 679). Even if these figures are adjusted for price inflation, increases would be substantial by most standards; however, these total costs must be viewed in light of the fact that after controlling for inflation, the real value of AFDC benefits has deteriorated by 40 percent in the last two decades (Committee on Ways and Mean, 1993, p. 615). In 1970 the average monthly payment to an AFDC family was $178; in 1992 the average was $388; had AFDC kept pace with inflation, the average AFDC payment would have been $644 (Committee on Ways and Means, 1993, p. 615).

The scenarios are similar in other major public assistance programs. Caseloads in the Supplemental Security Income (SSI) program for poor people with disabilities continue to grow rapidly; SSI payments also remain modest, although there is a federally funded minimum that is adjusted annually for inflation. Caseloads in the federally funded Food Stamp Program have been at all-time highs. Caseloads and costs will also continue to grow substantially in the Social Security insurance program for workers who incur disabilities (SSDI). Of course, increases in all these programs will continue to pale in comparison to the Social Security retirement program. As caseloads and costs continue to increase, the eligibility criteria for all these entitlement programs will become more selective and payments will become more penurious. One recent effort to reduce SSI and SSDI caseloads is that in 1994 Congress passed, and President Clinton signed, the Social Security Independence and Program Improvements Act. The act contains serious consequences for alcoholics and drug addicts: "For SSI recipients, benefits would be terminated after 36 months, regardless of treatment availability. For SSDI beneficiaries, the 36-month time limit would only be applied once treatment becomes available" (National Association of Social Workers, October 14, 1994, p. 9).

Herrnstein and Murray's (1994) suggestion that we return to the pre-1960s era when children of single women tended to be made available for adoption at birth, and the House Republican "Contract with America" that proposed placing the children of the poor in orphanages, are examples of this growing conservatism. Many get-tough welfare-reform proposals are making headway, but orphanages were dropped from the contract after heavy criticism. There are hardly enough suitable substitute care placements for children who suffer extreme neglect or abuse, let alone for children of parents whose only "crime" is that they are poor. The use of orphanages even flies in the face of current child welfare practice in which family preservation is preferred over substitute care when it seems that neglectful or abusive parents can be helped to provide a suitable home environment for their children (see, for example, Fraser, Pecora, and Haapala, 1991).

The major exception in the trend toward greater residualism may be in health care for the poor and near poor (see Chapters 4 and 6). Although plans for a national health care program were defeated in 1994, there is hope for some type of compromise because health care is a universal need, because 35 to 48 million Americans are without regular health care coverage (see Committee on Ways and Means, 1993, p. 295; Executive Office of the President, Office of Management and Budget, 1994, p. 177; "48 Million Uninsured," 1992), because many are underinsured ("The Doctor Is In," 1989), because health care costs continue to rise (even though the rate of health care cost inflation has slowed in the last few years, health care inflation remains higher than inflation in general), and because the demand for health care grows greater each year as more medical advances occur and the population ages.

Republican opposition to a true universal health care program has been strong, perhaps because Republicans did not want to agree to the major social welfare reform of the last third of the century while a Democratic president and a Democratic Congress were in power. The Republican version of a plan for national health insurance will be substantially more modest than President Clinton once dreamed, but with a Congress that is now Republican controlled, and perhaps with the election of a Republican president in 1996, Republicans might be willing to break the gridlock they have created and take credit for health care reform for the first time in the nation's history. But if there is no progress on health care reform, the gap between the two tiers of the system of care for health, mental health, and substance abuse problems (see McNeece & DiNitto, 1994)—in which many poor and near-poor people have very limited access to services—will grow even wider.

Workfare, Not Welfare

Work requirements will continue to be the centerpiece of public assistance reform. Demographic trends tell us why. As more mothers (both in single-parent and two-parent families) of preschool- and school-age children have gone to work, the idea that welfare should be provided so that mothers can stay at home to care for their children has become obsolete. Since the 1960s, amendments to the Social Security Act have increased the emphasis on requiring AFDC parents to work. Single parents receiving AFDC used to be exempt from work requirements if their youngest child was under age 6 (the age at which children generally enter first grade). Today they may be obligated to meet work requirements if their youngest child is age 3 or older, and they can be obligated to work if their youngest child is at least 1 year of age if the state in which the family resides has chosen this option.

In a review article, Goodwin (1981) described workfare programs as a waste of time because most welfare recipients would prefer decent jobs and because workfare did not improve participants' job skills and it did not reduce the costs of welfare. Feminist Barbara Ehrenreich (1987) further criticized workfare, saying that "we are being asked to believe that pushing destitute mothers into the work force (. . . for no other compensation than the welfare payments they would have received anyway) is consistent with women's striving toward self-determination" (p. 40). To be fair, many families have yet to be affected by AFDC work requirements because states have neither sufficient job and training programs nor sufficient child care placements to enforce them, but the trend is clearly toward work.

The Job Opportunities and Basic Skills (JOBS) program (part of the Family Support Act of 1988) places greater pressure on states to see that more parents receiving AFDC meet work requirements even though it is unlikely that many states will be able to generate enough decent job training or jobs to raise many recipients out of poverty. As some social scientists have described the situation, "while parents on welfare may no longer be idle, most are likely to remain poor" (Gideonse & Meyers, 1989, p. 39). But workfare is here to stay. President Clinton has vowed to turn welfare offices into employment offices. The title of his welfare reform proposal, the Work and Responsibility Act, reflects this theme. Other innovative options include New York State's Child Assistance Program which reduces the family's AFDC grant by only 10 cents for every dollar earned if the family's income is below the federal poverty level.

The IRS, Not HHS

During the last few decades the Earned Income Tax Credit (EITC) has become a more politically popular way of helping the working poor than public assistance programs. This credit originated in 1975 to assist low-income working families with children. The amount of the EITC has increased substantially in recent years, and in 1994 a smaller EITC became available to low-income workers without children. The EITC is an income tax in reverse (also known as a negative income tax). Rather than the worker paying a tax to the federal government, the government makes money available to workers through the Internal Revenue Service (IRS). In 1994 workers with one child whose family income was less than $23,755 were able to receive a maximum EITC of $2,038 (the income ceiling and the amount of the credit are greater with each additional child in the home); workers between the ages of 25 and 64 without children who earned less than $9,000 could receive up to $306. Even though the EITC generally does not result in a reduction of public assistance (food stamps, AFDC, or Medicaid) benefits, this approach to helping low-income households is popular with most people because it rewards work.

Although the amount paid to families may be reduced, another advantage of the EITC is that it makes use of the federal tax system, the mechanism by which the middle and upper classes receive many of their social welfare benefits. The middle classes receive social welfare benefits primarily in the form of income tax deductions for property taxes and the interest paid on home mortgages and through other mechanisms such as student grants and loans to attend college. The upper classes also receive benefits in the form of various tax breaks for business expenses. Although there have been calls from Democratic and Republican camps to eliminate much of the help provided to upper- and even middle-class Americans, when the IRS is involved the term *welfare* is not used. In fact, use of the IRS rather than the

U.S. Department of Health and Human Services (HHS) to assist poor working people normalizes the way assistance is provided to the poor. The poor then get their help from the government in the same way that the middle and upper classes do. A negative income tax (NIT) that would replace public assistance programs was suggested by economist Milton Friedman (Friedman & Friedman, 1979), and President Richard Nixon proposed a NIT in the form of the Family Assistance Plan (FAP) in the 1970s. Although unsuccessful at the time, in the years ahead the more politically successful attempts to reform public assistance will make use of the tax system, not the welfare system.

Majorities or Minorities?

The ethnic composition of the U.S. population is changing rapidly. By 2050 non-Hispanic Whites may be only 53 percent of the U.S. population instead of the 75 percent that they are today (Usdansky, 1992), and this will have implications for social welfare policy.

The largest social welfare program in the country—the Social Security retirement program—has long treated members of certain ethnic groups unfairly in at least some respects (Gnaizda & Obledo, 1985). For example, the life spans of black and Hispanic Americans are shorter than those of whites, and thus blacks and Hispanics collect Social Security retirement benefits for a shorter period of time even though they are taxed at the same rate as whites. In fact, Gnaizda and Obledo (1985) point out that since the median life expectancy of Hispanics is about 64 years, half will never collect retirement benefits. In order to adequately support the elderly population, younger members of all ethnic groups will have to pay increased Social Security taxes. But the burden is heavier for black and Hispanic Americans because Social Security retirement and disability taxes are regressive (lower-paid workers end up paying a higher percentage of their total income in taxes than higher-paid workers), and members of these ethnic groups are overrepresented among the ranks of lower-income workers.

Better news is that in recent decades more members of ethnic minority groups have fared well in the job market as a result of increased education and antidiscrimination policies; as a result, they will fare better with respect to Social Security benefits on retirement. In addition, as women of all ethnic groups slowly narrow the income gap with men, their benefits are also rising, and more women will collect Social Security retirement benefits based on their earnings records rather than those of their husbands.

Other legislation with implications for various ethnic groups is Proposition 187, passed in California in 1994. It would restrict almost all services now available to undocumented individuals in California. Although it apparently reflects the sentiments of those who went to the polls, it is at odds with federal policies that, for example, allow for the children of undocumented individuals to receive a free public school education, and undocumented individuals are already prohibited from participating in most federally supported social welfare programs. Many aspects of Proposition 187, also referred to as Save Our State (SOS), are unlikely to hold up under the scrutiny of the courts, but there will be further efforts to restrict the social welfare benefits available to immigrants (both undocumented and documented) as domestic problems mount, despite research that shows that immigrants pay their way in work effort and taxes (see Richardson, 1993, for a review).

Conservatives and Centrists, Not Liberals

The 1994 elections portend an increasingly conservative agenda for the country. Republicans now hold the majority of Senate seats for the first time since the 1986 elections. They also hold the majority of governorships for the first time since 1970, and more striking is that they currently hold the majority of House seats for the first time since 1954. In addition, as the true liberals on the Supreme Court have retired after holding on as long as they could, the high court now has now emerged as a more moderate force in public policy.

At least for the time being, more Americans will lean to the conservative side because so many are working- and middle-class individuals who are struggling to get by without those benefits labeled welfare. The rising incidence of social problems and the often erroneous ideas that social programs do not work have led to a preference for control strategies, such as building more prisons (which don't work either), rather than social welfare strategies, such as public assistance benefits that would reach poverty thresholds or a livable minimum wage.

We are now also contending with the agenda of the radical right, or the religious right, as it prefers to be called, which still sees no need for sex education other than the "just say no" abstinence approach. The size of the religious right is unclear, but it is well organized and highly committed. Those characteristics will continue to allow it to influence public policy well beyond the size of its membership. Pro-choice forces have been able to hold their own against the opposition of the religious right and other conservatives by being just as organized in their efforts to preserve reproductive freedoms.

The Private Sector, Not the Public Sector

The trend toward privatization that is prominent in many facets of social welfare services will continue to gain momentum. Privatization has already been an important force in the operation of jails and prisons, elementary and secondary schools, residences for people with mental retardation and other developmental disabilities, and mental health and chemical dependency treatment programs. Privatization will continue because entrepreneurship is the American way. Initially, mental health and mental retardation services were not privatized, not only because of the stigma associated with these disabilities but because most people could not afford to purchase these services. When service providers and insurers saw the potential market in these areas they moved in.

Many social workers favor privatization, as evidenced by the growing number who work full-time or part-time in private-sector agencies and in independent private practices. Perceptions are that public service is stifling to professionals and that private work is better for one's "personal well-being" (Jayaratne, Davis-Sacks, & Chess, 1991). As the eligibility criteria for public assistance payments and publicly funded social services grow increasingly stringent, and as payments decrease and the scope of services becomes more limited, social workers will become further disenchanted with government work. They will be propelled in even greater numbers to the private sector, despite current exhortations from academic circles that the profession has abandoned its mission to serve the poor and disenfranchised.

Privatization will continue to increase in the area of child support enforcement (CSE) as public CSE agencies encounter even greater difficulty in keeping up with the demand to locate absent parents and to collect from them. It will continue to expand in the justice system, and more probationers will be assessed fees to cover the costs of their supervision. Parents will be expected to foot the bill for care of children under the supervision of the juvenile justice system, and parents who become clients of child protective service agencies will also be assessed a fee for the services they and their child receive (Gustavsson, personal communication, December 7, 1994), especially as more private contractors are paid to assist these families. Privatization will grow despite concerns about governments abrogating their responsibilities (Bendick, 1989), about maintaining the quality of services, and about the co-optation of alternative service organizations by governments (Smith & Lipsky, 1993).

Income Inequality, Not Income Equality

While the country concerns itself with how to control the growth of the welfare establishment, it is destined for greater income inequality, which will increase the need for social welfare benefits. A common method of assessing income inequality in the United States is to divide the population into quintiles from the lowest to the highest in income. For many decades the lowest quintile slowly gained in income share. For example, according to the U.S. Bureau of the Census, from 1936 to 1970 the lowest quintile went from 4.1 percent to 5.5 percent of all personal income, whereas the highest quintile lost ground, going from 51.7 percent in 1936 to 40.9 percent in 1970. In the last few decades the trend has been reversed. The lowest quintile lost ground, dropping to 4.4 percent by 1992, whereas the highest quintile gained, increasing to 44.6 percent by 1992.

As greater income inequality has resulted in the need for more social welfare services, it has also resulted in more polarization among the classes. Duncan, Smeeding, and Rodgers (1992) of the Survey Research Center at the University of Michigan describe "a tidal wave of inequality" occurring between those with more skills and work experience and those with less of both, with these trends affecting men and women and people of all ethnic groups. In the years ahead, there will be even greater disparities between the poor and the nonpoor with respect to education, job preparation, and income. Unless attitudes toward public assistance and other social supports take a sharp turn, poverty among children in the lower-income classes will continue to increase, because their parents will have less recourse to methods of supporting them.

The paths to greater income equality include (1) a more progressive tax structure, (2) a higher minimum wage, (3) more educational and job opportunities, and (4) more generous public assistance and social insurance benefits for those who are poor. Option 2 seems the most likely because it rewards work, but if history is any lesson, the minimum wage can be expected to increase only very slowly.

Computers, Not Cash or Paper

It may not need saying, but in the years ahead the system for delivering social welfare benefits will become increasingly computerized. Paper transactions in welfare, as in business matters, will be a thing of the past. Electronic benefit transfer (EBT) has already been tested extensively in the Food Stamp Program, and it will soon render the debate over whether to give stamps or cash almost obsolete. In some locations EBT is also being used to deliver AFDC, child support, and WIC benefits. There are many advantages to EBT. For example, it costs the government about 4 cents to do an electronic transfer, compared to about 30 cents to issue a check (Food and Nutrition Service, 1991); issuing food stamps because of the complex process involved is more costly.

EBT makes use of a plastic debit card like those used at commercial automated teller machines and is not without risks. Computer hackers can break into systems, making theft of benefits by computer a distinct possibility, and there have already been reports of scams to defraud EBT systems (Fritz, 1995).

In the child support enforcement system, interstate and intrastate tracking of parents will become increasingly sophisticated, resulting in nationwide dragnets. Computerization will also result in more sophisticated monitoring to detect fraud and abuse by clients, social welfare workers, vendors, and others in social welfare programs. Fingerprinting recipients to prevent others from using their benefits and to prevent recipients from collecting multiple benefits in the same program will become commonplace.

The Clinton health care plan contained the use of a health security card (see Chapter 7) that would be issued to all eligible participants. Recent suggestions to control immigration have included a national identity card. Such cards can make use of on-line computer systems that are linked to a central computer or off-line systems that rely on smart cards. Smart cards contain a computer chip that holds information and do not require a connection to a central computer. There is the potential for electronics to vastly improve the delivery of social welfare benefits. There is also the potential for problems, such as invasion of privacy, as fear of Big Brother watching Americans ever more closely mounts. Groups such as the American Civil Liberties Union will certainly view these suggestions closely.

Despair or Hope?

Of course, there is hope for the future of social welfare policy. Social workers and other human service professionals bring this hope to their work every day. Without it they would not even bother to show up at the office. What are these hopes? They exist in programs that recognize the strengths of the people served. For example, researchers have pointed out that mothers receiving AFDC have more recent work experience and cycle on and off welfare more than has been recognized (Spalter-Roth, Hartmann, & Andrews, 1992). Programs such as CAP (mentioned earlier in this chapter) capitalize on this strength.

There is hope because the issues of gay men and lesbians as parents and serving in the military have been broached, even if current policies are not yet different enough from past policies to suit most social workers. There is hope as more women have been appointed to high-level posts in the Clinton administration than under other presidencies, and because more women and ethnic minorities are serving in elected positions in Congress and at state and local levels than ever before. There is hope because Americans are a giving people. They give of their time and of their money to assist others. They are concerned about their neighborhoods and they strive for the best for their families. There is hope because Americans do not want to see rising child poverty. Americans have been very successful at improving life conditions for older Americans, and concerted efforts can do the same for children. There is hope as college and university enrollments in social work education and other human service programs are increasing again, and as social work faculty and practitioners debate curricula that will best prepare professionals for the challenges ahead.

Conclusion

In this chapter I have taken the position that social welfare policy will become increasingly residual in nature. There is no denying that signs point in this direction. I wish I could look even further ahead to a time when the pendulum might swing again to the type of social awakening that occurred in the United States in the 1930s during the New Deal and in the 1960s with the Great Society. It is difficult to envision liberal transformations of social welfare policy as the population grows ever larger and the demands placed on governments to serve the people increase even further. Canada and European and other countries with much more universal social welfare provisions are also feeling the strains and discussing the need to resort to more residual approaches to social welfare and to restrict their immigration policies. Even among the strongest advocates of increased social welfare benefits, there is a reality that indicates that Congress's inability to control spending and balance the budget is like a speeding locomotive that has lost its brakes, and that the full impact of the crash will come when Generation X is old enough to take over the White House and Congress and becomes responsible for the care of the baby boom generation. If current conservative political trends continue to prevail, social workers will face even greater challenges in upholding the ideals of social and economic justice for all members of society, and this is our call to greater social activism in the years ahead.

References

Bendick, M., Jr. (1989). Privatizing the delivery of social welfare services: An idea to be taken seriously. In S. B. Kamerman & A. J. Kahn (Eds.), *Privatization and the welfare state* (pp. 97–120). Princeton, NJ: Princeton University Press.

Committee on Ways and Means, U.S. House of Representatives. (1993). *Overview of entitlement programs: 1993 green book.* Washington, DC: U.S. Government Printing Office.

Congressional Quarterly. (1994, January 22). *Congressional Quarterly Weekly Report*, p. 121.

DiNitto, D. M. (1995). *Social welfare: Politics and public policy* (4th ed.). Needham Heights, MA: Allyn & Bacon.

The doctor is in . . . but not for everybody. (1989, July–August). *Highlights* (Newsletter of the American Association of Retired Persons Volunteers), p. 7.

Duncan, G., Smeeding, T., & Rodgers, W. (1992). Why the middle class is shrinking. Ann Arbor, MI: University of Michigan, Survey Research Center.

Ehrenreich, B. (1987). A step back to the workhouse? *Ms., 16,* 40–42.

Executive Office of the President, Office of Management and Budget. (1994, January). *Budget of the United States Government, fiscal year 1995.* Washington, DC: U.S. Government Printing Office.

Food and Nutrition Service. (1991). Government agencies test a new way to deliver benefits. *Food and Nutrition, 20*(2), 2–3.

48 million uninsured in U.S., study says. (1992, March 1). *Austin American-Statesman*, p. A14.

Fraser, M. W., Pecora, P., & Haapala, D. A. (1991). *Families in crisis: The impact of intensive family preservation services.* New York: Aldine de Gruyter.

Friedman, M., & Friedman, R. (1979). *Free to choose: A personal statement.* New York: Harcourt Brace Jovanovich.

Fritz, M. (1995, January 14). Crooks abuse food stamp cards. *Austin American-Statesman*, p. A17.

Gideonse, S. K., & Meyers, W. R. (1989, September/October). Why the Family Support Act will fail. *Challenge, 32,* 33–39.

Gnaizda, R., & Obledo, M. (1985, Spring). 1983 Social Security reforms unfair to minorities and the young. *Gray Panther Network*, p. 12.

Goodwin, L. (1981, Fall). Can workfare work? *Public Welfare, 39,* 19–25.

Handler, J. F., & Sosin, M. (1983). *Last resorts: Emergency assistance and special needs programs in public welfare.* New York: Academic Press.

Herrnstein, R. J., & Murray, C. (1994). The bell curve: Intelligence and class structure in American life. New York: The Free Press.

Jayaratne, S., Davis-Sacks, M. L., & Chess, W. A. (1991). Private practice may be good for your health and well being. *Social Work, 36*(3), 193–272.

Kingson, E. R., & Berkowitz, E. D. (1993). *Social Security and Medicare: A policy primer.* Westport, CT: Auburn House.

McNeece, C. A., & DiNitto, D. M. (1994). *Chemical dependency: A systems approach.* Englewood Cliffs, NJ: Prentice Hall.

National Association of Social Workers. (1994, October 14). *1994 government relations wrap-up.* Washington, DC: Author.

National Association of Social Workers. (1994, December 14). *Communications with members of Congress on the new House Republican welfare reform proposal, "The Personal Responsibility Act."* Washington, DC: Author.

National Association of Social Workers. (1994, December). *Federal waivers for state welfare reform projects.* Washington, DC: Author.

Nichols, M., Dunlap, J., & Barkan, S. (1992). *National general assistance survey, 1992.* Washington, DC: Center on Budget and Policy Priorities and National Conference of State Legislatures.

Richardson, M. (1993). *Theories of migration and U.S.-Mexico integration.* Los Angeles: UCLA Graduate School of Architecture and Urban Planning.

Smith, S. R., & Lipsky, M. (1993). *Nonprofits for hire: The welfare state in the age of contracting.* Cambridge, MA: Harvard University Press.

Spalter-Roth, R. M., Hartmann, H. I., & Andrews, L. (1992). *Combining work and welfare: An alternative anti-poverty strategy.* Washington, DC: Institute for Women's Policy Research.

Stockman, D. (1975, Spring). The social pork barrel. *The Public Interest, 39,* 3–30.

Towle, C. (1965). *Common human needs* (Rev. ed.). New York: National Association of Social Workers.

U.S. Bureau of the Census. (1975). *Historical statistics of the United States: Colonial times to 1970,* Part 1, Bicentennial Edition. Washington, DC: U.S. Government Printing Office.

Usdansky, M. (1992, December 4–6). Minorities are headed toward the majority. *USA Today,* pp. A1, A8.

Chapter 25

The Future of Political Social Work

KAREN S. HAYNES, PhD
University of Houston

Definition

The belief that all social work is political represents one end of a spectrum of opinion in the social work profession. That notion is supported by the reality that social work practice, historically and presently, deals with a purposive heuristic framework that includes system variables; includes interventions that range from consciousness raising to reallocation of resources; and targets particularly the have-nots for services. The historical connection with reform movements as well as current concerns about empowerment provide credence to this position.

However, the belief that all social work is political is far from reality; few social workers are trained in or employed within the political arena. The history of social work's connection to advocacy is juxtaposed onto today's reality of the preponderance of social work education curricula, faculty, students, placements, and practice that would be defined as political. Although it is possible, and in fact probably even necessary, to promote politicized social work practice in a broad context, this chapter will focus on a narrower definition.

For the purposes of this chapter, political social work practice will encompass those roles and tasks relevant to future social work practice in policy-making settings. This includes but is not limited to the electoral arena, executive-level policy making, and policy implementation. The reason for the narrowness of the definition is that this aspect of social work practice in the past has been even more ignored and maligned as inappropriate for social workers than other roles, and yet it is my belief that it is essential to the purpose and success of all social work practice in the future.

Additionally, this narrower definition has been chosen because there are other chapters in this book that relate to areas that would be included within the larger definition, such as Chapters 20, 22, and 23.

Political social work practice is crucial to the profession because it legitimizes social work's role in the policy-formulation stage as well as in the policy-implementation stage. Without social workers at the policy table, directly or through their chosen representation, social work practice will continue to function in a reactionary manner and will be forced to make the best of impossible policies and regulations, and social workers will continued to feel overwhelmed by the enormity of social problems laid at their feet.

Unfortunately, after more than 100 years, this role has not yet been accepted as a legitimate one within our profession. The 1993 Abramovitz/Bardill debate most dramatically encapsulated the competing arguments of our present day (Abramovitz & Bardill, 1993). Abramovitz argues against the false dichotomy of debating personal treatment versus social change, whereas Bardill upholds the necessity for increased clinical skills and experience of students (Abramovitz & Bardill, 1993). I refute both the argument regarding the mutual exclusiveness of these approaches and the argument concerning ideological incompatibility and the "curriculum space."

Furthermore, I believe that the future of political social work practice is essential to the future of all social work practice; that political social work has achieved some legitimacy recently; and that there are trends within and without social work practice that predict its future growth. Following a brief history, the rest of this chapter will describe those future trends.

History and Current Status

Our history in this arena of practice is both inconsistent and unimpressive to date. This is quite obviously due to the profession's ambiguity regarding this practice arena and the resultant lack of educational content and direction.

Despite what might appear to be an early positive harbinger of social work political roles with Jeannette Rankin's inauguration into Congress in 1917 as the first woman and the first social worker, there are only three social workers in the U.S. Congress in 1994.[1] In almost 80 years, this does not signify progress in or acceptance of political social work practice.

Between these dates we have recorded the names of a few social workers in the political arena, but their numbers are not large. As recently as the mid-1980s the National Association of Social Workers (NASW) had no centralized information regarding the numbers of social workers holding political office, and, worse yet, refused to help with the collection of national data on social workers in the political arena. Finally, in 1991 NASW published its first edition and in 1993 its second edition of social workers in elected political office. This 1993 edition includes only 165 social workers in all levels of government, from U.S. Congress and state legislatures to local school boards (National Association of Social Workers, 1993).

Although curricula in the 1960s became more activist in focus with community-organizing content, this was short-lived. As soon as the 1970s began, with a federal focus on accountability, macro practice in most MSW programs quickly shifted to management and planning, and, unfortunately, when community organization was deleted as a major method, the language, as well as the skills of advocacy, disappeared also.

Connected to the pursuit of professional stature, specialized clinical practice and scientific research methodology became the yardstick by which to measure effective MSW programs and, consequently, effective practice. It was not until 1982 that the Council on Social Work Education's (CSWE) Curriculum Policy Statement and Accreditation Standards included advocacy and political action. According to the 1982 CSWE Curriculum Policy Statement, "the knowledge and skills students accumulate in social welfare policy and services should prepare them to exert leadership and influence as legislative and social advocates, lobbyists, and expert advisors to policy makers and administrators." The 1992 Curriculum Policy Statement further strengthened the commitment to social justice. Its statement of the purpose of social work includes "the pursuit of policies, services and programs through legislative advocacy, lobbying, and other forms of social and political action, including providing expert testimony, participation in local and national coalitions and gaining political office" (Council on Social Work Education, 1982, 1992).

Worse yet, the National Association of Social Workers Code of Ethics in its 1969 revision actually moved away from this language, and the current Code includes minimal reflection of advocacy as a professional mandate. The current code does include one explicit statement about political activity: "The social worker should support the formulation, development, enactment and implementation of social policies of concern to the profession." However, at the NASW Delegate Assembly in 1994, one of the Practice Advancement goals established was to increase the number of social workers in elected public office and political appointments at all governmental levels.

The direction and written prescriptions of our professional associations have great impact for those currently in practice and to those educating future professionals. Explicit exclusion of roles and areas of practice provide clear signals of the appropriateness and relevance of professional social work roles. For political social work, consequently, it was important that the NASW publication *Choices: Careers in Social Work* included politics as a career choice for the first time in its 1993 edition (National Association of Social Workers, 1993).

The entrance of BSWs into the profession and the accreditation of BSW programs in the early 1970s opened the door to definitions of a more generalized (thus less clinically specialized) practice, and within that definition advocacy became a renewed concept. However, although the language was in the curriculum, it was a mistake to assume that the entry-level professionals would be the ones to assume the high-level policy-making positions in the electoral or appointed political arena. Consequently, one might argue that the groundwork for more political social work practice was laid with the introduction of BSW education in the United States, but these BSWs had nowhere to pursue this avenue, because at the same time most MSW programs were replacing community organization content with program evaluation, program planning, and fiscal management.

A review of the summary curricula of the approximately 114 MSW accredited programs in 1994 reveals that 7 had a community organization or community development concentration; one had a concentration in social development; one described a social justice and empowerment practice concentration; and one (at my university) had a political social work concentration (Council on Social Work Education, 1993; Fisher, Haynes, Latting, & Buffum, 1994; Fisher, 1995). Therefore less than 10 percent of the MSW programs describe anything resembling a politicized social work practice concentration. Add to that the fact that approximately only 5 percent of MSW students in these 10 programs are enrolled in these political concentrations, and we are not, nationally speaking, preparing many political social workers.

For what kinds of roles and jobs does one prepare political social workers? Probably the most obvious are those roles in elected office from city level to the federal government: on local school boards and city councils, in state legislatures, and in Congress. Also, working in the electoral arena are those social workers who are staff aides to these elected officials and who may be as central in the passage of legislation as the people for whom they work.

Social workers can have careers as political paid lobbyists for advocacy groups or for an array of client organizations from the formal social work groups to special-interest social welfare groups. Political social work also includes those high-level political appointments at federal or state levels, such as a state Commission of Human Services, Child Welfare, or Mental Health or as the U.S. Secretary of Health and Human Services. These positions are crucial in the implementation phase of rule writing, in the budget-allocation process, and in setting the agenda for the entire state or nation in this field of practice. Social workers engaged in political social work may also run or work in campaigns, although this role is more likely to be as a volunteer or a short-term one.

Like Specht and Courtney, I am concerned with the increasing abandonment of our profession's traditional mission and clientele; I am tired of the ideological debate of the political correctness of political social work. But unlike Specht and Courtney (1994), I am unconvinced that the profession must chose between mutually exclusive paradigms.

Harbingers of Change

There are, however, a number of indicators external to the profession as well as within it that bode well for increased interest in political social work and increased entrance into political social work practice. The changes within the profession to accept and support political social work will hopefully continue and strengthen while external factors will simultaneously push and pull more social workers into the political arena.

Forces within the Profession

1. Political Social Work Connects to Case and Class Advocacy

Although political social work may still be viewed as innovative, it certainly is not without precedent or without a recent and expanding literature to sustain it (Mahaffey & Hanks, 1982; Humphreys, 1986; Haynes & Mickelson, 1991: Mary, Webb, & Newell, 1989). And

. although this chapter is focused on macro political practice, the clear connection between what C. Wright Mills called private troubles and public issues remains. In fact, some of the curriculum developments have focused on practice approaches that account for *both* personal and social change. "Essentially, the orientation stresses that personal and social problems are perceived as manifestations of entrenched structural inequalities related to class, gender, and race that are not amenable to change through traditional measures, and it clearly recognizes the need for both personal and social change" (LeComte, 1990, pp. 34–35). Acknowledging the limits of the social work profession, the argument is that effective social work education must include analysis of power and political dialogue as integral aspects of the social worker–client relationship (Carniol, 1990).

In fact, Carniol (1990) asserts the following concerning the dilemma of being explicitly political:

> Curiously, professionals who are accepting of the status quo and its downward flow of power are not seen as being political. Yet when social workers support an upward flow of power they are accused, at least by some, of being "political," that is, of doing things viewed as "unprofessional." (p. 134)

2. Both Professional Associations Have Increasingly Supported This Specialization

The Council on Social Work Education has not only included more and stronger language relative to advocacy, lobbying, and political office holding but through its recent Millennium Project will provide more flexibility for extended time frames for innovative curriculum design. Through expansion of the experimental programs, alternative, extended time lines to test programs, innovative programs, and new visions for social work practice can be experimented with without jeopardizing accreditation. This should allow for political social work concentrations not to have to be identical to the traditional concentrations relative to content, sequencing, or admission of students. It will also provide greater flexibility for nontraditional forms of supervision for students in political placements.

The National Association of Social Workers has become more involved in, invested in, and supportive of political social work and political activity during the last decade than ever before in its political history. They have been in the forefront as spokespersons with position statements about both health care reform and welfare reform. The association has increased the sophistication and impact of its PAC and it has begun the data collection about, and included the acknowledgment that, political social work is a career path and that increasing numbers of social workers are pursuing it.

Earlier in this chapter it was noted that only 165 social workers were listed in the 1993 publication of NASW of social workers in elected political office. However, the positive side is that this is almost a 50 percent increase over the numbers included in the first publication in 1991. Also, according to this same source, in the 1992 election 10 social workers sought Congressional offices; 2 for the Senate and 8 for the House. Only the three noted above were successful. Another 10 ran unsuccessful state legislative campaigns. The good news is that there are 25 percent more social workers in state legislatures than were known in 1991, 30 percent more at county level positions, and almost 50 percent at the school board level. Although the increase portends an optimistic trend, the numbers are hardly sufficient to suggest a major social work presence in the electoral arena yet.

Given that this practice arena includes appointed policy-making positions, it is equally important to note that five social workers were selected by President Clinton to serve as assistant secretaries serving under cabinet members during the first two years of his term.[2] This is four more than at any other time in our professional history. And, although there is no comprehensive list, we know that social workers have played roles in political campaigns and serve in staff positions in other political offices.

3. Demographics of Social Work Students Has Changed

Certainly since the inception in 1974 of accredited BSW programs, the demographics of the student population in social work programs has changed. Obviously, there are more social work students, and the majority of the BSW students are younger students; recently the age distribution of MSW students has changed, with a greater percentage of students under 30 years of age. Although some faculty bemoan the lack of maturity and work experience, the possibility for reduced cynicism and greater commitment to different client populations and ideologies exists.

Social work's historic commitment to diversity has promoted greater diversity among social work students than among most other professional student cohorts. Diversity in race, ethnicity, gender, age, disabilities, and sexual preference are usually found among social work student populations. The obvious and anticipated consequences of this diversity is the concern for all voices to be heard, and for groups not to suffer because of discrimination and stereotyping. Other consequences might be the shift in importance to forms of practice in which political social work connects to these nontraditional students in particular as a viable and necessary form of achieving social justice.

Forces External to the Profession

In addition to these professional changes, a variety of other forces are likely to positively effect the roles and numbers of social workers in the political arena. These are not included in priority order or in a causal sequence, although many are obviously interconnected. The 1993 liberalization of the 1939 Hatch Act, term limitations, and dialogue about reducing political action committee support may reduce some barriers. The increased percentage of women voters, of women running for offices, and women as fund-raisers also may be congruent with social workers' engaging in political activity. Technology also has allowed us to watch directly the political process, lobby via fax and e-mail more quickly, and connect to voters via sophisticated mailing procedures.

1. Women Are Participating in Politics in Larger Numbers

Only in 1984 did women's voter participation exceed men's for the first time, and by 1992 that election year was heralded as the "year of the woman." In the less than 10 years between these two events, the proportion of people who believed that "the country would be governed better if more women held political office" increased from 28 percent in 1984 to 61 percent in 1992, according to a *U.S. News and World Report* poll. Given that the majority of social work practitioners are women, the more women who see political office as viable and run, the more credence and possibility it will give to social workers to enter the electoral political arena. And despite the fact that the 1994 elections did not continue as dramatic an increase, the gains for women were one more in the Senate, for a total of eight women Senators, and 10 more women in the House, for a total of 48 women in the House.

2. The Strength of Political Incumbency Will Be Reduced

Term limits, retirements, and redistricting may allow the potential for a new cadre of political office holders, including social workers, to seek, run for, and win office. Additionally, new routes to national offices are being found and are working. Big-city mayoral positions and statewide elective offices are now increasingly serving as springboards to national elected office. As many as 100 seats may become available through these means to candidates in the near future (Aburdene & Naisbitt, 1992).

3. Campaign Fund-Raising and Financing Will Need to Improve

Although social work political action committees were started in the mid-1970s at the national as well as at state levels, in 1994 they are neither as sophisticated, as monied, nor as comprehensive as many other PACs. However, the social work profession has become more sophisticated regarding candidate support, both for social workers and for pro–human-service candidates, and have provided financial as well as in volunteer support. Additionally, EMILY's list provided an excellent example relative to support for women candidates and a strategy for getting around campaign finance reform. This is not to say that women have not given financial contributions to campaigns, but EMILY's list targets women to give money only to women candidates (Hirshmann, 1993). Increased sophistication about campaign support has helped social work realize that if the financial contribution cannot be great, early contributions bring a greater return for the investment than do later ones.

4. Social Work Issues Have Become the Political Issues

Education, day care, family leave, abortion, and poverty are less and less viewed as women's issues and increasing viewed as the mainstream domestic agenda. Clearly, they connect to central social work tenets and to many of our social work client populations. These are issues about which social work has information, a value-based ideology, and a historical commitment. And, given that the issues have become mainstream, social work will see itself as an informed player, and thus these issues may serve to both pull and push more social workers into the political arena.

5. 1993 Hatch Act Revisions Permit Greater Involvement

In 1939 the federal Hatch Political Activity Act was enacted in reaction to a patronage system, and because the Civil Service Commission didn't cover many of the new New Deal employees. Over time, however, the perceptions plus the reality of limitations or political activity in this law may have done more to violate First Amendment rights than to preserve political neutrality, and this continues to pose real and imagined threats to social workers. The federal Hatch Act spawned numerous state Hatch Acts that prohibit the same type of partisan political activity for employees whose positions are state funded. However, the 1993 revision to the federal law did expand the off-duty political activities that were permitted and better defined the prohibited activities (Thompson, 1994). With greater clarity and more permissible off-duty activities, more social workers can engage in more political activities without fear of a loss of a federal or state job.

6. Technology Will Increase Access to the Political Process

Cable television has permitted a larger audience to monitor federal and state legislative processes. Interactive satellite linkages now provide opportunities for direct and immediate interaction. Fax and electronic mail provide quick transmittal of information as well as of positional statements. Knowledge of the political process, access to it, and influence in it have increased, and consequently opportunities for social workers have broadened.

Increasingly sophisticated and accessible databases are being used and will be used to target individuals for extremely personalized messages about issues and candidates. Political polling changed more during the past decade than during the past 50 years, and the changes have been such that they can be used by smaller campaigns rather than in advances in the techniques themselves (Selnow, 1994).

7. Lobbying Rights for Nonprofits Have Been Expanded

The curtailment in the percentage of a nonprofit's budget that could be spent on lobbying as defined by IRS quite directly can negatively affect those agencies' abilities to influence legislation in favor of human services issues. In 1990 the IRS and the Treasury released regulations that support the expanded lobbying rights of nonprofit organizations and provide a more flexible framework for nonprofits' efforts to guide and influence legislation (Code of Federal Regulations, 1994).

Vision for the Future

A political activist must predict that political social work will become a legitimized activity within social work practice and social work education by the year 2000. Indeed, it seems likely that if this does not occur, the profession will have made no strides in bridging the increasingly wide gaps between the haves and the have-nots and between private troubles and public issues.

A political social work faculty must anticipate that although the tension between social work education and social work practice regarding who leads has not diminished, the changes that will have the most dramatic and long-lasting impact on political social work will be curriculum changes in social work programs. Redirecting the newer professionals during their socialization within professional social work programs is the easier change effort.

Therefore, it is my hope and prediction that by the year 2010 our profession and professional education will have changed in the following ways:

1. BSW programs will increasingly value the advocacy perspective within the generalist framework and increasingly teach policy from a politicized context, teach generalist practice with equal attention to advocacy, and foster placements in legislative offices as constituent case managers.

2. MSW programs will continue to reidentify and recommit to public social services and will have increased concern about equity, access, and affordability to a variety of services. Consequently, programs will better balance content to equally attend to the therapies and the advocacies of case and class and will develop entire concentrations in political social work. Within these programs, entire courses on lobbying, effective use of the media, campaigning, and fund-raising will be offered rather than only as a topic within a macro practice course.

3. Doctoral social work programs will refocus their curricula and outputs such that important career paths include high-level policy positions as well as social work education, research, and administration.

4. Social workers will run for office in larger numbers. They will find the local arena not only easier to enter but also a logical springboard to state and national offices if they so desire. Once elected, they will continually identify themselves as social workers and provide opportunities and mentorship for other social workers wishing to pursue similar career paths.

5. Lobbying will become a well-defined social work role. Social work agencies will look to social workers to fill these positions, and lobbying organizations assertively reach out to social workers to hire them for a wide array of human service organizations and associations.

6. Social workers will finally grasp that technology works in their favor in the political arena, and political social workers will become more knowledgeable about and sophisticated in using these tools for their roles in lobbying, campaigning, and polling the public (or their constituencies) about issues.

7. NASW will continue to track and count social workers in elected political office and add to that database social workers who are in significant appointed political positions. NASW will aggressively seek out social workers in these positions and support research on their career paths, the connectedness to their educational preparation, and advice to the profession, and will publish the same.

8. The CSWE will recognize political social work as a specialization, will begin to count the students in these concentrations nationwide, and will include them in its annual statistics.

Conclusion

Political social work must become a viable and legitimate field of practice before the end of this millennium if social work is to continue as a profession whose primary focus is on the disadvantaged, disenfranchised, and oppressed. There is no question that social work education must take the lead in this endeavor, and that both professional associations must strongly support all necessary actions. Clinical social work need not be abandoned or reduced, but merely balanced to provide equal attention, fervor, status, and legitimacy to political social work.

It is my premise that all social work is political; thus my conclusion is simply that we should become explicitly and purposively so That social work acknowledge and claim its legitimate place in the policy-making and policy-implementing processes seems a logical maturational step in our profession's progress.

To do social work and to be a social worker requires commitment to social work's historic mission and to the goals of social justice. The meaning of politics and its practice is essential to that commitment, and we must ensure that the profession has skilled practitioners to lead us there.

Notes

1. Senator Barbara Mikulski, Maryland; Representative Ron Dellums, California; and Representative Ed Towns, New York.

2. These five are Wardell Townsend, Assistant Secretary of Agriculture; Wendy Sherman, Assistant Secretary of State; Fernando Torres-Gill, Assistant Secretary for Aging in the Department of Health and Human Services; Ada Deer, Assistant Secretary for Indian Affairs in the Department of the Interior; and August Kappner, Assistant Secretary for Vocational and Adult Education in the Department of Education.

References

Abramovitz, M., & Bardill, R. (1993). Should all social work students be educated for social change? *Journal of Social Work Education, 29*(1), 6–18.

Aburdene, P., & Naisbitt, J. (1992). *Megatrends for Women.* New York: Villard Books.

Carniol, B. (1990). Social work and the labor movement. In B. Wharf (Ed.), *Social work and social change in Canada* (pp. 114–143). Toronto: McClelland & Stewart.

Code of Federal Regulations. (1994). Internal Revenue Service, 26, pp. 12–19, Code 501(c)-3.

Council on Social Work Education. (1982, 1992). *Curriculum Policy Statements.* Alexandria, VA: Author.

Council on Social Work Education. (1993). *Summary Statistics.* Alexandria, VA: Author.

Fisher, R. (1995). Political social work. *Journal of Social Work Education, 31*(2), 194–203.

Fisher, R., Haynes, K. S., Latting, J., & Buffum, W. (1994). Empowerment-based curriculum design: Building a program in political social work. In L. Gutiérrez & P. Nurius (Eds.), *Education and research for empowerment practice* (pp. 127–136). Seattle: University of Washington Press.

Haynes, K., & Mickelson, J. (1991). *Affecting change: Social workers in the political arena.* New York: Longman.

Hirshmann, S. (1993). Emily's list: Chicks with checks. *American Spectator, 26*(4), 20.

Humphreys, N. A. (1986). *Education for social workers: Political practice.* Unpublished final report submitted to The Lois and Samuel Silberman Fund.

LeComte, R. (1990). Connecting private troubles and public issues in social work education. In B. Wharf (Ed.), *Social work and social change in Canada* (pp. 31–51). Toronto: McClelland & Stewart.

Mahaffey, M., & Hanks, J. W. (Eds.). (1982). *Practical politics: Social work and political responsibility.* Silver Spring, MD: National Association of Social Workers.

Mary, N. L., Webb, C., & Newell, J. (1989). Social and political activism among social work educators. Paper presented at Annual Program Meeting, Council on Social Work Education, Chicago, IL.

National Association of Social Workers. (1993). *Choices: Careers in social work.* Silver Springs, MD: Author.

National Association of Social Workers. (1993). *Social workers serving in elective offices 1993.* Silver Springs, MD: Author.

Selnow, G. W. (1994). *High-tech campaigns: Computer technology in political communication.* Westport, CT: Praeger.

Specht, H., & Courtney, M. (1994). *Unfaithful angels: How social work has abandoned its mission.* New York: The Free Press.

Thompson, J. (1994). Social workers and politics: Beyond the Hatch Act. *Social Work, 39*(4), 457–465.

Part VIII

Future Directions

The final part of the book takes a broader view of the profession of social work. In Chapter 26 Matt Howard and Dow Lambert present a well-documented, thorough critique of the paucity of practice-relevant scientific information in social work and what that observation bodes for the future of the profession. It is not a pretty picture; we hope that it will be read with great interest by future researchers. In the final chapter, Paul Raffoul summarizes the future responses that social work might make to the current technological revolution that is already confronting our society and the profession. He also examines the anticipated value conflicts that this revolution is having and will continue to have on social work in the future. It is an optimistic view of how we might take advantage of this technology; it provides a balance to the sentiments expressed in the previous chapter in the section. Both chapters are perhaps correct; one sees a cup that is half empty, the other a cup that is half full.

Howard and Lambert have examined the state of the profession from a research point of view, beginning with their analysis of the failure of the empirical practice movement of the past two decades. The result of their analysis is an identification of the reasons for the deficient production of practice-relevant scientific information by the profession, the quality of the social work literature, and the deficient dissemination and utilization of scientific information. The implications for the future of social work knowledge are grim and deserve careful consideration by all readers of this text. Some questions that might encourage change in the future include the following:

1. How have inadequate production and utilization of practice-relevant scientific information damaged social work's credibility as a profession?

2. Do you agree that deficient dissemination of scientific information to practitioners and deficient utilization of practice-relevant scientific information are both identified as impeding the establishment of empirically based modes of clinical conduct?

3. Detailed practice guidelines (standards, protocols, parameters, and algorithm) have been suggested as one means of providing practitioners with user-friendly clinical guidance. What impediments can you identify to implementing this suggestion by the authors?

In the final chapter one of the coeditors has examined the general question of what social work can do to address the changes mandated by the technological or information revolution. Within this chapter, anticipated value conflicts of the profession are also described as we enter this information revolution for the second decade during the next century. Curious readers will want to answer the following questions:

1. How will social work's response to the information revolution change as we as a society become more comfortable with technological innovations and access to information becomes more universal?

2. What additional value conflicts can you identify that social work must consider in order to ensure a more egalitarian access to computers, information, and technology for the future?

3. What is your view of the future of social work in relation to technology? Is it positive, negative, or both?

Chapter 26

The Poverty of Social Work

Deficient Production, Dissemination, and Utilization of Practice-Relevant Scientific Information

MATTHEW OWEN HOWARD, PhD, and M. DOW LAMBERT, PhD
University of Washington

As the twentieth century draws to a close, heralding a new era for social work practice, many observers believe that the empirical practice movement of the past two decades has faltered, if not failed entirely. Deficiencies in the production, dissemination, and utilization of practice-relevant scientific information continue to undermine efforts to foster empirically based practice. Clinicians and policy makers complain about the insufficient quantity and poor quality of empirical findings available to guide their practice efforts. Social and political scientists, unschooled in traditional social welfare concerns, provide most of the data used by decision makers. Epstein (1992) observed that

> important social problems are far more commonly addressed in the general political and intellectual life of the nation by economists, psychologists, psychiatrists, political scientists, and so forth. I cannot ever remember seeing a social work author appear in the Scientific American, the New York Review of Books, the New York Times Magazine, or the American Scholar. Apparently our culture turns to disciplines other than social work for commentary on social problems, the substance of social work itself. (p. 526)

Information useful in selecting and implementing social service interventions has been poorly disseminated and infrequently utilized. Physicians, psychologists, lawyers, and professionals in other fields scrutinize new reports, debating their practice implications, whereas many, if not most, social workers consider scientific evaluations irrelevant to their professional conduct. Empirically based clinical guidelines continue to proliferate throughout medicine and other practice areas (for example, see Walker, Howard, Lambert, & Suchinsky, 1994; Walker, Howard, Walker, Lambert, & Suchinsky, 1995). However, scientifically supported parameters for social work practice are virtually nonexistent. Social work's failure to develop and promulgate systematic protocols for social service interventions could have serious consequences for social work practice in the 2000s.

Inadequate production and utilization of practice-relevant scientific information have damaged social work's credibility (Fraser, 1994; Proctor, 1994). Social work's continued viability in the increasingly competitive managed care environment of the twenty-first century may depend critically on its ability to generate and apply scientific findings informing practice efforts. We examine the scope of current deficits in knowledge production, dissemination, and utilization, and envisage a possible future for social work characterized by vigorous production of research and informed application of the most promising interventions. A less sanguine outcome for social work practice in the 2000s, wherein practice efforts continue to reflect unsupported biases and therapeutic fads and fashions, is an unfortunate alternative possibility. It is not inconceivable that the antiempirical stance of many practicing social workers could lead to the demise of the profession itself.

I. Deficient Production of Practice-Relevant Scientific Information

A. Human Capital Issues

Few Doctoral-Level Graduates

A small number of doctoral graduates in social welfare are produced annually. Doctoral graduates have always constituted a minuscule proportion of students receiving graduate degrees in social work. In the academic year 1964–65, 1.2 percent ($n = 39$) of the 3,245 graduate social work degrees awarded were doctorates; by 1989–90, this proportion had risen to 2.4 percent ($n = 247$ of 10,310 graduate degrees awarded) (Ginsberg, 1992). An average of 4,170 MSW students graduated annually between academic years 1964 and 1969, compared to an annual mean of 9,282 MSWs between 1985 and 1990. On average, 61 Ph.D.'s in social work/social welfare were awarded annually between 1964 and 1969, compared to an annual mean of 252 between 1985 and 1990. By comparison, 5,272 doctoral engineering degrees, 2,238 doctorates in chemistry, and 526 doctorates in foreign languages were awarded in 1990–91 (U.S. Department of Education, 1993). It is clear that graduate schools of social work do not produce the critical mass of doctoral students needed to sustain energetic data-generating activities. Social work research and practice efforts in the 2000s would be greatly enhanced by vigorous efforts to attract a larger number of students to doctoral-level preparation. Conversely, failure to increase the number of doctoral graduates will ensure that social work research continues at a sluggish rate.

Inadequate Research Training

Training experiences of doctoral students may not adequately prepare them for research careers. Graduate schools of social work are populated by a significant number of instructors who lack the training and experience to teach students research methods. Between 1986 and 1990, 43 to 45 percent of the faculty members of graduate schools of social work were not themselves recipients of doctoral-level training (Spaulding, 1991).

In 1990, 61 percent of faculty members teaching in schools of social work nationwide were 45 years of age or older; 5 percent were under 35 (Spaulding, 1991). Thus, many faculty members received their graduate education in an era when research methods now considered basic had not been developed. Spaulding's (1991) findings indicated that a small proportion of graduate social work faculty members are recently trained doctorates exposed to the latest in substantive findings and methodological techniques. Green, Hutchinson, and Sar (1992) found number of years since graduation significantly negatively correlated with average annual total scholarly productivity for the large group of doctoral graduates they studied.

Empirical evaluations of social work graduate education are surprisingly few in number. Jenson, Fraser, and Lewis (1991) interviewed directors, or their designates, of all doctoral programs (*n* = 47) listed in the directory of the Group for the Advancement of Doctoral Education (GADE), noting that 78 percent of doctoral programs had no research-related prerequisites. One-fifth of doctoral programs required one or fewer research classes for graduation; more than a quarter (26 percent) required one or fewer statistics courses. The majority (57 percent) of doctoral programs required two statistics courses and nearly half (46 percent) required two research classes. These standards do not ensure adequate levels of research skills, especially considering the scant amount of course work devoted to research by MSW programs (*M* = 6.4 semester hours for the 90 accredited MSW programs in 1987) and the elementary nature of such instruction (Fraser, Lewis, & Norman, 1990).

Recent findings of the GADE Task Force on Research Curricula (1994) are consistent with those presented above. Two-thirds of the 39 doctoral programs assessed reported no entry-level research or statistics-related prerequisites. A large proportion of programs did not require completion of a research practicum (41 percent) or made participation optional (15 percent). Advanced statistical and methodological procedures were generally not taught at the application or mastery levels.

Doctoral program directors participating in the investigation by Jenson et al. (1991) reported that 54 percent of the faculty members teaching in 47 social work doctoral programs were not engaged in funded research. This finding may account for the observation that only 30 percent of doctoral students were involved in an ongoing research project. The National Institute of Mental Health recently established the Task Force on Social Work Research to examine factors contributing to the dearth of federally funded grants awarded to social workers (Austin, 1991). Jenson et al. (1991) concluded that

> research training in social work is a prisoner of an out-dated educational paradigm. Focused largely on casework training at the MSW level, this paradigm insures that doctoral students will enter doctoral programs with weak research methods and statistics backgrounds. In the absence of greater vertical integration

of research content, social work appears likely to remain a profession dependent, in large part, on other disciplines for knowledge generation. The fundamental structure of social work education must be reconsidered if the profession is to make a serious effort to generate its own research knowledge. (p. 37)

Fraser, Jenson, and Lewis (1993) argued that the process of research education in schools of social work begins anew at each level of training (that is, BSW, MSW, Ph.D./DSW). Consequently, social workers do not gain expertise in advanced statistical and methodological aspects of research. A new curriculum study, Fraser et al. (1993) contended, building on the Hollis and Taylor (1951) and Boehm (1959) reports "could provide a forum for differing opinion and a structure through which the profession might make critical decisions regarding the future of social work education" (p. 60). Social work practice in the 2000s will benefit from faculties with doctoral-level training, and from graduate programs requiring more extensive and sophisticated methodological and statistical preparation, and research experience in the form of practicums and paid research assistantships.

Deficient Scholarly Productivity

Approximately half of all doctoral graduates do not publish following graduation. Baker and Wilson (1992) counted the number of articles published by 284 doctoral graduates during the year they graduated and the following 6 years. Graduates published an average of 1.2 ($SD = 2$) articles in journals listed in the Source Index of the *Social Sciences Citation Index* (SSCI) (Institute for Scientific Information, 1989); half published no articles. Nearly half of the respondents to Green, Hutchinson, and Sar's (1990) survey of doctoral graduates published no articles in peer-reviewed social work (47 percent) or non–social work (47 percent) journals following graduation. Green et al. (1992) noted that the modal number of articles, books, book chapters, and book reviews published by social work faculty members in 1989 was zero for each publication category. Mean annual productivity rates were low (for example, 0.32 and 0.42 refereed social work and non–social work journal articles published annually, respectively) and indicated that doctoral graduates were as likely to publish in non–social work journals as in social work journals.

Abbott (1985) reported that 175 students graduating from 21 social work doctoral programs between 1960 and 1974 published an average of 0.25 ($SD = 0.42$) articles per year in peer-reviewed journals between 1976 and 1981; 46 percent published no articles during the follow-up interval. The investigations of Abbott (1985) and Green et al. (1992) are marred by low response rates (50 percent and 56 percent, respectively), suggesting that the true failure-to-publish rates for social work doctoral graduates may be even higher.

Green et al. (1990) reported that 20 percent of the 932 school of social work faculty members they studied had published no articles, and less than 12 percent had published more than 20. Social work "failure-to-publish" rates were twice those of academics in other disciplines, and high-frequency (21 or more articles) publishers were underrepresented relative to other fields. Fraser (1994) asserted that "a small core of scholars, perhaps 200 in all, produce at rates comparable to those of faculty in other professions."

Faculties of schools of social work differ widely with regard to publication practices. Baker (1994) examined 50 schools of social work with doctoral programs, noting that mean publication rates for the period between 1974 and 1989 ranged from 0.11 to 5.9. Klein and Bloom (1992) found the mean number of citations to the faculties of four schools of social work in 1989 ranging from 0.9 to 4.1.

Factors contributing to low rates of scholarly productivity among doctoral graduates and faculty members warrant investigation. The degree to which social work is dominated by a small group of researchers, relative to other disciplines, and the potential consequences of this concentration of research activity on the profession's growth should be examined. If social work practice in the 2000s is to have an adequate empirical foundation, efforts to increase the scholarly productivity of doctoral graduates, particularly the half that publish nothing, should be initiated. If conditions contributing to the small number of doctoral students who publish following graduation are not effectively addressed, social work practice will continue to founder in the future.

B. Quality of the Social Work Literature

Publishing Trends

Many observers decry what they view as the excessive rate of modern scientific publication. Critics argue that pressures to publish or perish have distorted the process of scientific communication, leading to piecemeal publication of results, publication of trivial findings, and to the creation of scores of unread journals. Hamilton (1990) noted that 74,000 scientific journals were listed in Bowker/Ulrich's compendium and presented findings indicating that 55 percent of reports published in the top 4,500 scientific and social scientific journals between 1981 and 1985 were not cited during the five years following their publication. Additional analyses suggested that an even larger proportion of social science articles were uncited.

Trends in social work knowledge generation via publication are difficult to assess, given the interdisciplinary nature of the field and attendant difficulties in identifying the core literature. Cnaan, Caputo, and Shmuely (1994) observed that previous estimates of the number of social work journals ranged from 50 to 250 depending on how *social work journal* was defined. Mendelsohn listed 138 journals in his book *An Author's Guide to Social Work Journals* (1992), many of which are publications of professional or specialty groups not directly associated with the social work profession; 29 journals included the term *social work* in their titles. Mendelsohn (1992) acknowledged that his guide is not exhaustive, noting that the "number of journals devoted to social work, social welfare, and the human services has increased significantly [since the mid-1980s]" (p. ix). We expect that social work's literature base will continue to grow in the 2000s, but whether the quality of the literature will rise concomitantly is an open question.

Quality of Editorial Board Members and Manuscript Reviews

Few studies have examined the research productivity of social work journal editorial board members. Pardek (1992a) conjectured that research in this area was sparse because "critical examination of social work editorial boards could be aversive to editors and perhaps result in deleterious consequences for the critic" (p. 487). Pardek (1992a) compared 69 members of five social work journal editorial boards (*Child Welfare, Jour-*

nal of Social Work Education, Families in Society, Social Work, and *Social Service Review*) to 165 editorial board members of five journals of the American Psychological Association (*Journal of Abnormal Psychology, Journal of Applied Psychology, Journal of Counseling Psychology, Journal of Educational Psychology, Journal of Personality and Social Psychology*), in terms of the total citations to their published works in the 1989 edition of the *Social Science Citation Index.* He found that psychology journal editorial board members had significantly higher median citation counts than social work editorial board members, concluding that "editorial board members of psychology journals . . . excel over social work editorial board members in the area of scholarly publishing. . . ." Pardek speculated that "many social work editorial board members did not achieve board membership on the basis of scholarly publishing in professional journals" (pp. 492–493).

Epstein (1992) stated that the National Committee on Inquiry of the National Association of Social Workers (NASW) attempted to "banish" him from social work following publication of his study concluding that social work manuscript reviews were frequently incoherent, inaccurate, and otherwise reflective of poor attention to relevant scientific details. Epstein (1990) submitted "dummy" manuscripts to journals for review, a procedure employed earlier by Mahoney (1977), but of obviously debatable acceptability. The furor occasioned by Epstein's (1990) and Pardek's (1992a) reports (Fortune, 1992; Gillespie & Khinduka, 1992; Hopps, 1992; Lindsey, 1992; Reamer, 1992; Schuerman, 1992) suggested to some observers that individuals charged with gatekeeping publication in social work journals may be resistant to an open evaluation of their decision-making protocols.

Epstein (1992) considered Pardek's (1992a, 1992b) findings indicative of the "poor intellectual climate of the field," commenting that

> social workers on editorial boards are drawn out of the undistinguished base of social work academics. Large numbers of tenured professors, even in prominent schools of social work, have never published anything. Others' productivity halted after being awarded tenure. Many appointments to social work faculties have little to do with teaching, scholarly, or intellectual competence. They seem to have a lot to do with the traditional varieties of corruption (nepotism, cronyism, trading favors, and the fecundity of incompetent selection committees in replicating themselves) and their New Age variants (compensatory appointments on the basis of gender, race, sexual preference, and ethnicity and political correctness). An undergraduate degree in social work today does not certify literacy. A graduate degree does not certify competence. An appointment to a social work faculty does not certify merit. (p. 527)

The chief difference between psychology and social work, Epstein contended, is not so much the quality of their research as the degree to which they accept the "governing logic of scientific proof." Epstein believes that social work research has been hindered, to put it mildly, by the rampant antiempirical subjectivism characterizing the field, the absence of critical debate, and the eschewal of quantitative methods. If the role of research in social work practice is appreciated more fully in the future, editorial boards will reflect this change and include more productive and influential members of the social work research community.

Low Impact of Social Work Journals

Various views are voiced concerning the relative impact of social work journals. Pardek (1992b) noted that only one social work journal, *Child Abuse and Neglect,* had an SSCI impact factor (number of times the average article in a journal is cited in a given year) exceeding 1, whereas numerous psychology, sociology, and political science journals had impact factors greater than 1. This observation, in conjunction with Cheung's (1990) findings indicating that social work journals cited psychiatry, sociology, and family studies journals 4.7, 5.4, and 2.3 times more often between 1981 and 1985 than they were in turn cited by journals in these respective fields, was viewed by Pardek (1992a) as evidence that scholars in related disciplines do not regard material published in social work journals seriously. Epstein (1992) considered the impact rating of *Social Work* (0.73 in 1989) astoundingly low, given its large circulation. The impact rating of *Social Service Review* (0.45 in 1989), arguably the most prestigious social work journal, approximates the median impact score (0.38) for all 1,383 journals evaluated in the SSCI. A larger corpus of well-trained researchers should lead to greater consumption of practice-relevant research in the future, raising the impact of social work journals.

Poor Quality of Published Research

Fraser, Taylor, Jackson, and O'Jack (1991) and Glisson (1990) assessed research methods used by investigators publishing in 15 social work journals between 1985 and 1988. Articles utilizing systematic data collection and analytic procedures were considered research based; fewer than half met this criterion. Experimental designs were used in less than 6 percent of research-based investigations. Most research-based reports relied on rudimentary descriptive or univariate analytic approaches, leading Fraser et al. (1991) to conclude that the social work literature he reviewed evidenced a paucity of sophisticated quantitative and qualitative evaluations.

Fraser (1993) extended earlier work by incorporating 263 studies from three additional social work journals and assessing the comparative utilization of research methods by social work and non–social work authors. Nearly 77 percent of reports published by non–social workers were research based, compared with 28 percent of reports published by social workers. Fraser (1994) concluded that "the methods presented in the core literature are often based on no discernible systematic information collection and analysis strategy . . . the quantitative or qualitative systematic methods that are used are often elementary, and expose findings to a host of alternative explanations . . . the methods used by social workers who publish in the core literature appear weaker than those used by non–social workers" (p. 254). The poor quality of social work research reflects inadequacies in the research education of graduate social workers and in the evaluation of published manuscripts. If more social workers receive better research training in the future, the demand for high-quality research will increase and tolerance of poorly conducted or rudimentary research will decline.

II. Deficient Dissemination of Scientific Information to Practitioners

Many social workers do not rely on published empirical findings for guidance in clinical decision making (Kirk, 1990; Schilling, 1990; Schilling, Schinke, & Gilchrist, 1985). Poor training in research methods, limited available time and resources, organizational impediments to knowledge generation and utilization, and the perception that published reports are of limited relevance may account for clinicians' failure to apply scientific findings in practice settings. One explanation has been termed the *technology-transfer* problem. As the corpus of practice-relevant scientific information accrues exponentially, many professions are confronting the issue of how best to disseminate scientific information to practitioners. Methods such as newsletters and popular research digests are used to bridge the age-old divide between the findings of researchers and the needs of practitioners.

Detailed practice guidelines (also referred to as standards, protocols, parameters, and algorithms), based on the best available scientific evidence and expert opinion, are one promising means of providing practitioners with user-friendly clinical guidance based on recent research. More than 1,500 clinical guidelines, most of relatively recent origin, have been published within the medical profession (Walker, Howard, Lambert, & Suchinsky, 1994). Consensus-based prescriptive standards for clinical interventions are largely, if not wholly, absent from the social work data base. We recently reviewed guidelines development efforts in the chemical dependency treatment area (Walker, Howard, Walker, Lambert, & Suchinsky, 1995). Although many organizations and professional groups were actively establishing clinical standards in this area, NASW and other social work organizations were not.

Although guidelines are not a panacea for all that ails clinical social work, recent findings suggest that they promote selection of effective and cost-effective treatment modalities and help standardize delivery of care (Institute of Medicine, 1990, 1992). Other methods of disseminating research findings to practitioners and encouraging provision of high-quality care should be developed and evaluated.

Poor dissemination of practice-relevant empirical findings exacerbates problems associated with the limitations of the social work data base and contributes to the low level of research utilization by social work practitioners. If social work practice is to thrive in the future, clinical guidelines will be needed, addressing important areas of service need and identifying the most effective treatments available. If the social work field does not produce these guidelines and substantiate their efficacy empirically then other professions will do it for us.

III. Deficient Utilization of Practice-Relevant Scientific Information

Published proceedings from a conference convened in August of 1988 examining "Empiricism in Clinical Practice: Present and Future" suggest that the empirical practice movement and associated methodologies (such as single-case evaluation) have gained less than widespread acceptance among social work practitioners (for example, Gingerich, 1990). In the keynote address, Briar (1990) observed the following:

> That the empirical practice movement has had little impact on the profession at large other than social work education is not surprising for two reasons. One reason is that advocates of empirically based practice have made little effort to reach the profession at large, beyond publications and sessions at a few conferences. Second, many researchers have greater access to social work education than to organized social work. If we researchers think it is important to have a greater impact on the profession at large, other than the long-range impact through students, then we will need to consider what it would take to accomplish that goal. (p. 6)

In a similar vein, Gingerich (1990) asserted that

> it is probably accurate to say that today, social work practice is based largely on "practice wisdom," rather than on empirically tested interventions. The inherent difficulties involved in developing and testing social work interventions and the scant resources devoted to research and development suggest that it will be a long time before it can be claimed that social work practice is empirically based. (p. 15)

> LeCroy (1990) distinguished between *research utilization* and *knowledge utilization,* arguing that practitioners tended to rely on experiential knowledge "because the information practitioners need is instrumental rather than scientific. Practitioners have a different end view from scientists—one that may not necessitate an optimal solution. Such practical ends are easily satisfied by experiential forms of knowledge. The result is that practitioners achieve their ends without the need to engage in systematic modes of inquiry or consultation with scientific research" (p. 263).

> Schilling (1990) offered useful recommendations for increasing utilization of empirically supported interventions and suggested that researchers consider the degree to which the scientific literature provides a basis for informed clinical judgments before they blithely refer clinicians to it.

> Many prominent social workers lament the low degree of reliance on empirical findings evidenced by many social work practitioners. Even more troubling is the internecine conflict between researchers and practitioners that continues to impede the establishment of empirically based modes of clinical conduct.

Implications for the Future of Social Work

Social work scholarship is produced at relatively low levels because few students with doctoral-level research training graduate annually, and those that do tend to be relatively advanced in age with foreshortened research careers. Future efforts to recruit larger numbers of promising students into the field earlier in their careers will enhance the growth of the social work data base. Insufficient research and statistics training at the MSW and doctoral levels, both in amount and sophistication, contributes to relatively low rates of scholarly productivity among doctoral graduates and social work faculty members. In the future, social work students preparing for careers as clinician–scientists will be exposed to diverse clinical settings and patient populations and will participate in integrated educational experiences preparing them in advanced statistical techniques and rigorous evaluation methodologies. Schools of social work currently are environments in which federally funded research projects and research assistantships are few in number, prolific researchers are rare, and many faculty members themselves are not the beneficiaries of doctoral-level training. Deans and other opinion leaders among social work faculties in the twenty-first century will be exemplars of the scientist–practitioner model, and schools of social work will be populated by faculty members with doctoral-level training. Additional attempts to create research-friendly environments within schools of social work will be undertaken.

Important questions have been raised regarding the scholarly productivity of leaders in the field, such as deans, directors of doctoral programs, and journal editorial board members. The Task Force on Social Work Research (1991) reported that fewer than 900 persons had published research in the field since 1985 in a profession of more than 400,000 practitioners. Thus the direction that social work research takes is dependent largely on the work of a small cadre of researchers. Social work journals have less impact than journals in many other fields, and a large proportion of the articles they publish are not research based or use rudimentary statistical techniques. If social work successfully addresses its current crisis, social work research and the journals publishing practice-relevant scientific information will have a far greater impact on the field. As more social work researchers produce more and better empirical work, social work journals will become more influential in guiding the direction of the field. Editorial boards will be composed of highly trained clinical scientists attuned to substantive and methodological issues in their respective fields. Empiricism will become the accepted epistemology of the social work field and the general level of intellectual discourse will rise accordingly.

The Task Force on Social Work Research (1991) suggested that the field was in crisis vis-à-vis its scholarly foundations, but Fraser (1994) commented that "to be in a crisis, the state . . . described should have arisen suddenly. It has not . . . [it] is the result of years of relatively little action (in part because the problems are not easily addressed), a public policy environment that has been hostile to scholarly inquiry . . . and other factors, such as the failure of research curricula to keep pace with the growth of research methodology" (pp. 260–261). In the twenty-first century social work will begin an equal partnership with other professions and scholarly disciplines. Psychiatrists, psychologists, public policy analysts, and others will increasingly attend to the findings of research conducted from a social work perspective. As the profession grows more adept at demonstrating the efficacy and cost-effectiveness of its interventions, social workers will gain credibility and increased access to federal funding.

Deficient social work research production and poor dissemination of relevant empirical findings contribute to the underutilization of empirical findings by practitioners. Proctor (1994) and Kirk (1990) suggested that the rift between clinicians and researchers has recently narrowed, and that the profession increasingly values research. Technical developments will lead to better dissemination of scientific information to clinicians in the future. Clinicians will access clinical guidelines on-line, helping them to employ the most cost-effective treatments available. Probable outcomes of treatment will be assessed in individual cases by reference to large databases describing therapeutic outcomes of similarly afflicted individuals with conditions of varying severity receiving different treatments. Social workers using the World Wide Web (or one of its future incarnations) will stay abreast of the scientific literature, network with colleagues around the world, and participate in national on-line video conferences to share and gain from the clinical experiences and insights of other professionals. Research utilization by practitioners will increase as the quality and relevance of research grows and as practitioners become more sophisticated consumers of published evaluations.

Fraser et al. (1993) argued that a continuum of education and experience is needed, integrating statistical and methodological training across master's, doctoral, and postdoctoral levels. A sequenced approach would help eliminate redundancy in programming at different educational levels and would facilitate presentation and acquisition of advanced research techniques. One challenge to the profession, Fraser (1994) argued, is to establish a "culture of scholarship" at more schools of social work by increasing social and material rewards for research and adjusting workloads for scholarly involvement. Proctor (1994) echoed this theme, describing the role of tangible supports in producing climates enhancing research productivity of faculty, students, and agency staff: "Deans and directors need to boldly and repeatedly remind the faculty the knowledge is prized and knowledge-generating activities are to be protected. Enhancing the profession's knowledge must be central to the mission of social work education" (p. 4). Proctor (1994) argued that better connections between research and practice could be fostered by creating research partnerships between schools of social work and service agencies.

Innovative efforts to encourage research and publishing by faculty members need to be promoted. Berger (1990) discussed "The Getting Published Program" in the Department of Social Work, California State University (Long Beach), and its role in increasing faculty publication rates. Schilling et al. (1985) examined ways researchers could publish their findings that would be of greatest interest to practitioners.

Additional efforts to attract more students to doctoral-level social work careers early in their collegiate years would likely be rewarded. The physician–scientist model applied in some medical schools is one approach that should be considered. Promising students could elect early in graduate school to enroll in a course of studies that would prepare them for advanced practice and research roles in the field. Increased doctoral training capacity and concomitant recruitment of promising doctoral students would increase the rate of knowledge accrual in the field. Increased federal funding of social work research proposals would serve the field well by increasing research opportunities for students within schools of social work. Proctor (1994) noted a number of reasons for optimism as social work approaches the twenty-first century: (1) In 1993 five individual social work organizations united efforts with the goal of improving social work research; (2) 20 schools of social work submitted proposals in response to NIMH's announcement for Social Work Research Development Centers; (3) movement toward the establishment of a Society for Social Work Research increased; and (4) the Group for Advancement of Doctoral Education began work aimed at developing model statistics and research methods curricula.

Efforts to improve the empirical foundations of social work practice will grow increasingly important as social work enters the twenty-first century.

If social work should fail to redress prominent impediments to its continued viability in the twenty-first century (that is, its limited data-generating and utilizing capacities), its future may be far less bright than depicted above.

References

Abbott, A. A. (1985). Research productivity patterns of social work doctorates. *Social Work Research and Abstracts, 21*(3), 11–17.

Austin, D. M. (1991). *Report from the Task Force on Social Work Research.* Berkeley, CA: National Institute of Mental Health, Social Work Task Force on Research Conference, School of Social Work.

Baker, D. K. (1994). *A bibliometric analysis of academic productivity in social work: The utility of CD-ROM-based bibliographies.* Unpublished manuscript, University of Oklahoma, Norman.

Baker, D. K., & Wilson, M. V. K. (1992). An evaluation of the scholarly productivity of doctoral graduates. *Journal of Social Work Education, 28*(2), 204–213.

Berger, R. M. (1990). Getting published: A mentoring program for social work faculty. *Social Work, 35*(1), 69–71.

Boehm, W. W. (1959). *Objectives of the social work curriculum of the future, Volume I.* New York: Council on Social Work Education.

Briar, S. (1990). Empiricism and clinical practice. In L. Videka-Sherman & W. J. Reid (Eds.), *Advances in clinical social work research* (pp. 1–7). Silver Springs, MD: National Association of Social Workers.

Cheung, K. M. (1990). Interdisciplinary relationships between social work and other disciplines: A citation study. *Social Work Research and Abstracts, 26*, 23–29.

Cnaan, R. A., Caputo, R. K., & Shmuely, Y. (1994). Senior faculty perceptions of social work journals. *Journal of Social Work Education, 30*(2), 185–199.

Epstein, W. M. (1990). Confirmation response bias among social work journals. *Science, Technology, and Human Values, 15*(1), 9–38.

Epstein, W. M. (1992). A response to Pardek. Thump therapy for social work journals. *Research on Social Work Practice, 2*(4), 525–528.

Fortune, A. E. (1992). More is not better—Manuscript reviewer competence and citations: From the past-editor-in-chief of the *Journal of Social Work Education. Research on Social Work Practice, 2*(4), 505–510.

Fraser, M. W. (1993). What can we conclude about the status of research in social work? *Social Work Research and Abstracts, 29*(2), 40–44.

Fraser, M. W. (1994). Scholarship and research in social work: Emerging challenges. *Journal of Social Work Education, 30*(21), 252–266.

Fraser, M. W., Jenson, J. M., & Lewis, R. E. (1993). Research training in social work: The continuum is not a continuum. *Journal of Social Work Education, 29*(1), 46–62.

Fraser, M. W., Lewis, R. E., & Norman, J. L. (1990). Research education in M.S.W. programs: An exploratory analysis. *Journal of Teaching in Social Work, 4*(2), 83–103.

Fraser, M. W., Taylor, M. J., Jackson, R., & O'Jack, J. (1991). Social work and science: Many ways of knowing? *Social Work Research Abstracts, 27*(4), 5–15.

GADE Task Force on Research Curricula. (1994). *Research and statistics training in social work doctoral programs.* Paper presented at the Annual Program Meeting of the Group for the Advancement of Doctoral Education, Seattle, WA, October 6–8, 1994.

Gillespie, D. F., & Khinduka, S. (1992). A response to Pardek. From the Associate Editor and from the Chair of the Editorial Board of the *Journal of Social Service Research. Research on Social Work Practice, 2*(4), 511–514.

Gingerich, W. J. (1990). Rethinking single-case evaluation. In L. Videka-Sherman & W.J. Reid (Eds.), *Advances in clinical social work research* (pp. 11–24). Silver Springs, MD: National Association of Social Workers.

Ginsberg, L. (1992). *Social work almanac.*Washington, DC: National Association of Social Workers.

Glisson, C. (1990). *A systematic assessment of the social work literature: Trends in social work research.* Unpublished manuscript, School of Social Work, University of Tennessee, Knoxville.

Green, R. G., Hutchinson, E. D., & Sar, B. K. (1990). *The research productivity of social work doctoral graduates: 1960–1988.* Richmond: Virginia Commonwealth University School of Social Work.

Green, R. G., Hutchinson, E. D., & Sar, B. K. (1992). Evaluating scholarly performance: The productivity of graduates of social work doctoral programs. *Social Service Review, 66*(3), 441–466.

Hamilton, D. P. (1990). Publishing by—and for?—the numbers. *Science, 254,* p. 133.

Hollis, E. V., & Taylor, A. L. (1951). *Social work education in the United States: The report of a study mode for the National Council on Social Work Education.* New York: Columbia University Press.

Hopps, J. G. (1992). A response to Pardek. From the Past-Editor of *Social Work. Research on Social Work Practice, 2*(4), 497–498.

Institute of Medicine. (1990). *Clinical practice guidelines: Directions for a new program.* Washington, DC: National Academy Press.

Institute of Medicine. (1992). *Guidelines for clinical practice: From development to use.* Washington, DC: National Academy Press.

Institute for Scientific Information. (1989). *Social sciences citation index.* Philadelphia, PA: Author.

Jenson, J. M., Fraser, M. W., & Lewis, R. E. (1991). Research training in social work doctoral programs. *Arete, 16*(1), 23–38.

Kirk, S. A. (1990). Research utilization: The substructure of belief. In L. Videka-Sherman & W. J. Reid (Eds.), *Advances in clinical social work research* (pp. 233–250). Silver Springs, MD: National Association of Social Workers.

Klein, W. C., & Bloom, M. (1992). Studies of scholarly productivity in social work using citation analysis. *Journal of Social Work Education, 28*(3), 291–299.

LeCroy, C. W. (1990). Opening the door to knowledge utilization. In L. Videka-Sherman & W. J. Reid (Eds.), *Advances in clinical social work research* (pp. 261–264). Silver Springs, MD: National Association of Social Workers.

Lindsey, D. (1992). Improving the quality of social work journals: From the editor of *Children and Youth Services Review. Research on Social Work Practice, 2*(4), 515–524.

Mahoney, M. (1977). Publication prejudices: An experimental study of confirmatory bias in the peer review system. *Cognitive Therapy and Research, 1,* 161–175.

Mendelsohn, H. N. (1992). *An author's guide to social work journals* (3rd ed.). Silver Springs, MD: National Association of Social Workers.

Pardek, J. T. (1992a). Are social work journal editorial boards competent? Some disquieting data with implications for research on social work practice. *Research on Social Work Practice, 2*(4), 487–496.

Pardek, J. T. (1992b). The distinction and achievement levels of social work editorial boards revisited. *Research on Social Work Practice, 2*(4), 529–537.

Proctor, E. K. (1994). *Research and research training in social work: Climate, connections, and competencies.* Paper presented at the 7th National Symposium on Doctoral Research and Social Work Practice, Ohio State University, Columbus, OH, April 15–16, 1994.

Reamer, F. G. (1992). A response to Pardek. From the Editor-in-Chief of the Journal of Social Work Education. *Research on Social Work Practice, 2*(4), 501–504.

Schilling, R. F. (1990). Making research usable. In L.Videka-Sherman & W. J. Reid (Eds.), *Advances in clinical social work research* (pp. 256–260). Silver Springs, MD: National Association of Social Workers.

Schilling, R. F., Schinke, S. P., & Gilchrist, L. D. (1985). Utilization of social work research: Reaching the practitioner. *Social Work, 30*(6), 527–529.

Schuerman, J. R. (1992). A response to Pardek: From the editor of *Social Service Review. Research on Social Work Practice, 2*(4), 499–500.

Spaulding, E. C. (1991). *Statistics on social work education in the United States: 1990.* Alexandria, VA: Council on Social Work Education.

Task Force on Social Work Research. (1991). *Building social work knowledge for effective services and policies: A plan for research development.* Austin, TX: Capital Printing.

U.S. Department of Education. (1993). *Digest of education statistics.* National Center of Education

Statistics. Washington, DC: U.S. Government Printing Office.

Walker, R. D., Howard, M. O., Lambert, M. D., & Suchinsky, R. T. (1994). Medical practice guidelines: An overview. *Western Journal of Medicine, 161*(1), 39–44.

Walker, R. D., Howard, M. O., Walker, P. S., Lambert, M. D., & Suchinsky, R. T. (1995). Practice guidelines in the addictions: Recent developments. *Journal of Substance Abuse Treatment, 12*(2), 63–73.

Chapter 27

Social Work and the Future

Some Final Thoughts

PAUL R. RAFFOUL, PhD, LMSW-ACP
University of Houston

Whether your personal metaphor for the future is a great roller coaster on a moonless night; a mighty, rapidly moving river; a great ocean; or an entirely random colossal dice game, it is certain that you have a picture in your mind about the future.

Based on the contributors to this book, the future of social work, for most of the authors at least, portends to be rather grim and suggests the question, "Is there a future?" If our next president is a staunch conservative with a limited budget for social welfare and entitlement programs, the question may be moot. Some final thoughts then about the future of social work are in order, followed by a brief discussion of how social workers might prepare for the changes that technology will bring and the anticipated value conflicts accompanying those changes for the profession and its future mission.

Whether or not you agree entirely with the authors assembled in this volume, it is clear that our profession will be facing some difficult choices in the near future during a chaotic and uncertain period in our country's history. *Politically* there is now a major shift under way in the party leadership of our government, which is talking (and acting more and more) as though "business as usual" will be very different in the next few years. *Socially,* according to the demographic projections by Murdock and Michael (Chapter 1), the rapid growth in the sheer numbers in the dependent population in our country will require changes in the way we do social welfare "business" or it will not be able to survive financially to help anyone. Each social work contributor has described within a particular field of practice a future that involves change, either from within the profession as described by John Longres in Chapter 22 (micro versus macro emphasis) and Linda Reeser in Chapter 23 (vision versus mission) or from outside in terms of our social agenda for youth (Rosemary Sarri, Chapter 14) or strategies of social justice and equality (Gutiérrez and Nagda, Chapter 20). It is time to change, they argued, from strategies of social control to social justice and equality in an increasingly diverse world. Simultaneously, Reeser and others argued for changes in social work education that are built on a social justice and human diversity framework within our curricula. This is a call to return to our empowerment tradition as social workers. It will require social workers to be political, to be educated in and then to use these skills to work for a more equitable society. John Longres explained the implications of radical social work for the current debate regarding macro verses micro curricular emphasis and their relevance for ameliorating inequality. The current debate on social work's visions of practice may stimulate a revival of radical thinking. Economic class distinctions need to be reemphasized as a way of unifying the working class and making them less susceptible to conservative proselytizing. At the same time Linda Reeser spoke about our private visions versus our public agendas; the advancement of the specialization debate in education; and the expanding privatization of social work practice, which limits those who can be served by social workers. She called on educators to talk about these issues with students to prepare them for the realities of practice both now and in the future.

There is a current malaise in the public's attitude toward politics, politicians, and government, especially at the national level. Reeser argues for grassroots community-organizing work now to seize this opportunity, assisting people in the community to gain political skills and to realize their strengths to create community-based institutions of economic and political power. This is the multicultural human service organization (HSO) described by Gutiérrez and Nagda. This position also strengthens Karen Haynes's belief that *all* social work is political and must be an integral part of the training that social workers receive in their educational program.

Do We Have the Political Will to Change?

The challenge for the future is to work on resolving these serious issues identified in the previous chapters. It is difficult to predict exactly what the future will require of the profession and its members. From the contributions in this volume, it is obvious that a change in the way social work is taught, practiced, and, yes, even how we conduct and disseminate research (see Chapter 26) is necessary to meet the anticipated needs of people in the future. Do we as a profession have the willpower to make the necessary changes? Do we have the energy to work for a better fit between our purpose and mission as a profession and what we do as social workers? Are we committed to social justice, equality, and social change? If not, why not? Do we really have a choice? What are our alternatives?

How Do We Create This Change?

First, we need to identify the need for change. Circulating thoughtful ideas, such as are contained in this book, about current trends and future needs will begin to create the atmosphere for debate, which is critical in initiating change. Throughout our short history, as noted by John Longres, social workers have often debated their role as social change agents. The current debate seems to link public with private services and the changing political climate that is currently impacting on both areas for social workers. This question also crystallizes the polarities in social work practice at the present time: individual clients' problem-solving versus ameliorating larger social problems such as injustice, inequality, loss of status, and social class conflicts. This information will enable social work to begin to examine the many issues that need to be resolved internally (among ourselves) so that we can begin to move ahead as a unified profession with a common vision and contemporary (or more traditional) mission. With this unified mission we can then begin to organize our membership, our clients, and the public into our social justice and human equality movement. We must do both: unify within our ranks and then proselytize to others. Mission and movement are both required in order to make this shift.

Once we have resolved issues related to our political will, then (and only then) will questions about technological change be relevant. All of the technology in the world will be of little use if we have no viable profession in which to apply and use it.

Technology and Social Work

It is apparent that the computer revolution begun in the early 1980s has impacted our society as a whole in many ways. The profession of social work has finally moved "beyond the keyboard" and the rather tenacious myth that computers were only a tool for research and statistical analyses, and has begun to embrace this new tool of technology (see Chapter 2). In the near future, the notion of ubiquitous computing will be firmly established as a part of our social mores. According to a recent issue of *PC Magazine* (Machrone & Raskin, 1994), by 1999 ATM backbones and widespread access to high-speed data transmission lines will make out-of-office computing links nearly as fast and transparent as local area networks (LANs) are now. Printers with walk-up wireless connections will be commonplace in the office. Credit card–operated versions will be in airport terminals and hotel lobbies. Many of us will not even work out of a traditional office anymore. "By 1996, along with your gas and electric bill, you'll receive an itemized bill for information" (p. 152).

But where does this technological rat race lead? When does it stop? Can we ever get ahead? There is a truism called Moore's Law (after Gordon Moore, a pioneer computer chip designer and engineer), which says that the computer speed and processing power available on one computer chip would double every 18 months. "The process of permanent technological revolution is more appropriately stated as computerized planned obsolescence" (Sterling, 1994, p. 13).

For some in social work this technological revolution provides an opportunity to move more rapidly into the mainstream of modern computing. For people who are positively oriented toward this technology it is an exciting time in our history (see, for example, Negroponte, 1995). But for many it is also a time of increasing concern (see, for example, Stoll, 1995). As we begin to feel the impact of this information technology and the computer revolution, it is increasingly difficult not to think about how we will be affected by the social changes we are about to experience, if we haven't begun to experience them already. It is a time of great anticipation, with seemingly endless opportunities, and yet some of us move quite reluctantly with the technological changes, continuously dealing with the social and human implications of the changes that are taking place all around us. What exactly are we worried about?

Some of the sources of our anxiety are justified and have been previously identified by Reamer (1986) in terms of the ethical dilemmas of personal privacy (how much detail should clients be given about the security of their information?), use of technology in behavior control, and a wide range of complex ethical issues in health care (such as creating life, enhancing the quality of life, or ending life). Cwikel and Cnaan (1991) also described seven ethical issues of the practitioner–client relationship (beneficence, equality of access, promotion of common good, preservation of individualized care, maintenance of flexibility in treatment, links with community networks, and use of treatment time). For others the discomfort with technology remains a personal issue, a matter of attitudes and prior personal experience with machines and technology that are difficult to overcome (Pinkerton & Raffoul, 1984).

Although the future of social work is not totally dependent on changes in computers and technology and their impact on society, it is one opportunity to begin to move the profession into the next century with new vigor and energy. If we can take full advantage of this new product of technology, the personal computer, and put it to use, helping us operationalize our vision and implement our mission, perhaps it can be the key to opportunity for the next century.

What Can Social Work Do to Prepare for These Changes?

We need to take advantage of the efficiencies of time and cost available from ubiquitous computing and high-tech inventions *if* they make our work more productive, by enabling us to spend less time doing repetitive, busy work and more time with clients, policy issues, and other professional concerns. Through mandatory computer literacy training we can begin to increase the use of computers in the profession beyond accounting and word processing services. At all three levels of education we need to insist that students learn how to use the keyboard and to mandate a computer literacy requirement upon admission to all graduate programs. (It is probably not too far off when all reputable colleges will have such requirements for admitted freshmen). Master's-level students should be encouraged to utilize the variety of computer programs available as another tool for enhancing their practice (see Nurius & Hudson, 1993). Doctoral students should be encouraged to write their own programs and to use this technology for advancing new knowledge and expanding the number of specific programs available for social work practice. What about practicing social workers already finished with their formal training?

Taking Advantage of the Superhighway

Becoming a literate on-line e-mail user is often the first opportunity to access the Internet (or Information Superhighway or Cyberspace) for many social workers. However tentatively we begin to use our personal computers for more than word processing, once we begin message communication, exploring the Internet is often the next step in the learning process. It is the most unstructured and time-consuming activity to engage in with a personal computer (at least at the present time). There are presently over 10,000 discussion groups, called newsgroups, on the Internet. They cover every conceivable subject or special interest groups (SIGs) ranging from support groups for cancer patients (alt.support.cancer) to devoted followers of the Grateful Dead. Social workers could encourage use of the Internet by establishing dedicated interest groups on-line for specific interests: a FIELD group, SOCWORK group, DRUGABUSE group, mental health group, and health care group have already been formed. All opinions found in a newsgroup or on-line forums have the same apparent weight. It is important to give everyone a chance to be heard in order to ensure that access is as ubiquitous as the subjects that are discussed. It is a basic value of social work to respect individual rights and equality of access. There is a role for social workers in this newly available communication medium. It is a tremendously popular form of direct person-to-person communication that is organized not from the top down by one person but by many to many on a level playing field. This medium could be used to further publicize the mission of social work both to the public and to other social workers. A recent advertisement concerned a renegade band of conservative activists that have formed a private forum on CompuServe called TOWN HALL® to "share ideas, express opinions, conduct research, and develop strategies leading to what they hope will be a 'political and cultural revolution' in America" ("Renegade Band of Conservatives," 1995, p. 5). Why can't social work do the same? Why don't we do it now? (A list of many of the contributors' e-mail addresses is provided at the end of this chapter.)

The volume and kind of information available on the Internet, however, are also a source of distraction, confusion, and even an unproductive waste of time:

> What the Internet hucksters won't tell you is that the Internet is an ocean of unedited data, without any pretense of completeness. Lacking editors, reviewers or critics, the Internet has become a wasteland of unfiltered data. You don't know what to ignore and what's worth reading. (Stoll, 1995a, p. 41)

Questions remain: How can you "look someone in the eye" on the Internet? How will people be affected by the change in status associated with electronic communications?

The Internet makes possible a genderless form of communication, without faces or real names, visual cues, body language, or involuntary forms of communication. All interaction is limited to the written output from a keyboard with alphanumeric characters as they appear on a glass screen. There is a sense of democracy, equality, and sameness to the medium that is unique and without boundaries.

> While the Internet beckons brightly, seductively flashing an icon of knowledge-as-power, this nonplace lures us to surrender our time on earth. A poor substitute it is, this virtual reality where frustration is legion and where—in the holy names of Education and Progress—important aspects of human interactions, are relentlessly devalued. (Stoll, 1995a, p. 41)

Anticipated Value Conflicts for Social Work

1. Widening the Gap between the Haves and the Have-Nots

General participation in the Information Revolution assumes access to personal computers as well as ability to use them comfortably. Such is not the case yet in our society.

The richer the family, the more likely it is to own and use a computer, according to 1993 census data. White families are three times as likely as Blacks or Hispanics to have computers at home. Seventy-four percent of Americans making more than $75,000 own at least one terminal, but not even one-third of all Americans own computers. A small fraction, only about 7 percent, of students' families subscribe to on-line services that transform the plastic terminal into a telecommunications port (Wallis, 1995, pp. 49–51).

Cyberspace may be everywhere in America, but it is not yet representative of it. A recent *Newsweek* poll (Alter, 1995) found the inhabitants to be younger, more educated, and more affluent than the country's general population. There is a greater proportion of White men who tend to be Republican. Among those on-line, 48 percent identify with the GOP, and only 24 percent with the Democrats (Fineman, 1995, pp. 32–33). At a time when some people define success as the ability to use computers and gain access to cyberspace, the question to be raised is, Will the new technology only widen the gap between young and old, rich and poor, educated and uneducated, Blacks, Whites, and Hispanics? (Ratan, 1995, p. 25).

> The stakes are high. Access to the information highway may prove to be less a question of privilege or position than one of the basic ability to function in a democratic society. It may determine how well people are educated, the kind of job they eventually get, how they are retrained if they lose their job, how much access they have to their government and how they will learn about the critical issues affecting them and the country. . . . **"All this disparity comes to a head in this statistic: a working person who is able to use a computer earns 15% more than someone in a similar job who cannot."** (Ratan, 1995, p. 25)

The current popularity of computers has also not been equally shared among the sexes. In fact, current surveys identify a gender gap between school-aged boys and girls. The gap reportedly begins in elementary school where girls use computers to solve a math problem less frequently than boys (only 59 percent, compared to 69 percent for boys). By the age of 17 the gap is 46 percent versus 60 percent. In a poll of high school students that asked how many 17-year-olds have had a course in computer programming, it was 28 percent of the girls compared to 36 percent of the boys. Because women will be two-thirds of the new entrants into the workforce, this current trend is anticipated to increase the salary gap between the sexes in the next century. At home, men and boys use computers more often. One study shows that boys are three times as likely to enroll in computer clubs and summer classes than girls. Even on-line, women are in short supply. Only 10 to 15 percent of users of on-line services are women.

There is also an age gap to be considered: "Of the 100 million Americans who use computers at home, school or work, nearly 60 percent are 17 or younger, according to the census. Children, for the most part, rule cyberspace, leaving the over 40 set to browse through the almanac" (Levy, 1995, p. 52).

2. New Privacy and Confidentiality Issues

Future communication will require new rules for protection of privacy and confidentiality (see Chapter 2). No longer can one assume that a message to one person will be seen or read only by that person. Rules yet to be defined will require that personal identifiers be limited to protect the rights of others. Professional boundaries will have to be redefined for what is appropriate to write or say in written form over the Information Superhighway. Even passwords, scramblers, or other encryption schemes the government develops will not protect individuals from computer hackers attempting to violate the integrity of any system designed to protect users of the Internet. Like other dilemmas and unanswered questions of the digital age, traditional approaches simply will not work. New assaults on personal freedom and privacy occur daily. According to a recent *Newsweek* telephone survey of adults, 85 percent are concerned about pornography being too available to young people through the Internet; 80 percent are concerned about being harassed by 'virtual stalking' through unwanted messages on the Internet; and 76 percent are concerned about being harassed by real stalking from someone they first meet on the Internet.

Conclusion

There is something special about this cyberspace experience that causes some peoples' imagination to go crazy, from one extreme to the other: Either one reacts with anxiety and fear of the consequences or one acts with excitement and enthusiasm about the future and the many possibilities. Although it is difficult to predict all the changes that will come about as a result of the computer revolution currently under way, it is clear that changes have begun to occur, and they will affect the practice of social work and the development of social welfare policy. If history repeats itself, as it often does, results of the current technological revolution will take longer to reach fruition than predicted. But when the changes of this technological revolution finally occur, its effects are likely to be more profound and widespread than anyone imagined or predicted.

Although not all the future issues in social work can be addressed by technological innovations, new and more powerful computers, or access to the information highway, they do represent potential resources for making the future a better place for all. If we can assist those who do not have access to computer equipment through donation of used equipment, grants to community centers, and the like, we can ensure that the technological revolution does not widen the gap between the haves and the have-nots.

In addition to preparing ourselves technologically for the future, we have to continually ask some basic questions about social work's principal mission(s). If we really are concerned about matters of social justice, equality of access and opportunity, and so forth, then we need to take a long, hard look at where we are going as well as how we are going to get there. As important (and wonderful) as this new technology is, the future of the social work profession will not be defined by its technological capabilities but by its values.

With our common vision of equality and a mission of social justice for all, we can use technology to help provide more resources to more people. I hope that social workers who read this book will be better prepared for this day.

References

Alter, J. (1995, February 27). The couch potato vote. *Newsweek,* 34.

Cwikel, J. G., & Cnaan, R. A. (1991). Ethical dilemmas in applying second-wave information technology to social work practice. *Social Work, 36*(2), 114–120.

Fineman, H. (1995, February 27). The brave new world of cybertribe. *Newsweek,* 30–33.

Levy, S. (1995, February 27). TechnoMania. *Newsweek,* 26–40.

Machrone, B., & Raskin, R. (1994, December 20). Gazing into cyberspace. *PC Magazine, 13*(22), 152.

Negroponte, N. (1995). *Being digital.* New York: Alfred A. Knopf.

Nurius, P., & Hudson, W. W. (1993). *Human services practice, evaluation and computers: A practical guide for today and beyond.* Pacific Grove, CA: Brooks/Cole.

Pinkerton, G. L., & Raffoul, P. R. (1984). Professional colleagues: Confronting the attitudes of professionals toward computers. In M. D. Schwartz (Ed.), *Using computers in clinical practice* (pp. 61–66). New York: Haworth Press.

Ratan, S. (1995, Spring). A new divide between haves and have-nots? *Time, 145*(12), 25–26.

Reamer, F. G. (1986). The use of modern technology in social work: Ethical dilemmas. *Social Work, 31*(6), 469–472.

Renegade band of conservatives gathers on CompuServe to start a revolution, save money. (1995, April). *CompuServe,* p. 5.

Sterling, B. (1994). Opening keynote address. In T. J. Courville & P. R. Raffoul (Eds.), *Proceedings of the Ninth Annual Futures Conference: Vol 9. Year 2000 & beyond: Information technology for social work—Visions, choices, ethics* (pp. 8–27). Houston: University of Houston, Graduate School of Social Work.

Stoll, C. (1995a, February 27). The Internet? Bah! *Newsweek,* 41.

Stoll, C. (1995b). *Silicon snake oil: Second thoughts on the information superhighway.* New York: Doubleday.

Wallis, C. (1995, Spring). The learning revolution. *Time, 145*(12), 49–51.

List of Contributors with E-mail Addresses

Diana DiNitto
University of Texas at Austin
School of Social Work
ddinitto@mail.utexas.edu

Maxine Weinman Epstein (Peggy Smith)
University of Houston
Graduate School of Social Work
mwepstein@uh.edu

Wallace A. Gingerich
Case Western Reserve University
Mandel School of Applied Social Sciences
wjg4@po.cwru.edu

Stephen Gorin
Plymouth State College
Social Work Program
sgorin@psc.plymouth.edu

Ronald K. Green
Case Western Reserve University
Mandel School of Applied Social Sciences
rkg3@po.cwru.edu

Lorraine Gutiérrez
University of Michigan
School of Social Work
lorraing@umich.edu

Yeheskel (Zeke) Hasenfeld
UCLA
School of Social Welfare
ilo5zek@mvsoac.ucla.edu

Karen Haynes
University of Houston
Graduate School of Social Work
kshaynes@uh.edu

Karen A. Holmes
University of Houston
Graduate School of Social Work
kaholmes@uh.edu

Matthew O. Howard
Director, Drug Abuse Treatment Services
matth@u.washington.edu

Siri Jayartne
University of Michigan
School of Social Work
sirijay@umich.edu

Gayle Klaybor
5438 Edith
Houston, TX 77096
socwpt@uhupvm1.uh.edu

M. Dow Lambert
University of Washington
mdl3@u.washington.edu

Jean K. Latting
University of Houston
Graduate School of Social Work
jlatting@uh.edu

John Longres
University of Washington
School of Social Work
longres@u.washington.edu

C. Aaron McNeece
Florida State University
Institute for Health and Human Services Research
amcneece@garnet.acns.fsu.edu

Dianne H. Montgomery
Florida State University
School of Social Work R-91
dmontgom@mailer.fsu.edu

Steve H. Murdock
Texas A&M
Department of Rural Sociology
Center for Demographic and Socioeconomic Research
and Education
smurdock@rsocsun.tamu.edu

Paula S. Nurius
University of Washington
School of Social Work
nurius@u.washington.edu

Robert I. Paulson
Portland State University
Regional Research Institute
rip@rri.pdx.edu

Paul R. Raffoul
University of Houston
Graduate School of Social Work
praffoul@uh.edu

Linda Reeser
Western Michigan University
School of Social Work
linda.reeser@umich.edu

Rosemary C. Sarri
University of Michigan
Institute for Social Research
rcsarri@r.imap.id.umich.edu

Kim Strom
University of Minnesota
School of Social Work
strom015@gold.tc.umn.edu

Bruce A. Thyer
University of Georgia
School of Social Work
bthyer@uga.cc.uga.edu

Rebecca J. Walker
University of Kentucky
College of Social Work
rwalk1@ukcc.uky.edu

Kennard Wellons
University of Kentucky
College of Social Work
wellons@ukcc.uky.edu